Day by Day

IN THE UPPER ROOM

Day by Day

IN THE UPPER ROOM

Expositional Meditations

CHUCK GIANOTTI

ECS

MINISTRIES

The Word to the World

Day by Day in the Upper Room
Chuck Gianotti

Published by:
ECS Ministries
PO Box 1028
Dubuque, IA 52004-1028
phone: (563) 585-2070
email: ecsorders@ecsministries.org
website: www.ecsministries.org

First Edition 2016

ISBN 978-1-59387-284-7
eISBN 978-1-59387-458-2

Code: B-DBDUR

Copyright © 2016 ECS Ministries

Other books by Chuck Gianotti:
Biblical Foundations
Cosmic Drama: Men, Women & the Church
Day by Day in the Gospel of Matthew
Day by Day in Galatians, Ephesians, Philippians & Colossians
Day by Day in Hebrews
The Formation of the New Testament
Leadership Qualities
Leadership Principles
Practical Ministry

Printed in the United States of America

To the brothers and sisters at Crossroads Bible Fellowship (Rochester, NY), who have been a source of encouragement and joy to me for 20 years as we have worked toward becoming a community of believers like those of the Upper Room.

ACKNOWLEDGMENTS

No author can claim sole credit for his work, as there are many involved in supporting roles—from editors (the faithful Ruth Rodger and Erica Fitzgerald), those who provide feedback (the faithful readers of the E-Meditations blog, the original form of these meditations), my wonderful wife (life partner and encourager in all things, Mary), to the publisher (ECS Ministries, Rob Tyler and Mark Wainwright who have encouraged me in writing this series of "Day by Day" books). This is not to mention the many other hands that, though involved to a lesser extent, have contributed to the final book you hold in your hands.

Thanks above all to God, whose name we seek to magnify through this study of the Upper Room discourse of our Lord. It is only by His strength and inspiration that anything we do brings Him the glory, appropriate to the eternal Son of God.

–Chuck Gianotti, 2016

PREFACE

How does one fill up a page of notes on a single verse or even two verses—and then do it for five days a week for 52 weeks? That is a daunting proposition to be sure. I have drawn my challenge from a book written more than 100 years ago, "Our Lord Prays for His Own." That 480-page masterpiece by Marcus Rainsford (1820–1897) focuses on one solitary chapter in Scripture, John 17, which we traditionally call the High Priestly prayer of our Lord. Every verse is examined, meditated upon, expounded and enjoyed for the ultimate value of listening closely to the intimate conversation of our Lord Jesus with His heavenly Father.

Making no pretense to compare with such a monumental work as Rainsford's, I have endeavored in this book to present the larger context of the Upper Room Discourse (John 13–17), of which the High Priestly prayer is the grand finale. These five chapters contain the final conversation Jesus had with His disciples before His crucifixion. Herein we find some of the most engaging and profound insights into the Son's relationship with the Father. We also discover startling truths for all believers for carrying on successful ministry without Jesus being physically present.

The atmosphere that the twelve (then quickly reduced to eleven) experienced was foreboding and troubling. Jesus appeared to be dashing their dreams and hopes. Yet for us who know the end of the story, the truths ascend to the spiritual heights. The inspired human author, John, writes with simple words and with elementary grammar and sentence structure, but God has sovereignly appointed him to not only take us soaring, but also to take us diving into the depths of spiritual insights. No superficial reading will suffice to gain the heart of God as revealed herein.

It remains for the reader to judge whether these meditations will in any way scratch the surface of doing justice to the Upper Room Discourse. We present it with the hope that you will be challenged to go higher and deeper in knowing and loving the Lord Jesus Christ. For in Him, we know God.

And the Word became flesh, and dwelt among us, and we saw His glory, glory as of the only begotten from the Father, full of grace and truth.

–John 1:14

No one has seen God at any time; the only begotten God who is in the bosom of the Father, He has explained Him.

–John 1:18

NOTES FOR USING THIS BOOK

This *Day by Day* series fills a gap between the typical daily devotional readings (very brief) and in-depth commentaries (very long). It is designed to provide meaty exposition in bite-size amounts for the busy Christian.

This installment of expositional devotions will take you through one year of reading in the Upper Room Discourse (John 13–17), one or two verses at a time. This is not meant to be a dry commentary, but to help you fall more in love with and be amazed by the Lord Jesus Christ. My desire is that you would come to know about the love relationship between the Father and the Son, and His invitation for us to join them in that circle of affection.

You will notice that these expositions are divided to suit a typical five-day work week. We suggest you conclude each reading with a few minutes in conversation with the Lord, using the prayer at the end of each day's meditation as a springboard for adding your own thoughts.

We have also included suggested readings for the weekends from the rest of the Gospel of John (which will provide the greater context for the Upper Room discussion) and also from the book of Acts (which shows the historical context of how the Upper Room instructions played out in the lives and ministry of the apostles).

Upper Room Outline

John 13-17

Initial
Preparation

The Upper Room

John 13–17

Intimacy with the Lord on the human front reached its zenith in the Upper Room, the scene of the Last Supper of our Lord with His disciples, the night before His crucifixion. Jesus' final briefing for them to carry on His mission lies exposed for all to read. Like the proverbial "fly on the wall," we are afforded the opportunity to listen in on this "by invitation only" gathering. The interaction contained herein has captivated Christians for its insights into the inner workings of that first band of disciples who forsook all to follow Christ.

Since Jesus Himself did not write down any of His teachings (that we know of), we completely depend upon the "apostles' teaching" to convey the true message of the Savior of the world (Acts 2:42). In these few hours together, with the disciples unsuspecting that Jesus would be dead in less than 24 hours, they (and we) learn about serving one another, God's shepherd heart, the seeds of His betrayal, the hope for the future, the Holy Spirit, abiding in Christ, warning about persecution, the promise of peace, the resurrection and the intimate prayer of Jesus with the Father.

In the Upper Room, Christians have found great comfort and guidance. We learn about the heart of our Lord and Savior Jesus Christ; He really does care for those who follow Him. He washed their feet for the here and now held before them a vision of eternal life and a heavenly home for the future. Although not specifically mentioned, we know from the synoptic gospels (Matthew, Mark and Luke) that the Upper Room experience included what Christians call "The Last Supper," their final meal together before His death.

The most hallowed ground of all comes in chapter 17, in what some have called the Lord's High Priestly prayer. There, we see the most extensive prayer of our Lord and what He requests of His Father. He asks for restoration of His glory, and He prays for His immediate followers as well as those who will one day come to faith in Him, through their witness.

Yes, this section of Scripture covers much ground that is rich and deep, unparalleled as literature and unsurpassed in its glory. It has inspired the fascination and imagination of untold numbers of Christians for about 2,000 years. Using simple language, yet employing lofty concepts, the gospel writer has captured for us the culmination and summation of Christ's teachings. In beginning this expositional devotional series, our hope is that you the reader would sense God's invitation to join Him in the Upper Room.

Lord, open our ears and the eyes of our hearts as we enter the Upper Room.

The Context

John 13–17

Context is important to understanding a story. In our passage of John 13-17, there are different levels of contexts. The first, of course, is the physical context, namely Jerusalem (12:12), during a supper (13:2), just before the Passover celebration (13:1), the night before His betrayal and death (18:1). From the parallel passages in the other gospel accounts we know this "Upper Room" discussion took place in a large upper room of the house belonging to an individual whose name is unknown to us (Mark 14:15). The room had been prepared for the Passover meal by an advance team of two of His disciples (Mark 14:13).

The literary context, on the other hand, looks at the placement of this passage in the flow of John's gospel account. In contrast to the other accounts, John focuses on only a few events in the life and ministry of Christ. For example, only seven of the miracles of Christ are recorded. But the telling of each event is accompanied by an extended discourse or explanation, relating the event to spiritual truth. Here we have the event, without miracle, extending five chapters, a significant amount of space for a book of 21 chapters. John explains his rationale for the material he included: "Therefore many other signs Jesus also performed in the presence of the disciples, which are not written in this book; but these have been written so that you may believe that Jesus is the Christ, the Son of God; and that believing you may have life in His name" (20:30-31).

This Upper Room discourse is the longest we have of Jesus' teachings in all of the gospel record and so deserves the special attention we are giving it. We learn of the passion of this Man with His most intimate followers, on the penultimate day of His ministry: the day before His once-for-all-time sacrifice, as the book of Hebrews so carefully describes it. This day in the Upper Room is preparatory to the greatest day in the existence of this universe, the day God provided the final solution to what began in the fall in the Garden of Eden (Genesis 3).

The personal context is that of the writer himself, the apostle John. We know him to be the author because of the humble references to "the disciple whom Jesus loved" (John 13:23; 19:26; 20:2; 21:7) correlated with the complete absence of any named reference to John in the book along with the placement of the other disciples. Early Christian tradition names him as the author, and the earliest manuscripts we have attach his name as the author. To be sure, the Upper Room discourse is written for us as an eyewitness testimony of one who was especially beloved of the Lord.

Lord, help me know for sure that I, too, am a beloved disciple.

The Passover

John 13:1

¹ Now before the Feast of the Passover, Jesus knowing that His hour had come that He would depart out of this world to the Father, having loved His own who were in the world, He loved them to the end.

The Upper Room discourse took place in the context of the Passover Feast. Core to Jewish religious life was the celebration rooted in the Exodus story, when God liberated their ancestors from bondage in Egypt. This annual feast reminded every succeeding generation of the major theme of their existence: they were a redeemed people, special to God among all the nations of the earth. It was exceptionalism at its finest, defined by the eternal, almighty God of Creation, the God of Abraham, Isaac and Jacob. He is the One who identified Himself to Moses as "Yahweh," the name that means He will be everything Israel needs Him to be as they traverse the geographic and time landscape of God's plan for the world.

The Passover specifically recalls the sacrificial lamb that was offered up to protect the households of Israel (Ex. 12–13). God had sent a destroying angel to kill the firstborn throughout Egypt, as the final plague against all those who rebelled against God's word through Moses. Every household that in faith smeared the lamb's blood on the doorposts was protected from the destruction of the "Passover" angel. As barbaric as that may seem to our present-day sensibilities, the resolution is certainly simple. Only those who rejected God's word would suffer the calamity.

So as Jesus spoke with His disciples, the imagery of rebellion, judgment, sacrificial substitution, faith and redemption were very much on the forefront of the disciples' consciousness. Jesus would certainly have been fully aware of this setting and took full advantage of it. In fact, one could say the Feast itself was intended by God to have been the ages-long pointer, not only to the redemption that took place during the Exodus, but also to the more perfect Exodus and redemption that God was going to provide. Not just an earthly liberation from political domination, with which Israel struggled almost their entire existence, but a liberation from the spiritual domination of sin and death. Everything Jesus had to say was against the backdrop of the Passover. And John brings this to our attention, as readers today, so that we will understand the connection, that Jesus' soon-coming death was a direct fulfillment of the inherent prophecy of the Feast of Passover. With that in mind, Jesus begins His final conference with the disciples before His death.

Lord, I am excited to listen in on the words of life that Jesus is about to share with His disciples. Help me to think deeply and reflectively, so that I may grow.

The Omniscience of God

John 13:1 (cont.)

---

¹ Now before the Feast of the Passover, Jesus knowing that His hour had come that He would depart out of this world to the Father, having loved His own who were in the world, He loved them to the end.

Twice we see Jesus "knowing" in this, the first part of the Upper Room discourse: once in our verse for today and once in verse 3. This could be a reference to what theologians call the omniscience of God and therefore an indication of Jesus' deity. His knowing could also line up with the role of a prophet, who was given a special vision of the future. At any rate, this "knowing" was divine in nature and makes it clear that Jesus entered the final stage of His earthly mission knowing full well the great implications. "His hour had come."

Death was the very reason He had come into the world. His mission was to die. This might seem odd to some, except that the death of Christ, as symbolized in the Passover celebration, and in particular, the Passover lamb, was and is central to God's redemption of people to Himself. This is "the hour" for which Christ came into the world.

Knowing the end was coming and "having loved His own," He set His mind on continuing to love them to the very end, that is, until He died. His composure was remarkable. Most humans, when facing death, become preoccupied with their own experience; it is extremely difficult to focus on anything else. Yet here was Christ concerned about loving His disciples, not settling for any minimization or "justifiable" lessening of His love. Even when excruciatingly fastened to the cross, He was concerned about His own mother and assigned John to look after her as his own mother (John 19:26). And He did not reject them when they denied Him and turned their backs on Him.

Genuine Christian love is not simply an act one does on occasion when the time calls for it. That kind of love comes and goes. Christ's love was a state of being, not just some action divorced from character. The phrase "loved them to the end" indicates an ongoing, perpetual love. This love was not just something that Jesus did better than most; it was characteristic of who He was and is. He is love! Later in His life, John echoed this: "Beloved, let us love one another, for love is from God; and everyone who loves is born of God and knows God. The one who does not love does not know God, for God is love" (1 John 4:7-8). Since Jesus loved His own until the end, should we not fan the flame of our love so that it will become like His?

Lord, I am amazed that Your love for me will never be exhausted. You will love me also to the very end of my life and into eternity. Praise to Your Name.

The Battle Lines Drawn

John 13:2

² During supper, the devil having already put into the heart of Judas Iscariot, the son of Simon, to betray Him . . .

Characters in the story come to the fore. Christ, of course, is front and center, and "His own" are there as well, that is, the disciples. The timing is "the hour," the culmination of His mission on earth. The final scene is on stage and the act is opening. We also find the antagonist lurking in the background. Comparisons with Satan working against God through Adam and Eve are hard to miss. So also is the similarity of that sinister arch-enemy of God working to dethrone the Sovereign of the universe by attempting to coerce that righteous man Job to curse God. Here we see the ugly visage of the devil working in the heart of Judas Iscariot to betray Christ.

Jesus knew He would be betrayed, having previously told the disciples, "Did I Myself not choose you, the twelve, and *yet* one of you is a devil?" (John 6:70). That betrayal is not set in motion until verse 21, but clearly the seeds have been planted. In fact, the seed had been planted in the Garden of Eden, when the serpent (2 Cor. 11:13; Rev. 12:9; 20:2) tempted Adam through his wife, Eve, to reject God's sovereignty in their lives.

Yet at an even deeper level, the betrayal of the Creator God of the universe began in the heart of Satan himself. In clear allusion to Satan, Isaiah wrote: "How you have fallen from heaven, O star of the morning, son of the dawn! You have been cut down to the earth . . . you said in your heart, 'I will ascend to heaven; I will raise my throne above the stars of God . . . I will ascend above the heights of the clouds; I will make myself like the Most High'" (Isa. 14:12-14).

Satan has committed his entire existence to attempting to dethrone God, to rise above Him. Since there is no possibility of anything or anyone being greater than the Creator of all things, the most he could possibly imagine is only a likeness, because it is eternally obvious that he is not the Creator. The history of the universe is the history of Satan's cosmic struggle to usurp God's place of honor and glory, His throne. Yet the universe is not dualistic, in the philosophical sense of two equal and opposite forces vying back and forth, like the yin and yang of Chinese mysticism. While God and Satan are opposites, they are certainly not equal! Like a spiritual chess game, Satan tries to check the Master, only to be checkmated in the end.

Christ, fully aware of Satan's move and knowing the ultimate outcome, sat with His disciples in the Upper Room preparing them for the final act.

Lord, I bow before You as a created being, made in Your image.
You are God and I am not. And for that I am so thankful.

WEEKEND READING

Saturday – John 1:1-18
Sunday – Acts 1:1-26

PERSONAL REFLECTIONS

_____
_____
_____
_____
_____
_____
_____
_____
_____
_____
_____
_____
_____
_____
_____
_____
_____
_____
_____
_____
_____
_____
_____

Week 2

Day 1

Knowing What Was His

³ Jesus, knowing that the Father had given all things into His hands, and that He had come forth from God and was going back to God,

Second on Jesus' list of things known was that "the Father" had assigned ownership to Him over all things. We already know from John 1:3 that all things were made through Him. In Colossians, we learn that "by Him all things were created, both in the heavens and on earth, visible and invisible, whether thrones or dominions or rulers or authorities—all things have been created through Him and for Him" (Col. 1:16). Though that passage in Colossians was written long after the Upper Room discourse took place, the Lord Jesus already knew His ownership and entitlement. He was heir to the Father's wealth, and it already was His.

He set it all aside when He took on the outer appearance of a human servant (see Philippians 2:7). This may very well be. He temporarily turned away from His "wealth," as the apostle Paul conveys: "For you know the grace of our Lord Jesus Christ, that though He was rich, yet for your sake He became poor, so that you through His poverty might become rich" (2 Cor. 8:9). His "wealth" with His Father in glory did not prevent Him from doing the Father's will and coming into this world of spiritual poverty. He left ownership of everything safe with His Father when He became part of that which He Himself owned and created.

We must note the significant point that what He owned was what the Father had given to Him. Christ, though being co-equal with God, was in the Trinitarian relationship with the Father. Theologians call this the eternal procession of the Son from the Father. In His role as the second person of the Trinity, He was on the receiving end of the Father's loving generosity. From eternity past, in the inner sanctum of the Godhead, the unity and perfection of God was expressed in the relationship of love, with the Father giving and the Son receiving. That is perfect, infinite and unified love!

There are two other things that Jesus knew as He began the Upper Room discourse. He was fully cognizant that He was sent from the Godhead and that He was returning to God. Having already established that Jesus "was God" (John 1:1) and that the Pharisees understood Jesus to teach His equality with God (John 8:58-59), we have no fear of using the terms "God" and "Father" interchangeably. Because Jesus was certain of His relationship with God, He could face the coming hours of His suffering. We too need to be certain.

Lord, I believe Your "divine power has granted to [me] everything pertaining to life and godliness, through the true knowledge of Him . . ." (2 Peter 1:3).

First Things First

. . . ⁴ got up from supper, and laid aside His garments; and taking a towel, He girded Himself.

So begins the premium illustration of Philippians 2:7-8, the model for us to follow in our behavior toward one another. Imagine in your mind's eye the Creator and Sovereign of the universe, who is high and lifted up, the train of whose robe filled the temple, the Alpha and the Omega, Wonderful Counselor, Mighty God, Everlasting Father, Prince of Peace, the Eternal King of Glory, the great I AM—imagine this One arising from supper, where the aroma of the Passover meal still hung in the air, the taste of lamb, bread and wine still lingering on their palates—and taking on the form of a servant.

Join with the disciples in astonishment as they look up from their reclining position with legs stretched back from the table, resting on one elbow finishing their meals, to see Jesus straightening Himself up and taking off his dinner clothes. And then He wraps a towel around his waist. What could this mean? How unusual.

The Lord Jesus never ceased to amaze them—no, confuse them. He was not afraid to touch lepers or hang out with known sinners, prostitutes and even the hated tax collectors. He took the time to sit children on His knee and to teach and talk to women and Samaritans. He walked on water, stilled the storms, verbally excoriated the formidable Pharisees and commanded demons. Yes, the disciples were quite familiar with the unusual. But no, they never got used to it: "What manner of man is this . . . ?" (Mark 4:41 KJV).

No mention here of anyone else getting up. It may be the disciples were still eating, or they were mesmerized. Or it may be somewhat a casual outplaying of the beginning of the story. But it strikes me as parallel with so many times in life where God begins to work, and yet we followers of Christ sit by watching, unaware or unconcerned, maybe even confused. We become so engulfed in our own activities, thoughts and daily lives while Jesus is thinking about something else. To be sure, we all have needs that require attendance, but even in those things, what are the thoughts that occupy us?

For Jesus, the big picture was not satisfying His earthly needs, nor even the religious observance of the Passover meal. He has His mind set on a much larger picture, and it begins with His taking on the "form of a servant." For, indeed, it was the job of a servant to wash the feet of the guests. In a day when sandals and unpaved walkways were the norm, such a task was a customary element of hospitality. And Jesus was not above doing it. Are we? Am I?

Lord, help focus my life on being a servant for others, like Christ was and is.

No Delegating Servanthood

John 13:5

⁵ Then He poured water into the basin, and began to wash the disciples' feet and to wipe them with the towel with which He was girded.

Minor details that fill out the story, on the way to a great moral lesson of serving one another? No, nothing the Lord did—and nothing recorded by inspiration of the Holy Spirit—is minor or included for literary purposes only. Some simple observations may be helpful in gaining deeper insights. First, we must notice that Jesus poured the water Himself. There was no regalia of ornate attendants doing His bidding here. No musical accompaniment or pre-washing, so that this Great One would not have to soil His hands. This was not simply a symbolic gesture divorced from the dirt of life. This was not done on a performing stage with the curtain pulled back for a huge audience to applaud. And certainly it was not an ostentatious show of faux-humility. Jesus did not dress up, but rather dressed down as appropriate for the task.

One cannot help but think how this might be played out today, by those who claim to be "servants" of God. The feet of selected worthies would be pre-washed and sanitized and even perfumed, and the event attended with great pomp and vestures created to regale the one who would imitate symbolically the Lord. The pageantry indeed would be great.

Not so with the Lord. In a humble upper room, with a gritty band of fishermen, tax collectors, zealots and others, Jesus handled their dirt-caked, earth-trodden feet. There was no pre-washing for ceremony. No delegating to those lower on the social order. He even filled the basin Himself.

The Jewish mind might even make the connection with the great bronze laver/bowl outside of the tabernacle in the wilderness, where the priests would wash their hands and feet before going near the altar to offer sacrifices (Ex. 30:18-19). Yet with His hands, which needed no ritual cleansing, Jesus washed the disciples' feet, which were muddied by the dirt of the world. Certainly there was about to be a sacrifice, and that of the very One washing their feet.

Finally we observe the towel He used to wipe their feet, taken from around His waist. Like the woman who washed His feet and then wiped them with her hair, that which was her glory (John 12:3), Jesus used the towel that covered His body to wipe the disciples' feet, a most un-glorious action. The Lord stooped low to be a servant of those whom He highly regarded. Yes, having loved His own, He loved them to the end.

Lord, I am humbled by this example of loving and serving others. I am not worthy to ascend to the position of being served by You. But here am I, Lord.

How Would I React?

John 13:6

⁶ So He came to Simon Peter. He said to Him, "Lord, do You wash my feet?"

First recipient in this normally routine domestic chore was Peter. Hardly would anyone have rejected such an offer of hospitality in that culture; it was an expected courtesy from any decent host. But Jesus was not the host, and He was not the host's servant, in the normal sense. In fact, He was the greatest of the guests there, and the dinner in many ways was in His honor. To be sure, He called for the meal to be performed at this specific location, but things as they happened broke with the normal customs of the day.

Possibly the host or the owner of the home where they met was chagrined for not providing that service himself, but that sentiment seems unimportant to our storyteller. What does get noticed is Peter's quite understandable reaction. It was a response of incredulity.

How would James and John have reacted? They, as it was famously noted in another place, desired to sit at Jesus' side in the kingdom (Mark 10:37). They desired the first place. To have the Master wash their feet—and theirs first—might have helped them gain the prestige they so desperately desired.

How would Judas have felt? Would he have objected with indignation, insisting the home owner should have provided that service? After all, he seemed to pride himself in correcting Jesus at other times, as when the Master allowed the expensive perfume to be poured out on His feet, when the betrayer asserted that it should have been sold and the money given to the poor (John 12:4-5).

Thomas? Might he have doubted Jesus' lordship in performing such a menial task, the way he doubted Christ's resurrection from the dead? Could Andrew have wondered about the value of Christ's action, the way he questioned the value of the boy's meal in the hands of the miracle worker? (John 6:8-9).

Peter was incredulous, in a state of consternation. This is the one who recognized that Jesus was the Christ, the Son of the living God. This is the one who said, "Lord, if it is You, command me to come to You" (Matt. 14:28) and walked on water. This is the one who was chastised for his faltering faith when he sank amid the howling storm, taking his eyes off the divine Water-Walker.

How would I have felt if I were there? Would I have allowed Jesus to wash my feet? Do I resist being indebted to another's service? Do I doubt God in the details? Do I have ulterior motives? Am I too proud to be served by God? Do I recognize my need? Am I astonished by what Christ has done for me?

Lord, "I stand amazed in the presence of Jesus the Nazarene, and wonder how He could love me, a sinner, condemned, unclean."

Delayed Appreciation

[7] Jesus answered and said to him, "What I do you do not realize now, but you will understand hereafter."

A young seminarian, bored with a minute point of theology, sardonically intoned to his professor, "I don't see the relevance of this." The man of God responded, "Although you don't see the importance of this truth now, someday you will need it." Later in life he grew to understand what might be called "delayed appreciation for profound truth."

To Peter's initial objection and astonishment, Jesus recognized that Peter would not fully appreciate what was taking place. After all, what Jesus knew that Peter did not was that in a few short hours, Christ would be hanging on the cross, dying for the sins of the world. He would be resurrected three days later, then after another short while, He would be physically taken up from them to return at a later undisclosed date. What Peter didn't know at that time was that he, along with the other disciples under the power of the Holy Spirit, would soon be launching a worldwide, epoch-making movement called the Church.

One can understandably cut Peter some slack in not comprehending this humble servant-like act of Jesus, His first act in the Upper Room in preparation for the end—which, as it turns out, was really the beginning.

How often does God do things that we don't understand? If you walk with the Lord for any length of time, you find that that is "typical" of how God does things. One of those truths that we have an extremely difficult time grasping is that through serving comes greatness. Who of us would have ever thought that a good battle plan for fighting a foe is to die? That is completely counterintuitive, or to put it more bluntly, ridiculous from our limited human perspective. Yet, in the cosmic battle of evil versus good, of Satan and his forces assaulting God (and eventually His church), the ultimate battle plan is for the Captain of the Lord's army, the Lord of hosts, to lay down not just His weapons but His life. How can one understand that?

In the Upper Room, as things unfolded, did Peter sense the foreboding darkness that was coming? It did not seem the time for pleasant niceties of foot-washing, the tide seeming to be turning against them. One day later Peter did come to appreciate that even in the midst of conflict and persecution, humility was to be central to Christian behavior. He later wrote to the scattered, persecuted Christians, "Clothe yourselves with humility toward one another, for God is opposed to the proud, but gives grace to the humble" (1 Peter 5:5).

Lord, help me to appreciate the importance and absolute centrality of humbleness and serving for being effective in spiritual warfare.

WEEKEND READING

Saturday – John 1:19-34
Sunday – Acts 2:1-13

PERSONAL REFLECTIONS

_____
_____
_____
_____
_____
_____
_____
_____
_____
_____
_____
_____
_____
_____
_____
_____
_____
_____
_____

Fellowship with Christ

John 13:8

> [8] *Peter said to Him, "Never shall You wash my feet!" Jesus answered him, "If I do not wash you, you have no part with Me."*

Stark relief—that's what Peter provides to the Upper Room story. Almost the foil. In his honest, though impetuous, reaction, he provides Jesus with opportunity to further elucidate His message. This Passover Supper was not going well, in his mind. It would be one thing for Peter to have accepted one of the other disciples' washing his feet, establishing that he was the greater among them, something over which the disciples can be found arguing in the Upper Room (Luke 22:24). Foot washing was something that a lesser person would do for the greater person. But it was entirely another thing for Jesus, who was clearly greater than all of them, to wash Peter's feet. The most prominent of the disciples would not stand for this.

Peter's flat-out refusal, in no uncertain terms (using the strongest possible negative construction in the Greek language), has the force of "Absolutely not!" He wouldn't even hear of it. He could not imagine a scenario in which he would allow Jesus to wash his feet. While we may quietly chide Peter that he would soon have to eat his words, do we not do the same when we quietly refuse the Lord's leading in our lives? We know we should trust Him when we begin to sink in the waters of discouragement and difficulty.

Jesus responds quickly and tersely. This was not a time to equivocate or mollify. Although not as harsh as when He met Peter's resistance to going to Jerusalem with "Get behind me, Satan" (Matt. 16:23), Jesus adroitly retorts that this washing of Peter's feet was absolutely necessary, non-negotiable for fellowship with Christ. Literally, without this, Peter would have "no part" with Christ, that is, no sharing with Christ. He is not talking about the washing of regeneration taught elsewhere in Scripture and soon alluded to in this story. It has to do with fellowship.

Whatever the meaning (as we will see shortly), the essential thing at this juncture is that Jesus' washing Peter's feet was absolutely essential, non-negotiable. If Peter had won the argument, he would have ironically lost fellowship with the Lord. Our fellowship with Christ flows out of His serving us. And fellowship with Him is the most important thing.

One is reminded that Paul made the right decision when faced with suffering. Rather than refuse it, he desired to experience the fellowship of sharing in Christ's suffering, in the midst of his own suffering (Phil. 3:10).

Lord, as humbling as it is, I thank You for being my servant. Knowing that humbles my heart and enflames in me the desire to be a servant to others.

Faith to Fellowship

John 13:9

---

[9] "Then, Lord," Simon Peter replied, "not just my feet but my hands and my head as well!"

Peter has been much maligned by Christians for his impetuousness, and this may not be altogether misplaced. However, we must tread carefully lest we inadvertently judge ourselves in the process. To be sure, Peter tended to either lag behind Jesus or sprint ahead. His impulsive resistance to the foot washing turned to a knee-jerk over-embrace. "If Jesus thinks I am not following along with Him, then I'll not only embrace what He is doing but add some of my own improvements." He wasn't thinking too deeply at this point, but you can't fault him for his loyalty, bungling as it was.

Sometimes in our desire as Christians to be loyal to Christ, we vacillate to the extremes. How many of us have with heartfelt conviction asserted ourselves in a renewed commitment to one or more of the spiritual disciplines, proclaiming (at least to ourselves) that now we are going to take our faithfulness to new levels? That New Year's promise to read my Bible every day for 30 minutes (or thereabout) begins to waffle at the three-week mark. Our vow to tell someone about Christ every week falls off target quickly. Our resolution to bring our eating under control by adding a day of fasting once a week loses its thrust after one or two efforts. We either sprint out full speed ahead, or we lag behind—neither of which keeps pace with the Lord's work in our life.

We easily make promises we cannot keep, offering to the Lord more than He has asked for. What we really need is to allow the Lord to wash our feet on a regular basis. That means coming to Him for daily forgiveness for sins, just like we take care of our personal grooming every morning. We need the cleansing of Christ in our lives, much as the people walking on the dry, dusty roads of the first century needed their feet washed on a regular basis.

Some Christians fall into abject confession of the same things over and over again, taking even this to an extreme. It is as if every sin uncovers the defeating thought that all previous confessions weren't enough. Yes, while we continue to sin (see 1 John 1:8), we have already, as genuine Christians, been cleansed from our eternal sin and our salvation is secured. All the sins that condemn us have been washed away in the one-time spiritual baptism when we were redeemed, the event of which water baptism is a symbol. But our daily sins, which hinder not our salvation but our fellowship with the Lord, need daily confession and forgiveness. Faith in salvation breeds faith in forgiveness daily.

Lord, I confess my daily sins to You and believe You forgive me for every one.

Hints

[10] Jesus answered, "Those who have had a bath need only to wash their feet; their whole body is clean. And you are clean, though not every one of you."

Contrasting most other NT documents, this gospel writer spoke in picturesque story form with much dialogue. Simple language and vocabulary characterize his communication, but don't be fooled into thinking that his thoughts and ideas are simple. Interestingly, only John's account of the gospel does *not* include Jesus' comments about *becoming* like a child in relationship to the kingdom of God (see Matthew 18:14; Mark 10:15; Luke 18:17). To be sure, as a result of faith, we become the "children of God" (John 1:12), but in John's focus, simple language was not an effort to reduce the message to its simplest form. God used John's language to convey profound, powerful truths that did not depend on erudite wording.

Inspired as he was by the Holy Spirit, John now spoke of a different shade of meaning to the feet-washing incident. It was more than an example of humility (about which he would speak in verse 14). Obvious to every resident of Palestine, dinner guests would have needed some freshening up after arriving in sandal-clad feet, even if they had bathed before arriving. But Jesus added what might have seemed odd to the disciples: "You are clean, though not every one of you." He subtly moved from talking about the feet not being clean, to not everyone present being "clean."

The next verse makes it clear that Jesus was referring to His betrayer, but the disciples did not know that yet. In fact, much of what He had to say caused a great deal of consternation and self-reflection as the story unfolded. Here, though, it probably stirred up at most a slight raise of the eyebrow.

Religious people, those with little study of the Scripture, often completely miss the levels of meaning in the teachings of Christ. He was a master at teaching clearly, and at the same time He infused His communications with shades and depth that take a life time of study to plumb. In the disciples' case, it took the death and resurrection of Christ for them to fully realize that their number had been compromised and they as a group needed to be "cleansed." That took place in Acts 1:15-26: when awaiting the Pentecostal coming of the Holy Spirit, they brought their number back up to twelve, identifying Matthias as the replacement for Judas, who had committed suicide. At that time, they all recognized the prophetic nature of Judas' betrayal and replacement; they were not prepared or capable of understanding it before then.

Lord, help me to see the "odd" or difficult things in Your word
as gateways into deeper understanding of Your ways.

Evidence of Deity

John 13:11

[11] For He knew the one who was betraying Him; for this reason He said, "Not all of you are clean."

Jesus knew Judas was going to betray Him. We know it already, because most of us have heard the stories of Jesus Christ repeatedly. Plus John had already made reference to it in 6:71 and 12:4 as well as earlier in this chapter (13:2). The first-century Christians who were reading the Gospel According to John for the very first time most likely were well acquainted with the betrayal story from the accounts of Matthew, Mark and Luke, which had long been in circulation, for anywhere from 20 to 40 years. The disciples, in the chronology of the Upper Room events, were not yet privy to this knowledge.

On a side note, the early Christians did not think of the four gospel accounts as four separate gospels. They understood the Gospel to be singular—there was only one life and one message, which was/is the Good News of Jesus Christ. By the beginning of the second century, Christians customarily referred to the four "accounts" of the one Gospel. Fittingly, the titles given to the four writings were "According to Matthew," "According to Mark," etc., John's account was the last of the four to be written and circulated. And by the beginning of the second century, we see all four accounts being circulated in one collection.

Back to our story. We readers are given the inside of Jesus' meaning at a juncture in the story when the disciples didn't know it. And it raises for us questions the disciples did not even conceive. First, was this prophetic premonition or simply wise discernment? This is only problematic if one eliminates the supernatural out of the starting gate. In John's perspective, Jesus is "the Word" and the "only begotten of the Father." It was John who preserved for us Jesus' words, "Before Abraham was, I am," which to the Jewish mind of that day amounted to a claim to deity, and incurred their attempts to stone him. At the minimum, Jesus had "foreknowledge" and could see what was going to happen. Further, being familiar with OT prophecies, as later discovered by the eleven disciples (Acts 1:16-26), a betrayal was inevitable. So, yes, Jesus' knowledge was prophetic, contrary to what those of a more liberal view of Scripture and the life of Christ would have us to believe. There is no question that John portrays Jesus as the Christ, the Son of the living God. "These have been written so that you may believe that Jesus is the Christ, the Son of God . . ." (John 20:31). And His foreknowledge is one evidence of this.

Lord, I do believe that You are the Christ, the Son of God. And I believe that You know all things before they happen. There are no surprises with You.

Stretching Comprehension

John 13:11 (cont.)

[11] For He knew the one who was betraying Him; for this reason He said, "Not all of you are clean."

A second question arising from this verse is this: if Jesus knew Judas was going to betray Him, why didn't He stop the betrayal? Jesus could have revealed the plot to the other eleven, and their loyalty to Christ might have kicked in. After all, Peter later was quick with the sword to defend Jesus before the arresting mob (John 18:10)—might he have used it on Judas? At the very least, Jesus could have shamed Judas by confronting him publically.

But Jesus' knowledge of the future extended beyond Judas' actions. He had come for the purpose of dying for the sins of the world, so He could not stop Judas without stopping the entire process. Just like He could not respond to the taunt, "Save yourself and come down from the cross" (Mark 15:30), without undermining the greater purpose of saving the world.

But wasn't there a way other than treachery? Was not Judas included in the beginning of the Upper Room event, where ". . . having loved His own who were in the world, He loved them to the end" (13:1)? Certainly the God of the universe could have devised another way. But could it be He wanted to both show us the extent of Jesus' love to the entire world, even to one who would betray Him, and also warn us that following Christ outwardly can hide a bent heart? But Judas rejected that love and suffered the consequences that even Christ's love could not alter, since in fact that love was rejected.

A third question arises. Why did Jesus choose Judas in the first place, if He knew him to ultimately be a betrayer? In fact, John does not shy away from making this fact absolutely clear. Jesus had already warned the twelve, "Did I Myself not choose you, the twelve, and *yet* one of you is a devil?" (John 6:70). This falls in the purview of the doctrine of election, which we will encounter again in John 15:16. His foreknowledge and election are inescapably intertwined, and pondering these things will stretch the deepest thinking about God. It does not admit to superficial formulations or pat answers. Make no mistake, Jesus chose Judas, knowing that Judas would betray Him. However, Judas would be held fully responsible for his actions. God operates in dimensions beyond us, and it makes sense that there are some things too difficult for us to reconcile, this being one of them. But John, using simple language, certainly taxes our comprehension. Yet, at the same time, we sense the superiority of a God who does all things well, though they are hard to understand.

Lord, help me trust You in those complexities of Your ways that stretch my comprehension. You are infinitely good and wise; You make no mistakes.

WEEKEND READING

Saturday – John 1:35-51
Sunday – Acts 2:14-36

PERSONAL REFLECTIONS

_____
_____
_____
_____
_____
_____
_____

_____
_____
_____
_____
_____
_____
_____
_____
_____
_____
_____
_____
_____

The Wait of Questions

John 13:12

12 So when He had washed their feet, and taken His garments and reclined at the table again, He said to them, "Do you know what I have done to you?"

When Jesus asked a question, He was not looking for information. Being the master teacher that He was, the goal was to draw His listeners into an indelible learning experience. Some things are best learned in perplexing situations. His comments so far served to knock the disciples off balance, as evident from Peter's response. Now Jesus wanted to drive home at least one of the points He was trying to communicate.

Of all the gospel writers, John reveals the teaching side of Jesus more than the others. The number of stories included by John reflects a distinct selectiveness, as he explains later in John 20:30-31. But those he does include come with great details of Jesus' conversations surrounding those events. And in the Gospel According to John, Jesus shows many layers of meaning to his actions.

In the preceding verses, the aim was to give forewarning of Judas' betrayal (he was the member of disciples who was not "clean," the uncleanness that had to be removed). Now the Lord is taking the disciples to another level of meaning in His actions, namely that the way of the follower of Christ was the way of servanthood.

Jesus could have simply sat the disciples down for a three-year academic program of classroom lectures. "Here is the truth; now write this down and memorize it." He could have provided His teaching strictly in monologue form, but instead He often taught with questions, creating a problem or illustration first and then inviting the disciples to contemplate the meaning. The world may call this the Socratic method of teaching, but Jesus is the greatest Teacher of all.

Does this not reflect how the Lord often teaches us, how He takes us to deeper levels of understanding of Himself and His ways? When we don't understand why things are happening, that can become the greatest time of learning. When heaven is silent, when God does not answer prayer, when our faithful living does not result in well-being, when pain is unrelenting, when disappointments travail us. Then it is like Jesus' washing the disciples' feet without immediately telling them why. To be sure, He did answer the question, but it is important to note that He wanted them to ponder it first: "Do you know what I have done to you?" God leaves us to wait and ponder so that we can more readily appreciate the answer when it is given. And sometimes the wait can be a lifetime.

Lord, help me to understand when questions arise in my mind that You are in the process of teaching me deeper truths about Yourself and Your ways.

Teacher and Lord

John 13:13

13 "You call Me Teacher and Lord; and you are right, for so I am."

Meekness does not negate objective acknowledgment of one's status. Christ had no problem acknowledging that He was in fact Teacher and Lord over the disciples. He provides the perfect example of true humility. False humility denies reality. The "ah shucks, I'm nothing" persona brings self-aggrandizing, prideful attention to one's self. The most humble thing a person can do is to confidently serve in the capacity of his giftedness and purpose. Jesus is the prime example of humble confidence.

Consider for a moment some of the titles and descriptions Jesus had. Besides being Teacher and Lord, He was Emmanuel (God with us), Son of God, and Son of David. In the book of Revelation He takes on the names firstborn from the dead, the Alpha and Omega, Lord God, the First and the Last, Living One, Creator, Lion of the tribe of Judah, Root of David, the Lamb, Shepherd, Christ, Faithful and True, Word of God, King of kings, Lord of lords. Elsewhere He is the Only Begotten, My Beloved Son, Rabboni, Rabbi, Master, I Am, Son of Man.

Here in John, Jesus centers on two titles which His disciples mainly used. The first refers to His role in teaching them about God and life, and the second refers to His relationship to them and all of creation. He is Teacher and Lord.

Jesus is our Teacher as well. He teaches us through the recorded words of the gospel writers. There we have preserved the greatest teaching of all time, for it comes straight from the mouth of the Creator God, who inhabited His creation in the form of a human being. Jesus taught using questions, stories, illustrations and life experiences. He taught using parables, proverbs and propositional logic. He modeled what He taught, and did not call His disciples to do anything that He Himself didn't already do (except for confessing sin, see Hebrews 4:15). Paul used the Lord as his model: "Be imitators of me, just as I also am of Christ" (1 Cor. 11:1). We do well to listen and follow the teaching of the Lord.

He is also Lord. He has authority over not only believers, but also unbelievers. One day, ". . . at the name of Jesus every knee will bow, of those who are in heaven and on earth and under the earth, and . . . every tongue will confess that Jesus Christ is Lord . . ." (Phil. 2:10-11). We believers acknowledge and bow before Him now. We join with the apostles in following Jesus, not just because He is a good teacher, but because He is Lord. And we want to grow in increasingly seeing Him that way in our lives.

I call You Lord because I humbly submit to Your authority in my life in every area. There are no hidden places that I keep back for myself.

Oughts and Shoulds

14 "If I then, the Lord and the Teacher, washed your feet, you also ought to wash one another's feet."

Contemporary Christianity is in a backlash mode, like a pendulum swinging away from religious obligations to religious freedoms. After all, if we are saved by grace apart from the works of the Law (Rom. 3:28), then we should not be required to live by a NT version of the Law. It seems there is an invisible sort of Christian "Sanhedrin" that has defined what good Christians are to look like. These laws may come as direct statements on moral behavior or innuendo, or through modeling (whether subtly or not) when exhibited by the older generation or leaders of the church. And so people (especially younger people) go searching for a freer atmosphere, where grace and love and freedom predominate rather than the straight-jacket of conformity.

Many times the pendulum of Christian behavior does need to move away from so-called outward legalistic codes. Paul emphatically addressed this when he asked, "If you have died with Christ to the elementary principles of the world, why, as if you were living in the world, do you submit yourself to decrees, such as, 'do not handle, do not taste, do not touch!'" (Col. 2:20-21). He goes on to add, "These are matters which have, to be sure, the appearance of wisdom in self-made religion and self-abasement and severe treatment of the body, *but are* of no value against fleshly indulgence" (Col. 2:23).

But we need to be careful, for pendulum swings rarely stop in the middle, but sway to unhealthy extremes. We see from our passage today that being a follower of Christ *does* carry a non-negotiable obligation: "You ought to wash one another's feet." Jesus' word here is unmistakable: the obligation is similar in nature to a financial debt. If we are going to follow Christ then we must do as He says! Non-optional.

This "ought" of Christ is far more difficult than keeping up with someone's checklist of Christian behaviors, ratings of movies watched, where we draw the line on language that is emphatic, crude or profane, the degree and style of one's modesty, length of hair, or number of church meetings attended, etc. No, the obligation of following Christ is much more demanding than that. We are to serve one another, humbly, treating others as superior, more worthy than ourselves. We can keep all the Christianized laws perfectly, yet not be a servant like Christ—and thus fail. Which of these do you want?

Lord, I don't want to waste my time with legalistic codes of behavior; rather I want to be a servant like the Master, treating others as better than myself.

Servanthood Multiplication

John 13:15

15 "For I gave you an example that you also should do as I did to you."

Modeling is big in Christianity. Not the showing of fashions, but the emulation of behavior and attitudes. Our primary example is found in the Lord Jesus Christ, yet there are times when Paul invites others to follow his example as well. Some might be tempted to think this takes away from patterning our lives after Christ and redirects us to follow a mere human. But Paul takes seriously the Lord's teaching on this matter. He modeled his life after Christ, precisely when he invited people to model their lives after him. Listen to how he phrases it: "Be imitators of me, just as I also am of Christ" (1 Corinthians 11:1; see also 1 Corinthians 4:16; Philippians 4:9). In fact, he tells the Christians in Philippi to follow the example of "those who walk according to the pattern you have in us" (Phil. 3:17). Further, Paul presents himself to the Ephesian elders as an example of shepherding God's people (Acts 20:13-38).

Christians often stumble on a false sense of humility when thinking about this. "It is presumptuous for anyone besides Jesus and Paul to say, 'Follow my example.'" However, we must take modeling seriously and soberly as a core responsibility of the Christian life. When a parent teaches a child how to tie a shoe, the parent will say, "Here, watch me do it, then you try." There is no sense of pride or presumption in that. It is simply the parent sacrificing time in order to responsibly show another human being (the child) a basic skill of life. We Christians, likewise, sacrifice our time and energies to help other Christians through our service of modeling servanthood to them.

Now, being a model is not the ultimate goal of our lives. Rather, it is the ministry of servanthood multiplication, if we might call it that. Jesus, in the Upper Room, is training the twelve to be servanthood multipliers. He wants them to not only serve one another, but to be models of serving. To do as Jesus did to them meant more than just becoming humble enough to serve one another. It meant an intentional way of life that consciously spurs others on to similar acts of servanthood. Like the writer of Hebrews says, "Let us consider how to stimulate one another to love and good deeds . . ." (Heb. 10:24). These are not Pharisaical, superficial, self-centered good deeds done for show; they lift our serving to another level. There, like Jesus, we serve others sacrificially, but also spur them on to serve others, who will in turn serve others. Is this not simply another form of teaching similar to 2 Timothy 2:2?

When serving, bring along one or more to serve with you. After serving someone, you might even say, "As I have served you, so also serve others."

Lord, help me be a servant who helps multiply the company of servants.

Master and Slave

John 13:16

16 "Truly, truly, I say to you, a slave is not greater than his master, nor is one who is sent greater than the one who sent him."

Had Jesus not begun this with the double "truly," we might miss the import of His statement. It is like He is saying, "Now listen carefully, hear me, this is important . . ." We are reminded of when Jesus spoke in parables to the multitude and said, "He who has ears to hear, let him hear" (Mark 4:9). Focus, guys! Core to being a disciple of Christ is to always keep in mind that He is greater than we will ever be. We are simply His servants. In some regards, we are like slaves who have resigned their will to the one who is greater. This comes *before* we can appreciate His later comment about them being no longer slaves, but friends (John 15:14-15). We are not "friends" of Christ because we choose to be, and we are not on the same level as Christ even though He later calls us friends. He is still the Master, and we are not!

John is the only gospel writer to record the double "truly" phrase of Jesus (the others only record the single "truly"), and it occurs 25 times in John. While Jesus most likely taught in Aramaic, as many scholars and historians tell us, the gospel writers all rendered His teaching in Greek, thus the various ways of conveying the Master's teachings. However, the record of this statement in the Upper Room is unique to John. Matthew and Luke both tell us that Jesus spoke at other times of the slave not being greater than his master. But they don't include Jesus repeating Himself in the Upper Room as John did. This is not surprising, because John included considerably more details of this conversation that others leave out.

Indeed, in the Upper Room Jesus speaks of things that most people will never understand because of their lack of faith or superficial faith. Seeing ourselves as "slaves" of God smacks of religious fundamentalism and extremism. Some religions describe their relationship solely in those terms, which in reality is slavery to someone's interpretations of the Scripture. But Jesus calls His disciples to understand that since they have already voluntarily become His followers, they must obey what He commands them. His commands, contrary to earthly constructs, are based in His love and sacrifice of Himself, as He is about to explain further. That is a missing element in false religions.

Obeying God and being loved by Him weave together beautifully and bring wholeness, spiritual oneness. But it begins with rightly understanding the relationship we have with God. He is Master, and we are His servants.

Lord, when I am my own master instead of You, life becomes a fundamental failure. But with You as my Master, life is an integral whole. I am loved.

WEEKEND READING

Saturday – John 2:1-12
Sunday – Acts 2:37-47

PERSONAL REFLECTIONS

_____
_____
_____
_____
_____
_____
_____
_____

_____
_____
_____
_____
_____
_____
_____
_____
_____
_____
_____
_____
_____
_____

Beatitude in Brief

¹⁷ "If you know these things, you are blessed if you do them."

Blessing is what God loves to do. And throughout the teachings of Jesus, He talks about blessings. Probably the most well-known teaching on this subject is the eight-fold blessing of the beatitudes. The most surprising, counter-intuitive notion is that blessing doesn't come in the way one might think. Who would have thought that blessing would come to those who are poor in spirit, who are meek or who suffer persecution? Here in the Upper Room, which of the disciples had anticipated Jesus' teaching here that blessing comes to those who serve others, illustrated by Jesus in the washing of their feet? How, if we are honest, can one be blessed through serving others?

Serving others can be drudgery. Your service can be misunderstood, taken for granted, expected or unappreciated. Someone once said, "I don't mind serving, but I don't like be treated like a servant!" Yes, serving is hard. And by all observation the company of those who serve as Jesus served is a small fraternity indeed.

People serve for a variety of ulterior motives. There is the false show of humility. Conversely there is pompous serving for praise. There is "paying one's dues, before the big reward." But Jesus spoke of a genuine serving of others, putting their needs ahead of one's own. Is this not what Paul wrote to the Philippians? "Do nothing from selfishness or empty conceit, but with humility of mind regard one another as more important than yourselves; do not *merely* look out for your own personal interests, but also for the interests of others. Have this attitude in yourselves which was also in Christ Jesus . . ." (Phil. 2:3-5).

Serving is the way of Christ. "The Son of Man did not come to be served, but to serve, and to give His life a ransom for many" (Matt. 20:28). And if we want to be like Christ, then we need to become those who serve like Christ. And if He could wash the disciples' dirty, stinking feet, then is there any service too low for us, who are not greater than Jesus, our Master?

Think of the mother who lovingly serves her children by changing their diapers, cleaning up after them, patiently teaching. Or the man who visits his aging mother in a nursing home each week. Or the church elder who visits a church member in the hospital, the business man who jump-starts a subordinate's car, the individual who stops at an accident to help tend the injured.

Notice, Jesus says it is not just knowing about serving that brings blessing. It is the actual serving. The blessing is real, for in serving like the Master, you have the confidence that you are acting in His will and for His pleasure.

Lord, make me a servant so that I may know the pleasure of serving with You.

Chosen Betrayal

John 13:18

18 "I do not speak of all of you. I know the ones I have chosen; but it is that the Scripture may be fulfilled, 'HE WHO EATS MY BREAD HAS LIFTED UP HIS HEEL AGAINST ME.'"

The most incredibly ironic, "didn't-see-that-coming" plot twist ever written is this story of Judas' betrayal of Jesus. So mind-boggling, the disciples were at a complete loss as to whom Jesus was referring (vs. 22). The word that probably most aptly describes this is treachery. The dictionary definition of treachery seems almost defined by this story: "Violation of allegiance or of faith and confidence," "harmful things that are done usually secretly to a friend, or your own country," "betrayal of trust."

Judas, who is more fully disclosed as the story progresses but whom anyone familiar with Christianity well knows, fulfills the role to which Jesus refers, that of duplicity. Indeed, when the vast majority of people abandoned Christ as His teachings began to command total commitment, Judas stayed with those whose view was expressed by Peter, "Lord, to whom shall we go? You have words of eternal life" (John 6:68). Yet even then Jesus warned, "Did I Myself not choose you, the twelve, and *yet* one of you is a devil?" (John 6:70).

So we see that despite the outward show of loyalty to Christ, Judas did not fool the Master of the Universe, who became flesh and "dwelt among us." From the earliest times of Jesus' separating out those who were devoted to Him from those who were committed to their own well-being, the two-faced conniver was not "hidden from His sight." Little did he realize that "all things are open and laid bare to the eyes of Him with whom we have to do" (Heb. 4:13).

Jesus knew full well, and now was warning His closest followers in the Upper Room on the night before His death, that one of them would betray Him. Make no mistake, this did not catch Him by surprise. He knew of it; it was prophesied in Scripture, as He quoted Psalm 41:9 to them. The worst possible sin we can imagine against Jesus, to betray Him from within the close intimate circle, was all part of the plan. The difference between God's foreknowledge and God's sovereign plan runs fairly thin at this point. Jesus says, "I know the ones I have chosen," and that included Judas (see again John 6:70). The gospel that records "that whoever believes in Him" also speaks of God's choosing. Lest we bog down in theological controversy, we rest in the universally accepted truth, as we see here in the Upper Room story of betrayal, that nothing is beyond God's control, nothing can thwart His plan. Not even evil.

Lord, thank You that You not only know about my trials at hand, but You also continue to be in absolute control of what happens to me, no matter what it is.

Similarities

John 13:18 (cont.)

18 "I do not speak of all of you. I know the ones I have chosen; but it is that the Scripture may be fulfilled, 'HE WHO EATS MY BREAD HAS LIFTED UP HIS HEEL AGAINST ME.'"

New Testament use of the Old Testament at times challenges the interpreter of Scripture. Here Jesus Himself quotes from Psalm 41:9 and says that Judas' treachery was prophesied well ahead of time, more than 1,000 years before. Yet in that same Psalm, the writer says, "O LORD, be gracious to me; Heal my soul, for I have sinned against You" (Ps. 41:4). But we know that Jesus ". . . has been tempted in all things as *we are, yet* without sin" (Heb. 4:15). So Jesus quotes from a Psalm about David, who acknowledged his sin, but says one of the verses there applies to Himself.

Books have been written about understanding the various ways the NT writers use the OT Scriptures, whether quotations, allusions or simply references. Psalm 110, for example, is quoted in the NT as having primary fulfillment in Christ, but the original context presents a difficulty. "The LORD says to my Lord: 'Sit at my right hand . . .'" (Ps. 110:1). Jesus plays up that difficulty in His dialogue with the Pharisees (Matt. 22:41-16)—how can David say, "The LORD says to my Lord"? It simply cannot be understood apart from the knowledge that the Messiah Himself was God. Sometimes, as in Isaiah 7:14 (the son to be born), there is a near fulfillment that applied to the time of writing in the OT but has a greater fulfillment in the life of Christ. Then there is Psalm 22, which Jesus quoted on the cross: "My God, my God, why have You forsaken me?" (Matt. 27:46). He used typical Rabbinic methodology in quoting the first verse to refer to the entire Psalm, which describes His dying experience followed by resurrection.

Here in John 13:18, we have a case where Jesus takes a single verse and applies it to His situation of betrayal, and uses the word "fulfilled" without inferring that any of the rest of the Psalm applies to Him (especially not the verse about sinning). He sees in David's experience of betrayal at the hand of, scholars suggest, Ahithophel, his one-time friend (2 Sam. 15:31), a parallel with His own betrayal by Judas. In fact, it would be someone who was at that very Passover meal in the Upper Room "breaking bread" with Christ. Jesus was not referring to the entire Psalm, but pointing out a verse all Jewish people would have been quite familiar with, and flagging His warning to the disciples with it. At this, the atmosphere in the room continued to darken.

Lord, even though adversity is known well ahead of time, and though my life may seem dark, I am encouraged that You are still in control of all things.

That You May Believe

John 13:19

[19] "From now on I am telling you before it comes to pass, so that when it does occur, you may believe that I am He."

Prophecy at its most basic is simply telling ahead of time what will happen. With mere humans, some may have remarkable intuition, a sense of what will happen based on insights about present activities and behaviors. Others are adept at so-called fortune telling, by casting future predictions in such general or ambiguous terms that the predictions could fit almost anyone's future experience, or at least be manipulated to fit what does happen. Still others go back and rewrite their predictions or claim to have made the predictions that fit the circumstances. All of these are not the substance of genuine prophecy as talked about in Scripture.

In our passage in the Upper Room, Jesus tells His disciples ahead of time that one of them will betray Him. First of all, this is no mere mortal speaking, but the incarnate Son of God, the one who, though presently living in time, is nonetheless timeless. He who said, "Before Abraham was, I am" observes all of time in the present tense—so the future is not unknown to Him. So what He has to say is not simply premonition. He is not just surmising from a remarkable ability to read a person's face and know what he is thinking. This is not just a matter of the Master who knows well the tendencies of His disciples. This is the God who created their minds, but who also created time. Mind boggling as it may be, God created all things at every single point in time—past, present and future—from a position outside of time. He is not subject to the sequence of before and after as though He were traveling through time. To be sure, the incarnation teaches us that the infinite, timeless God intersected in time and space in becoming human. But He did not cease to be God. So when Jesus tells His disciples that something will happen, you can count on it happening.

Secondly, His "prediction" is specific and therefore could have been verified. Although we have no biblical evidence that the disciples wrestled with the statement intellectually, they certainly wrestled with it emotionally, such an unthinkable thing that one of them should actually betray their Master.

But Jesus didn't tell them to satisfy an intellectual curiosity about the verifiability of prophecy. Rather, He told them so that they would believe that "I am He"—that they would come to know Him as He really is, the God-man, identified with the Creator God of the universe.

Lord, when I see all the things that have happened just like You said they would, I am increasingly driven in faith to understand You better.

That You May Believe (cont.)

John 13:19

---

19 "From now on I am telling you before it comes to pass, so that when it does occur, you may believe that I am He."

One of the unique phrases as recorded by John the gospel writer is Jesus' use of "I am." With simple yet powerful imagery, Jesus was the Master of metaphor. Seven times He identifies Himself with "I am . . .":

- ➤ I am the Bread of Life (John 6:33, 48)
- ➤ I am the Light of the World (John 8:12; 9:5)
- ➤ I am the Door (John 10:9)
- ➤ I am the Good Shepherd (John 10:11)
- ➤ I am the Resurrection and Life (John 11:25)
- ➤ I am the Way, Truth and Life (John 14:6)
- ➤ I am the Vine (John 15:1)

Yet even more basic to who Christ is, is the name found in the abbreviated, condensed form, "I am," without any further qualifier. He is the "I am." We see this clearly in John 8:24, 28 and the well-known verse "Truly, truly, I say to you, before Abraham was, I am" (John 8:58). Here in our verse, the same truncated phrase actually occurs, though the translators wrestle with how best to render it, since "I am" in English is an incomplete sentence. The NASB and NKJV translations italicize the word "He" as in "I am *He*"), while the NIV renders it, "I am who I am." The NLT reads, "I am the Messiah." Literally, the underlying Greek of our verse today reads "I am," identical with John 8:58!

This "I am" reflects back on the Greek translation of Isaiah (which was the common OT version in use during Jesus' time), where the identical underlying words are used repeatedly from chapters 41–48 (for example, Is 41:4, 43:13, 46:4, 48:12). The phrase emphasizes God's uniqueness as the One who is the answer to all Israel's needs, and is unlike false gods. The Jewish mind understood the connection Jesus was making between Himself and Yahweh when they tried to stone Him in John 8:59. The disciples may very well have made the connection as well, but they were probably still reeling from the talk about a betrayer in their midst. There was much in the Upper Room that was confusing to them. But Jesus was preparing them for their post-resurrection ministry. He didn't expect them to understand the connection at that point. We conclude, then, that accurately telling the future about His betrayer became an authenticating sign that Jesus was in fact the Messiah, God come in the flesh.

Lord Jesus, as I see one more evidence of You being God in the flesh, I praise You unashamedly. You are not just a prophet, but God to be worshipped.

WEEKEND READING

Saturday – John 2:13-25
Sunday – Acts 3:1-26

PERSONAL
REFLECTIONS

The Receivers

²⁰ "Truly, truly, I say to you, he who receives whomever I send receives Me; and he who receives Me receives Him who sent Me." John 13:20

Ambassadorship implicitly befits those who follow Jesus. We carry this responsibility because of our association with Him—really, whether we want to or not. John, many years before recording Jesus' words here, had heard them firsthand in the Upper Room with his very own ears. He writes as a personal eye-witness, as he does in his first epistle: ". . . what we have seen and heard we proclaim to you also, so that you too may have fellowship with us; and indeed our fellowship is with the Father, and with His Son Jesus Christ" (1 John 1:3).

In this scene, etched deeply in John's memory and after years of reflection, Jesus summarizes the core truth presented earlier in this gospel account: "But as many as *received* Him, to them He gave the right to become children of God, even to those who believe in His name . . ." (John 1:12). As children of God, we "receivers" of Christ now represent Him, similar to how a child represents his family. And this representation has a direct linear path: he who receives us as followers of Christ essentially receives Christ, which means he receives God, the One who commissioned Christ.

Now what does it mean for someone to receive me, a Christ follower? We understand this to refer to a person receiving my message of Christ that I share with them. In receiving me, they accept the message that I communicate by my words and my life, the Good News of Christ. This of course assumes I have genuinely received Christ, as John 1:12 explains, and therefore am genuinely a child of God. So someone receiving me means they are receiving a child of a God and what I stand for. This puts that person in line with John 1:12, and thereby he can also become a "receiver" of Christ and a child of God. And by receiving Christ, they are receiving God Himself.

The importance of this cannot be missed. Jesus introduces this with, "Truly, truly." Believers are critical to the propagation of the message of Christ, and the Lord wants His Upper Room audience to understand this foundational principle of the Great Commission. Again, the disciples won't understand this until after the resurrection, when Jesus would no longer be physically present with them. Only then would it make sense why it is significant for people to receive believers. Because that is how they will know about Christ. That is how they will come to know Christ.

Lord, I want to be an effective testimony for You so that others might come to receive You as I have.

Troubled Spirit

John 13:21

²¹ When Jesus had said this, He became troubled in spirit, and testified and said, "Truly, truly, I say to you, that one of you will betray Me."

Calm, cool and collected, Jesus seemed to be calm up until this point. But that was now changing. Though Son of God, He was also human with the full range of emotions. Facing the troubling truth of betrayal by one of His own disciples, the Master became agitated. The word used here, "troubled," has as its most basic meaning, "to be shaken, stirred up." When used to describe a person's emotional state, it carries the sense of inner turmoil and unsettledness, being greatly disturbed. It is the same reaction Jesus had after Lazarus died—when Jesus saw Mary weeping, "He was deeply moved in spirit and troubled."

This is the beginning of His passion, that is, the strong emotional reaction to the events leading up to and including His crucifixion. His incarnation was not a "piece of cake" as some might think, nor was His dying. While retaining full deity, He was also fully human. The mystery of the two natures combining in one individual stretches the capacity of human contemplation. Because of His deity, He had absolute foreknowledge; in particular, His betrayal by Judas was no surprise to Him. Yet for the God who created time and is outside of time and therefore not subject to the time sequences of before and after—for this God to intersect *with* time as the incarnation depicts, means that things will happen or exist that would otherwise be impossible. Here we have the God-man, Jesus, "becoming," that is, experiencing a change of His emotional state.

This is not the "process theology" that some theologians hold to, where God is mutable, that is, He is "in process" and changing, depending on how creation turns out. On the contrary, we believe God is *immutable*; He does not and cannot change (Ps. 55:19). At times God appears to change, like the wind seems to change when we turn around and walk into it. But God Himself does not change.

But in becoming a human, the God-man's foreknowledge did not stem His human emotional response. He was troubled that one of His closest followers was about to betray Him. This hit Him hard, for He loved Judas as He did all the disciples. And He knew this was the catalyst that would ultimately lead to His death. The fuse was about to be lit; Judas would soon leave to report to the religious leaders and collect his bounty. The spiritual battle was beginning and would escalate to the point of no return.

Lord, thank You for entering into the depths of human pain and emotion and the experience of being betrayed. Thank You that You will never betray me.

Horror of Realization

John 13:22

²² The disciples began looking at one another, at a loss to know of which one He was speaking.

W e the readers already know what the principle support actors in the play do not, namely, which of them would betray the Master. They had no clue. In fact, the story line has revealed that individual, Judas, much earlier and prepared us for this eventuality. God's unveiling the truth to us today, 20 centuries later, comes at a different pace and sequence than it did to the original disciples.

Why is this important to note? Because from a literary point of view, though the disciples were living the story in "real time," we all learn from their experience. This is the essence of wisdom, to learn from others' experience, which is moderated to us by the divine Author through the pen of the apostle. He was not only selective in which historical material he included (John 20:31) but was also purposeful in how he arranged and conveyed those things. The goal was so that ". . . you may believe that Jesus is the Christ, the Son of God; and that believing you may have life in His name" (John 20:31).

We see the disciples completely dumbfounded, having absolutely no clue about who would betray Jesus. To be sure, they had argued among themselves about who was the greatest among them (Luke 22:24), but the thought that one of them might betray Jesus was unthinkable. At this point, the story is left ambiguous. Were they each searching among the others or were they looking about defensively? The former seems more likely than the latter, but things would ultimately crash down on them all when in the end they all failed Him.

At the least, their eye contact must have blindingly eclipsed everything else. How could this be? They had all expressed loyalty to the One for whom they had left all to follow. Yet the Lord had already dropped an ominous bomb in referencing Psalm 41:9. Peter had already been rebuked by Jesus over having his feet washed. This also added to the fact that Jesus insisted that none of them were completely "clean" and that they all needed feet washing, and this by their Master no less. Things were becoming unsettled, and fast.

Nothing more tragic can happen than when a follower of Christ turns away. The apostle Paul expressed this deeply, "For many walk, of whom I often told you, and now tell you even weeping, *that they are* enemies of the cross of Christ, whose end is destruction . . ." (Phil. 3:18). While Judas represents the ultimate in betrayal, his story strikes sobering fear in all of us: "Is it I?"

Lord, thank You for the warning, which strikes fear in my heart. I never want to be like Judas and betray You in even the smallest way.

Whom Jesus Loved

John 13:23

²³ There was reclining on Jesus' bosom one of His disciples, whom Jesus loved.

In stark contrast with the betrayer, we find the disciple "whom Jesus loved." Could this be the author's method of making sure the reader sees the contrast? He knew Jesus loved him; there was no doubt as he penned this account. But that would seem too finitely human to think John would be making a personal statement of his own fidelity here. Rather, we believe the unflinching purity of motives here, as controlled by the authorship of the Holy Spirit. John was indeed beloved by Christ, but that did not give him any sense of superiority over the rest. To be sure at the time, there may have been some rivalries, as when he and his brother James desired the positions of prominence in the coming kingdom. But those feelings were long gone by the time John wrote this gospel account on the island of Patmos, some 60 years later, and from a point of theological reflection.

It may seem odd to describe the situation as John "reclining on Jesus' bosom." But the custom of eating in those days often involved the dinner guests reclining on the floor, with body and feet extended away from the low dinner table. Typically, individuals would support their upper body on one elbow while eating. So it is easy to imagine John leaning back onto Jesus' chest.

While this verse is clearly a setup for what comes next—Peter asking John to interview Jesus privately about the identity of the betrayer—we must spend time contemplating the significance of John's including this detail. The intimacy the disciples experienced was one of committed love—not theirs but Jesus'. John's self-image was that of "one of His disciples, whom Jesus loved." This is the same word for Jesus' love for "His own" (plural) expressed at the beginning of this Upper Room narrative (John 13:1). Jesus loved them all with an "agape" kind of love. Loyal, committed, sacrificial. He loved them ultimately, and this would be fully demonstrated soon (see Romans 5:8). So whatever we say about John's self-reference, we should come short of saying the Lord loved John *more* than the others.

What we can say is that John saw himself not in terms of *his* loyalty to the Lord (like Peter, who vowed to defend Jesus to the death), but in terms of the Lord's love for him. He continually saw himself as "the disciple whom Jesus loved" (see also John 19:26, 20:2, 21:7, 20). We all, who are blood-bought children of God, can say with John that we are disciples whom Jesus loves. It is all about His love for us, not our loyalty to Him. We are His beloved.

Lord, though I strive to serve and love You with all my heart, it is You who first loved me, and I rest in Your love. I too, like John, am Your beloved disciple.

The Big Question

²⁴ So Simon Peter gestured to him, and said to him, "Tell us who it is of whom He is speaking."

Indications of an eyewitness testimony, John pictures for us the gesture of Peter. The two must have been some distance apart at the dinner table as they reclined, but close enough to carry on a somewhat private conversation; possibly Jesus was preoccupied in conversation with someone else and Peter mouthed the question to John. As in all cultures, a dinner party invokes many side conversations, and this may very well have been the case. The whole record of the Upper Room conversation in this gospel account would not account for the whole conversation taking place, judging from a mere time perspective.

Why would Peter not have asked Jesus directly; why go through John? Was it just a matter of position at the table? That seems hardly likely since the number in the Upper Room would not prevent someone even at the far end of the table from speaking up in everyone's hearing. Certainly Jesus' speaking to the whole group would indicate that. Could it be that Peter was conferring with the "inner circle" (which would ostensibly include James as well) for the purpose of discussing this matter of betrayal with Jesus more privately? In that way, Jesus could confide in them, and then they could take care of the matter for Him.

Or could it be that Peter was still smarting from Jesus' rebuking him for resisting the foot-washing, and therefore was a bit reticent to address this new issue? We will never know for sure, but our suspicions are with the last suggestion: Peter was beginning to feel less confident in Jesus' approval of him. With all the assertions of loyalty coming yet, we can possibly see an increase in uneasiness on all the disciples' parts, especially Peter's, culminating with his adamant and strong vow of loyalty that he would never deny Christ. Was he speaking out of a fomenting insecurity? The truth is that he eventually denied Christ three times, so we know how it ended up. Such strong proclamations often reveal one's trying to prove himself. So his reticence in the Upper Room to speak about the betrayer may have been the beginning of Peter's self-doubt.

In Peter, we see a humility lesson in the making. We are called upon to be loyal to Christ, and we dare not set a lower goal than that. At the same time, we are called to humility by the recognition of our human failings. The balance point between these forms the fulcrum of spiritual life that is following Christ.

Lord, I humbly follow You loyally and boldly, recognizing that my walk is not yet perfect. But my goal is to never deny or betray You.

WEEKEND READING

Saturday – John 3:1-21
Sunday – Acts 4:1-12

PERSONAL REFLECTIONS

_____
_____
_____
_____
_____
_____
_____
_____
_____
_____
_____
_____
_____
_____
_____
_____
_____
_____
_____
_____
_____
_____
_____

Leaning on Jesus

John 13:25

²⁵ He, leaning back thus on Jesus' bosom, said to Him, "Lord, who is it?"

John was in the privileged position, at the side of the Lord Jesus in the Upper Room, close enough to lean back against Jesus as they reclined around the dinner table, as was customary in those times. Any joviality was quickly replaced by ominous dark clouds. Matthew, one of those in the room, remembers the introspection caused by Jesus' comments about betrayal, as he wrote, "Being deeply grieved, they each one began to say to Him, 'Surely not I, Lord?'" (Matt. 26:22). The NIV puts it this way; "Surely, you don't mean me?" The NLT has it, "Am I the one, Lord?" The reason for variety in translation is that they are all encompassed in the original language here. The disciples all were asking the question, but expecting, yea hoping, for a negative response.

Clearly, the hint of self-doubt or at the least the hint that Jesus might have doubted them was in the air. Unimaginable and completely unexpected. Each vouched for his own loyalty by stating the incredulous, almost while beginning to doubt Jesus: "How could You doubt my loyalty to You? Don't You know, don't You see how much I have sacrificed to follow You? I can't believe You would think that about me. You don't, do you?" Couple that with the natural self-doubt most people carry about, especially those in the presence of someone far superior to themselves. Jesus was leaving them hanging, and it was simply not tolerable.

John alone among the gospel writers remembers the intimate details recorded in our passage today, probably because only he and Peter may have been privy to them. Maybe the plan was to whisper to Jesus in a side, quiet conversation—so in case it was to be one of them whom Jesus suspected, they could deal with this privately, away from the hearing of the others. Be that as it may, an answer must be found to who the betrayer was.

John doesn't record the self-doubts of all the others, but only the question he asked of the Master: "Lord, who is it?" Who is the guilty party that would so treacherously betray the Lord they had all come to love and for whom they had sacrificed so much? What John and Peter would do with the knowledge we can only surmise.

But they weren't afraid to ask. It must have been a hard question to ask. The unity and camaraderie of this band of men was about to be forever disrupted. It would never be the same again. Disloyalty, when found, irreparably changes everything. Little did they know that the answer to the question was someone whose name would forever be associated with betrayal.

Lord, thank You that in Your love, You are always loyal to me.

Bread Dipping

²⁶ Jesus then answered, "That is the one for whom I shall dip the morsel and give it to him." So when He had dipped the morsel, He took and gave it to Judas, the son of Simon Iscariot.

Never one to give a simple answer, Jesus answers John (and Peter's question) somewhat cryptically. The "morsel" is literally a piece of bread—not the yeast-raised kind of our day, but probably a flat bread. The dipping was probably into wine or some kind of meat juice. And the action of Jesus, it is said, was a sign of respect shown by the host of a meal to an honored guest. Others think it was something done for all the guests, with Judas, in this case, being the first. Minor details, but rich in ironic symbolism.

Jesus had told them long before that there was among them one who did not truly believe: "'But there are some of you who do not believe.' For Jesus knew from the beginning who they were who did not believe, and who it was that would betray Him . . . 'Did I Myself not choose you, the twelve, and *yet* one of you is a devil?' Now He meant Judas *the son* of Simon Iscariot, for he, one of the twelve, was going to betray Him" (John 6:64, 70-71). Jesus had just winnowed down the huge crowds to just a few true believers by His difficult teaching, "Truly, truly, I say to you, unless you eat the flesh of the Son of Man and drink His blood, you have no life in yourselves" (John 6:53). He raised the stakes of belief to complete commitment, and "[a]s a result of this many of His disciples withdrew and were not walking with Him anymore" (John 6:66). The remaining small number included Judas, who would outwardly walk with those who said, "Where would we go? You have words of eternal life. We have believed and have come to know that You are the Holy One of God" (John 6:68-69). But he would prove to be not only an unbeliever, but also a traitor.

This Judas was the son of a man named Simon Iscariot. Indeed, a son brings dishonor also to his father's name. Judas' life affected so many! His name always appears last in the lists of disciples, and he is to be distinguished from another disciple named Judas, who was the son of a man named James (Luke 6:16).

Did the betrayer suspect that Jesus was aware of his traitor's heart? We don't know how long even Judas himself was aware of the extent to which his unbelieving heart would take him. But in this despicable individual we find the ultimate application of Jeremiah's prophecy, "The heart is more deceitful than all else and is desperately sick; who can understand it?" (Jer. 17:9). But for the grace of God, there go I.

Lord, "I do believe; help my unbelief" (Mark 9:24) so that I never betray You.

The Penultimate Move

²⁷ After the morsel, Satan then entered into him. Therefore Jesus said to him, "What you do, do quickly."

One cannot worship the risen Savior without contemplating His rejection and suffering. Dark and gloomy as it is, scenes like this passage weave the black background against which the brilliant glory of the Savior shines. On so many levels this verse draws us deeper into the spiritual battle that has raged on since the beginning of creation, a veritable chess match whose stakes are nothing short of cosmic. The most powerful force of all God's creation (Ezek. 28:12) has been locked in continuous maneuvering to checkmate his Creator, and the universe is his chess board. We see in the first chapters of the book of Job the overriding, defining narrative describing the root issue: whether a human being would inevitably curse his Creator if blessing were removed.

Satan now was making his penultimate move. Judas' leaving to start the process of betrayal was the big setup for the crucifixion. The irony of this is that the devil knew full well that he was not surprising Jesus, for he knew that Jesus was the "Son of the Most High God"—if his minions knew it, then certainly he would have known it as well (Mark 5:7). Yet desperate was the devil to play on, despite the inherent futility. What must he have thought when Jesus even encouraged the action, and to do it with haste? This was not the time to delay the game, as had been the case in the past, when He said, "My time is not yet here" (John 7:6). Jesus was in full control of the game.

Contrived paranormal movies cannot compare with this moment of demonic possession. The very arch-enemy of God, Satan himself, enters the body of one of the twelve. While previously the devil interacted directly with Christ in the wilderness temptation, here we find him embodying himself in a human for the task of betrayal. While he could have used other supernatural means, he resorts to betrayal, treachery and deception. These are his "best," most effective moves. Jesus saw this clearly when He confronted His unbelieving detractors: "You are of *your* father the devil . . . He was a murderer from the beginning, and does not stand in the truth because there is no truth in him. Whenever he speaks a lie, he speaks from his own *nature,* for he is a liar and the father of lies" (John 8:44). In the Upper Room, Satan lives up to his billing. But though he was planning the move that would secure his goal of supremacy over God, he was about to fall prey to the checkmate that would be heard throughout eternity.

Lord, I marvel at how Your every move is perfectly crafted
to show the shining brilliance of Your glory.

None the Wiser

John 13:28-29

[28] Now no one of those reclining at the table knew for what purpose He had said this to him. [29] For some were supposing, because Judas had the money box, that Jesus was saying to him, "Buy the things we have need of for the feast"; or else, that he should give something to the poor.

Superficial reading of this verse may breed incredulity. How could the disciples have not understood what was really happening after what Jesus said? After all, He told them the meaning of dipping the morsel of bread and giving it to one of them. As with all of Scripture reading, we must approach it with an open, studious mind, digging deeper than the surface. Significant events are often conveyed in rather brief form, so it makes sense that all the details are not given. As much as possible we need to recreate the scenario in a way that makes sense.

The orientation of this meal for at least 13 people (possibly there were others with them), the method of seating (or we should say reclining, with legs and feet extending away from the table), the mood and the confusion all play a role in picturing what was happening. So unimaginable was it that any of them would betray the Master, around whom they had gathered and for whom they sacrificed everything, that even the suggestion of betrayal brought absolute confusion. To be sure, they had all struggled with understanding their enigmatic Leader, and they had all fallen short of His expectations; Peter was the most noteworthy example of this when Jesus said to him, "Get behind Me, Satan! You are a stumbling block to Me; for you are not setting your mind on God's interests, but man's" (Matt. 16:23). Pretty harsh interpretation of Peter's actions. But treachery? It couldn't be!

Now Judas appears to have been the treasurer of the group; he "had the money box." It was he who expressed overt concern for the poor (John 12:3-5) coupled with indignation over a lavish honor bestowed on Jesus. His issue was ". . . not because he was concerned about the poor, but because he was a thief, and as he had the money box, he used to pilfer what was put into it" (John 12:6). By the time of the Upper Room, his duplicity was exposed by Jesus, as Matthew records: "And Judas, who was betraying Him, said, 'Surely it is not I, Rabbi?' Jesus said to him, 'You have said *it* yourself'" (Matt. 26:25). Apparently no one else heard this interchange.

The self-doubts, unbelief and confusion of the disciples blinded them to the meaning of Jesus' words. How much does that also happen to us?

Lord, I confess to wallowing in self-doubts and superficial thinking, which blind me to understanding Your Word. Thank You for not giving up on me.

Forgiveness Trumps

John 13:30

[30] So after receiving the morsel he went out immediately; and it was night.

No time to waste, the betrayer exited the intimate circle of fellowship—and fast was the fall thereof. Sometimes when the tares among the wheat have participated for so long in the close interaction of the family of believers, we are surprised at their seemingly quick rejection of Christ and abandonment to the world. But the inner workings of the heart are seldom obvious. So what looks like a quick desertion from the faith is nothing more than the climax of a long simmering unbelief. Such was the case with Judas.

The die was now cast and Jesus encouraged its timely dispatch. The Sabbath was well entered, the calm before the storm. Behind the scenes, the crescendo builds toward the climax. This is the last we see of Judas until after this last dinner of our Lord was completed and the company retreated to the garden for the fateful kiss.

Judas would miss everything else in the Upper Room. Fellowship was irreparably broken; things would never be the same. Indeed his life span on this earth was going to be cut short by suicide. What bad timing—his demise came just hours before the Savior's death on the cross for the sins of the world. Unlike Peter the denier, Judas the betrayer removed all possibility for repentance and restoration. Even Thomas the doubter was not rejected by the Lord (John 20:28-29). All the other disciples, the "abandoners" (Matt. 26:56), found forgiveness and ultimately carried on as Jesus' appointed eye-witnesses (Acts 1:8) and messengers of His teachings (Acts 2:42). But not Judas!

Matthew alone records the turncoat's obituary (Matt. 27:1-10); John the beloved, having the closest relationship with our Lord, does not even mention the treacherous kiss (Luke 22:47-48). Yet it was not that Judas' sin was, in its essence, worse than denying Christ or doubting Christ or abandoning Christ. Judas' door-slamming, unforgiveable sin was that he prevented any opportunity for forgiveness. He would never hear Christ's restoring words, "I will be with you to the end of the ages." His suicide erected an eternal roadblock to repentance. "It is appointed for men to die once and after this *comes* judgment . . ." (Heb. 9:27).

The betrayer was not unforgiveable. The Sovereign of the universe can forgive whom He will. He took a Christian-killing kicker of the goads (Saul of Tarsus) and not only saved him but used him to reach the lost Gentiles (as Paul the apostle). God could have done that with Judas. The difference? Repentance!

Lord, help me to never have a hardened heart, to never wallow in my grief and resist Your kindness of forgiveness. Your forgiveness is greater than all my sin.

WEEKEND READING

Saturday – John 3:22-26
Sunday – Acts 4:13-31

PERSONAL REFLECTIONS

_____
_____
_____
_____
_____
_____
_____
_____
_____
_____
_____
_____
_____
_____
_____
_____
_____
_____
_____

Winnowed Down

John 13:31

[31] Therefore when he had gone out, Jesus said, "Now is the Son of Man glorified, and God is glorified in Him . . ."

The group of disciples is now further reduced, after the initial decrease from the multitudes to relatively few in number. In John 6, Jesus made clear that following Him required nothing short of an all-out commitment. "As a result of this many of His disciples withdrew and were not walking with Him anymore" (John 6:66). He gave the twelve opportunity to bail out as well (John 6:67-69), but they—including Judas—affirmed their allegiance to Him. Yet even at that time He made clear to them, "Did I Myself not choose you, the twelve, and *yet* one of you is a devil?" (John 6:70). Finally, the group is now culled down to eleven; the devil and his work among them is done, and the tempter won't return until the garden—not Eden this time, but Gethsemane.

What a contrast with other interactions with demonically influenced people. The norm was for Jesus to cast out, or exorcise, the demon, as for example in Mark 5, where a "legion" of demons were expelled from a single man. But here, Satan, the prince of the demons, was not cast out of the man Judas, but Judas went out, and presumably Satan with him. Could not have Jesus exorcized Satan? Of course. At the beginning of His earthly ministry, during the temptation in the desert, Jesus commanded Satan with a simple word: "Go, Satan! For it is written, 'You shall worship the LORD your God, and serve Him only'" (Matt. 4:10). No fight, no struggle. Satan left. That could have happened in this case with Judas just as easily. We know from a theological perspective that this betrayal was prophesied and thus was part of God's ultimate plan. But it may well have been that Judas was completely confirmed in his own heart, that there would have been an unwillingness on his part to alter his plans of betrayal. His heart, like Pharaoh's of the Exodus story, was completely hardened.

So Judas and his "complicitor" were not privy to this intimate conversation. Of course, Satan can read this tome of John's as well as we can, so he is cognizant *now* of the Upper Room conversation. But at the time, he was the swine before whom Jesus was not about to cast His pearls. This was a select audience; the half-hearted followers, self-serving religious folks and demons were not privileged to sit among these favored ones, these loved ones.

We are about to see Jesus in His most transparent moments, in His passion, His struggles and His death. As with the eleven, we too prepare to "share in the fellowship of His suffering." The depths and heights of His glory eclipse all else, so that even when despair comes, faith does not give up.

Lord, I am ready to listen to Your preparation for those who have left all.

Magnification to the Nth

John 13:31 (cont.)

³¹ Therefore when he had gone out, Jesus said, "Now is the Son of Man glorified, and God is glorified in Him . . ."

With Judas now gone, the about-to-be-crucified Savior of the world begins to take His faithful disciples deeper in their preparation for His departure. As yet, they had absolutely no idea what the next 24 hours would hold for them. Yes, Jesus talked about a betrayal, and in their minds Judas had gone out on a grocery run. And to be sure, Jesus was acting a bit strange with washing their feet. Little did they suspect that in less than one full day, their world would be shattered. Little did they comprehend the glory of God—glory that had been veiled since the dawn of creation but that was about to break out in magnificent light. The love of God for His fallen image bearers would be demonstrated in all its brilliance. For God would soon be reconciling the world to Himself through Christ's death on the cross. This was not just a return to a pre-fallen Edenic state, but to a new, glorious existence where the grandeur and splendor of God would be manifested far greater than ever before.

No, the disciples had no idea, but Jesus was preparing them for it. What began the Upper Room experience in John 13:1 ("Jesus knowing that His hour had come that He would depart out of this world to the Father") now begins to unfold. Jesus wants to tell them about it before it comes, so that when it does come they will understand and be able to act upon their preparation.

The hour of Jesus' glory had come. Thirteen times in the Upper Room Jesus spoke of glory. The term "hour" obviously doesn't mean the literal 60 minutes during which Jesus was then speaking. It is a prophetic figure of speech, often used to refer to the appointment of God's cataclysmic working in the world. We tend to think of the glory coming as having to do with the resurrection, and that is certainly a part of it. However, the resurrection might be better understood as the evidence of glory, the ratification of it. But the essence of glory is something else, something greater, something far more—well, glorious.

Jesus did not come into the world to be resurrected, although that certainly proved Him to be the Son of God with power (Rom 1:4). He came into the world to save sinners. And in this we find the pinnacle of the glory of God, a glory whose contemplation can never be exhausted. Like a magnifying glass, the death of Christ brings an eternal, ever-amplifying, ever-enlarging understanding of the character, qualities and attributes of God. The cross is the ultimate, climactic and complete theology of God.

Lord, help me see Jesus in all His glory, the perfect expression of God.

Glory Abounds

32 ". . . if God is glorified in Him, God will also glorify Him in Himself, and will glorify Him immediately."

Glory is what God is all about. Five times the word "glorify" appears in this and the preceding verse. The disciples were being introduced to an unveiling of God in a way that was previously unimaginable. They were going to see the glory of God like it had never been seen or understood before. In the darkening gloom, while they could only see confusion and seeping depression, Christ spoke of the brilliance of what was about to take place—like a football coach challenging his team to see their monumental loss as the best thing that could have happened because of a higher principle in view.

To glorify means to magnify, to enlarge the view of something, as we mentioned before. To help others see the great and wonderful that is truly there. The Hebrew concept of glory comes from the idea of weightiness. An architectural column was said to be glorious because of its girth and solidness. The word "glory" came to be used of the weightiness of one's character. So to glorify a person was not to simply embellish his image, but to reveal the weightiness of his character, who he really is. A painting, for example, can be seen simply as a work of art. But a good curator can explain the painting, its background, the ideas reflected, the subtleties, the lighting—all of which help the viewer grow in appreciation for the masterpiece. He has "glorified" that work of art. A maestro can interpret the score of a music piece, focusing in on the various instruments, tones, rhythm and emphases, to bring concert-goers to a greater understanding and enjoyment of the beauty and symphonic resonance of the masterpiece. That glorifies the music and the composer. In the same way, glorifying God puts forth His character and nature in a way that makes us see how great He really is.

Four aspects of glory are seen in these five usages of the word "glorify" in verses 31-32. First, "The Son of Man is glorified." The life and character of Jesus Christ has been laid out for all to see. The gospel accounts, like a magnifying glass, reveal the exquisite picture of Christ—not just what He taught but who He was. He is "the Christ, the Son of the Living God." No more will John use the phrase "Son of Man" as a title for Christ. He has been magnified as the Savior sent into the world to save those who have gone astray. The Son of Man has been glorified; He is the Son of God.

Lord, thank You that You have revealed to us that Jesus was more than just a good teacher and prophet. He is the exalted Lord and Christ, the promised Messiah.

Glory Reflexively

John 13:32 (cont.)

32 ". . . if God is glorified in Him, God will also glorify Him in Himself, and will glorify Him immediately."

Secondly, "God is glorified in Him." "He has explained *Him*," John writes in his account (John 1:18). The word "explained" means to fully bring out the essence of something, to "exegete" it. Jesus has helped us see God more clearly, how great He is.

Third, "God will glory Him in Himself." If God is indeed seen most clearly in Jesus, then God will in the future continue to do the same thing, namely, to use Christ as a magnifying glass through whom He Himself is seen more clearly. In other words, glory gives rise to more glory. And as we grow in our understanding and knowledge of Him and His glory (2 Peter 3:18), we are ". . . being transformed into the same image *from glory to glory*, just as from the Lord, the Spirit" (2 Corinthians 3:18, emphasis added). Mundane life for us is profoundly changed, and changed continually as we grow in Christ.

Christ's glory reveals His absolute perfection. For anything less, a magnifying glass reveals imperfections. Closely examining a beautiful flower shows the many imperfections not seen in a casual glance or by the naked eye. But when Christ magnifies God, we see only endless perfection. Just as scientists in their study of the human body find increasingly complex and beautiful design, bone and muscle placements, connections, arrangements, cells, DNA, atoms and sub-atomic particles, through Christ we see the absolutely astounding beauty and flawless perfection of God. There are no aberrations. The more we search for God in Christ, the more we discover untold, unimaginable wonder. While at a general level the universe declares His glory (Rom. 1:19-20)—the contemplation of which can be overwhelming considering the vastness and wonder of the universe—Christ brings details into focus like a telescope, or enlarges like a microscope that which we couldn't see otherwise. And at every level God is seen to be completely and absolutely perfect.

Now, here is the third movement of glory: God will *continue* to magnify Christ in God Himself, so that in turn God Himself will be glorified (yes, I know that can sound confusing). It is like making a big deal about an extremely high-resolution camera because it shows great detail of the object. Like glorifying the mirror in a telescope or the lens in a microscope that help you see the details so much more clearly and accurately, God will glorify Christ and continue to do so, because it will help us see God Himself better.

Father, when I contemplate Your perfections as seen in Your Son, I am overwhelmed with how perfect He is. Help me to stay focused on Him.

Glory Immediately

John 13:32 (cont.)

32 ". . . if God is glorified in Him, God will also glorify Him in Himself, and will glorify Him immediately."

Finally, the fourth movement of glory is that God "will glorify Him immediately." This is where things become concrete, where glory becomes tangible, down to earth. This glory is not just some ethereal, esoteric concept or some religious experience intended for the monastics. This glory will immediately take place in less than 24 hours, not at all understood at first, but three days later revealed. Ironically, we tend to think of the resurrection of Christ as the event of glory, picturing the empty tomb with light shining out, brilliant angels, etc. But the glory of God in Christ was His reconciling the world to Himself. The resurrection is the final glory seen, but when we turn the magnifying glass on the cross, that is where we see the character of God on full display. Easter was proof of what Good Friday accomplished: the glorious deed was the cross.

That is why Paul writes in his quest to know Jesus (Phil. 3:10a) that he wanted to know the power of His resurrection (Phil. 3:10b). But the holy grail, as it were, was to know the "fellowship of His sufferings, being conformed to His death . . ." (Phil. 3:10c). This was the ultimate glory for the follower of Christ, because the cross is where Christ was most magnified. This truth so affected the apostle that it eclipsed all other earthly glories. His mantra was, "May it never be that I would boast [find glory in], except in the cross of our Lord Jesus Christ, through which the world has been crucified to me, and I to the world" (Gal. 6:14). The cross represents the transforming glory of God.

Back in the Upper Room, Jesus would soon say to Philip, "He who has seen Me has seen the Father" (John 14:9). We need to keep looking to Christ and through Christ to see the Father, particularly as Christ was fulfilling the will of the Father in dying on the cross. We need to turn the magnifying glass on Him and examine the unending glory of God, His character and His essence as displayed on the cross. The well of truth will never cease to satisfy the thirsty soul; Christ will never cease to satisfy the heart's greatest desires.

We remember the summary of Hebrews 1:3: "He is the radiance of His [God's] glory and the exact representation of His nature . . . when He had made purification of sins, He sat down at the right hand of the Majesty on high." This is the glory of God. This is our glory—to bask in the light of His glory. We never strive for a higher goal than when we strive for Christ.

Father, I too glorify Christ, for He perfectly reveals You. Show me increasingly how great He is. I want to see Him, to know Him and to love Him.

WEEKEND READING

Saturday – John 4:1-14
Sunday – Acts 4:32–5:16

PERSONAL
REFLECTIONS

_____
_____
_____
_____
_____
_____
_____
_____

_____
_____
_____
_____
_____
_____
_____
_____
_____
_____
_____
_____
_____
_____

Going Away?

John 13:33

³³ "Little children, I am with you a little while longer. You will seek Me; and as I said to the Jews, now I also say to you, 'Where I am going, you cannot come.'"

With great affection, Jesus refers to His disciples as "little children." John, the gospel chronicler, stands alone in recording Jesus' reference to the disciples with this word. While the regular word for children (Greek: *teknon*) is used by Jesus elsewhere (e.g. Mark 10:24), only the beloved disciple John noticed and recorded the diminutive form (Greek: *teknia*), a term of endearment—and He used it only after Judas had left. The only other place in the NT this word form can be found occurs in John's first epistle, where he refers to his readers seven times as "little children." He certainly emulated his Master well. In using this word, John captures and embodies the intimate relationship that Christians experience first with the Savior and then with those whom we disciple. In his elderly years (he penned the Gospel According to John and his epistles circa AD 90–95), he wrote as a fatherly figure (because of his age), but also as a spiritual father (regardless of age) to those whom he desired to see grow into spiritual maturity.

Jesus now drops a bomb: He's going to leave the disciples, and so the urgency for final instructions. He's leaving, and they can no longer follow Him. He had already said this to the "Jews" before: "For a little while longer I am with you, then I go to Him who sent Me. You will seek Me, and will not find Me; and where I am, you cannot come" (John 7:33-34). (In John's writings, the term "Jews" refers to the Israelites in general, and probably the Jewish leaders in particular.) The Jews had understood Him to mean that He would leave the physical land of Israel and go to the Jews scattered around the empire. Another time when He reiterated these words they thought He might be speaking of suicide (John 8:21-22). So the *words* were not new to the disciples, but now these words were being directed at them! They would soon be without Jesus. They had not yet heard Jesus' post-resurrection promise, "Lo, I will be with you always, even to the end of the age" (Matt. 28:20).

For now, He was going to be with them only a little longer, a matter of a few hours, and He still had much to say. But they would discover after Pentecost a new and greater presence of the God whom they served, in the person of the Holy Spirit—about whom Jesus had yet much to teach them in the Upper Room. But first things first, He next speaks to them about love, the foundation of everything else He wants to teach them.

Lord, while I would absolutely love to have You here physically with me, I believe by faith that You are with me in a greater way, by Your Spirit.

A New Kind of Love

John 13:34

34 "A new commandment I give to you, that you love one another, even as I have loved you, that you also love one another."

Love is central to Christianity, so central that even non-Christians recognize it as the "supposed" defining characteristic of those who claim to follow Christ. We believers do not always live up to this commandment, but it is the gold standard for Christian behavior. But in what sense was it new, as Jesus says here in the passage for today?

It was not new in its time sequence, in that love was required also in the Old Testament—for example, Leviticus 19:18 states, "You shall love your neighbor as yourself." Certainly Jesus had given the commandment to love early in His ministry: "You have heard that it was said, 'You shall love your neighbor and hate your enemy.' But I say to you, love your enemies and pray for those who persecute you . . ." (Matt. 5:43-44). Even in the Gospel According to John, He had already commanded His disciples to love (see John 15:12, 17).

What was new is not the timing of the command but the nature of the command. In the OT, they were to love their neighbor. Jesus taught them to love their enemies. The newness, though, is found more in the way they were to love: "even as I have loved you." This puts love into a whole different category, an impossible kind of love, one that can only happen by the power of the Holy Spirit, whom Jesus has more to say about shortly.

The disciples have yet to see the love of Christ expressed in its fullest, ultimate way. Yet, Jesus speaks of it as past tense. Little did they realize the love it required for the Creator God of the universe to condescend in humility to take on the form of a human being, a "servant" as Paul says in Philippians 2:7-8. He left His glorious throne at the right hand of the Father to come and die for the sins of those who rejected Him. He came to live as a human and lay His human life down for us. This was love at its finest. So yes, Jesus had already loved them by the fact that He was there in the flesh. But His love was about to be made perfect in His ultimate sacrifice. We readers of this passage, who have read the Upper Room discourse many times before, can't help but anticipate Jesus' clarification of this two chapters later: "Greater love has no one than this, that one lay down his life for his friends" (John 15:13).

Truly, as John says elsewhere, "In this is love, not that we loved God, but that He loved us and sent His Son *to be* the propitiation for our sins. Beloved, if God so loved us, we also ought to love one another" (1 John 4:10-11).

Lord, I can't thank You enough for loving me and giving Yourself to die in my place. This motivates me to love others as You have loved me.

Highest Love Standard

John 13:34 (cont.)

[34] *"A new commandment I give to you, that you love one another, even as I have loved you, that you also love one another."*

S tandards of love can be self-defining and relative. To love as you have been loved depends upon the love with which you have been loved. If God is the one who has loved you, and indeed He has, then the standard is quite high. This leads to the so-called "love, period" sort of love. There can be no keeping score with God, no out-loving Him. We can't get Him to love us more. He has loved us so completely and graciously, how can we not love Him back in like manner?

Yet how can we love Him the way He has loved us? His is so much greater, more holy than ours. His is absolutely perfect. We can never love like He does. But love, when understood properly, is something that a finite being can do just as thoroughly as the Infinite. Love is defined not in terms of giving what we don't have, but in giving what we do have. I give simply of myself, and that is like God. I mimic Him, who gave of Himself, so I give of myself. We are called to love as He loved. And that is something that is humanly possible, if understood humbly but correctly.

The word "love" as used here by Jesus is the Greek word "agape," which means a sacrificial love. Before the Christian era, the word did exist, but it was not common. In Greek and especially Roman culture, sacrificial love was not held as a high character trait but more as a weakness. Status was not attained through sacrificing oneself for others but by establishing one's superiority over others. It was the Christian community that adopted and popularized the word to convey the attitude of God toward us so that it came to be the defining characteristic quality (see the next verse) of the followers of Christ.

So while the world says, in effect, "Love your neighbor as they have loved you," and the Law of Moses says, "Love your neighbor as yourself," Jesus says, "Love one another, even as I have loved you." Anything less than Jesus' standard becomes completely relative, circumstantially based. If my love for someone depends upon his love for me, then the least fault in his love toward me (and be sure that he will have faults in his love for me, as I too will have for him), will lead to a diminishing of the love both of us actually express. This becomes a vicious cycle that degenerates into no love at all. Further, the faulty thinking of today that says I must first love myself before I can adequately love others falls flat before Jesus' words here. The higher standard is Jesus' love.

Lord, I want to love others with the highest possible standard, with the love You have for me. But Lord, I need Your help to do this.

The Mark of a Christian

John 13:35

[35] *"By this all men will know that you are My disciples, if you have love for one another."*

Talk, liturgy, doctrinal correctness, moral faultlessness, wisdom—all are good things, but they do not mark us out as Christians. Many religions of the world espouse these things, or claim so. Of course the central truth claim of Christianity is unique: that we are sinners who have offended a holy and righteous God; we are incapable of saving ourselves, and therefore God took the initiative in saving us through the substitutionary atonement of Jesus Christ on the cross. We enter into that salvation by faith through grace and not by any meritorious works of our own. But knowing and believing all that does not *mark* us out as followers of Christ to non-Christians.

Many "Christians" proclaim in the public square edicts on morality and righteousness, only to evoke the scorn of the world as misguided, out-of-touch ignoramuses (at best) or pompous, self-righteous fundamentalists (at worst). Such "Christian" bantering, even in the name of Christ, does not mark a person out as a genuine follower of Christ.

Jesus proclaimed in the Upper Room in no uncertain terms that sacrificial love provides the undeniable trait which distinguishes a genuine Christian. Specifically, He refers to the twelve loving one another, but we know that since "God so loved the world," our love should extend beyond the brotherhood of believers. But notice the priority: "So then . . . let us do good to all people, and especially to those who are of the household of the faith" (Gal. 6:10). There is a benefit to being part of the camaraderie of Christian fellowship. So we especially take to heart Jesus' command to love one another. And the world notices.

Even the most ardent atheist uses the "Christ love standard" in his attempts to undermine the Christians' witness, in essence using Jesus' own standard against those who claim to be His followers today. The point is that the world knows the standard for Christians; Christ knows it (obviously). Therefore, the question remains: do we who are Christ-followers know it? This is the key operative truth of evangelism: loving people into the family of God. When non-believers see us caring for each other, sharing one another's burdens, looking out for each other, praying for each other and sacrificing for each other—and also by extension doing these things for the people outside of the faith—they will begin to see the love of God in Christ, who is in us. And this will lead them to ultimately discover a love beyond which there is no greater: Jesus died for us.

Lord, help me love my Christian and non-Christian
neighbors in the way Christ loves me.

Follow—Not Now But Later

John 13:36

³⁶ Simon Peter said to Him, "Lord, where are You going?" Jesus answered, "Where I go, you cannot follow Me now; but you will follow later."

All the talk of love seemed to miss Peter, the consensus spokesperson for the twelve. Praise God for this character in the story that gives divine Authorial opportunity to address very natural human concerns and foibles. Apparently there was only so much they could take in, but the most pressing issue needing clarification was not the love commandment, but the "Where I am going, you cannot come" comment (vs. 33). They had turned their backs, burned their bridges to follow Jesus. Earlier, "Peter said to Him, 'Behold, we have left everything and followed You; what then will there be for us?'" (Matt. 19:27). There was no turning back. If Jesus left them, they would be completely lost. Another time, when the vast majority of "disciples withdrew and were not walking with Him anymore" (John 6:66), Peter confessed, "Lord, to whom shall we go? You have words of eternal life" (John 6:68). They had stuck their proverbial necks out, gone beyond the point of no return. Was everyone else right? Were these eleven fools for continuing to follow Christ?

"No way," we project in Peter's mind. He, for one, was not going to give up easily. Still calling Him Lord, Peter (dare we presume to read his mind) begins to suspect that maybe Jesus thinks he doesn't measure up or isn't loyal enough to Him and His cause. But not willing to sit around and guess, he ventures a clarification question: "Lord, where are you going?" If Jesus wouldn't take them along, then fine, Peter would find his own way.

Jesus essentially repeats Himself: "Where I go, you cannot follow Me . . ." But graciously He adds, ". . . now; but you will follow later." In other words, this is only a temporary hiatus in their physical proximity. There was a place where Jesus had to go it alone, a task that He had to accomplish solo. But Peter (and by implication the others) would later be able to rejoin Him. There would be a day when they too would follow Him in death!

This teaching would later become a great source of comfort to all believers. Although Jesus did reunite with them for a little while after the resurrection, He left again at His ascension. The expectation of His return is what keeps us encouraged in His absence. Most would die and also follow Jesus in resurrection. But there are some who will be ". . . caught up to meet the Lord in the air, and so we shall always be with the Lord. Therefore comfort one another with these words" (1 Thess. 4:17-18). Whether we join Christ through death or in the rapture, praise God we will be joining Him where He has gone!

Lord, I am so looking forward to being reunited with You at Your coming.

WEEKEND READING

Saturday – John 4:15-26
Sunday – Acts 5:17-32

PERSONAL REFLECTIONS

_____
_____
_____
_____
_____
_____
_____
_____
_____
_____
_____
_____
_____
_____
_____
_____
_____
_____
_____
_____
_____
_____
_____

Loyalty Asserted

³⁷ Peter said to Him, "Lord, why can I not follow You right now? I will lay down my life for You."

L oyalty asserting, Peter proclaims his fidelity. If anyone was devoted to Christ it was this man. Allegiance was his middle name—at least that is what he wants to convince Jesus of. He is the same one who, when seeing Jesus walking on the water in the midst of the storm, was willing to risk his life to be with his Master. "Lord, if it is You, command me to come to You on the water" (Matt. 14:28). And leaving the other gunnel-hugging disciples, he dared to do what normally would be called foolish: he stepped out of the boat and walked on water at the Lord's command.

Then there was the time when Jesus spoke of going to Jerusalem, where He would suffer and be killed (and also be raised up again—but Peter missed that part). This disciple expressed his consternation at the thought: "Peter took Him aside and began to rebuke Him, saying, 'God forbid *it,* Lord! This shall never happen to You'" (Matt. 16:22). Although Jesus sternly rebuked him, "Get behind Me, Satan! You are a stumbling block to Me" (Matt. 16:23), you must admire this disciple's devotion to his Master. Who can forget Peter's impetuous initiative to provide housing for Christ on the Mount of Transfiguration? Or his frequent speaking out before any of the others had a chance to say anything?

Yes, Peter, of all the disciples, was loyal to Christ. Not that the others weren't, but he stood out among those who had left all to follow Jesus. So now, as we might expect, at Jesus' announcement that where He was going the disciples could not come, Peter speaks up. "If loyalty is the issue, Jesus, I'm Your man. How could You not possibly want to take me along?"

Peter misses a few things of significance, as we often do as well. First, we sometimes have *no idea* what the Lord is doing. Peter saw only the physical suffering, for which he was ready to defend Jesus to the death. How often do we only see the surface of our situation and not the bigger picture? The spiritual battle for the souls of men is at stake. Second, we often over-estimate our loyalty to Christ. Self-preservation, as Peter was about to learn, is an extremely strong instinct. Third, sometimes we cannot possibly understand what is coming, even if God were to explain it to us. Jesus had already told Peter of the resurrection (Matthew 16:22, as noted above), but he couldn't hear it.

Although Peter was sinking into a confusing panic, Jesus was not deterred in His training of the twelve. They must go through this perplexity.

---

*Lord Jesus, when I am confused and perplexed, I want
to see You and hold on to Your promises.*

Context for Mercy and Grace

John 13:38

³⁸ Jesus answered, "Will you lay down your life for Me? Truly, truly, I say to you, a rooster will not crow until you deny Me three times."

Second bomb dropping, Jesus gives the haunting assessment of Peter's claims to loyalty. What could this brave disciple be thinking in this moment? The Master has absolutely no confidence in him. Peter knows the Lord has an uncanny ability to predict the future. After all, this is the One whom he had previously proclaimed as "the Christ, the Son of the living God" (Matt. 16:16). How could he directly contradict the Son of God?

Worse than being chided for resisting Jesus' decision to go to Jerusalem or being addressed as "Satan" (Matt. 16:23), this charge of impending disloyalty must have been crushing to the one who was overzealous in his presumptive attempts to protect Jesus from opposition. After three-plus years of following Christ, in the end Peter was going to fail. He could protest no more—the Lord had spoken definitely; what would be the use? End of story, right? Wrong.

Again, the reader, even in the gospel writer's day, was already aware of how the story goes from here, for the other gospel accounts had already been in circulation for a number of years. Every one of the four chroniclers records this statement of Jesus to Peter. His legacy of failure is recorded indelibly for all generations to come. But again, that is not the end of the story, and we err to think this failure defines Peter. In truth, we must not allow any of our own failures to define us either.

The end game is what God does about our failure and how we respond to that. We know how the story plays out, with Jesus meeting Peter after the resurrection. Ignoring his failure, the Lord tells him three times to shepherd God's people. Peter's failure became simply a foundation or context for showing God's great mercy and grace in using broken and failing people to do great, responsible work for Him. Probably in his own mind he could rival Paul's statement, ". . . Christ Jesus came into the world to save sinners, among whom I am foremost *of all.* Yet for this reason I found mercy, so that in me as the foremost, Jesus Christ might demonstrate His perfect patience as an example for those who would believe in Him for eternal life" (1 Tim. 1:15-16).

Could this indelible experience of failure and restoration be reflected in his writings later to the scattered Christians? "[C]lothe yourselves with humility . . . for God is opposed to the proud, but gives grace to the humble. Therefore humble yourselves under the mighty hand of God . . ." (1 Peter 5:5-6).

Lord, never let me forget Your graciousness and mercy in overlooking my failures and disloyalty, and still wanting to use me to serve You.

New
Relationships

Fear Not

¹ "Do not let your heart be troubled; believe in God, believe also in Me."

Never has there been a more timely message than this one. In the face of growing despondency and confusion, when everything looks to the disciples like it is going downhill fast, Jesus counsels them to believe in Him. Raw, audacious, blind faith. Not blind in the sense of stupidity or ignorance, but blind in the sense of holding on to Jesus when nothing else makes sense, even when He doesn't make sense.

They had been afraid before when all seemed lost. Remember when Jesus came walking on the water in the midst of a monster storm that had even the most experienced, weather-hardened fishermen among them frightened out of their minds? Then Jesus calmly spoke, "It is I; do not be afraid" (John 6:20).

That was part of the training of the twelve then, but things were different now. In the Upper Room He was not offering His presence to them. In the storm event, He did offer His presence to them; in fact, He got into the boat with them. But now He has told them He is leaving them and they cannot follow Him. So how could their hearts not be troubled?

The Master cuts to the quick in His hard-core training of the eleven. At the core is faith in Him, just like they had faith in God. No clear teaching on the deity of Christ can be found. The same kind of faith that they had in the God of (what we now call) the Old Testament, they should now have in Him, Jesus. If He were not God, then Jesus would be uttering blasphemy. He asks the same level of faith, putting Himself on the same level with God. It is like He is saying, "Listen carefully to Me; understand what I am saying. What is about to happen will rock your world. Everything changes."

Of course, for God, nothing changes. But the ramifications of their leaving all and fully committing to Jesus are eternal in scope, epic in history, and profound in concept. When Peter confessed, "You are the Christ, the Son of the living God" (Matt. 16:16), eternity pivoted. When Martha spoke similar words— "Yes, Lord; I have believed that You are the Christ, the Son of God, *even* He who comes into the world" (John 11:27)—death gave way to life.

The message stays the same today. No matter what we are facing, no matter how difficult our life, no matter how impossible things look, the message of Christ remains the same: "Do not let your heart be troubled; believe in God, believe also in Me." In the dark night of the soul, God calls us to believe He is there with us and He is good. We have nothing to fear. We have Him.

Lord Jesus, though I am discouraged and feel defeated, beaten down and fearful, I reach out, against all I feel, and dare to believe and trust in You.

Better than Imagined

John 14:2

2 "In My Father's house are many dwelling places; if it were not so, I would have told you; for I go to prepare a place for you."

Heaven is going to be better than you or I can imagine. The Lord uses images from our experiences to describe our ultimate living situation after death— each image designed to excite the soul to the highest level of anticipation. In the OT, God used the image of an elaborate Bedouin tent and its furnishings to convey the eternal state. He said to Moses, "See that you make *them* after the pattern for them, which was shown to you on the mountain" (Ex. 25:40). What better way to convey the best possible kind of life to a nomadic people living in the desert, than a rich, ornate and huge tent? The writer to the Hebrews spoke of that tent (called the Tabernacle) as a "copy and shadow of the heavenly things . . ." (Heb. 8:5). A great amount of space is given to its descriptions: gold-covered tables, elaborate altars, an ark, angelic images, embroidered curtains and walls. Never has there been a tent so lavish.

In the book of Revelation, the eternal state is pictured as a beautiful city that will far outshine any Roman city. In fact, at the time of writing, the city of Rome was at or near its historical peak in terms of majestic, elaborate architecture and opulence. Yet in all its glory it was nothing compared to a city whose streets are paved with gold, whose gates are like enormous pearls (Rev. 21:21). To a Christian living at that time such an image would have been enticing.

In the time of the Upper Room, a different image is presented. The disciples typically would have lived in stone or crude brick homes, covered with a sort of mud plaster or stucco. The average working-class person (which was the vast majority of the population) subsisted in modest-sized homes of not more than a few rooms with limited space. The poorest lived in one-room, square buildings. Only the extremely wealthy (a sliver of the population) had large, opulent homes, the kind only dreamed about by the rest of the people. But Jesus informs His fearful, insecure disciples of their future destination. That is where He is going, where they cannot yet go. He will prepare it for them. It will be a huge mansion, with many rooms. And it will surpass any palace of any emperor of Rome or any other empire.

The point is that God invites us to imagine heaven with Christ as far exceeding our wildest dreams! And whatever you can imagine, heaven will be even greater. If Jesus could say the least in the kingdom of heaven is greater than John the Baptist (Matt. 11:11), then we can conclude that the least aspect of life in heaven is greater than the greatest possible aspect of life here on earth!

Wow, Lord. I can hardly wait to be with You in heaven!

Preparing the Best Place

John 14:3

³ "If I go and prepare a place for you, I will come again and receive you to Myself, that where I am, there you may be also."

Finally, Jesus assures them that His leaving them will only be a hiatus, a temporary situation. They could not possibly imagine life without Christ; they had given up everything to follow Him, to be with Him. They were not committed to the *cause* of Christ; they were committed to the person of Christ. Without Him, there was no cause. He was the cause!

The teachings of Christ are wrapped up in the person of Christ, because so much of what He taught was designed to reveal who He was and is. Yet today many claim to follow Jesus' teachings but are not committed to Him personally. Jesus didn't leave that as an option. To be sure, many follow the so-called "golden rule," and life is better for it. Some trace their non-violence ethic back to Him (and to Gandhi, Martin Luther King, Jr. and others)—all which is good "humanitarian" stuff. But Jesus' teaching included an all-out commitment to Him in everything He taught. The disciples in the Upper Room got that, and that is why Jesus' bombshell that He was leaving them was so disconcerting.

This verse provides the salve for the earlier shock. The teaching of Christ's return, as a result, composes a major teaching of the NT and of Christianity historically. Great systems of theology have wrestled with the details of eschatology, as scholars have named it, the study of the future and end times. Jesus gave very little detail, but He incited their imagination and anticipation. His goal was not to give them "correct" theology, but to whet the greatest yearning of their souls, that is to be with Christ. He gives no time table, but this truth of His return would bring hope and anticipation to millions of Christians for many centuries into the future.

The apostle Paul wrote these encouraging words of hope: ". . . in the future there is laid up for me the crown of righteousness, which the Lord, the righteous Judge, will award to me on that day; and not only to me, but also to all who have loved His appearing" (2 Tim. 4:8). Do you love the idea that Jesus is returning? John loved His appearing, as reflected in this: "Beloved, now we are children of God, and it has not appeared as yet what we will be. We know that when He appears, we will be like Him, because we will see Him just as He is" (1 John 3:2).

In his final written words, the beloved apostle pens this revelatory interaction with Jesus, the One Who loved him: "He who testifies to these things says, 'Yes, I am coming quickly.' Amen. Come, Lord Jesus" (Rev. 22:20).

Lord, I too am looking for Your return. Amen, Come, Lord Jesus!

WEEKEND READING

Saturday – John 4:27-38
Sunday – Acts 5:33-42

PERSONAL REFLECTIONS

_____
_____
_____
_____
_____
_____
_____
_____

_____
_____
_____
_____
_____
_____
_____
_____
_____
_____
_____
_____
_____
_____
_____

The Way Already Known

John 14:4-5

⁴ "And you know the way where I am going." ⁵ Thomas said to Him, "Lord, we do not know where You are going, how do we know the way?"

Simple language to convey a seismic change in thinking, Jesus simply says, "You know the way where I am going." Yet they could not go there yet ("Where I go you cannot follow Me now, but you will follow later" 13:36). Jesus needs time to prepare the place (14:2-3) after which He would return to receive them and then allow them to follow Him to that place. We who are reading this might ponder, what is time to God for whom a day is as a thousand years and a thousand years as a day (2 Peter 3:8)? But to the disciples at that moment any separation would seem an eternity.

Their idea of following Jesus was going to change from a physical activity to a spiritual one, a paradigm shift of enormous magnitude. The disciples already "knew" the way, Jesus calmly says. The Greek word here is *oida,* which reflects a knowing that comes from careful, reflective thinking. The subtle chide is this: "Think about what I have been teaching you all along!" What Jesus is telling them is really not something new. Thomas, the disciple much maligned (possibly unjustly) for his honest expressions of doubt, questions what must have been lingering in the minds of his fellow disciples in the Upper Room. How can one possibly know the *way* to a place when they didn't even know *where* the place was?

That is actually quite a natural question, from a human point of view. The problem was that Jesus was taking them to a super-human point of view. He was changing their entire view of faith and spirituality. Up until now, religious life for Jewish people was mostly practiced in the external realm of the physical world: physical sacrifices at physical locations (i.e. at the temple in Jerusalem). The land was prominent in Jewish thinking and existence. To the average Jew of the first century, religious life had to do with the tangible, the earthly.

Jesus was refocusing them on the spiritual, away from the physical. The disciples were thinking in terms of which roads to walk on to follow Christ. But the place He was going was a spiritual place, and it required a new, a spiritual way to attain it. It was already in their grasp, but they were not yet ready to lay hold of it. In one sense they had already done so in following Christ, but the new way required, made it absolutely necessary, for Jesus to leave them and come back later. Then they would be able to follow Him by the way He had already taught them. The picture now is ready for sharper focus.

Lord, I have neighbors, friends and relatives who have not yet come to know the true way to God. Help me be the messenger to show them that Jesus is the Way.

The Deity of Jesus

John 14:6

⁶ Jesus said to him, "I am the way, and the truth, and the life; no one comes to the Father but through Me."

R inging through the centuries, the centrality of the person of Jesus Christ for all of existence is proclaimed, and that by none other than Jesus Christ Himself. This overlays and penetrates every religious effort, every philosophical pursuit and every advice for wise living. This is one of the most important verses that demonstrates the deity of Christ.

Some have objected that the historical Jesus Christ never claimed to be God, that this was just an overlay that later Christians gave to the Christ "myth." However, the historical record does not support this objection. (Considering the historicity of the Upper Room account and the gospel narratives in their entirety is beyond the scope of this book.) Jesus certainly gave the impression of Himself as being on the order of deity by His actions and teachings.

For example, He forgave sins, which even Jesus' detractors said only God can do (Mark 2:7-11). He took on the unique appellation that the Jews recognized only applied to Yahweh of the OT, when He said to the Jews, "Truly, truly, I say to you, before Abraham was born, I am" (John 8:58). The Jews, in response, tried to stone Him, the punishment for blasphemy. A short while later they tried again with this explanation: "For a good work we do not stone You, but for blasphemy; and because You, being a man, make Yourself out *to be* God" (John 10:33). So we see that Jesus' contemporaries, and not just His close followers, understood the import of His statements and claims. They had no doubt Jesus was making Himself out to be God!

But no less important, this very band of men, although struggling in the Upper Room with their world that seemingly was caving in on them, came to believe that Jesus was God. John the gospel chronicler makes this clear in the prologue of his biography of Christ: "In the beginning was the Word, and the Word was with God, and the Word was God . . . And the Word became flesh, and dwelt among us, and we saw His glory, glory as of the only begotten from the Father, full of grace and truth" (John 1:1, 14).

The apostle Paul, who formerly tried to snuff out the followers of Jesus (identified in the record by his Hebrew name Saul), joined the chorus proclaiming Christ's deity: "For it was the *Father's* good pleasure for all the fullness to dwell in Him . . . For in Him all the fullness of Deity dwells in bodily form . . . (Col. 1:19; 2:9). There is nothing more divine about God than about Jesus.

Jesus, my Lord and my God. I worship You as the Creator God of the universe, the second person of the Trinity. One God in three persons. Blessed Trinity.

I Am the Way

⁶ Jesus said to him, "I am the way, and the truth, and the life; no one comes to the Father but through Me."

There is one, and only one way to God, and that is through the Lord Jesus Christ, the One who lived in history. All roads do *not* lead to God, contrary to popular religious sentiment. This is one thing that is absolutely clear in the New Testament scriptures.

Christians are often accused of being narrow-minded and exclusivistic, which does not go over well in the prevailing pluralism and multi-culturalism of our day. Yes, there is a fundamental truth to the uniqueness of Christianity, but it is not because of Christian arrogance. The distinctiveness goes back to the originator of Christianity, Jesus Christ Himself. He said, "I am the way . . . no one comes to the Father but through Me." Christians are simply repeating what their Lord and Master said about Himself. A statement like this renders the dismissive comment that "Jesus Christ was a great moral teacher, but not God" as nonsense. If Jesus is not the only way, then His statement disqualifies Him from the patronizing praise of being a great moral teacher.

On the other hand, the uniqueness of Christ is a great truth. And by definition truth is narrow, because it does not permit falseness. An airport runway is narrow, but it is good. The roads we drive on are narrow. The laws of gravity are "narrow" in that every time you drop something, you can count on it dropping. We live in a world that continuously operates based on the so-called "laws of nature;" things always work in a certain, narrow way, and they don't work if done in a different way.

The real problem with the "narrowness" of Jesus' statement is that the human soul wants its freedom, like an airplane pilot wanting his freedom to land the plane perpendicular to the runway. He can do that, but only at the risk of his well-being. Reactions abound, but these are mostly non-objective concerns. "What about those who never hear of Jesus? If He is the only way, then it's not fair to them." Yet, as we are compelled to teach Third World people about health and hygiene, Christians likewise are compelled to teach people who don't know about "The Way." Thus the Christian missionary endeavor: precisely to tell those who don't know.

This isn't a new concept for the disciples in the Upper Room. Jesus had already taught them that He was the Door to the sheepfold (John 10:9). God has provided a way back to the Creator, against whom we have all rebelled.

Father, I believe Your Son is the only way back to You, and I believe in Him. Help me to never forget those who have not yet heard this truth.

I Am the Truth

John 14:6 (cont.)

6 Jesus said to him, "I am the way, and the truth, and the life; no one comes to the Father but through Me."

Philosophers seek the truth. Libraries on university campuses around the nation have written over the front entrance to their sacred halls, "Ye shall know the truth, and the truth shall make you free." This quote comes from none other than the Lord Jesus Christ (John 8:32). Yet so often the pursuit of truth has become secularized, where the concept of spiritual truth has been demoted to something less than true truth. In other words, spiritual truth in our secular world has been relegated to a sub-speciality of truth seeking, one that is not necessary but pays some condescending respect to religious tradition. Once theology was considered the queen of the sciences, and philosophy its handmaiden. Now, the hard sciences seem to be the clamor in education, with the humanities dominated by secularism, and religious thought a distant third, if at all present.

Jesus' clarion proclamation cannot be written off so easily, the echo of which is still etched in architectural stones, and the Scripture continually being preached. Truth, if anything is true at all, is centered squarely on the Author of truth. One can no more pursue truth without Christ than breathe without air. To build life or a world absent Christ is to build a house on the sand, without a solid foundation. Again, this is not new teaching (see Matthew 7:24-27). Jesus is bringing together numerous thoughts in summary, memorable fashion.

So if what Jesus says is true (and we believe it is truth)—that He is the truth—everything in life changes. Certainly we can learn about computers, social constructs, history, mathematics and how to get along with our neighbors, but to be truly educated we must learn Christ. If He is the truth, we must study Christ. Paul puts it this way: "I [want to] know Him and the power of His resurrection and the fellowship of His sufferings, being conformed to His death . . ." (Phil. 3:10). He was all about Christ.

The apostle Paul warned the Ephesians against fleshly living and concluded, "But you did not learn Christ in this way, if indeed you have heard Him and have been taught in Him, just as truth is in Jesus . . ." (Eph. 4:20-21). The greatest endeavor any human can pursue is the knowledge of Jesus Christ. As John puts it, "No one has seen God at any time; the only begotten God who is in the bosom of the Father, He has explained *Him*" (John 1:18). So we study and learn Christ, because it is in Him that we learn about the Father.

Lord, I have come to know You through Your Son the Lord Jesus Christ. Every day I grow in that understanding, so that I will become more like You.

I Am the Life

John 14:6 (cont.)

⁶ Jesus said to him, "I am the way, and the truth, and the life; no one comes to the Father but through Me."

"Life ain't nothin' but a funny, funny riddle . . ."—so goes a catchy country song. Apart from Christ, our human existence can be confusing, frustrating, making no sense. Popular philosophers have asked, "Why do bad things happen to good people?" or "What's the point? You live, you die, the world goes on without you." Things can be going well, but then an arbitrary event happens that changes everything, inexplicably. People are searching for purpose and significance, to give some sensible framework for understanding what life is all about. The result is many religions, philosophies, worldviews and self-help books—all claiming but not delivering the answer to the riddle of life.

In the cacophony of life noises, the words of the Lord Jesus Christ ring out: "I am the life." Not "I am *a* way of life" or "I am a pointer to life." These things are true, but they don't do justice to His words. He said, "I am *the* life." We cannot let the simple wording lull us to simplistic thoughts.

Again, Jesus is not teaching anything new here, but summarizing what He has been getting at all along. Even John, the writer of this gospel account, assesses Jesus' life this way: "In Him was life, and the life was the Light of men" (John 1:4). He is the essence of life, the very core of life. He gives life meaning, because He is "the life," and ". . . in Him all things consist." (Col. 1:17 NKJV).

He restores and raises to resurrected life, because He is "the life." Jesus said to Martha at the time of Lazarus' death, "I am the resurrection and the life; he who believes in Me will live even if he dies, and everyone who lives and believes in Me will never die. . . ." (John 11:25-26). To believe in Christ is to have life all through time and space, because He is the central core of existence. "He who believes in the Son has eternal life . . ." (John 3:36).

When we make Him the central focus of our life, the target of our pursuit for meaning and significance, then we have discovered that life is no longer a riddle, but a wonderful, fulfilling way to order our lives. "The thief comes only to steal and kill and destroy; I came that they may have life, and have *it* abundantly" (John 10:10). To live with any other focus is to live a failed life. "He who loves his life loses it, and he who hates his life in this world will keep it to life eternal" (John 12:25). That's because Jesus is "the life"; nothing else can substitute. Paul puts it this way: "For to me, to live is Christ . . ." (Phil. 1:21).

Lord, for me to live is Christ, and to die is to be with Him in glory, thus gain!

WEEKEND READING

Saturday – John 4:39-45
Sunday – Acts 6:1-15

PERSONAL REFLECTIONS

_____
_____
_____
_____
_____
_____
_____
_____
_____
_____
_____
_____
_____
_____
_____
_____
_____
_____
_____
_____
_____
_____

That I May Know Him

⁷ "If you had known Me, you would have known My Father also; from now on you know Him, and have seen Him."

They just didn't get it yet—or we should say, they just didn't get Jesus yet. Not quick studies, these disciples! But dare we judge them from the vantage point of having read the entire story of Christ repeatedly, as well as the divine commentaries on the spiritual life and truth in the epistles? Give the disciples, especially Thomas at this juncture, credit for searching, asking and wrestling with what Jesus is saying and portending. The Lord always responds to genuine inquiry.

Jesus gently chides that they had spent enough time together for the basic truths about Jesus and the Father to be obvious by now. His form of comment was meant to challenge the disciples to think back over everything they had seen Jesus do and heard Jesus say. Is it not true that faith that is growing is a faith that is always being stretched? The same goes for spiritual knowledge. Spiritual understanding must be challenged with ignorance in order to grow. And the Lord is not in the business of revealing deeper truths about Himself to people who are too lazy to recognize and confront their ignorance about Him.

Thomas and the other disciples had certainly come to a much greater understanding of who Jesus was/is than anyone else. They had left all because He had the words of life. They had confessed that He was the Christ, the Son of the living God. But there was still much to learn. Knowledge begets knowledge. A Christian can never rest content with what he has already learned, or he stagnates, becomes complacent and ceases to grow. This is profoundly true when we consider the infinite nature of Christ, His unlimited glory, His unrelenting love, His endless mercy and grace. An eternity is not enough to exhaust the joy of discovering the "glory to glory" that we uncover and gaze on, as we grow in our knowledge of Him.

Peter came to understand this and passes on his great admonition as he closes out his writing ministry: ". . . but grow in the grace and knowledge of our Lord and Savior Jesus Christ. To Him be the glory, both now and to the day of eternity. Amen" (2 Peter 3:18). The exploration of glory is the *crème de la crème* of Christian endeavors. Paul reveals his ultimate motivation in life and ministry: "that I may know Him . . . I press on toward the goal for the prize of the upward call of God in Christ Jesus" (Phil. 3:10, 14). All other pursuits are hopelessly inferior. So Jesus tells the disciples their education is just beginning!

Father, I too want to know Your son, the Lord Jesus Christ and to grow in understanding Him, so that I will come to know You better.

Not Just Enough

John 14:8

⁸ Philip said to Him, "Lord, show us the Father, and it is enough for us."

As Thomas slinks into the background, Philip takes his turn, the third one of the disciples to venture an interaction with the Lord. Not wanting to be overly ambitious and risk rebuke, his concern is not to go where Jesus was going, or even to know the way. He had seen Peter's rebuke when stumbling over the feet washing incident and his rebuffed claim of loyalty. Philip's request was simple, not overly demanding, yet at the same time it offered what seemed like a simple request. Like the others, he seemed to be tracking ever so slightly with the Lord's words, but at a very superficial level.

"Show us the Father," he asks, and that will be sufficient. Satisfactory was what he was shooting for. It was a good request, though, wanting to see the One whom Jesus so intimately called "Father." To a Jew, this request bordered on futility, since it had been clearly taught that no one can see God and live (Ex. 33:20). Philip and the rest were about to discover a new understanding of what it means to "see" God: to perceive Him in the incarnate Christ. The aged John, writing years later, came to understand this truth quite well when he wrote, "No one has seen God at any time; the only begotten God who is in the bosom of the Father, He has explained *Him"* (John 1:18). The disciples in the Upper Room were just being introduced to this idea.

Indeed the disciples would eventually learn that Jesus was "enough" to satisfy the righteous demands of the holy law of God—for God was in Christ reconciling the world to Himself on the cross. The depth of understanding expands as we contemplate this incarnate truth. The Father is revealed in the Son, because the Son is the incarnate God, "the express image" (Heb. 1:3 NKJV) of God. To be sure, it is indeed "enough" to see the Father. But the Father must be seen in the Son, or the Father cannot be seen at all.

Jesus would not allow Philip, or his fellow disciples, or even us today, to be satisfied with a limited, superficial understanding. One day's knowledge is not enough for tomorrow's spiritual growth. The Christian life is a continual, ongoing exploration and discovery of God. This pursuit of the knowledge of God is never finished, because He is of infinite proportions in every category of thinking or existence. We never arrive where we fully know Him. We can know Him more fully than we did before, but there is always infinitely more to know about Him. And the more we know about Him, the more we know Him, and therefore the more we become like Him—until "He appears [when] we will be like Him, because we will see Him just as He is" (1 John 3:2).

Lord, I look forward to learning more of You in Your Word, in life and in glory.

Go Where the Evidence Leads

John 14:9

⁹ Jesus said to him, "Have I been so long with you, and yet you have not come to know Me, Philip? He who has seen Me has seen the Father; how can you say, 'Show us the Father'?"

Gently reproving Philip, the Lord challenges him that he should already know these truths about Christ. How could Philip ask a question like that when he had been with Jesus for so long? But like us all, the disciples were slow to learn. However, it may not be that the Lord is disappointed in Philip, as it may seem on the surface. Rather, being the master Teacher that He was, this chiding was a means to forcing the disciples to think back over His teaching the previous three-plus years. His present Upper Room interaction sheds much light on His earlier training sessions with them.

In hindsight, we can see His enlightening words in a new way. Everything Jesus did should now be starting to make sense to them. He had been doing the very things that God does—the resemblance to deity certainly raised their suspicions in that direction, but the implication of their Master being God was almost too much for their monotheistic minds to go there.

What did they think when Jesus forgave the sins of the paralytic deposited through the roof into His presence? "The scribes and the Pharisees began to reason, saying, 'Who is this *man* who speaks blasphemies? Who can forgive sins, but God alone?'" (Luke 5:21). What were the disciples, his close followers, thinking when that happened? They were not deterred from following Christ, but were still clinging to their monotheistic belief.

This wasn't just a one-time deal that could be misinterpreted. Remember the time when Jesus was a dinner guest of a Pharisee named Simon? A woman of ill-repute had washed His feet with her tears and hair, and as a result Jesus forgave her of her sins? The other dinner guests aghast exclaimed, "Who is this *man* who even forgives sins?" (Luke 7:49). This would be shocking for any monotheistic Jew to hear concerning a mere mortal. Or what about when Jesus walked on water? It was the disciples who wondered, "What kind of a man is this, that even the winds and the sea obey Him?" (Matt. 8:27).

The most obvious scenario was when Jesus had told the Jews, "I and the Father are one" (John 10:30). When the Pharisees tried to stone Him, He asked them why. "The Jews answered Him, 'For a good work we do not stone You, but for blasphemy; and because You, being a man, make Yourself out to be God'" (John 10:33). Yes, there had been plenty of evidence that Jesus was God. Jesus is God!

Lord Jesus Christ, You are my Lord and my God. And I praise You.

Above All Else

¹⁰ "Do you not believe that I am in the Father, and the Father is in Me? The words that I say to you I do not speak on My own initiative, but the Father abiding in Me does His works."

Yes, there was enough evidence linking Jesus to God, as Jesus indicated in verse 9. Ignorance was not the problem; unbelief was. We present-day readers may miss the claim to deity here. Even though Jesus used the term "Father" and not "God," it was very clear that He was referring to God. In verse 1, He says, "Believe in God, believe also in Me," and then immediately follows that with, "In my Father's house there are many dwelling places" (vs. 2), equating "the Father" with "God." Beginning in John 1:14, we are set up to see Jesus as the Son and the God of Israel as the Father.

The Lord frequently referred to the God of Israel as "My Father" (John 2:16; 5:17, etc.). In fact, to the Jewish leaders such language amounted to blasphemy: "For this reason therefore the Jews were seeking all the more to kill Him, because He not only was breaking the Sabbath, but also was calling God His own Father, making Himself equal with God" (John 5:18). They caught the nuance of uniqueness in His words.

Yes, the disciples must have understood the same thing—that Jesus was not referring to God in the same way as all other observing Jews. But they couldn't bring their monotheistic minds to fully go where the evidence led. The implications of it would shake their belief system at the roots. There is one and only one God! Deuteronomy 6:4 was branded in the minds of all Jews: "Hear, O Israel! The Lord is our God, the Lord is one!" And Isaiah, "You are My witnesses . . . Before Me there was no God formed, and there will be none after Me. I, even I, am the Lord, and there is no savior besides Me" (Isa. 43:10-11). "I am the first and I am the last, and there is no God besides Me" (Isa. 44:6).

There was no refuting this. Fundamental to all Jewish belief is a hard-core monotheism: there is one and only one God. Yet here was Jesus making overtures that even the Pharisees did not miss. If their assessment was wrong, Jesus had plenty of opportunity to correct them. But here in the Upper Room, the disciples see their Master, the One to whom they had pledged undying loyalty, affirming the implications of His words: "I am in the Father, and the Father is in Me." Their allegiance to this One whom even the winds and sea obeyed, this One who forgives sin, trumped all their fears of the implications of His words about the Father. Yet it was difficult to accept the logical conclusion.

Lord, like the disciples in the Upper Room, sometimes I do not understand Your ways and Your mind. But I am devoted to You above all else.

One God, Father and Son

John 14:10 (cont.)

[10] "Do you not believe that I am in the Father, and the Father is in Me? The words that I say to you I do not speak on My own initiative, but the Father abiding in Me does His works.

Balancing incredulity with love, Jesus does not reject the disciples for their unbelief, though that is the one thing He chides them most about in His training of them. Even in the case of Judas, it was that disciple who rejected Jesus, not Jesus rejecting him. Faith is the key issue, because it is faith that leads to true obedience. So Jesus questioned their lack of faith in His teachings. But He doesn't give up on them; this is His final pre-crucifixion prepping of them for a world-shaking, lifelong ministry of carrying His message into the lost, broken world, which is in need of a Shepherd and a King.

At this juncture, the gravity of Jesus' claim to deity on the same level as God the Father would lead to one of two conclusions: either 1) Jesus was wrong (to the Jews the easiest, most natural conclusion) or 2) His claim to be deity was theologically correct. Certainly, those who can move beyond the condescending nonsense of Jesus' being nothing more than a good teacher and a prophet, must hold that He was simply wrong. They have only two positions to take concerning Jesus: 1) He was delusional about being divine (which has tremendous implications about Jesus' credibility mental state), or 2) He was quite arrogant (which calls into question his ethical and moral integrity).

In the best possible argument that philosopher of religion can muster, it is impossible for a man to become God, for if God created the universe, then it is inherently self-defeating to argue that a part of His creation become Him.

Yet Jesus said clearly that this was not of "[His] own initiative." He didn't just think up the idea of becoming God and then somehow make it happen. That is not what He said at all. What He did say was that God was "abiding in Me" and doing "His works [in Me]." God had invaded humanity, not vice versa. Man did not become God, but God became a man. And that is *not* impossible.

The idea that God became a man was not compatible with Jewish theology as understood from the Old Testament. But the gospel writer John wants us to see that connection from the beginning of this biography of Jesus: "In the beginning was the Word, and the Word was with God, and the Word was God." For those religions that teach Jesus was a god, but not the same as God the Father, John would respond with Isaiah that there is only one God: the Father is God and Jesus is God. This is the profound truth that, together with the Holy Spirit, we call the Trinity. All based on the authority of Jesus Christ Himself.

Lord, I worship You—Father, Son and Holy Spirit.

WEEKEND READING

Saturday – John 4:46-54
Sunday – Acts 7:1-29

PERSONAL REFLECTIONS

Believe Me or My Works

John 14:11

[11] *"Believe Me that I am in the Father and the Father is in Me; otherwise believe because of the works themselves."*

Question gives way to command. "Why don't you believe?" gives way to "Believe Me"—not strictly a command, but what is called a "hortatory" statement, an exhortation. Jesus urges Philip and the others to believe, to go where the evidence leads. Their faith has a solid foundation on which to build, but it is still faith. Not blind, but reasonable faith.

Too often faith is portrayed as believing in something that is not real or doesn't exist, but if you believe, then whatever you believe is true or real for you. That is not the kind of "faith" to which Jesus is calling His disciples. They had had three-plus years with Him; there was sufficient evidence in His teachings, interactions and love. In essence, faith does not have to do with believing *things*, but believing a person. It has to do with believing Jesus. It is not just believing about Him, or as a result of Him, or even "in" Him. It is believing Him. That includes everything about Christ, including His teachings and the things He points to. And it includes believing in Him as having a personal relationship. It means everything that Jesus is: Savior, Messiah, Master and King, Friend, Shepherd, the Way, the Truth, the Life, the "I am." He is the Door, the Light, the Living Water. He is the Son of God. That is all wrapped up in His statement, "I am in the Father and the Father is in Me."

Plan A is backed up by Plan B. Jesus said that if they have difficulty in accepting all that because of His teachings, then they can believe because of the sign-evidence. When He taught in the synagogue in Nazareth early in His earthly ministry, He quoted Isaiah 61, "The Spirit of the LORD is upon Me, because He anointed Me to preach the gospel to the poor. He has sent Me to proclaim release to the captives, and recovery of sight to the blind, to set free those who are oppressed . . ." (Luke 4:18). Then He said these evidences or Messianic qualifications were fulfilled in Him: "Today this Scripture has been fulfilled in your hearing" (Luke 4:20).

Everything He did pointed to who He was. And that demanded a response—not just an acknowledgement, but belief. So in the Upper Room, Jesus calls on His disciples to make that final step in following Him and fully believe what He is saying, that He truly is the Messiah, the Sent One of God, God in the flesh. They were going to need that kind of faith in a few hours, when the One in Whom they believed would be dead. When all would seem lost.

Lord, I believe in You even though it goes against all that I can see and touch.

Power of the Promise

John 14:12

12 "Truly, truly, I say to you, he who believes in Me, the works that I do, he will do also; and greater works than these he will do; because I go to the Father."

Spoken to the future apostles (who they were going to be), not the present ones (who they are now in the Upper Room), this statement of Jesus would probably lie dormant for the time being. We the readers know where this is going and how God will tremendously fulfill this promise for the followers of Jesus Christ for 2,000 years. But in the darkening atmosphere in this Palestinian house, He was preparing them, training them for life without Him (physically).

They needed to know His promise *before* the crucifixion and resurrection. Though the power of the promise would remain hidden during the terrible time of Jesus' torture, crucifixion and death, the disciples would probably have wrestled with everything He said just hours before. What would those things mean then, as Jesus was dying or when He was dead in a grave? Indeed, the promises of God become most precious precisely when we are not experiencing the fulfillment of them, when things couldn't possibly get darker. The sustaining power of His promises is that they give us hope in our darkest moments, when we cannot see their fulfillment—when God seems to be "not there," when we are not hearing from Him. That is when His promises germinate and bear the fruit of hope.

The specific promise is reminiscent of 2 Kings 2:9-10, when Elisha was promised a "double portion" of the prophet Elijah's spirit, which translated into twice as many miracles being performed. Here Jesus promised that believers in Him would perform similar kinds of works and even "greater" ones than Jesus performed. These were the powerful, confirming signs He did to demonstrate that He was the Messiah. These would happen at the hands of His followers.

Clearly the men in the Upper Room, the original apostles, performed great miracles. At last count in the Upper Room Jesus had eleven disciples (maybe a few women as well, though that is nowhere stated), and in the Upper Room just prior to Pentecost, there were 120 people (Acts 1:15). Then, at the preaching of Peter, 3,000 were saved and baptized, while a short while later the number grew to 5,000 (and that's not including women and children). Already in a few days, the crowd of followers was comparable to what Jesus had at His largest count (5,000 in Mark 6:42). In fact, miracles at the hands of the apostles preponderate (see Acts 4:16; 8:13; 19:11; 2 Corinthians 12:12; Hebrews 2:4).

Lord, Your promises give me hope, even in dark times when I feel alone and abandoned. I believe because of Your power in me, I will someday prevail.

Miracle-Working Apostles

John 14:12 (cont.)

12 "Truly, truly, I say to you, he who believes in Me, the works that I do, he will do also; and greater works than these he will do; because I go to the Father."

Did Jesus speak generically when He made this promise concerning "he who believes in Me," in which case it extends to all believers? Or was He talking specifically concerning those out of the masses who had believed in Him to this point, that is, the eleven disciples?

The case can be made for specificity, in that we do see the apostles uniquely endued with miraculous powers. To be sure, they were promised perfect recall of all Jesus taught (John 14:26), something which most Christians today do not have. They were to be the uniquely authorized witnesses of Christ's message (Acts 1:8). Confirming this, shortly after Pentecost, we find Peter and John healing the lame man at the gate called Beautiful (Acts 3). The writer of Acts comments: "With great power the apostles were giving testimony to the resurrection of the Lord Jesus . . ." (Acts 4:33). "At the hands of the apostles many signs and wonders were taking place . . . to such an extent that they even carried the sick out into the streets . . . so that when Peter came by at least his shadow might fall on any one of them . . . bringing people who were sick or afflicted with unclean spirits, and they were all being healed" (Acts 5:12, 15-16).

Paul, in defense of his own apostleship, though not one of the original apostles, said, "The signs of a true apostle were performed among you with all perseverance, by signs and wonders and miracles" (2 Cor. 12:12). The writer of Hebrews tells us, "God [was] also testifying with them, both by signs and wonders and by various miracles and by gifts of the Holy Spirit according to His own will" (Heb. 2:4). We take the "them" to be the apostles.

Historically when God moved in His largest, most unprecedented ways, He accompanied His movement with miraculous signs. The Exodus from bondage in Egypt and entry into the Promised Land were accompanied by the confirmatory, miraculous events at the hands of Moses and Joshua. The succession of miracles during the ministries of Elijah and Elisha warned of punitive captivity for national disobedience against God. Now, during the change of dispensations to spiritual freedom and the new covenant under the ministry of Jesus and His apostles, we again see the confirmatory miraculous signs. Though miracles do happen at other times, historically the outpouring seems largely confined to times when God was changing how He was dealing with His people. That is the case with the apostles of Jesus Christ.

Lord, thank You for confirming Your message through the apostles so that we have the message preserved for us today.

Miracle-Working Believers

John 14:12 (cont.)

12 "Truly, truly, I say to you, he who believes in Me, the works that I do, he will do also; and greater works than these he will do; because I go to the Father."

One of the challenges of the Upper Room teaching is determining how much is aimed specifically at the apostles and how much is for all Christians. Certainly the promise of perfect recall (John 14:26) was intended for the eleven (and also the twelfth when added later in Acts 1), to aid them in their propagating the message of Christ. After all, it was "the apostles' teaching" to which the early church was continually committed (Acts 2:42). The only way we would know what Jesus taught was through the apostles' teaching.

But Christians for years have found great comfort and help in the Upper Room teaching. Concerning the "greater works" promised, certainly there are situations where miracles occurred in the New Testament at the hands of non-apostles. For example, the first non-apostle miracle in Acts is at the hands of Stephen, who "full of grace and power, was performing great wonders and signs among the people" (Acts 6:8). He was one of the seven selected to oversee the serving of food to the widows of the early church. Another of the seven, Philip performed "signs and great miracles" (Acts 8:13). Even though Paul had similar signs ("extraordinary miracles" in Acts 19:11, see also 2 Corinthians 12:12), he was not one of those in the Upper Room, or numbered among the twelve.

We see the gift of "miracles" was given with no restriction to just the apostles (1 Cor. 12:10; 12:28). But then Paul teaches that not all are workers of miracles (1 Cor. 12:29), so the promise in the Upper Room was clearly not inclusive of all believers. Yet many today feel that the miraculous sign gifts continue into the present based on Peter's Pentecostal sermon quotation of Joel in Acts 2:17-21. We would point out that not all of Joel's prophecy has been fulfilled; for example, the sun has not turned dark or the moon into blood. Israel's rejection of Christ, even though the message continued on in the apostles, put Joel's prophecy on hold.

The truly miraculous does not seem to be occurring today as it did in the days of Jesus and the apostles, despite current claims to the contrary. But that is only when we focus on the outwardly miraculous. The genuine, undeniable miracle of changed lives through the testimony of believers through the ages has resulted in the miracle of new birth that far exceeds the number of followers Jesus had during His earthly ministry. And that is the "greater works" that we believers do collectively.

Lord, I want to experience Your promise in doing the work of sharing the message of Christ with a lost and broken world in need of redemption.

Ask In My Name

13 "Whatever you ask in My name, that will I do, so that the Father may be glorified in the Son. 14 If you ask Me anything in My name, I will do it."

Pithy statements on prayer abound. Nothing is more simple and to the point, and "pithy," than Jesus' own statements about prayer. The verse for today is one of those. He invites His followers to request anything of God in the name of Jesus Christ, and He promises to answer the request. Is this a blank check for gaining wealth or power or prestige? We just need to claim what is ours by faith? Hardly. But then what do we make of this statement?

First, the invitation is to *ask*. Nothing is said about demanding, holding God to His word or claiming (all popular but erroneous notions of prayer today). Asking implies humility, need, ceding control. Prayer is not a way to "turn the hand of God" as though we know better than the sovereign, infinitely wise, all-knowing Creator and Sustainer of the universe, who sees all and is everywhere present. We mere human creatures are invited not to direct God or tell Him what to do, but to simply ask in humility. In this asking, there is an implicit acceptance of whatever answer God gives, whether yes, no or wait. What a wonderful thing for Jesus to leave the men in the Upper Room, an invitation to ask God for what they need.

Second, the asking must be in Jesus' name. We must take this in connection with the preceding verse. We are invited to ask for God's help in doing the kinds of things Jesus was doing—and even greater things. It is a truism that God's ways will not lack God's resources. He would never make a promise for us for which there are not enough resources to bring it to pass. But rather than simply make all His promises manifest for us in a passive way, He invites us not as peons, but as partners with Him in His work. So rather than just give us what we need, He invites us to see the need and then ask Him for the resources to accomplish what He wants for us. That is more like a partnership than an unthinking slavish, hireling relationship.

Third, notice the response to the request is "I will do," not "I will give." God will sometimes give us something we ask Him for, but more importantly, He "will do" for us what we ask. He Himself is the answer, not what He gives us. The answer we need is not a thing but a person—a divine Person.

As followers of Christ, we should live in the light of His promise and His presence, and we should ask Him for the resources to do His work.

Lord, help me see clearly the work You have for me to do, and to fearlessly and confidently bring my needs to You, so that You can enable me to do that work.

WEEKEND READING

Saturday – John 5:1-17
Sunday – Acts 7:30-53

PERSONAL
REFLECTIONS

_____
_____
_____
_____
_____
_____
_____
_____
_____
_____
_____
_____
_____
_____
_____
_____
_____
_____
_____
_____
_____

Ask in My Name (cont.)

John 14:13-14

¹³ "Whatever you ask in My name, that will I do, so that the Father may be glorified in the Son. ¹⁴ If you ask Me anything in My name, I will do it."

Martha had already concluded that Jesus had special inside access to God, as she exclaimed to Him, "Even now I know that whatever You ask of God, God will give You" (John 11:22). Now the disciples are being offered the same access. We have mediated access when we come to the Father "in Jesus' name." This is more than just tacking that phrase onto our prayer requests. It means we come with the needs for serving the way Jesus served. We represent Jesus' interests in the world, on His behalf. He has sent us into the world to preach the Good News (Mark 16:15), as His ambassadors (2 Cor. 5:20). And we need His provision to do His work, which will be greater in and through us than what He did Himself during His earthly lifespan.

We must be clear. The goal in our asking is that Jesus might be glorified. We as His followers ask the Father for things that will help us magnify Jesus, that the world might see Him more clearly, that He would get the attention. That is the Father's goal, and that must be ours.

Now if it is God's will for us to glorify Christ, He delights to answer prayers that line up with that goal. John put it this way: ". . . if we ask anything according to His will, He hears us. And if we know that He hears us *in* whatever we ask, we know that we have the requests which we have asked from Him" (1 John 5:14-15). So if we ask God for anything that He desires to happen, then why would He not give us what we request if the goal is to glorify Christ?

It is interesting that instead of just loading us up with what we need at the moment of salvation, God leaves many things for which we must ask. While it is true that we have already been given everything we need for life and godliness (2 Peter 1:3), it lies dormant, waiting to be activated through prayer. This is not like a soldier going to the quartermaster and being assigned what the army says he needs. No. Rather the Christian goes about seeking to do the "greater works," discovers his need and approaches the divine Quartermaster, the Supplier of all the resources he needs to do those things. Like when Jesus told the disciples to feed the 5,000 (Mark 6:37), the disciples came to see their inability to accomplish the feat. Facing their inability placed them in a position to see Christ's ability. So God takes us into the "greater works" endeavor and then waits with anticipation for us to see the need for His help. He delights to answer us then.

Lord, my desire is to glorify the Lord Jesus Christ through my life.
Help me hone my requests to only those that will bring Him glory.

Ask in My Name (cont.)

John 14:13-14

[13] "Whatever you ask in My name, that will I do, so that the Father may be glorified in the Son. [14] If you ask Me anything in My name, I will do it."

The "anything in My name" covers a lot of ground. What are those things that would be appropriate requests? Obviously, anything that is designed for my particular enjoyment or comfort does not fit the context of this command, namely glorifying Christ. But what are some of the things we need that God does want to provide?

Sometimes our prayers, as we suggested before, might be for activating the things He has already given us that are lying dormant or are in need of strengthening. We might ask for patience, stamina, grace, mercy, strength, wisdom, insight, gentleness, skill, protection, power, sound mind, and infinitely more. These are all things that God has willed for us, so we can be assured that He will give these to us (or, should we say, activate these things in us), so that we can better glorify Christ.

Scripture is filled with the promises of God, the blessings of God, the character of God—all are ours, ready for use, application and experience: ". . . His divine power has granted to us everything pertaining to life and godliness, through the true knowledge of Him who called us by His own glory and excellence" (2 Peter 1:3). But why do some Christians experience the abundance of life and spiritual resources when others do not? It is because some ask while others do not.

I think of a young man who needed to buy a vehicle. He was challenged to pray about the kind of car he should buy. The obvious choice for a young man like himself was a flashy, two-door sports car. But in prayer the Lord answered his desire to serve Him more faithfully and effectively, so he ended up buying a van, with multiple rows of seats—which would prove to be far more useful in his work with young people. The Lord gave Him wisdom to purchase the right vehicle.

Recently I heard of a woman from Jewish background who came to faith in Christ. Many in her family shunned her. With great desire to reach her people for Christ she prayed for God's help. In time, she became pregnant and gave birth to baby with Down syndrome. Her extended family began to warm up to her and offer assistance. The pathway to a more open relationship with them opened up, and with it, the opportunity to speak about Christ. She and her husband see their special-needs child as being God's blessing and help in their effort to reach others for Christ.

Lord, help me pray for the things that glorify Your Son.

Right Way Causation

15 "If you love Me, you will keep My commandments.

Repetition is a key to interpretation. Jesus uses the phrase "If you love Me . . ." repeatedly in the Upper Room. The grammatical form is identical to the previous statements of our Lord, "If you ask Me anything in My name . . ." In the Greek language, there are four different ways to make conditional statements, each carrying a sense not always conveyed well in the translation to English. In this case, "if" carries the sense of being hypothetical (Greek scholars call this a third-class conditional statement), with no sense that Jesus is assuming the case to be true. In other words, "If you love Me (and I am not stating whether or not you do love Me; I am making a hypothetical statement), then the following will happen." In this case, that which follows is keeping His commandments.

We must be careful in handling this text or we can fall into a works-oriented relationship with God. What is in question is the disciples' love for God, not their works or obedience. Now obviously the two are connected (as the book of James points out) but not in the wrong, causative sort of way. Jesus is not saying, "Keep my commandments, which is what is really the important thing here. When you do obey me, that will result in causing you to love Me." The apostle Paul embellishes this in his celebrated love chapter, 1 Corinthians 13, where he runs through a series of good things that Christians can do and how they can live, yet if they don't have love, it all is for nothing.

Jesus *is* saying the causative goes in the other direction. Genuine love for Christ will lead to good works, which are the evidence of authentic love. Real love will be displayed by acts of devotion. That is the nature of love. Just to be clear, Jesus is not saying, "The essence of Christian love leads to a works-oriented salvation." Absolutely not. Who of us could ever work or obey enough to rise to the level of love worthy of salvation?

But love is not just a word or a feeling. Love is an action, a movement from one person to another. And of all the writers of the NT, John uses this word the most. He was especially tuned to Jesus' words and most willing to record this aspect of the Master's ministry, because he himself understood that he was the one "whom Jesus loved" (John 13:23; 19:26; 21:20; etc.). The person who knows he is loved by God and who in turn responds in love—"[w]e love because God first loved us" (1 John 4:19)—will surely be the person who obeys what Jesus taught. And that is the goal of the Great Commission: to "teach them to observe all that I [Jesus] commanded you" (Matt. 20:20).

Lord, I love You and desire to obey You in every area of my life. Help me do so.

Trinity Introduced

John 14:16

16 "I will ask the Father, and He will give you another Helper, that He may be with you forever . . ."

New presence, in light of Jesus' imminent departure, will enable the disciples to carry on the mission, to carry the Good News to all the world. This Upper Room teaching is dense with meaning, promise and encouragement. Now for the first time Jesus tells of the provision that will be given them, something far better than having His physical presence with them.

Of particular interest is that we are beginning to see the intimacy of familial communication in the Trinity. The mystery is displayed, but the depths are unfathomable. Here we have God the Son talking with God the Father. Both are equally God, yet there is no thought of jettisoning the disciples' monotheistic belief. Yet why would God have a need to talk with Himself, so to speak? At this point, we beg limited, finite understanding of exactly how the idea of the Trinity can possibly be true. Faith in Christ, though, compels us to embrace this mystery. There is one God, who exists in three persons, without negating the truth of monotheism. He exists in community within Himself. The Scripture shows us Jesus, who presented Himself as God, whom the disciples came to believe was God, and whom the rest of the NT teaches is God.

Church history reveals that the nature of Jesus' identification as God consumed much theological debate and resulted in great councils to deal with the matter. There were, for example, the Nestorians, who separated out the divine nature of Christ from the human nature of Jesus. The modalists taught that God was one distinct, divine person who appeared in different forms. Adoptionism held the belief that Jesus was an ordinary man who became God.

The Nicene Council in AD 325 settled the matter of belief, though not the reality of the truth. The decision, as reflected in the Nicene Creed, states, "I believe in one God, the Father Almighty, Maker of heaven and earth, and of all things visible and invisible. And in one Lord Jesus Christ, the only-begotten Son of God, begotten of the Father before all worlds; God of God, Light of Light, very God of very God; begotten, not made, being of one substance with the Father, by whom all things were made . . . And I believe in the Holy Ghost, the Lord and Giver of life; who proceeds from the Father [and the Son]; who with the Father and the Son together is worshipped and glorified; who spoke by the prophets." This creed did not make these things so, but revealed that although the word "Trinity" does not occur in the Bible, the Scripture does indeed teach this truth.

Lord, I believe in You, One God in three persons: Father, Son and Holy Spirit.

Trinity Introduced (cont.)

John 14:16

16 "I will ask the Father, and He will give you another Helper, that He may be with you forever . . ."

Ever wonder what the Trinity members say to one another, this mysterious one God who exists in three persons? If you find that unfathomable to contemplate, you are in good company with great thinkers through the centuries since Jesus lived on this planet. We must be clear that we are not blindly trying to cover over a contradiction with theological nonsense, as some would think. The doctrine of the Trinity does not teach that there is one God, yet three Gods. That would be contradiction. Nor does it say that there is one divine person, yet three divine persons. Rightly understood, the Trinity is the belief that there is one and only one God, who exists in three persons, the Father, Son and Holy Spirit. Why do we believe that?

It is true, the actual word "Trinity" does not occur in the Bible. Of course, neither do many other terms we use to summarize theological concepts, like Christology (the study of Christ), Pneumatology (the study of the Holy Spirit), etc. They are simply convenient labels for identifying concepts that are biblical.

In the case of the Trinity, Scripture portrays Jesus as fully divine (see John 1:1; Colossians 1:29; 2:9; Hebrews 1:3). He did the kinds of things that only God can or should do. For example, He forgave sins (Luke 5:21), used the name of God for Himself (John 8:58) and accepted worship (John 20:28). Yet there is also a distinction, for we see the God-man Jesus calling on God the Father, as in today's verse, indicating the Father and Son have different roles. We use the words God the Father in contrast to God the Son.

Yet Isaiah repeatedly propounds that there is one and only one God. "Understand that I am He. Before Me there was no God formed, and there will be none after Me. I, even I, am the Lord, and there is no savior besides Me" (Isa. 43:10-11). So if Jesus is divine and there is only one God, then Jesus must be *the* God over all, the God of Abraham, Isaac and Jacob, the God of Moses, called Yahweh.

If Jesus is fully God, then what does it mean for Jesus to "ask the Father"? At its most fundamental level, we should not be surprised that there would be things about God's intersecting with this world that would be difficult for us finite creatures to understand. But God lays it out in familial terms to which we can more readily relate. The conversation within the Godhead is like a conversation between a father and son.

Lord, I readily admit that there are things about You that will remain a mystery to me. In faith I accept what Your Word says about you, Father, Son and Spirit.

WEEKEND READING

Saturday – John 5:18-24
Sunday – Acts 7:54–8:3

PERSONAL REFLECTIONS

_____
_____
_____
_____
_____
_____
_____
_____
_____
_____
_____
_____
_____
_____
_____
_____
_____
_____
_____
_____
_____

Holy Spirit Introduced

John 14:16 (cont.)

16 "I will ask the Father, and He will give you another Helper, that He may be with you forever . . ."

"**A**nother Helper" will be given to us at the Son's request. The third person of the Trinity is now in this world to be of assistance to us. Do you believe that? We think so little of the Holy Spirit in today's church, notwithstanding the penchant in some circles to exalt the Spirit's so-called manifestations.

That this Helper refers to the Holy Spirit is evident from the context. But notice first of all, Jesus wants us to have the Holy Spirit. The Son will ask (from our perspective, the Son already has asked) His Father to present us with this gift. And at the moment of our salvation, that is what takes place—we receive among other things, the Holy Spirit, the third person of the Trinity (see 2 Corinthians 1:22; Romans 8:9, 15; 1 Corinthians 6:19).

Second, the Holy Spirit is a person, not just a spiritual force or a figure of speech. Third, He is distinct from the Son and from the Father; He is not just an expression of the other two members of the Trinity. In the well-known Christian baptism formula, we are baptized in the name of the Father, Son and Holy Spirit (Matt. 28:19). All three are on equal basis, yet they are distinct.

Fourth, the Spirit will be ours forever. We are sealed permanently (Eph. 1:13; 2 Cor. 1:22), and we are secure.

Not to be missed, the Spirit is our Helper. He is a helper like Jesus (notice the word "another" Helper). He is in our lives in the absence of the physical Jesus. The disciples were concerned about Jesus leaving them, but He would give them the presence of deity in the person of the Spirit. His work in our lives will not be essentially different from Jesus' work. If that were the case, He would have used another Greek word, *heteros,* which means another of a different kind. But Jesus used *allos,* which simply means another.

The word "Helper" comes from the Greek word *parakletos,* which refers to one who comes alongside to help and encourage. He assists us in doing the "better works" Jesus spoke of earlier. Just as Jesus came into the world to help us return to God, that is, to *enter* His kingdom, the Holy Spirit has come to help us *live* in the kingdom of God here and now. Just like the apostles after the Day of Pentecost, believers today are completely dependent upon and empowered by the "help" of the Spirit. Without Him we can do nothing.

Lord, thank You for not leaving us alone, but giving us the power to accomplish Your purposes, Your great works here on earth.

Spirit of Truth

17 ". . . that is the Spirit of truth, whom the world cannot receive, because it does not see Him or know Him, but you know Him because He abides with you and will be in you."

Helper is synonymous with truth. That is the One the Father will be sending (in our case, has already sent), the Spirit of truth. Used 26 times in the Gospel of John, the first mention of truth is found in John 1:14: "And the Word became flesh, and dwelt among us, and we saw His glory, glory as of the only begotten from the Father, full of grace and truth." Jesus certainly taught truth, but He proclaimed that He was "the truth" (John 14:6). He is what is real; there is no falsehood about Him. The same can now be said of the Spirit. God does not lie, nor is He ever mistaken. Paul put it this way: ". . . Let God be found true, though every man be found a liar, as it is written . . ." (Rom. 3:4).

A number of things pertaining to the Spirit are enunciated here. The world cannot receive Him, similar to its inability or refusal to accept Jesus: "He [Jesus] came to His own, and those who were His own did not receive Him" (John 1:11). The world does not see or know the Spirit, just as with Jesus. "The Light shines in the darkness, and the darkness did not comprehend it" (John 1:5). Even the disciples had a hard time really knowing Jesus: "Have I been so long with you, and *yet* you have not come to know Me, Philip? . . ." (John 14:9). Yes, the Spirit is very similar to Jesus; the third person of the Trinity is similar to the second person.

However, unlike Jesus, who was soon to be leaving the disciples, the Holy Spirit would come and abide in them and be with them. The previous verse indicated that the Spirit would be with them forever (John 14:16). This was to be permanent. What was going to be oblique to the world would be manifest to the disciples. He would become very real to them.

While the disciples had grown quite fond of Jesus, even loyal to the point of giving up all to follow Him, it was going to be the Holy Spirit who would be with them forever and never leave them. The physical presence of the Godhead, incarnate in the person of Jesus Christ, would soon be leaving them, but the spiritual presence of God, in the person of the Holy Spirit, would always be with them—and with us. There is no room here for a theology that allows for being abandoned by the Holy Spirit. We do not need to pray the prayer of David, "Do not take Your Holy Spirit from me" (Ps. 51:11).

Lord, thank You for Your Holy Spirit, who has secured me and
all other true believers with His presence for all eternity.

Spirit of Truth (cont.)

John 14:17

17 "... that is the Spirit of truth, whom the world cannot receive, because it does not see Him or know Him, but you know Him because He abides with you and will be in you."

Truth, in the person of the Spirit, will be with us forever. In a world today where media has taken on the image of reality, truth is under attack. Someone has defined truth as that which corresponds to reality. But when reality is manipulated through the eye-gate, we find people, without any sense of obvious contradiction, saying such things as "What's true for you may not be true for me." Truth has become fluid. A new word has been invented, "truism," which refers to something that is not necessarily true, but it ought to be. So truth really has been commandeered by those who refuse to be ruled by objective reality but wish to create a reality of their own.

In the midst of all this, the Spirit of truth still reigns, and especially in believers in Christ. As the apostle Paul wrote, "Now we have received, not the spirit of the world, but the Spirit who is from God, so that we may know the things freely given to us by God . . ." (1 Cor. 2:12).

Three truths are laid out concerning our relationship with the Spirit of Truth. First, we know Him. Jesus said earlier, ". . . you will know the truth, and the truth will make you free" (John 8:32). We are free from the falsehood, pretensions and manipulated imagery of the spirit of the world, and we now walk in the Spirit of truth—because we know Him.

Second, the Spirit of truth abides with us. He remains, takes up residence in our lives. He makes Himself at home with us. We are His temple individually (1 Cor. 6:19). Where we go, the Spirit of truth goes with us.

Third, the Spirit of truth will be with us. His abiding will continue into the future, forever (see the previous verse, John 14:16). All three of these things picture for us a wonderful truth. As followers of Jesus Christ, though He is not with us physically, we have the ever-abiding presence of the Spirit of truth. He is a constant, shining light that pierces the darkness and shows us the way. He illumines the Scripture so that we can understand it. He quickens, that is, enlivens, the inner man so that we are moved to walk in that light. He helps us to distinguish between right and wrong, whether morally, philosophically or practically. The Spirit of truth helps us abandon the self-deceptions and insecurities and enables us to embrace the Word of truth. And this reflects the reality of God. Nothing but our own lack of faith can separate us from experiencing the truth of the Spirit of God.

Lord, help me to walk in the light of the Spirit of truth that You have given me.

Not Left as Orphans

John 14:18

18 "I will not leave you as orphans; I will come to you."

One great concern that good parents have for their children is to provide for them after they are gone. But a well laid-out will with a wealthy inheritance makes a poor substitute for a father. Although in His absence, the Father will give the Holy Spirit to His followers, there is still the sense of relationship with Jesus that they will miss. While the New Testament abounds with the teaching that Jesus is with believers now in a spiritual way, He leaves the disciples with the hope of His physical return.

Some have spiritualized Christianity to the point of being completely other-worldly. It is, in their thinking, unrelated to the tangible, real world, other than providing inspiration for living. In that view, it matters little whether Jesus was really God, or that God became a physical being. But our Lord doesn't leave us that option. He said He would be back, and He meant that physically.

The Christian life is one lived by faith. We are followers in the line of disciples that extends back 2,000 years, a line that continues on in hope that the Christ will return. It seems every generation—including the generation following the disciples—hopes theirs will be the one to see His return. Indeed, some among the Thessalonian believers struggled with the wait, being anxious that those who had died already would miss out on Christ's return (2 Thess. 2:1-2). Later they even feared that they themselves may have missed the event of Christ's return (1 Thess. 4:13).

Paul allays their and our anxiety over the long wait for Christ's return and encourages us to continue on in faith along with hope: "But we do not want you to be uninformed, brethren, about those who are asleep, so that you will not grieve as do the rest who have no hope. For if we believe that Jesus died and rose again, even so God will bring with Him those who have fallen asleep in Jesus. For this we say to you by the word of the Lord, that we who are alive and remain until the coming of the Lord, will not precede those who have fallen asleep. For the Lord Himself will descend from heaven with a shout, with the voice of *the* archangel and with the trumpet of God, and the dead in Christ will rise first. Then we who are alive and remain will be caught up together with them in the clouds to meet the Lord in the air, and so we shall always be with the Lord. Therefore comfort one another with these words" (1 Thess. 4:13-18).

Yes, Christ will return. That hope sustains us in our faith as we struggle through the difficulties and trials of life.

Lord Jesus, the hope of Your return comforts and encourages
me to continue on faithfully following in Your ways.

Coming Again

John 14:18 (cont.)

18 "I will not leave you as orphans; I will come to you."

"**O**rphaned" is how Jesus described to His disciples their lives without Him. What a terrible thing to consider, life without the personal presence of God. For many people their religion views God only as "the Master." To others He is the Great Omni-potentate who created all, and sits in the background, distant and uncaring for the most part. For still others, He is an impersonal force, or even a multiplicity of deities who have greater concerns than for us mere mortals. Only Christianity presents God as a personal Father, One whom we can address as "Abba, Father" (Rom. 8:15; Gal. 4:6). What an absolutely wonderful and amazing thing. Not only do we have forgiveness and eternal life granted us by the Almighty God, the Creator of heaven and earth, but we also have His presence in our lives. But what is even more astounding is that His presence provides a fatherly, intimate, familial relationship that is at once spiritual and mystical, tangible and real.

That Jesus is pictured (implied) here as a father image doesn't confuse the roles of the Trinity. He at other times referred to the disciples as "children" (e.g. John 13:33). He even used the imagery of a mother hen and her chicks in relationship with the people of Israel (Matt. 23:37). However, the unity of purpose with the Father would suggest that the Son is affirming that the Father would not leave them as orphans, but would provide a Fatherly presence for them. Praise God we as followers of Christ are never left as orphans.

This is all connected with Jesus' coming back to them. However, this cannot refer to His post-resurrection appearances, for that would have been a short-lived presence, 40 days to be exact (Acts 1:3). And if that were an eschatological reference to His coming in the last days, as depicted in His return at the end of the tribulation period, that would leave the disciples (and us) orphaned for these past 2,000 years. Such an interpretation seems highly unlikely.

Rather Jesus, in keeping with the rest of His teaching in the Upper Room, teaches them that He will return to them spiritually. In this sense the coming presence of the Holy Spirit would be the same as the presence of Jesus. Indistinguishable. We today are not orphaned, without the presence of God, because we now have God's presence, the Holy Spirit. And we can say, in the words of the Great Commission, that Jesus Christ, as God, is with us (Matt. 28:20) through the presence of the Holy Spirit, the third person of the Trinity—to the end of this age.

Lord, thank You for being ever-present with me through Your Holy Spirit. I am unworthy, but I am extremely blessed and thankful.

WEEKEND READING

Saturday – John 5:25-35
Sunday – Acts 8:4-24

PERSONAL REFLECTIONS

Better than the Physical Jesus

John 14:19

19 "After a little while the world will no longer see Me, but you will see Me; because I live, you will live also.

Oh, to have been there in the Upper Room with the disciples to see Christ in person—how could anything possibly be better than that? To experience His very real presence in person, to break bread with Him, to sit and listen to the living, breathing Son of God, to lap up every word, dwell on every facial expression. With the aroma of the Passover lamb roast wafting through the air, the warm bread and the sweet taste of wine lingering in our mouths. The foreboding, confusing words of the Master, teaching as a loving father preparing us for His trip away, where we could not go—all that would have been lost in the delight of having His presence with us. Caught up in the experience of the moment, we'd wonder, why does anything have to change?

Yet change had to come, and it would be for the better. In fact, what was coming would be far better than Jesus' physical presence. In simple terms, when He would return to them, they would see Him but the world would not. They would live, and by implication, the world would not. Things would hugely change.

In the Upper Room, there were severe limitations on Jesus, who had ". . . emptied Himself, taking the form of a bond-servant, *and* being made in the likeness of men" (Phil. 2:7). In His pre-resurrection "form of a bond-servant" He could not physically be everywhere present. While the disciples enjoyed His presence in the Upper Room, what about Joseph of Arimethea (Matt. 27:57), whom the Scripture states was a disciple of Jesus, or Nicodemus (John 19:39), who gave evidence of faith by assisting in the burial of the crucified Jesus?

But there was coming a time, which is now here, when the presence of Jesus through the Holy Spirit would be everywhere. That was why it was so significant at the Great Commission for Jesus to say to them, "And lo, I am with you always, even until the end of the age" (Matt. 28:20). His spiritual post-resurrection presence is far better than His physical pre-resurrection presence. And it is every bit as real; actually, by faith, the presence of the Holy

Spirit can be said to be "more" real. In fact, Jesus tells us in our passage for today, "Because I live, you will live also." This is life eternal—to truly know Him (John 17:3). This is abundant life (John 10:10). This is life indeed as God intends it. This is better than pre-resurrection, pre-crucifixion life. This is having the presence of Jesus in our lives forever and ever. Without end! Never to be orphans or separated from our heavenly Father.

Lord, I praise You for the life You have given me. This is true life indeed.

Triunity in Me

John 14:20

20 "In that day you will know that I am in My Father, and you in Me, and I in you.

Trilogies occur frequently in Scripture. The trilogy of Father, Son and Holy Spirit is the most central of course. But here we have the Father, Son and us. We take the liberty here to see ourselves in the "you" to whom Jesus addresses this comment. Certainly, the Upper Room apostles came to discover this truth beginning on the Day of Pentecost. Jesus would be physically leaving, but they would not be left alone as spiritual orphans with a distant, uninvolved God. He, the Creator God of the universe, the intimate Father of Jesus Himself, would take up residence in us via Jesus Christ. That needs some thought to appreciate it fully.

That the "day" in question refers to the time of the Spirit coming, beginning at Pentecost, has been addressed earlier. In Acts 2:3, the Spirit's coming was symbolized by the flames of fire that came down on the disciples. It is written that they were "filled with the Holy Spirit," and it happened to them individually ("on each one of them"). This presence would be distinct and personal. But more specifically, not just the Spirit but also the Father would take up residence in them as well, along with the Son—the Father by virtue of being in the Son (see also John 10:38). That makes the entire Trinity. What an amazing thing—the triune God being "in" us!

Now what is meant by "in?" Since God is spirit, and clearly physical-spatial considerations are not in view, there must be something other than the image of our physical bodies carrying around the presence of God. It is similar to the way the Shekinah glory resided in the tabernacle of Israel, though even Solomon admitted that no house on earth could contain the God of the universe (1 Kings 8:27). The Greek word can be translated "with" or "among." We understand this to mean that God would be with them spiritually—no less real than His physical presence but far better, as we have already seen. Christians live in both the physical and spiritual realms, eternally attached and irrevocably intertwined with God. There is a unique, special union of the Christian with God that can only be described as God being "in/with/among" us in the fullest sense.

But notice also, the Christian is also in Christ. Although hard to imagine in concrete terms, the sense is that we are aligned with the life and purpose of Christ. As Paul says, "For me to live is Christ . . ." (Phil. 1:21) and ". . . Christ lives in me; and the *life* which I now live in the flesh I live by faith in the Son of God . . ." (Gal. 2:20).

Lord, Your presence in my life motivates me to align my purposes with Yours.

Loved by My Father

John 14:21

21 "He who has My commandments and keeps them is the one who loves Me; and he who loves Me will be loved by My Father, and I will love him and will disclose Myself to him."

Young or unlearned Christians can stumble over this verse. Does not Jesus teach in John 3:16 that God loves the whole world? And does not Paul lay out clearly that before we ever loved Him, "God demonstrates His own love toward us, in that while we were yet sinners, Christ died for us" (Rom. 5:8)? How then can Jesus teach that the Father's love for us depends upon our love for Him?

We need to take all of Scripture into account. First, the same chronicler, the "beloved disciple," in his first letter 40-plus years later, wrote that any love we have originates from God: ". . . love is from God; and everyone who loves is born of God and knows God" (1 John 4:7). Our ability to love is catalyzed by God's sacrificial love for us: "In this is love, not that we loved God, but that He loved us and sent His Son *to be* the propitiation for our sins" (1 John 4:10). Succinctly he adds, "We love, because He first loved us" (1 John 4:19). So in what sense does Jesus explain that God's love is contingent upon our love?

Remember in context Jesus had already told them, "If you love Me, you will keep My commandments" (vs. 15). The evidence of our love for Christ is our obedience to His commands. It does no good to say we love Him if we do not do anything He asks of us. Love is not a feeling but a response to Christ. Jesus is simply making a statement that the one who obeys Christ is the one who truly loves Him. Just as loving one another is the evidence that we are Christ's disciples (John 13:35), so also obedience is the evidence that we love Christ.

But this love is a response to the love of God in Christ. So, yes, God loves the world and everyone in it (see 1 John 2:2)—that is the beginning point. Through faith, His disciples respond to that love by loving God in return and following Jesus. God then responds to our obedient love with a special or increasing love as a Father loves his children. The growing reciprocity of God's initiating love increasingly energizes our responsive love, so that we ". . . being rooted and grounded in love, may be able to comprehend with all the saints what is the breadth and length and height and depth, and to know the love of Christ which surpasses knowledge, that [we] may be filled up to all the fullness of God" (Eph. 3:17-19). So we can say like John, "By this the love of God was manifested in us, that God has sent His only begotten Son into the world so that we might live through Him" (1 John 4:9).

Lord, I love You because You have infused me with Your love through Christ.

Judas, the Good One

John 14:22

[22] Judas (not Iscariot) said to Him, "Lord, what then has happened that You are going to disclose Yourself to us and not to the world?"

Unfortunate to have the same name as the traitor, this disciple presents the fourth and last question to their Lord in the Upper Room. In John 16:17, they had wished to ask another question for clarification, which the Lord knowing, answered anyway even though they didn't actually ask Him. We know little about this disciple, except that he is distinguished as the son of James (Luke 6:16) and possibly went by the name Thaddaeus (see Mark 3:18, where only one Judas is named among the twelve).

In actuality, of the twelve, we know virtually nothing about four of them (Bartholomew, James the son of Alphaeus, Simon the Zealot, and Matthias, who replaced Judas Iscariot). Such does not make them insignificant in the least. As part of the twelve, they were privy to the Master's teachings and were the faithful band of men Jesus deputized as His official witnesses (Acts 1:8). It was to their teaching that the early church was "continually devoting themselves" (Acts 2:42). Although the history of what happened to the twelve apart from the biblical record is sketchy and based on what is called "tradition," that is, other writings beyond Scripture, it is believed that this Judas died as a martyr in AD 65 in Syria.

His question, probably on the minds of the others as well, was one for clarification. How would it be that the followers of Christ would see Him but the world would not? At this juncture, the disciples probably were still imagining Christ's coming in the fullness of the kingdom, victorious over the Roman system, which had subjugated the Jews in their own land. Not since before the Babylonian captivity had Israel been an independent nation, with aspiration to influence the world, and in the terms of the Abrahamic promise, be a blessing to the world. How could this happen, in Judas' mind, if Jesus was not going to disclose Himself to the world?

Isn't this a question we all ask, in one form or another? How often have we wished God would manifest Himself in a tangible way by speaking with a booming voice out of heaven or performing an incontrovertible miracle or even coming in person so that people would believe in Him? Yet to this day, God has not disclosed Himself to the world. He only reveals Himself to those who come by faith, who become His followers. He is not hiding, for He taught that those who seek will find. Seeking Him in faith is required for the disclosure of God.

Lord, thank You for revealing Yourself to me through Your Son, the Lord Jesus Christ. I desire to learn more of You, so therefore I seek You all the more.

Divine, Triune Occupation

John 14:23

²³ Jesus answered and said to him, "If anyone loves Me, he will keep My word; and My Father will love him, and We will come to him and make Our abode with him."

Straight answers Jesus gave to the disciples in the Upper Room, though clouded emotions and thick heads cannot always hear straight. Jesus answered Judas (not Iscariot, we must continually make that clear for this poor son of James) in the singular, though without doubt the other ten were listening over his shoulder (the other, nefarious Judas had already left, as recorded in John 13:30). What Jesus had said previously at least two times, He reiterates again so there is no doubt about the ground rules for after He was gone: how to have an ongoing intimate relationship with God.

The evidence of genuine love for Christ shows in how a person responds to His teachings. Is that not one of the two key aspects of the so-called Great Commission, where Jesus, after the resurrection and just before His ascension to heaven, and before the coming of the Holy Spirit, charged His disciples to make disciples by 1) baptizing them and 2) teaching them to obey all that Christ commanded them (Matt. 29:18-20)? Evangelism (bringing people to faithful identification with Christ) and love (leading people to obey Christ). This constitutes a return to the proper relationship that was abandoned at the tree in the Garden of Eden. Obedience is the truest test of genuine love for God. Although love is not mentioned in the Great Commission, Jesus certainly made clear the relationship between love and obedience in the Upper Room.

There is no confusion here with salvation by works, for that is not at all what Jesus taught. If we bring up the Law, Jesus' answer was that the Law is summed up not in a merit-based effort, but in love for God and our neighbor (Matt. 22:37-40). So the Great Commission is to bring people to faith (the evidence of which is baptism) and love (the evidence of which is obedience). This is a far cry from earning salvation through obedience. Obedience is not the cause, but the result, the outward action. The reality is love (see 1 Corinthians 13:13).

And so Jesus reiterates what He said in verse 21. When we love Him, we enter into a relationship with God that is like living together in the same house. He takes up the familial closeness only experienced by those who live, eat, work and sleep together. The Christian, together with God the Father, God the Son and God the Holy Spirit ("We") become a nuclear family unit. There are no closed doors; our lives have come under divine, triune occupation.

Lord, welcome to my life. I continually open every door to You for Your full possession. Teach me to live in the faith that You really do reside in Me.

WEEKEND READING

Saturday – John 5:36-47
Sunday – Acts 8:25-40

PERSONAL REFLECTIONS

_____
_____
_____
_____
_____
_____
_____
_____
_____
_____
_____
_____
_____
_____
_____
_____
_____
_____
_____
_____
_____

Growing Love

John 14:24

24 "He who does not love Me does not keep My words; and the word which you hear is not Mine, but the Father's who sent Me.

Making sure they don't mistake what He is saying, Jesus repeats Himself in the negative. Before, He said, "If anyone loves Me, he will keep My word." Now He asserts that "He who does not love Me does not keep My words."

The positive is a universal though indefinite statement applying to "anyone;" the negative uses an intensified singular focus, "he," making this very personal. Imagine each of the disciples reviewing in his own mind whether this applies to himself. Can we not admit what we ourselves might be thinking? "Have I done enough to show the Lord that I love Him?" Certainly, Peter had already asserted his commitment to even die for Christ. According to Matthew, they had already wondered about themselves at the talk about a betrayer, where each one said, "Lord, is it I?" (Matt. 26:22). Who might Jesus have been looking at during that brief moment? Judas (not Iscariot)? Or was it like those liturgical pictures of Jesus where His eyes seem to pierce you from whatever angle you view it? If the eyes of the Lord pierced my soul, would He see my love for Him? Would He just be able to assess my love for Him by my actions?

If I do not love Christ, then why in the world would I want to keep His words? Oh, to be sure, there is societal pressure, even the benefits of Christian fellowship by outwardly donning obedience to the Bible (at least in the obvious ways) that will motivate a person to live Christianly. The Pharisees excelled in this kind of living—outwardly impeccable, but in reality lacking love for God or neighbor. They loved their righteousness. God can see the difference when He observes our actions.

Notice the difference in the negative statement. Jesus refers to "My words," whereas He used the singular in the positive statement, "the word." Again, the specificity leads us to the idea that it is not just a "pick and choose" approach to obedience, where we can claim faithful obedience in a certain percentage of our actions and attitudes. James, in his letter, said that if we have broken the least of the commandments, we have essentially broken the entire law (James 2:10). Let there be no mistaking this point. If we love Christ, then there is nothing He commands us that we would not be willing to do for Him. High standard, high calling. So we study His love for us so that we grow in our love for Him. We aren't there yet, but we desire to grow in His love.

Lord, help me love You more by showing me the depths of Your love for me.

His/Their Word

24 "He who does not love Me does not keep My words; and the word which you hear is not Mine, but the Father's who sent Me.

Word of Christ versus the word of the Father? Which is which? If Jesus Christ is God, then is not the word of the Father the same thing as the word of the Son? The Christian concept of the Trinity contains within it mysteries and seeming anomalies, though when correctly understood they are not contradictions. We have already pointed out that the one true God exists in three persons. This is not three Gods but one God. Yet the Bible presents God as Father who is distinct in some way from God the Son. And both are distinct in some way from God the Holy Spirit. Yet the Bible presents all three as not just equal to God, but all three are in fact God.

Here we find one of the distinctions between God the Father and God the Son. There is the Father's word, and there is the Son's word (implied in this verse). The Father has "sent" the Son in a fashion that is uniquely one-way, that is, the Son did not send the Father. Theologians call this the eternal procession of Jesus from the Father. Furthermore, theologians talk about the Holy Spirit eternally proceeding from the Father and the Son.

We take this verse to mean that Jesus is not giving new teaching on this subject, but that God (the Father) had made this idea known long before Jesus was born and carried on His earthly ministry. From the beginning Jesus had quoted the OT Scriptures (God's Word), e.g. during the wilderness temptation, where Jesus quoted OT passages to the devil rather than using His own words (Matt. 4:1-11).

This is similar to wording Paul uses when speaking to the issue of marriage: "But to the married I give instructions, not I, but the Lord, that the wife should not leave her husband . . ." (1 Cor. 7:10). In other words, he is relying on the teachings of Jesus in making His point (see Matthew 5:32; 19:6). Yet a few verses later he says, "But to the rest I say, not the Lord, that if any brother has a wife who is an unbeliever, and she consents to live with him, he must not divorce her" (1 Cor. 7:12), emphasizing that this is new revelation. The latter is no less inspired then the former, but just clarifies the source of revelation.

So the Lord in our passage for today is clarifying that what He is teaching is no new revelation, but has been the truth all along, as revealed in the OT. The point would stand on the authority of Jesus alone, but the reduplication and the divine emphasis add up to stressing this truth in the strongest possible way.

Lord, I want to be obedient to Your Word because I love You. Thank You for making it absolutely clear that I can't win Your love, but only respond to it.

His Word in Red

John 14:25

25 "These things I have spoken to you while abiding with you."

R ed letter Bibles are helpful for identifying the direct teachings of Jesus, but they are no more important than any other teachings found in Scripture. Some erroneously attribute more weight to quotations of Jesus as though they are unmitigated, straight from God's mouth. This is uninformed and even divisive. "All Scripture is inspired by God . . ." (2 Tim. 3:16). To elevate Christ's words above the rest of God's Word constitutes wrongly "dividing the word of truth" (2 Tim. 2:15 KJV). The apostles became very aware of this notion, as evidenced in Peter's referring to Paul's writings as being on the same level as "other Scripture" (2 Peter 3:16).

Some have suggested that there is a difference between inspiration at work in men as they interpret God's message to us, and the uninterpreted, direct quotations of God Himself, in the mouth of Jesus, as though no human intermediary was involved. However, this is patently false on a number of fronts. First, the gospel writers were selective in which words of Christ they included, as even a superficial comparison of the four accounts reveals. This emphasizes and thus interprets His teachings. Second, most scholars agree that Jesus probably taught in the common language of Palestine at the time, Aramaic. Yet our gospel accounts are written in Greek, which involved a human translation, which inherently requires some interpretation, as do all translations.

This does not diminish the teachings of Jesus. In fact, at this juncture in the gospel story, as He readies the disciples for the Holy Spirit's presence, they have already been learning the import of His teaching: ". . . they were amazed at His teaching, for His message was with authority" (Luke 4:32). They had heard Jesus contrast His teaching with the accepted rabbinical understandings by using the familiar formula, "You have heard it said . . . but I say . . ." in the Sermon on the Mount. He said, "Heaven and earth will pass away, but My words will not pass away" (Matt. 24:35).

So now in the Upper Room, Jesus wanted the disciples to remember His words, the ones He spoke while with them. Years later, John remembered well and wrote, "What was from the beginning, what we have heard, what we have seen with our eyes, what we have looked at and touched with our hands, concerning the Word of Life . . . what we have seen and heard we proclaim to you also, so that you too may have fellowship with us; and indeed our fellowship is with the Father, and with His Son Jesus Christ" (1 John 1:1, 3).

Lord, thank You for giving us Your Word. By it we can fellowship with You.

Perfect Recall

John 14:26

26 "But the Helper, the Holy Spirit, whom the Father will send in My name, He will teach you all things, and bring to your remembrance all that I said to you.

This verse adds two important truths to our understanding of the Holy Spirit. Let's look at the second truth first. Jesus promised the disciples in the Upper Room the gift of perfect recall. This coming Helper would "bring to your remembrance all that I said to you." What does it mean? It certainly and obviously can't mean all Christians will be given perfect recall. Most of us have a difficult time remembering many portions of Scripture even when we make a concerted effort to memorize the Bible. However, this would be a needed ability for the time after Christ left their presence. Human efforts to remember become easily clouded with time. Even two people can have significant differences in how they remember a shared experience.

In Acts, just before Jesus ascended into heaven, He spoke to the apostles (Acts 1:2) and said, ". . . you will receive power when the Holy Spirit has come upon you; and you shall be My witnesses both in Jerusalem, and in all Judea and Samaria, and even to the remotest part of the earth" (Acts 1:8). How would anyone know for sure what Jesus taught after He was gone? The early church looked to the apostles for that teaching. Immediately after Pentecost, we find that "[t]hey were continually devoting themselves to the apostles' teaching and to fellowship, to the breaking of bread and to prayer" (Acts 2:42). Why the apostles' teaching and not Jesus' teaching? Because the only way they would have known what Jesus taught was by what the apostles taught. We conclude, then, that the apostles were given perfect recall of all Jesus' teachings. And that was one of the two primary works of the Holy Spirit that Jesus spoke about in the Upper Room.

The apostles were to be Jesus' authorized witnesses about His life and teachings. That is why when they needed to replace Judas, we read Peter saying ". . . it is necessary that of the men who have accompanied us all the time that the Lord Jesus went in and out among us—beginning with the baptism of John until the day that He was taken up from us—one of these *must* become a witness with us of His resurrection" (Acts 1:21-22).

The other truth is that the Holy Spirit would teach the apostles that which was necessary to fill in the gaps. God would continue to teach them long after Jesus was physically gone. And praise God, we now have the benefit of this promise to them, for we can hold the written Word of God in our hands!

Lord, thank You for the assurance that what the apostles taught was accurate and true, both for the early church and for us today through Your written Word.

Peace Supernatural

John 14:27

27 *"Peace I leave with you; My peace I give to you; not as the world gives do I give to you. Do not let your heart be troubled, nor let it be fearful."*

Surprisingly, this is the first time the word "peace" is used in the Gospel of John. He uses it one other time in the Upper Room in 16:33, but not again until after the resurrection, where Jesus speaks peace to the disciples, again in a room (ostensibly the Upper Room). Other large-concept words abound in this gospel account like life, love and light. Emphasis can come with the vastness of repetition (as is the case of Luke's chronicle, which records "peace" numerous times), but emphasis can also come in an understated way. In the midst of the gospel of life, love and light, the idea of peace stands out subtly, yet starkly.

Probably for the first time we see that the disciples' spiritual high of walking with Jesus gets shaken to the core. Yes, there were times of fear before, as when struggling against the storms—the stories of which abound in Matthew, Mark and Luke. And Jesus spoke peace to them then. But their fears at those times concerned earthly things. In the Upper Room a different kind of fear was descending on them, the loss of their beloved Master, the One for whom they had given up everything to follow, the One in whom all their hopes rested. They were about to discover the depths to which their fears would be realized.

Jesus knew what it was like to be troubled. It was how He felt when He saw the people grieving for Lazarus at his tomb (John 11:33). He experienced a "troubled" spirit when He prayed to the Father in anticipation of His death on the cross (12:27). And the thought of one of the disciples betraying Him brought on this same feeling (13:21). So Jesus knows whereof He speaks, so He knows their need of a supernatural peace.

This peace He was offering them (and us) would be a supernatural harmony of soul and spirit, not just the assurance of personal well-being or even just an emotional sense of well-being. There are times when God seems silent and His promises seem distant. Times when our faith is shaken to the core and our hope wavers. Precisely at those times, when it seems God is simply not there, when we are tempted to feel that all we have lived and sacrificed for in believing in and following Christ is for nothing—*that* is when this promise of peace gets us through. It is at times like those when we hold on to the promise of Jesus' peace, which the apostle Paul describes as ". . . the peace of God, which surpasses all comprehension [which] will guard your hearts and your minds in Christ Jesus" (Phil. 4:7).

Lord, I cling to Your promise of peace and rest in it no matter the storm.

WEEKEND READING

Saturday – John 6:1-14
Sunday – Acts 9:1-19a

PERSONAL REFLECTIONS

Rejoicing He's Gone

John 14:28

²⁸ "You heard that I said to you, 'I go away, and I will come to you.' If you loved Me, you would have rejoiced because I go to the Father, for the Father is greater than I."

Pushing the envelope, Jesus not only broke the news to the disciples in the Upper Room that He would be leaving them and sending another Comforter who in many regards would be just like Him, but now He is saying the disciples should have rejoiced at this news. One would think this was a hard pill to swallow, from their perspective.

Jesus is not taunting them or overreaching in His expectations of them, which always were higher than they had attained at any given point. This is not a ceaseless carrot on a stick, always present but never truly attainable. No, Jesus' unique way of communicating effectively raises the bar that they will attain. Not once do we hear from the disciples after the resurrection, after the whole story of what Jesus was talking about in the Upper Room had taken place, that they ever complained about Jesus' absence or wished He were still there in His pre-resurrected presence.

To be sure, John finishes his inspired writings with "Amen. Come, Lord Jesus" (Rev. 22:20). And Paul wrote of his anticipation of being with the Lord when he wrote, "[I]n the future there is laid up for me the crown of righteousness, which the Lord, the righteous Judge, will award to me on that day; and not only to me, but also to all who have loved His appearing" (2 Tim. 4:8). But no one wished the pre-incarnate Jesus back. In fact, once the "another Helper" came, namely the Holy Spirit whom Jesus had promised them, the twelve apostles hit the ground running and began preaching Christ crucified.

They didn't wait around mourning Jesus' absence. In fact, in Peter's first sermon, on the very day the Spirit came upon them (Pentecost), he preached, "This Jesus God raised up again, to which we are all witnesses. Therefore having been exalted to the right hand of God, and having received from the Father the promise of the Holy Spirit, He has poured forth this which you both see and hear" (Acts 2:32-33). In that very first church plant from which the Word of God went out powerfully into all the world, "[e]veryone kept feeling a sense of awe . . . praising God and having favor with all the people. And the Lord was adding to their number day by day those who were being saved" (Acts 2:43, 47). So yes, though the disciples could not see it at the time in the Upper Room, they did come to rejoice that Jesus had gone back to the Father.

Lord, while my flesh at times desires to have been among those who walked with You on the earth, Your presence with me through the Spirit is all I need.

Greater than the Son

John 14:28 (cont.)

28 "You heard that I said to you, 'I go away, and I will come to you.' If you loved Me, you would have rejoiced because I go to the Father, for the Father is greater than I."

Greater than the Son, how can that be? The concept challenges us on a number of levels. First, the Bible makes a good case for the supremacy of Jesus Christ. How could any biblically compatible statement be made that puts something as a favorable comparison to Jesus, let alone a superior comparison? Jesus was the Word that was with God, that was God (John 1:1). He is the one of whom it is written, "For in Him all the fullness of Deity dwells in bodily form, and in Him you have been made complete, and He is the head over all rule and authority" (Col. 2:9-10). "He is the image of the invisible God, the firstborn of all creation" (Col. 1:15). "For it was the *Father's* good pleasure for all the fullness to dwell in Him" (Col. 1:19). "He is the radiance of His [God's] glory and the exact representation of His nature . . ." (Heb. 1:3). "For from Him and through Him and to Him are all things . . ." (Rom. 11:36). Jesus is no less than God, full deity. That is absolutely basic to Christian faith. So how could He say that "the Father is greater than I"?

Theologians wrestle with this (and I agree with them) by carefully wording the Trinity formulation. This is not a creation by an ecclesiastical court, but simply a recognition of what the Bible teaches in its whole scope. The earliest church councils dealt with the varying viewpoints of the Trinity. Jesus was God and the Father was God (and so also the Holy Spirit). They are all "co-equal," meaning they are all equally God, and there is only one God. Three persons, but not three Gods. It would be a logical contradiction to say there is one God, but three Gods. And it would likewise be a contradiction to say there is one person, but three persons. No, there is one God who exists as three distinct persons, separate in their relationships to each other, yet remaining a singular God.

Admittedly this concept of the Trinity requires faith, as it stretches us beyond the limits of our ability to fully understand. But so does the resurrection of Jesus from the dead. Our faith is in the message and truth of God as revealed in Scripture. And Jesus taught that the Father was greater than He. Jesus submitted to the Father's will for Him to die on the cross. Jesus said earlier, "I have come down from heaven, not to do my own will but the will of Him who sent me" (John 6:38). The sender is greater than the one sent. Jesus will shortly return from His mission on earth to the One who commissioned Him.

Lord, I am not surprised that there are some things I can't fully comprehend. It makes sense that my finite mind is limited in my contemplation of You.

Faith for Later

John 14:29

29 "Now I have told you before it happens, so that when it happens, you may believe."

A young man went to buy life insurance for the first time. When he saw the face value suggested by the agent, he became quite excited, having never had that much money in his entire life before. But then the realization set in that he would never see any of that money, but his wife and children would. That is the point of life insurance, and it was a stark discovery for him. Another person sets up his will to bequeath all that he has to those who survive him upon his death. Still another, with limited means, trains his children in all aspects of life, so that after his death, they will be fully capable for living life successfully and productively. Each of these prepared for others to live well after he departed this life. Some people give no thought at all to what happens after they are gone.

Jesus cared immensely for His followers and how they would fare after He departed. His work was not just to come to this world, minister and then provide the perfect atoning sacrifice. His mission was to continue on through His followers. So He could not leave them until they were fully prepared. His mission would not have been complete if He died for sins but did not prepare for the continuance of His message to the ends of the earth (Acts 28:18-20). While His disciples there in the room most certainly did not think they were ready for His departure, Jesus' training for them was nearing completion.

We have seen in the Upper Room so far that shortly after His departure (which they still could not fully comprehend, and which would be both "worse" and far more glorious than expected), the disciples would receive the Holy Spirit, who would be another Helper or Comforter just like Him. He was now giving them His final in-depth teaching, the instructions they would need after He was gone.

Jesus was fully aware that they did not understand what He was saying to them. He could have waited and given them this teaching after His resurrection, when it would have made more sense. But being the Master Teacher that He was, the plan was to give it to them before, to give greater clarity later to who He truly is. They would come to a greater depth of faith than they already had at that time. They would come to a profound understanding, beyond anything they could possibly imagine before the resurrection. To use the words of Peter at Pentecost, after the resurrection and ascension of Jesus, they came to ". . . know for certain that God has made Him both Lord and Christ . . ." (Acts 2:36).

Lord Jesus Christ, I bow before You and declare my allegience to You.

Ruler of the World

John 14:30

> [30] *"I will not speak much more with you, for the ruler of the world is coming, and he has nothing in Me . . ."*

Jesus is absolutely pure of all evil and gives no quarter to Satan. Jesus is connected to the Father, the God of Israel. To those who rejected Him, He asserted, "You are of *your* father the devil, and you want to do the desires of your father. He was a murderer from the beginning, and does not stand in the truth because there is no truth in him. Whenever he speaks a lie, he speaks from his own *nature,* for he is a liar and the father of lies" (John 8:44).

Satan had already begun his work in Judas Iscariot (John 13:2) and was about to finish his work through Judas (John 18:3-5). And when he was finished with Judas, the unfortunate pawn went and killed himself (Matt. 27:3-10). This erring disciple represents the epitome of Satan's attempts in humans (the Creator's image bearers) to rob God of His glory. Extreme Calvinists might say Satan was predestined by God Himself to do those things. But Jesus here disavows any thought that God's purposes may have intentionally included Satan. "He has nothing in Me," said the Master. The mystery of Satan's existence in a perfect creation is not resolved with extreme predestination theology.

Jesus was not fleeing because Satan was coming into the world. But what they could not fully understand then in the Upper Room is that Satan would be an instrumental cause of Jesus' leaving. The ultimate cause, of course, is Jesus' ascension to God in full glorification, His work being completed. But like a celestial Grand Master, the God who is supreme over all used the best hand Satan could play to bring him into checkmate. It would be supremely minimizing God to say He outwitted Satan—the match was not even close. Satan was playing on a limited-dimensional platform, whereas the God of infinity plays on an eternally multi-dimensional platform. Not in the same league at all.

Is it any wonder that Paul wrote, "For though we walk in the flesh, we do not war according to the flesh, for the weapons of our warfare are not of the flesh, but divinely powerful for the destruction of fortresses" (2 Cor. 10:3-4)?

So for a time, the ruler of the world (as Satan is referred to here) would have free reign, just enough rope to hang himself (interestingly pictured in Judas' suicide). His ultimate destiny? "Now judgment is upon this world; now the ruler of this world will be cast out" (John 12:31). But, if he is cast out, how can he still be actively influencing people now? One thing is certain: the victory is already complete. Whatever he is doing now, it is a losing battle for him.

Lord, thank You for Your victory over the deceiver, the ruler of this world.

Ruler of the World (cont.)

John 14:30

30 "I will not speak much more with you, for the ruler of the world is coming, and he has nothing in Me . . .

That Satan is still active in this world is made clear in many passages. We write about him not to give him glory and undue attention, but to warn. There is nothing more sinister to human beings than to be blinded to God's work in the world. John lays out this dichotomy at the very beginning of his gospel account: "The Light shines in the darkness, and the darkness did not comprehend it" (John 1:5). Christ comes as the light shining in the darkness; Satan comes blinding people to that light. He began this in the Garden of Eden, and he has been unwavering in continuing to do so.

Paul writes that ". . . the god of this world has blinded the minds of the unbelieving so that they might not see the light of the gospel of the glory of Christ, who is the image of God" (2 Cor. 4:4). The deceiver continues to be quite active. In writing to the Ephesians, Paul also says, ". . . you formerly walked according to the course of this world, according to the prince of the power of the air, of the spirit that is now working in the sons of disobedience" (Eph. 2:2).

Christians have been made to see. In the words of the man healed by Jesus of his blindness, we can say, ". . . one thing I do know, that though I was blind, now I see" (John 9:25). So now, our struggle is not in blindness but with the full knowledge that the light of the Gospel of Jesus Christ brings. We understand that "our struggle is not against flesh and blood, but against the rulers, against the powers, against the world forces of this darkness, against the spiritual *forces* of wickedness in the heavenly *places"* (Eph. 6:12). The unregenerate world still remains locked in the deceiver's grasp. But not believers. "We know that we are of God, and that the whole world lies in *the power of* the evil one" (1 John 5:19).

So what makes the difference? John again writes, "You are from God, little children, and have overcome them; because greater is He who is in you than he who is in the world" (1 John 4:4). Though Jesus is not physically in the world, and Satan has now come in some sense unfettered into the world that deceiver is a defeated foe, who blindly, rebelliously is going down—ostensibly not without a fight. But we have overcome the world because our Master, the Lord Jesus, before whom demons and Satan himself shudder, has overcome the world (John 16:33). We can therefore be of "good cheer," as Jesus said.

It remains then for us to continue walking by faith and in faith, for "Greater is He who is in us than he who is in the world."

Lord, the victory is Yours, and I choose to walk in light of the victory.

WEEKEND READING

Saturday – John 6:15-25
Sunday – Acts 9:19b-43

PERSONAL REFLECTIONS

That the World May Know

John 14:31

31 ". . . but so that the world may know that I love the Father, I do exactly as the Father commanded Me. Get up, let us go from here."

Everything recorded in the gospels about Jesus demonstrates His love for His father. Intentionally. Everyone knows that Jesus talked about loving one's neighbor and loving God. Although humans usually put those two points in that order, the Scripture always puts loving God before loving neighbor. But there is a greater message—that there is a love relationship within the Trinity. Those who deny the Trinity miss this huge fact. God is not simply an impersonal being who needs created humans in order for love to exist. To say, as John does in his first epistle, "God is love" (1 John 4:8, 16), is abstract to the point of irrelevance. Love is not merely a principle, a concept. Love is an active reality, independent of human existence. God was completely immersed in a love relationship within Himself. He needed nothing else to complete that love, for God was complete in His love within the members of the Trinity.

Admittedly, speaking about this enlivens the difficulty of our human understanding of the singularity of God with the plurality of the Trinity. We must live with that tension, which is more a limitation of human language and thought rather than of the concept of a singular God who exists as three persons. Jesus the Son loves the Father—we have that on inspired authority of Scripture. God is complete in that love.

God does not need love from any source outside of Himself, apparently by love's very nature (we should really say, by God's very nature). But there is an inherent flow outward. First it emanates out from each member of the Trinity toward one other—perfectly and completely. God loves, not because He lacks, but because He is perfect. He needs no other reciprocity, because His love is complete within the Trinity. So therefore, God can give love freely (the "love period" kind of love). And Jesus wants the world (over which Satan is currently ruling, see vs. 30) to know that He perfectly loves the Father and is absolutely committed to exactly and absolutely obeying His Father's commands.

That's how Jesus demonstrated His love for the Father, as He said, by doing "exactly as the Father commanded Me." That included what was coming next, and so the time had come to engage the "ruler of the world." It was time to face the final battle. He was about to continue modeling what He asks of the disciples: obedience to God.

Lord, I want the world to know there is a God who loves them, the proof of that being my commitment to loving You and loving them.

Engagement

John 14:31 (cont.)

---

[31] ". . . but so that the world may know that I love the Father, I do exactly as the Father commanded Me. Get up, let us go from here."

Just as He followed the Spirit's leading into the wilderness to be tempted by Satan at the beginning of His ministry (Matt. 4:1), so now Jesus submits to divine leading into the spiritual battle, where temptation again awaits Him. In the Garden of Gethsemane, the place of temptation (Matt. 26:41), He will be tempted to avoid His suffering, as evidenced three times in His prayer for the cup of God's wrath to pass Him by, but then He three times concludes, "Not my will but Yours be done" (Matt. 26:36-46). He was certainly led like a sheep to the slaughter (see Isaiah 53:7), and He would absolutely not disobey His Father.

Neither was His obedience a passive acquiescence. To use the words of the writer of Hebrews, He "resisted to the point of shedding blood" (Heb. 12:3). He endured the suffering with "joy" (Heb. 12:2) and became "obedient to the point of death, even death on a cross" (Phil. 2:8). So when Jesus told the disciples, "Get up, let us go from here," He was advancing to engage the "ruler of this world" (vs. 30) in final battle.

Interestingly, Jesus' relationship with and love for the Father are demonstrated through the adversarial agency of the unwitting tempter himself. The one who presumed to rule over the world could not gain mastery over Jesus, the One who was made "for a little while lower than the angels" (Heb. 2:7). The tempter found an impenetrable foe, an impervious barrier to world domination.

Only Jesus could say that Satan "has nothing in me" (vs. 30). He and Satan have absolutely nothing in common. The very thing that Satan is all about, namely temptation through lies and deceit (John 8:44), carries no sway with Jesus, because there is absolutely no operating principle within Christ that can give Satan's temptation any traction. To be sure, Jesus was tempted in every way as we are (Heb. 4:15), but those temptations had no power over Him. He was absolutely committed to do what the Father commanded. It was His "food" (John 4:34). With us, temptation finds common ground with our fleshly desires. But not so with Jesus. The sequence of temptation to sin as depicted in James 1:14-15 cannot even take root. He cannot be "carried away and enticed by his own lust" and so it cannot be said of Him that "when lust has conceived, it gives birth to sin; and when sin is accomplished, it brings forth death." The death He was about to die was not for Himself, but for the sin that had taken root in us to bring death to everyone. It was His joy to follow the Father's will to die for us (Heb. 12:2).

Lord, teach me to find joy, real joy, in doing as You command me in Your Word.

The Vine Metaphor

John 15:1

¹ "I am the true vine, and My Father is the vinedresser."

Master Teacher that He was, Jesus brought forward one of His farming illustrations. But we underestimate the divine Storyteller if we fail to recognize the exquisite plot lines at various levels. Many layers of meaning await the devoted believer revealing truth upon truth, the beauty of God's sweet communication to those who love Him and seek Him. This is what Jesus meant when He said, "Every scribe who has become a disciple of the kingdom of heaven is like a head of a household, who brings out of his treasure things new and old" (Matt. 13:52).

At this juncture, we aren't sure whether the group was now on the way from the Upper Room (in 14:31 Jesus said, "Let us go from here") and the rest of this discourse through chapter 17 was given on the way to Gethsemane, or whether they remained in the Upper Room as John 18:1 seems to indicate. Regardless, Jesus' teaching continued seamlessly.

On one level, interpreters of this analogy of the vine see Jesus teaching about individual spiritual growth—to continue in spiritual life one must remain connected to Christ. Yet at the same time, we recognize the vine motif that was often used in the OT to represent God's people. For example, Asaph wrote, "You removed a vine from Egypt; You drove out the nations and planted it. You cleared *the ground* before it, and it took deep root and filled the land" (Ps. 80:8-9). This was a clear reference to Israel (see also Psalm 80:8; Isaiah 5:2; Jeremiah 2:21; Hosea 10:1). Jesus is concerned about the health of the people of God, Israel. In this thinking, Jesus Himself is the vine, the true Israel.

Still another perspective is to see here the church, referred to elsewhere as the body of Christ. Jesus, then, is teaching ultimately about the health and growth of the new people of God, the church. This interpretation sees the church replacing Israel in the vine metaphor. But such would cause tension with Romans 11, which speaks of the Gentiles being grafted into the branches of the metaphorical tree, where clearly Israel comprises the so-called natural branches. Admittedly the plants are different (vine in John 15 and olive tree in Romans 11), but the concepts overlap. Jesus all along had been offering the long-awaited Messianic kingdom to the Jews, the people of God. Their rejecting it made room for Gentiles—but the vine did not change. God is still dealing with the people of God. To mix the two metaphors, Gentiles do not replace the natural branches, but are added alongside of those natural branches that are pruned.

Lord, I am grateful as a Gentile that You have given me the privilege to be grafted into Your vine, to become part of the people of God.

Growth Is God's Concern

John 15:1 (cont.)

[1] "I am the true vine, and My Father is the vinedresser."

Spiritual growth, whether individual or corporate, is first and foremost God's business. He is not only vitally interested in spiritual growth, but He is also the primary cause of it. As humans, we have a part, as seen in Jesus' commands to remain or abide in Christ. But our role is not causative but instrumental. To the prideful Corinthians, Paul spelled it out this way: "I planted, Apollos watered, but God was causing the growth" (1 Cor. 3:6).

Overshadowing all that Jesus is about to say about abiding in the vine, and the various layers of understanding what that means, two things stand out in stark relief. First, the vine He is talking about is Himself. Second, the primary responsibility for growth of the vine lies with the vinedresser, God the Father.

To be sure, as D.A. Carson puts it, "People don't drift toward holiness . . . [without] grace-driven effort." But our efforts are not the primary causative factor here. Paul expressed divine certainty to the Philippians: *"For I am* confident of this very thing, that He who began a good work in you will perfect it until the day of Christ Jesus" (Phil. 1:6). And to Timothy he breaks out in praise: "If we are faithless, He remains faithful, for He cannot deny Himself" (2 Tim. 2:13). The vinedresser is concerned about His vine, that it be fruitful. He will make it happen.

Now as will be seen, as Jesus unfolds the metaphor, the human element is necessary to the growth of the vine. However, this is secondary to the efforts of the vinedresser. In other words, we followers and believers of Jesus Christ are to make every effort to do the good works God created for us to do (Eph. 2:10), but we must remember that "it is God who is at work in [us], both to will and to work for *His* good pleasure" (Phil. 2:13). God works through our efforts in the same way a hand works through a glove. It is not the glove that does the work, but the hand working through the glove. So our efforts are like God's glove. He is the one doing the work.

And it is not as though God is rewarding our efforts and therefore working through us. No, the initiative lies with His desire for the growth of the vine, not with our faithfulness in living the right way. Our efforts are nothing more than a response of faith to His growth initiatives. We are the responders to grace, which may look very active from the human perspective, but we are really passive in respect to God. Any other way opens the door to boasting. With Paul we must say, "God forbid that I should boast except in the cross of our Lord Jesus Christ" (Gal. 6:14).

Lord, thank You for working in me to will and to do Your good pleasure.

Taking Up

John 15:2

² "Every branch in Me that does not bear fruit, He takes away; and every branch that bears fruit, He prunes it so that it may bear more fruit."

Jesus, continuing with the vineyard imagery, speaks of the standard practice of pruning, common for increasing fruitfulness of a plant. Macro-pruning cuts off branches from the trunk of the tree, increasing the fruitfulness of the other branches by preventing sap from being diverted to fruitless branches. Micro-pruning involves cutting offshoots from a main branch for similar reasons.

One interpretation of this is that a Christian who does not abide in Christ will lose his or her salvation. Appeal is made to verse 6, "If anyone does not abide in Me, he is thrown away as a branch and dries up; and they gather them, and cast them into the fire and they are burned" (John 15:6). But this makes too strong a connection between the figurative branches being burned and the experience of being cast into hell. The illustration of the branches being burned does not automatically imply that Christians are sent to hell for lack of abiding.

Others suggest that the phrase "takes away" really means "taking up," as it is used in John 8:59, where Jesus' detractors "picked up" stones to stone Him. The analogy then may give the sense that Christians who are not abiding are therefore not fruitful and will as a result be taken up to heaven, that is, die prematurely. This interpretation certainly accords with Paul's teaching in 1 Corinthians 11:30, where some believers in the Corinthian fellowship died because of their disrespect of the Lord's Supper. As Paul said earlier in that letter about those who do not build their lives on the foundation of Christ, their work will be judged: "If any man's work is burned up, he will suffer loss; but he himself will be saved, yet so as through fire" (1 Cor. 3:15). The analogies, though different, are similar enough to draw the inevitable comparison: unfruitful Christians are not in danger of losing their salvation but will be in danger of serious consequences, and in fact, loss of all rewards. And the imagery to convey this idea uses the concept of fire, where it is the Christian's work that is being burned up in judgment, not the Christian himself.

The ultimate goal is that Christians in particular, and the body of Christ in general, be fruitful. Jesus was about to leave the entire mission He had begun in the hands of His followers. He expected results, fruit. And that fruit was clearly to glorify the Lord Jesus Christ by bringing more people to faith in Him through the witness of His followers.

Lord, help me to be a fruitful follower of Jesus Christ. I want to join You in the work of spreading the Good News of forgiveness and life in Christ.

WEEKEND READING

Saturday – John 6:26-40
Sunday – Acts 10:1-23

PERSONAL REFLECTIONS

_____
_____
_____
_____
_____
_____
_____
_____
_____
_____
_____
_____
_____
_____
_____
_____
_____
_____
_____
_____
_____

What Is the Fruit?

John 15:2 (cont.)

² *"Every branch in Me that does not bear fruit, He takes away; and every branch that bears fruit, He prunes it so that it may bear more fruit."*

One can imagine the Lord holding some fresh fruit in His hand. While we may not know the kind of fruit Jesus may have been holding, we do understand He was speaking metaphorically, and therefore ask, what is the real "fruit" about which He was speaking? Some possibilities immediately come to mind, not least of which is the well-known fruit of the Spirit in Galatians 5:22-23. However, we should not too quickly assume that such wording elsewhere in Scripture means that the fruit here in the Upper Room is referring to the same thing.

Fruit is the result of life, and in this context, it is the goal of life. Often Christians confuse fruit with the means to life or even the abiding process itself. Abiding or remaining in Christ leads to fruitfulness, but abiding or remaining in Christ is not itself the fruit. What's the difference?

Some think serving is being fruitful, as though the end result of abiding in Christ is to become a servant. Witness the church that pushes people to volunteer or even to attend church services regularly, and that becomes the "evidence" of spiritual growth. After all, the Upper Room experience with Jesus began with a lesson in serving, "If I then, the Lord and the Teacher, washed your feet, you also ought to wash one another's feet" (John 13:14). We suggest that in Jesus' thinking here serving is not the fruit, but a means to being fruitful.

Or we might think of loving one another as the fruit Jesus has in view: "A new commandment I give to you, that you love one another, even as I have loved you, that you also love one another" (John 13:34). Again, while love is pictured elsewhere as the greatest of the three Christian virtues (the other two being faith and hope), this is not the ultimate fruit Jesus had in mind.

What about doing the works of Christ? "Truly, truly, I say to you, he who believes in Me, the works that I do, he will do also; and greater *works* than these he will do; because I go to the Father" (John 14:12). Or answered prayer (14:13), keeping Christ's commandments (14:23) or experiencing peace (14:27)? These are all objectives for disciples but not the ultimate goal.

While Jesus' mission can be stated in different ways, in the Upper Room He has already told them His goal: ". . . that the world may know that I love the Father" (John 14:31). The Christian's fruitfulness shines forth as the world comes to see Jesus Christ as the perfect manifestation of God's love. God is glorified in Him and through Him—and through us.

Father, help me be fruitful in showing the world how much Jesus loves You.

Pruning Clean

John 15:3

---

[3] *"You are already clean because of the word which I have spoken to you."*

Ritualistic cleansing tempts the interpretation we might give this passage, but this interpretation is without merit considering the context. The word "clean" occurs only in one other passage in the Gospel According to John, namely 13:10-11, where Jesus washed the disciples' feet. "Jesus said to [Peter], 'He who has bathed needs only to wash his feet, but is completely clean; and you are clean, but not all *of you.*' For He knew the one who was betraying Him; for this reason He said, 'Not all of you are clean.'" There He declared eleven of the disciples clean, but not Judas. We surmise then that Jesus had "cleaned" the band of disciples of dead branches, getting them ready for the fruitfulness that would begin on the Day of Pentecost, about 50 days later.

In the previous verse, we saw two words being used to describe the process of a vinedresser making the plant more fruitful. First, there is the taking away or lifting up of the unproductive branches. Then, there is cleaning or pruning of the productive branches so that they would be even more productive. By analogy, God is concerned about both the whole body of believers (the vine) and with individual believers (the productive branches). In application to the disciples, though, the removing of a dead branch (Judas) had already taken place (John 13:30). The other disciples had had their feet washed, symbolic of the fruitful branches being pruned back for more productivity.

While the vinedresser uses physical mechanisms to prune back the vine, God uses spiritual pruning shears, that is, His Word, to clean out that which hinders fruitfulness in our lives. "All Scripture is inspired by God and profitable for teaching, for reproof, for correction, for training in righteousness . . ." (2 Tim. 3:16). The pruning work of the Word of God is incisive: "For the word of God is living and active and sharper than any two-edged sword, and piercing as far as the division of soul and spirit, of both joints and marrow, and able to judge the thoughts and intentions of the heart" (Heb. 4:12). In reference to the church, God uses His Word to "sanctify her, having cleansed her by the washing of water with the word" (Eph. 5:26).

This is true for the body of Christ universal, the body of Christ local and the individual Christian. Without Christ physically present, the disciples and we have two things to equip us and make us useful for His mission: the Holy Spirit and the Word. The Spirit works through the Word to prune the dead, unproductive areas out of our lives.

Lord, thank You for Your Word that acts like pruning shears in my life. I want to be productive in helping the world know that You love the Father.

Abiding in the Vine

John 15:4

⁴ "Abide in Me, and I in you. As the branch cannot bear fruit of itself unless it abides in the vine, so neither can you unless you abide in Me."

Fruitfulness the goal, abiding the process. It is popularly said today that the Lord does not command us to be fruitful, only to be faithful. While technically that pithy statement may be true in a very narrow sense, God does in fact want us to be fruitful. One of His last commands to the disciples was to be fruitful in making disciples (Matt. 28:18-20). Granted the word "fruitful" is not used there, but the idea is clearly in focus.

The question really is, how does the Christian *become* fruitful? We cannot reach into our inner resources, within ourselves. We cannot dig deep enough, because we simply do not have the ability to be fruitful on our own. The analogy Jesus uses is so simple it needs no explanation. A branch does not have fruit-making ability; it must be fully connected to the plant stem. Our verse today is clear: we need to be vitally connected to Christ.

Now we have suggested earlier that Jesus is talking to His disciples, and therefore that they are already part of the body of believers. As it were, they were already abiding *with* Christ, as they were with Him since His baptism and now at the end, in the Upper Room for His final meal. But they needed to learn about abiding "in" Christ, for that is what would produce the fruitfulness after He was physically gone.

So what does it mean to abide? And why does the abiding go both ways, Jesus abiding in them, and they in Him? We stumble when we try to substitute other words than the metaphorical ones. But abiding seems to have in view the relationship with Christ that is *symbiotic*. We have a spiritual dependence on Christ and we are His hands, feet and mouth. We draw our spiritual sustenance from Him like a branch draws sap from the tree. Like branches are the outward manifestation of the tree, we are the body of Christ, through whom Jesus is at work in the world.

Suffice it to say presently that this relationship is absolutely necessary to accomplish anything of spiritual note for God. We may accomplish a great deal in this world, including large church edifices, expanding moral influence and profound Bible teaching. But unless we are abiding in Christ and He in us, then we have no genuine spiritual fruit of the sort Jesus talked about. Like building a house on the sand, accomplishing great things without abiding in Christ will only result in the loss of those very things we spent our lives accomplishing.

Lord, I confess to You all the things I have done in my own power and will, without abiding in Christ. I commit to turning away from all that.

The Divine Vine

⁵ "I am the vine, you are the branches; he who abides in Me and I in him, he bears much fruit, for apart from Me you can do nothing."

Metaphors are more powerful than similes, both figures of speech. Similes, using words like "as" or "like," compare something with something else, though implicitly acknowledge the comparison is not complete—"I am *like* a vine." Metaphors, on the other hand, strengthen the comparison by stating it in more definitive terms—"I am the vine," as we have in our passage today. Not just a lesson in literary style, this distinction serves to stress the weight Jesus puts on the analogy of Himself to the inter-workings of a vine plant and its branches. The comparison is a very close one.

Jesus is the vine. We, as His followers, are the branches. And in particular, we as branches can only bear fruit (whatever that might be) if we abide in Him. To do anything else would mean separation from the vine, from which we get our life-giving "sap." The imagery is clear. The question also is clear. What does it mean to abide?

First, notice the definite article "the." Jesus is not just any vine, or even one of a number of options. He is "the" vine, the one and only. This reminds of us of Jesus' exclusivist comments earlier: "I am the way, and the truth, and the life; no one comes to the Father but through Me" (14:6). Just as Christ is the only way to God, He is also the only way to fruitfulness. There is simply no other way. We can read all the Christian self-help books that fill our shelves, but apart from Christ we "can do nothing." Could it be that the "fruit" many Christians exhibit is more like paper images of Crayola colorfulness, taped onto the tree branches? The artistry may impress, but the results are nothing but colored paper. Not real fruit.

At the root of any Christian endeavor to promote spiritual growth and service must be a live, active, organic (as it were) connection with Christ. As Paul wrote, the path out of fleshly, unfruitful living for the carnal Corinthians remained the same as when he first preached the gospel to them: "For I determined to know nothing among you except Jesus Christ, and Him crucified" (1 Cor. 2:2). He wrote the Colossians, "Therefore as you have received Christ Jesus the Lord, so walk in Him" (Col. 2:6). The Christian begins his spiritual life through Christ and serves God through Christ. This analogy of abiding is similar to the analogy Jesus uses of building a house on the rock and not shifting sands. It comes back to our ongoing relationship with Him. We must abide in Him.

Lord, I come to You every day and abide, continually drawing on Your "every spiritual blessing" (Eph. 1:3).

Sharp Recall

John 15:5 (cont.)

5 "I am the vine, you are the branches; he who abides in Me and I in him, he bears much fruit, for apart from Me you can do nothing."

Imagine John, the gospel chronicler, writing this account many years after the fact. He had apparently made it into his 90s, as the second-century writer Irenaeus mentions his living until emperor Trajan's reign, which began in AD 98. The date he wrote his gospel account is not certain, but most conservative scholars put it between AD 85 and 90. And historians believe he composed this account while living in Ephesus, before his exile to the island of Patmos, where he wrote the Book of the Revelation (Rev. 1:9).

John, for one, knew the true value of Jesus' promise of perfect recall for all that He had taught the disciples (John 14:26). This disciple's mind was still sharp, his memory clear and his words inspired (2 Tim. 3:16). He had had much time to see the truth played out, of Jesus' illustration of being the vine and the requirement for fruitfulness being to abide in Him. Fifty to sixty years had passed between the time the Lord spoke those words and the time when John published them. He had witnessed the explosive Pentecostal event with its mass conversion (Acts 2). He had experienced miracles like Jesus had done (Acts 3). He was present at the Samaritans' baptism into Christ (Acts 8). Yes, he saw much fruit in the immediate aftermath of the beginning of the movement of the promised Holy Spirit. The disciples constantly preached Christ, and they saw great results. He must have continually seen fruit over the next half century until penning these words of Christ for all to hear: "Abide in Me" (vs. 4). There is no reason to believe otherwise.

So how do we abide in Christ? What does John have to say to us about this? Does he not begin with, "In the beginning was the Word . . ."? To abide in Christ means to immerse ourselves in His truth, His Word ("I am the truth . . ."). We need to be in the Word, studying the Word, meditating on the Word and living the Word. John tells us why he wrote his gospel account of the Lord: "These [things in this book] have been written so that you may believe that Jesus is the Christ, the Son of God; and that believing you may have life in His name" (John 20:30-31). Life in Christ is abundant (John 10:10), and therefore is a fruitful life.

Abiding in Him means drawing our life from Him like a branch draws sap from the stem of the plant. It means praying to Him, relying on Him, trusting Him and growing in "the grace and knowledge" of Christ (2 Peter 3:18). That is the only way to fruitfulness in the Christian life—to abide in Christ.

Lord, I want to be fruitful, so I abide in You and You only.

WEEKEND READING

Saturday – John 6:41-58
Sunday – Acts 10:24-48

PERSONAL REFLECTIONS

_____

_____

_____

_____

_____

_____

_____

_____

_____

_____

_____

_____

_____

_____

_____

_____

_____

_____

_____

_____

_____

_____

_____

_____

The Fruitless Christian

John 15:6

6 "If anyone does not abide in Me, he is thrown away as a branch and dries up; and they gather them, and cast them into the fire and they are burned."

Theological debates rage over this verse. Three main interpretations are offered by those of differing doctrinal persuasion. First, some see in this verse a Christian who loses his salvation. Clearly, the person (symbolized as a branch) was at one time connected to Christ (symbolized by the vine itself). But because of lack of faithfulness (symbolized by fruitlessness), he is separated from Christ and cast into hell (symbolized by cutting dead branches off the tree and burning them). In response to this interpretation, we point out that though the imagery of hell does at times include being a place of fire (Matt. 13:41-42), that does not automatically mean that the fire in this verse refers to hell. John has previously recorded that believers already have eternal life (John 3:36; 5:24; 10:28-29). Scripture teaches that the believer is secure and nothing can separate him from God's love (Rom. 8:29-39; 1 John 5:11-13).

The second interpretation is that the branch here that is thrown away and burned is the "professing" believer, who had the appearance of being in the vine but not the reality of it. In other words, he was not a true believer. That person is like a dead branch; there was never any fruit, and in the end he will be burned in the fires of hell. Though the idea of this is nonetheless true, it doesn't fit the analogy. The branch was indeed part of the vine in the illustration; it didn't just "seem" to be part of the vine. At best, this analogy leaves the question ambiguous, like the seed that falls on the rocky soil, whose faith fails for shallow depth or which falls on thorny soil and gets choked out by the cares of the world. Did they have genuine faith or not? The jury is still out.

The third, and preferable, interpretation is that this story of the branches being cut off does refer to genuine Christians who are not fruitful. Clearly, fruitfulness and not salvation is in view here. But what does it mean for those branches to be burned up, if not picturing hell? At times fire refers to God's judgment on fruitless works. For example, Paul wrote about the person who builds on the foundation of Christ with wood, hay and stubble rather than with gold, silver or precious stones: "If any man's work is burned up, he will suffer loss; but he himself will be saved, yet so as through fire" (1 Cor. 3:15). Christians all will stand before the "bema" judgment seat of God, where our deeds will be evaluated (2 Cor. 5:10)—not for our eternal destiny (i.e. the Great White Throne judgment, Revelation 20:11), but for our rewards.

Lord, though I am saved by Your grace and secure forever, I do not want to be fruitless in my life for You. I resolve to respond to Your love with my obedience.

The Fruitless Christian (cont.)

John 15:6

⁶ "If anyone does not abide in Me, he is thrown away as a branch and dries up; and they gather them, and cast them into the fire and they are burned."

Horror comes at the thought of not being fruitful as a Christian! How can that even be possible for those of us who have been blood-bought, grace infused and hope secured by the One from whom we can never be separated (Rom. 8:39)? Just as the grace of God is unfathomable, that is, that God can and does justify unrighteous sinners who place their faith in Christ (Rom. 3:26), so too it boggles the mind that sinners who have been justified by God's righteousness through faith would even think of sinning in any form. But it is true; we best admit it lest we be found calling God a liar (1 John 1:10).

Paul certainly struggled with sin (Rom. 7:14-25). He feared that he might do something that would disqualify himself from a reward in glory: "I discipline my body and make it my slave, so that, after I have preached to others, I myself will not be disqualified" (1 Cor. 9:27). So we are in familiar company.

Certainly, there is a place for Christians, as Paul writes, to "Examine yourselves! Or do you not recognize this about yourselves, that Jesus Christ is in you—unless indeed you fail the test?" (2 Cor. 13:5). But there is also a place for Christians to examine themselves concerning fruitfulness, and take action: "If you are living according to the flesh, you must die; but if by the Spirit you are putting to death the deeds of the body, you will live" (Rom. 8:13).

The solution to fruitlessness, then, is to put to death the old nature—and keep putting it to death. In the words of Romans 12:1-2, ". . . by the mercies of God . . . present your bodies a living and holy sacrifice, acceptable to God, *which is your spiritual service of worship.* And do not be conformed to this world, but be transformed by the renewing of your mind, so that you may prove what the will of God is, that which is good and acceptable and perfect" (Rom. 12:1-2).

Some might object, "If, as you say, a Christian is secure and not in danger of losing his salvation, what motivation does he have for being fruitful?" This is an amazing statement to make (for it really is a statement disguised as a question). It presumes the only reason for doing good is fear of hell's punishment. But the truly redeemed individual has become a new creation; old motivations have passed away (2 Cor. 5:17). The love of God produces in him the desire for fruitfulness. Indeed, for all of us, we love Him only because He first loved us (1 John 4:19). And our love for God motivates us to be fruitful—a far better stimulus to good deeds than fear of punishment.

Lord, I do love You and desire to be fruitful because this brings You pleasure.

The Key to Prayer

John 15:7

⁷ "If you abide in Me, and My words abide in you, ask whatever you wish, and it will be done for you."

Among the great promises about prayer in the Bible, our passage contains Jesus' simple invitation to "ask whatever you wish." What a fantastic, wonderful message. Leaders of big businesses pay enormous sums of money to hear the latest leadership gurus proclaim their "key" to successful leadership. Large organizations commission well-known sports heroes to come talk with their employees about commitment and motivation, paying large honorariums. Donors give huge "gifts" to gain gold-status subscriber privileges to meet the concert performers, media personalities or other famous people backstage. Some political contributors stream money to campaigns in order gain the ear of a politician.

Here we have a humble carpenter who "started from scratch" (so to speak), holding audience with a small group of followers—men who were about to launch a worldwide "organization" that would eclipse all other organizations that have ever existed. It has outlasted the mighty Roman Empire; it has spawned the largest-ever social movement to help the downtrodden, the sick and the disadvantaged; it has revolutionized more lives than any other movement the world has ever known. And at the center of it all is Jesus.

Who wouldn't pay all they had to sit in on that training session in the Upper Room, His last extended conference with them that we have a record of? In the midst of it, this nugget, this gem, this inspirational poster material statement rings forth and echoes down through the ages. One of the greatest sayings of all time, from the mouth of the Son of God. When He speaks, we need to listen!

The cost of this consultation is free. Bibles are free, online or in hotel rooms or just lying around somewhere. To hear Jesus' insights is indeed free, but to implement them carries a cost. That's where the prerequisite comes in. We who hear these words can ask God "whatever [we] wish, and it will be done for [us]." The prerequisite is to abide in Christ and have His words abide in us.

Psalm 37 resonated with this: "Delight yourself in the Lord; And He will give you the desires of your heart" (Ps. 37:4). The qualification for answered prayer is a dynamic, personal relationship with Christ. Answered prayer flows from lives that are intermingled with Him, enjoying His presence, infiltrated by and saturated in His word. Such a life makes requests even the Sovereign of the universe finds compelling. Why? Because those requests flow from an abiding, delighting heart that is aligned with Him.

Lord, let my prayers flow from a heart that has been transformed by You.

The Key to Prayer (cont.)

John 15:7

7 "If you abide in Me, and My words abide in you, ask whatever you wish, and it will be done for you."

That this verse is the key to prayer is not an overstatement. Every other verse on prayer in Scripture subsumes under this overarching principle. Many commentators and teachers provide all the requisite qualifications to keep us from seeing a blank check here. Others preach "name it and claim it," using verses like this. You can even ask for lots of money or an expensive car. No strings attached—or at least none other than superficial conformity to a prescribed set of rules.

Yet amidst the extremes, the simplicity of this verse must not be overlooked, as with all of John's account of the Lord's teaching. This promise is simple, yet profound; it deserves in-depth contemplation of its meaning. Jesus spoke about prayer often, beginning in the Sermon on the Mount: "Ask, and it will be given to you; seek, and you will find; knock, and it will be opened to you" (Matt. 7:7). Later, after His triumphal entry to Jerusalem and during the week before His crucifixion, He added the qualifier of faith: "And all things you ask in prayer, believing, you will receive" (Matt. 21:22). The overriding principle, though, is abiding in Christ and His word abiding in us. If these things are true, God will answer our prayer.

At the heart of the matter is the fact that God does wants to hear from us. He is not hiding behind some trick question, or waiting at the end of maze that we must figure out before He will hear us. He wants to be found, He wants to be asked, and He wants to give us answers. That is why He tells us in the simplest terms how to approach Him with our requests. This is not rocket science. He tells us to live our lives in intimate connection with Him and saturate ourselves with His word, not only in our minds, but also in our willingness to conform our lives to His teachings. Then He will answer "whatever [we] wish."

Since abiding in Christ (like a branch abides in a vine) and having His teachings abide in us (like a tender steak marinates in a great teriyaki sauce) are essential to discipleship living, it makes sense that asking God for anything must come from this context as well. Consider that He has called those that follow Him to a sacrificial lifestyle in order to accomplish humanly impossible things, namely to preach the powerful Word of God that changes lives for eternity and to love one another. We need powerful resources, divine help to accomplish this mission. Thus, God is our divine quartermaster, supplying us with the necessary resources to accomplish the job. All we need to do is ask!

Lord, I come to You today for what is need to accomplish Your will—today!

The Key to Prayer (cont.)

John 15:7

7 "If you abide in Me, and My words abide in you, ask whatever you wish, and it will be done for you."

S o why does God leave the divine resources on hold until we ask for them? Why not just put them on autopilot and skip the middle step of asking? Then He will supply what we need without depending on our erratic or inconsistent prayer life. After all, as Scripture says, "the Spirit Himself intercedes for us with groanings too deep for words; and He who searches the hearts knows what the mind of the Spirit is, because He intercedes for the saints according to the will of God" (Rom. 8:26-27). Further, ". . . we know that God causes all things to work together for the good to those who love God, to those who are called according to His purpose" (Rom. 8:28). It would seem, then, that asking God for anything would be superfluous. The Spirit prays for us; God is going to work everything out for the good. Why pray, then?

Jesus sees it as absolutely necessary for us to ask. His training of the disciples in the Upper Room was not preparing them to be automatons. He was training them to be partners with God, working together with Him in reaching the world. If efficiency were the goal, God could very well have cloned the human Jesus, placed His Spirit on all the clones and then the world would be reached much more "effectively," it would seem. But, just as God incarnated Himself in the person of Jesus, He wants to incarnate His word in us who are followers of Jesus and empower us with His Spirit. He wants to use our humanness, our "divine-image-bearing-ness" to reach the world.

So as He gave Adam and Eve human choice and responsibility, He gives the followers of Jesus the same God-like prerogative to voluntarily join Him in the mission to bless the world through the message of Christ. Thus, just as our abiding in Christ and having His word abide in us is subject to our volition, so also is requesting from God our hearts' desires.

This gives God great joy when He sees that the requests of our hearts ("whatever you wish") flow from lives that are abiding, that are delighting in the Lord (Ps. 37:4). Then we are functioning as originally intended, living out His image in our lives. And in our prayers we reflect back to Him the desires of His heart! And we grow as we increasingly recognize the real needs we have in fulfilling His mission for and through us. These are prayers He delights to hear; these are prayers He delights to answer. Oh, that we would abide in Him and that we would let His Word abide in us! That is preparation we need for serving the Lord in the power of the Spirit with the resources of God.

Lord, may I bring You joy by reflecting the image of Christ back to You.

WEEKEND READING

Saturday – John 6:59-71
Sunday – Acts 11:1-18

PERSONAL REFLECTIONS

Fruit Before the Toot

John 15:8

8 "My Father is glorified by this, that you bear much fruit, and so prove to be My disciples."

Reputation is important to God—that is, His reputation. Being created in His image, our main goal in life is to glorify God. We agree with the first point of the Westminster Shorter Catechism: "Man's chief end is to glorify God, and to enjoy Him forever."

The word "glory" comes from the Hebrew concept of "weightiness." The root derivation comes from describing columns holding up a building. They are substantial, weighty. In time, glory came to describe individuals who were weighty in character. To glorify someone came to mean enhancing others' appreciation of a person's character in some way, thus the idea of enhancing his reputation.

Today, God's reputation has taken a bad rap—not due to anything God has done, but because of misrepresentations about God and scandalous behavior of those who claim to be representatives of Christ. Not only have well-known preachers brought disgrace to His name, but on an individual level we also can easily misrepresent God by our behavior in our the workplace, community, neighborhoods and families.

As Christians, Christ followers, we represent Him as ambassadors (2 Cor. 5:20), and our main goal is to help others see what God is really like. To put it another way, we have the opportunity to add to God's reputation! And not just by our words, although people do need to hear the Word of God in order to be saved: "So faith *comes* from hearing, and hearing by the word of Christ" (Rom. 10:17). But our role also includes presenting God in a way that accurately reflects what He is like—particularly in our fruit bearing.

In other words, God's reputation is enhanced when we bear fruit that proves we are disciples of Christ. Jesus reiterates the principle He had already told them: "Each tree is known by its fruit . . ." (Luke 6:44; see also Matthew 7:20). The reality of our faith is proven genuine by our outward behavior, what people can see. Just a few minutes earlier in the Upper Room, Jesus had said, "By this all men will know that you are My disciples, if you have love for one another" (John 13:35). So the first and primary area of demonstrating genuine faith is in how we behave in love toward other Christians. There are many other addendums to proving our faith, but if faith cannot be worked out with those closest to us, then how can it be worked out toward our enemies? Tooting the gospel horn is nothing more than noise if there is lack of love among Christians.

Lord, convict me of any wrong attitudes I may have toward my fellow believers.

Fruit Before the Toot (cont.)

John 15:8

8 "My Father is glorified by this, that you bear much fruit, and so prove to be My disciples."

"That the world might know that I love the Father" is the ultimate fruit of our Christian lives (John 14:31). This is not a matter of verbally including a certain catch phrase in our witnessing, "Did you know that Jesus loves His heavenly Father?" Rather, it means that we ultimately lead people to the Trinitarian love that is perfectly expressed between the three persons of the Godhead, particularly as seen in Jesus' love for His Father. That love is what emanates out in Jesus' obedience in going to the cross (Heb. 5:8), for in that act He demonstrated His love for God (see John 14:31 again). And it is that love that motivated Christ to die for us (John 3:16). And finally, it is that love with which we respond: "We love because He first loved us" (1 John 4:19). Jesus said, "A new commandment I give to you, that you love one another, even as I have loved you, that you also love one another" (John 13:34). Is it any wonder that Jesus spoke of the two greatest commandments as loving God and loving one's neighbor (Matt. 22:37-40)?

So how do we Christ followers show that Trinitarian kind of love to one another and thereby glorify God to others? Church conflict, speaking ill of other churches or denominations, or failing to work together do not enhance God's reputation. Divorcing Christians communicate to the world that Christian love is really not all that exceptional. God-glorifying love is more than a good feeling when singing love songs to God. Rather, love that enhances God's reputation is a sacrificial love that emulates Jesus' love for the Father, as monumentally exhibited in His obeying the Father in going to the cross.

So the world needs to see that Christians do indeed love each other; that's the first step in learning about God's love. Some quickly offer judgmental sarcasm, saying that "other" Christians are so hard to love, as though the problem was inherently a Christian problem. Yes, because Christians are fallen humans, and because we ourselves (as in me and you reading this) are inherently sinful, love is difficult! Just as it is in the workplace when our associates or colleagues backstab, gossip, hold bitterness, act in pride or are easily offended, so these human fallibilities are exhibited in the church. Rather than justifying our criticism of fellow Christians on the premise that they should know better, we need to love others despite their human fallibilities, recognizing that we should know better, despite our human fallibilities. Who comes to your mind?

Lord, help me to love my brothers and sisters in Christ, just as You love me.

Abiding Love

John 15:9

⁹ "Just as the Father has loved Me, I have also loved you; abide in My love.

Flowing love, from the Father to the Son, and now to us—why would any believer not want to abide in Christ's love? Jesus' love for us is exactly the same kind of love that the Father has for Him. It is perfect and unblemished, and it flawlessly fulfills the 1 Corinthians 13 description of love:

Love is . . .
> patient, love is
> > kind *and* is
> > > not jealous;

Love . . .
> does not brag *and* is
> > not arrogant,
> does not act unbecomingly; it
> does not seek its own, is
> > not provoked,
> > > does not take into account a wrong *suffered,*
> > > > does not rejoice in unrighteousness, but
> rejoices with the truth;
> bears all things,
> > believes all things,
> > > hopes all things,
> > > > endures all things.
Love never fails.

This is the kind of love the world needs now. Love does not, as the famous movie quote goes, mean never having to say you are sorry. Rather it means never doing anything that requires an apology, because love always has the best interests of the other person in mind. God desires for us, as Paul prayed for the Ephesians, that we, ". . . being rooted and grounded in love, may be able to comprehend with all the saints what is the breadth and length and height and depth, and to know the love of Christ which surpasses knowledge, that you may be filled up to all the fullness of God" (Eph. 3:17-19).

Words, inadequate as they are in describing Christ's love, serve to catapult us into higher contemplation of what we mean to Him. He gave His all to save us from a lost eternity, but even more, He gave His all to redeem us for His own. How much more does He love us now that we are His and He is ours!

Lord, help me understand more fully the perfect love You have for me.

Motivating Love

John 15:10

[10] "If you keep My commandments, you will abide in My love; just as I have kept My Father's commandments and abide in His love."

So how do we abide in Christ's love? We abide in His love by keeping His commandments. That is the pattern we have from Jesus Himself, how He abided in His Father's love. Now, we need to be careful about how we understand this. Some erroneously get this backward, that if God sees us obeying His commands, *then* He will love us. The motivation of that is to do good deeds in order to procure or earn God's love. But that is impossible—we have all come short and could never live in such a way that we become worthy of a perfect love. In fact, the very act of doing the good works would undermine the thing that would make us worthy of love, namely, the good works would be done in self-interest, which is antithetical to love. It is "self-interest" because the motivation is to gain love. Does that not sound like a child who goes through life haunted by the fear of losing her or his father's love or never gaining it? Love that is earned that way is a fallacious love.

God's love, rather, is perfect, and He loves the unlovely, those requiring patience. He loved us "while we were yet sinners" (Rom. 5:8). He didn't wait for us to keep His commandments, because we have failed and come short of His glory (Rom. 3:23). We were already under judgment of God and dead in our sins, unable to do anything to merit His love. If we ever could merit God's love, then we would have something to boast about, but Ephesians tells us, "For by grace you have been saved through faith; and that not of yourselves, *it is* the gift of God; not as a result of works, so that no one may boast" (Eph. 2:8-9).

God's love is unconditional toward us, perfect and complete. But how do we live in the love, enjoying and relishing in it? By doing as Jesus says, just as Jesus does what His Father says. Where is the motivation in that, some might say? The motivation is the fact that we are loved by Christ. "There is no fear in love; but perfect love casts out fear, because fear involves punishment, and the one who fears is not perfected in love" (1 John 4:18).

Motivation by love always trumps motivation by fear. Certainly there is a sort of Machiavellian sort of efficiency to motivation by fear; that is the ultimate human manipulation of behavior. But such fear never accomplishes the glory of God. But when we abide in His love and extend that progression of love from the Father to the Son to us—and then to our fellow Christians and ultimately to the world—that is what brings glory to God.

Lord, because You love me, I want to do as You command. That is the desire of my heart, though I continually fail. Thank You for not condemning me.

Sustaining Joy

John 15:11

11 "These things I have spoken to you so that My joy may be in you, and that your joy may be made full."

Joy is not automatic, nor does it depend upon circumstances. Rather, joy is supernatural, completely independent of life's circumstances, just like God's love for us is independent of our earning His love.

Cults and abusers twist this teaching to absurd lengths, by manipulating emotions and making requests that are harmful to the individual. "If you love me, then you will do . . ." all sorts of evil, damaging things. This turns love into an emotional club to enforce behavior or compliance. Cults do that by keeping their members always needing more, like a child desperate for a father's love will do anything to get attention or find even a small shred of love.

God's love is not like that. It is not a reward or a carrot on the end of a stick that keeps a mule going forward. To be sure, there will be times when we trust in God's love over against the difficulties and hardships and sufferings of life. His love will never compel us to go against His revealed Word as we have it in Scripture. No prophecy or teaching can be legitimately given that contradicts the clear teaching of the Bible. This is why we so emphasize that every Christian must abide in the Word of God on a regular basis.

Jesus makes it clear that His goal for us is not our misery, but our joy. He will similarly state again before leaving the Upper Room, "These things I have spoken to you, so that in Me you may have peace. In the world you have tribulation, but take courage; I have overcome the world" (John 16:33). Joy and peace (along with hope) are "resources" we need as believers. But the greatest resource we need is love (see 1 Corinthians 13:13).

This is the abundant Christian life that Jesus spoke of earlier, "I came that they may have life, and have *it* abundantly" (John 10:10). Cult leaders destroy; Jesus gives life—and life abundantly, to the full. Such a life includes joy that is rooted in the awareness of and ever-increasing appreciation for His love.

There was coming a time, in less than 24 hours, when the disciples would not be feeling very joyful at all. In fact, all their emotions would soon be swallowed up in the pitch-tar blackness of grief. Did these words sustain them during the dark three days of Jesus' death and somehow keep them from the fate of Judas, who felt he had lost all? We do know that these words sustained them after Christ rose and ascended into heaven. And these words should encourage us in whatever circumstance of life we find ourselves.

Lord, thank You for Your love and joy, as You sustain me in my difficult times.

WEEKEND READING

Saturday – John 7:1-13
Sunday – Acts 11:19-30

PERSONAL REFLECTIONS

A Pleased Life

John 15:11 (cont.)

11 "These things I have spoken to you so that My joy may be in you, and that your joy may be made full."

The intimate circle of those who have forsaken all to follow Christ involves a fellowship of joy. While He spoke to the multitudes in parables, Jesus would follow with an explanation to His disciples. Now He again explains His teaching, this time the reason for teaching these things.

What things? In the space of a few hours Jesus had covered a lot of ground. He spoke of serving and being served (a lesson Peter had to learn specifically by submitting to Jesus washing his feet). But Jesus also spoke of leaving them, and of His suffering and dying. And He spoke of betrayal and denial from among their ranks. How could such sobering thoughts bring joy?

But He said all those things (among others) "so that My joy may be in you, and that your joy may be made full." Actually, joy was not an uncommon teaching in the Upper Room. Used six times, the word means the experience of gladness or feeling pleased. The only answer is that the joy He was talking about was not circumstantially sourced but grounded in something above and beyond the here and now. Though as believers, we are anchored in eternity, we so easily take our eyes off Jesus and look at the surrounding storms of life, and like Peter, we begin to sink away. Yet God wants us to be water-walkers, living out the supernatural enabling of the Holy Spirit. There is a joy in seeing the bigger picture and that the present difficulty is very small compared to what is coming.

Paul puts it this way: "For momentary, light affliction is producing for us an eternal weight of glory far beyond all comparison, while we look not at the things which are seen, but at the things which are not seen; for the things which are seen are temporal, but the things which are not seen are eternal" (2 Cor. 4:17-18). Does that thought not bring joy? There are better things ahead, and that will sustain us. The catalyst to joy, though, is faith (see Philippians 1:25). The truth of our position and the promises given to us do not automatically produce joy. The truth must be mixed with faith.

Jesus faced the disciples with the truth about what was about to happen. Their faith was in process and, as often was the case, they would fail the test of faith (e.g. Peter denying the Lord three times, the rest abandoning Him in His crucifixion). But the resurrection would change everything. Then their joy would be great, because the puzzle pieces of faith would finally fit together.

Lord, through faith I believe that even my most difficult times of life are nothing compared to the joy of knowing I will share in Your glory.

A Joy in Suffering

John 15:11 (cont.)

[11] "These things I have spoken to you so that My joy may be in you, and that your joy may be made full."

Life to the full (John 10:10) can be had even when hard times come. The more we know that before those experiences arrive, the better position we are in to experience supernatural joy. This is even more so when we fast forward our story from the Upper Room to the crucifixion and the post-resurrection experience. Think carefully of the difference.

As the disciples became reluctant participants in the unfolding drama, they fled the crucifixion, having abandoned Him (save for the minimal proximity of the disciple John). Peter was unwilling even to be associated with Him. How in the world could Jesus' words of a promised joy have any valid meaning? If anything, at the cross His words must have seemed pathetic, as those of a disillusioned positive thinker. How could those words have offered any comfort or hope when the One who healed others, raised them from the dead, gave them hope, was Himself beaten beyond recognition? The prophet wrote of Him, "His appearance was marred more than any man and His form more than the sons of men . . . He has no *stately* form or majesty that we should look upon Him, nor appearance that we should be attracted to Him" (Isa. 52:14; 53:2). But the disciples were not connecting those dots.

Before the resurrection, the suffering and crucifixion would seem meaningless. But after the resurrection, the words of joy Jesus spoke in the Upper Room would take on greater meaning at different levels. Obviously, there was joy at seeing Him again. Advance this joy up a notch at the next thought, that Jesus had beaten death and come back to life. Further, if death did not have mastery over their Lord for whom they dedicated their lives, then death had also lost its sting for them (1 Cor. 15:55-56).

But the words of Jesus had an even more profound effect on the disciples in the coming years of persecution. Since Jesus had spoken these words of joy to them *before* His suffering and crucifixion, that meant that joy could be experienced *in the midst* of suffering and *before* their resurrection. They could experience the presence of Christ *in* suffering. Paul, who was not present in the Upper Room, came to know this truth; his desire was to "know Him and the power of His resurrection and the fellowship of His sufferings, being conformed to His death . . ." (Phil. 3:10). We, therefore, come to know Christ more deeply when we are "fixing our eyes on Jesus, the author and perfecter of faith, who for the joy set before Him endured the cross, despising the shame . . ." (Heb. 12:2).

Father, help me see Your Son more clearly in the midst of my trials.

A Remembered Joy

John 15:11 (cont.)

11 "These things I have spoken to you so that My joy may be in you, and that your joy may be made full."

The words of Jesus echoed throughout Peter's life, so that in his later years he encouraged the scattered, persecuted believers with these words, ". . . though you have not seen Him, you love Him, and though you do not see Him now, but believe in Him, you greatly rejoice with joy inexpressible and full of glory . . ." (1 Peter 1:8). Peter wrote this around AD 62–64—after Jesus had been physically absent for over 30 years, after much suffering of his own, and just a few short years before his martyrdom (AD 67).

John was even more reminiscent in not only remembering Jesus' words and recording them here in his gospel account, but also in mimicking His words about joy in his first epistle: "These things we write, so that our joy may be made complete" (1 John 1:4). In his second letter, John builds on this: "Though I have many things to write to you . . . I hope to come to you and speak face to face, so that your joy may be made full" (2 John 12). His concern for their joy unmistakably reflects the Savior's concern for the disciples' joy in the Upper Room. He adds in his third letter, "I have no greater joy than this, to hear of my children walking in the truth" (3 John 4). Does this not reflect the Lord's heart?

The author to the Hebrews (unknown to us, yet amid many suggestions no one proposes that it was one of those present in the Upper Room) picked up on the relationship of joy with suffering. With the great examples of the past setting the standard, he challenges all believers, "Therefore, since we have so great a cloud of witnesses surrounding us, let us also lay aside every encumbrance and the sin which so easily entangles us, and let us run with endurance the race that is set before us, fixing our eyes on Jesus, the author and perfecter of faith, who for the joy set before Him endured the cross, despising the shame, and has sat down at the right hand of the throne of God" (Heb. 12:1-2).

Suffering, the bane of all human experience, the thing that has perplexed philosophers and thinkers from the beginning of time (think of Job and the question of suffering), finds meaning in Christ's sufferings and our sharing in them. Suffering is transformed from a thing to be avoided to a thing over which joy has victory. Joy does not remove it, but it supersedes it. Joy cannot be snuffed out by suffering. Because Christ suffered and died, suffering is not our bottom line. We can live a life of joy even in the midst of deep suffering. God will meet us there, like the fourth presence in the fiery furnace (Dan. 3:24-25).

Lord, when I am suffering, You are there with me. And in that I rejoice.

A Satisfying Community

John 15:12

12 "This is My commandment, that you love one another, just as I have loved you."

How interesting, love as a commandment. So much has been written on it in Christian circles that a short devotional cannot do justice to this statement by the Lord Jesus Christ in the Upper Room. First, Jesus lays out the overriding task for Christians in their community with one another. Second, this love is not a "feeling" kind of love. Psychologists tell us you cannot command a person to feel a certain way. Feelings come and go and are only indirectly controlled. Rather, this is an *agape* kind of love. It does not have the "magic" of intense eroticism (*eros* love), nor the warmth of brotherly affection (*philos* love). *Agape* was a word rarely used in pre-biblical Greek; it was the Christians who popularized it. While *eros* seeks its own benefit and *philos* seeks mutual benefit, *agape* seeks only the benefit of another.

This kind of love can be commanded; that means it is a choice that can be consciously and rationally made. But this is not a mechanical obeisance that Jesus called for, but rather an engaging choice to put others before oneself.

And while it is true that we should love our enemies, the priority is to love other Christians first. Some might think this encourages exclusivity and narrow-mindedness. However, *agape* love emanates from strength and security. The love between the Father and Son was complete, and it led to the Son loving the disciples. While perfectly satisfying, it was not exclusive. The divine love within the Trinity was characterized as a reaching out kind of love, flowing from the secure perfection of love within the Godhead. So too, the love of Jesus for His disciples should flow among the disciples. It was not enough that Jesus loved them; they needed to learn to love one another. So the love among the disciples should likewise overflow in their love for non-believers, just as Jesus' love for the Father overflowed to the disciples.

On a surface level, this makes sense. A community where people really do love one another attracts attention and invites investigation. Love is a compelling argument in favor of Christianity. Jesus had earlier spoken, "By this all men will know that you are My disciples, if you have love for one another" (John 13:35). It is to be the defining characteristic that the world sees. Now on another level this makes even more sense. Imagine, for a moment, a person comes to Christ as a response to God's love. But then the Christians are too busy loving non-believers to have time for him. No, disciples are to create a safe, secure and satisfying community of love, and it is out of this they can love the world.

Lord, help me love my fellow Christians the way You love me.

A Commanded Love

John 15:12 (cont.)

12 "This is My commandment, that you love one another, just as I have loved you."

Christians often seem to squabble a lot within churches, among churches, between denominations and doctrinal persuasions. A common criticism today is that individual Christians raise themselves up against "Christians" in general. To be sure there is a caricature of Christianity that the world has defined, and sometimes Christians join in the world's criticism, as though we agree with the world's condemnation of hypocrisy and hyper-conservatism. Strange bedfellows, though, for by doing that Christians inevitably place themselves on the pedestal of judgment over all so-called Christianity, as though speaking from a higher moral ground.

Yes, there should be self-judgment, but not on the world's terms. The world is no more able to judge hypocrisy than the Pharisees of old. Likewise, we ourselves need to be careful of that, for such criticism lands not far from home. We judge other Christians for narrow-mindedness, an unloving spirit, imbalance of focus, lack of evangelistic effort and unsound doctrine. We judge church leaders, church leaders judge parishioners, church leaders judge one another, etc. We compare ourselves and our ministries with others. Yet Jesus commands us to love one another!

One church is a mile wide in its outreach but an inch deep in its theology. Another is a mile deep in its theology but an inch wide in the evangelistic efforts. But is there love?

Jesus commanded many things, but few did He emphasize in this way: "This is My commandment . . ." The apostle John remembered this well: "Whoever keeps His word, in him the love of God has truly been perfected . . . Beloved, I am not writing a new commandment to you, but an old commandment which you have had from the beginning; the old commandment is the word which you have heard" (1 John 2:5, 7).

This command to love does not negate the importance of right doctrine, as though having love is all that matters. But without right doctrine there cannot be a genuine basis for loving with an *agape* love. It is all interconnected. The love between the Father and Son is a doctrinal truth about the Trinity. The love of God as expressed in Jesus' love for the world flows in grace from the Trinity to undeserving humans. That is doctrinal truth. So we can love one another and the lost world from the perspective and security we have in a perfect, sacrificial love from which we will never be separated.

Lord, help me love others with a truth-based, gracious and sacrificial love.

WEEKEND READING

Saturday – John 7:14-24
Sunday – Acts 12:1-19

PERSONAL REFLECTIONS

Greater Love than This

John 15:13

¹³ *"Greater love has no one than this, that one lay down his life for his friends.*

This verse is well quoted but rarely lived out (or should I say rarely "died out"?). It is the stuff of noble characters in fiction novels. But this should be normative Christianity. The call to Christian self-sacrificial love is well known and reaches its zenith in this assertion, the ultimate expression of love in action. This is the core of everything Jesus came to do and teach. This is the undoing of Eden's fall, when Adam and Eve acted in their own best interest, or so it seemed.

Self-sacrifice presents to us the opposite diametric of all sin as epitomized in the self-exalting, self-centered one, Satan. It was written of him, "But you said in your heart, 'I will ascend to heaven; I will raise my throne above the stars of God, and I will sit on the mount of assembly in the recesses of the north. I will ascend above the heights of the clouds; I will make myself like the Most High'" (Isa. 14:13-14). The universal struggle now resides in all of us, as we strive to give up the need to say "I" as saturated Satan's character.

Jesus came not just to teach this truth but to lead the way—to show it is not only possible, but that it needs to be the way of life for those who follow Him. This is not an "easy believism" preached to the masses. This is deep truth for those who are committed to Jesus as Messiah, the Christ. Let him who has ears to hear, hear, as Jesus would often say.

In a few short hours, this struggle would be maximized by the polar opposite strands of the redemption story's plot line. The major thread is, of course, Jesus dying on the cross as a substitutionary atonement for all mankind. The secondary thread was the disciples' sinking into that self-protection mode, escape at all cost, that demonstrated to them the depth of their self-centeredness. They were unable to even pray with Him without falling asleep. Peter would deny Him, not once but three times. We may recognize ourselves in the story and thus find their actions understandable. But make no mistake, in Jesus' most troubling time, they were consumed by their own self-preservation. They were unable to part with their most valuable possession, life itself.

We find this teaching hard to accept. We speak of self-preservation as a fundamental of human behavior, an inborn instinct that we share with all creatures. But that is not how God created humanity to be; we were to be different from the rest of creation. We were created in His image, and He is a self-giving God. Jesus came to restore us to that image.

Lord, loving as You love is impossible; I struggle with selfishness and am need of Your supernatural, miraculous help to do the impossible: to love sacrificially.

Greater Love than This (cont.)

John 15:13

[13] "Greater love has no one than this, that one lay down his life for his friends."

Love is the greatest of all Christian virtues (1 Cor. 13:13), and in our passage, Jesus identifies the greatest form of love: giving one's life for another person. Notice He doesn't speak of self-sacrifice as an end in itself, as though denying oneself intrinsically adds to one's merit. One can be sacrificial for the wrong ends. For example, an athlete denies himself many pleasures in life that others enjoy and endures much pain in training in order to reach his goal of victory in the games. Some train for years at great personal cost, dedicated to living a very disciplined lifestyle. But in the end, he enjoys the glory received for the victory he has achieved.

But this is not the "laying down his life" that Jesus spoke about; the goal is much higher. "Everyone who competes in the games exercises self-control in all things. They then *do it* to receive a perishable wreath, but we an imperishable" (1 Cor. 9:25). What we have in our passage today points to the ultimate, perfect goal that is worthy of complete self-sacrifice. Think of it like a boxing match between another person's interest versus our own interest. This is truly not just the fight of the century, but the struggle of all of life. Is the ultimate principle self-survival as evolutionists assert? Do I live my life for me, as humanism teaches? Am I the "master of my fate, the captain of my soul"? In the end is it all about me, number one? Or is it about living my life for the sake of others? Jesus answers that question in our verse for today. Love is the antithesis of self-centered living.

Of course, in marriage, we speak about love putting the other person first. But Jesus is speaking much more broadly than marriage. He speaks of sacrificial love as a lifestyle, as the core principle of life. If the greatest love is to sacrifice one's very life, then love must inherently be a core, saturating life principle. To see how deeply this must penetrate every corner of our lives, we only have to look at that great gospel verse as the model of what Jesus is asking us to do: "But God demonstrates His own love toward us, in that while we were yet sinners, Christ died for us" (Rom. 5:8). God loves both friends, as He spoke of in the Upper Room, and also sinners of all ranks. "For God so loved the world . . ." (John 3:16). He loves His enemies. Likewise, we must make sacrificial love our lifestyle and focus. In today's world the phrase "sexual orientation" is in vogue. For Christians, we need to be clear about our "love orientation." As William MacDonald wrote, "Some lay down their lives in a literal sense; others spend their whole lives in untiring service for the people of God."

Lord, let "love" be a lifestyle of sacrifice in my life and in my death.

Friends with God

John 15:14

14 "You are My friends if you do what I command you."

N ame dropping is the "art" of building oneself up by verbally associating with those of a higher status. In Canada, for example, most people can say they personally know or have met a professional hockey player. There is a theory called "Six degrees of separation" in which a chain of friendships connect any two people in the world. So that a friend of mine has a friend who knows someone else—through a series of six steps, that would associate me, for example, with the president of the United States.

Jesus offers to His disciples a direct connection of friendship with Himself that requires no intermediary steps, no "separation" to connect. It is a direct friendship. We can truly "name drop" and say, "I personally know Jesus Christ," and not just a friend of a friend of a friend of a friend of a friend of Jesus. As His disciples, we too can join the ranks of the inner circle of friendship, where we therefore know all of God's friends. For example, both I and Abraham are friends with God. What is said about Abraham is also true about me, "And Abraham believed God, and it was reckoned to him as righteousness, and he was called the friend of God" (James 2:23).

Now, Jesus conditions this friendship, we must note very carefully. He said, "You are My friends if you do what I command you." A contingent friendship. He is not talking about a casual relationship, but a friendship that is based on common goals. If we want to experience friendship with Jesus we need to get on board with His mission. No greater camaraderie have any two people than those who are on the same mission, pulling in the same direction, sacrificing all for each other and for the mission. Jesus came with a mission, and when we join Him in it, we experience friendship at the deepest level. This is not just an acquaintance relationship, but a growing, intimate connection built around a common focus: the glory of the Father.

Imagine for a moment, upon your home call to glory, the angels announcing, "Presenting, _____, a friend of the Lord Jesus Christ." What an experience that will be! Peter must have had that in mind when he wrote, "Therefore, brethren, be all the more diligent to make certain about His calling and choosing you; for as long as you practice these things, you will never stumble; for in this way the entrance into the eternal kingdom of our Lord and Savior Jesus Christ will be abundantly supplied to you" (2 Peter 1:10-11). What could be more abundant than joining the Son of God in His kingdom—as His friend?

Lord, I commit to living my life as Your friend, by
continuing to join in Your great mission.

Friendship with Jesus

John 15:15

[15] "No longer do I call you slaves, for the slave does not know what his master is doing; but I have called you friends, for all things that I have heard from My Father I have made known to you."

When did Jesus call His disciples slaves? Well, maybe not in those exact words, but certainly He referred to Himself as "master" and to them as "servants." Earlier in this Upper Room scenario, clearly Jesus said, "Truly, truly, I say to you, a slave [*doulos*] is not greater than his master, nor *is* one who is sent greater than the one who sent him" (John 13:16). More directly, He applied one of the parables directly to His followers: "So you too, when you do all the things which are commanded you, say, 'We are unworthy slaves; we have done *only* that which we ought to have done'" (Luke 17:10). Even in our rewards, Jesus invites us by use of a parable to see ourselves as slaves: "His master said to him, 'Well done, good and faithful slave. You were faithful with a few things, I will put you in charge of many things; enter into the joy of your master'" (Matt. 25:23).

Now, in the Upper Room, just before He dies, Jesus raises their status to that of "friend" and tells them to no longer think of themselves as slaves. The progression is important in that we cannot come to friendship with Him unless we first see our rightful place as His servants. In other words, we cannot simply choose to be Jesus' friend; He brings us into that circle of relationship. We must first see ourselves as slaves in order to position ourselves properly to receive His gracious invitation to friendship.

God is first and foremost Master; He is Lord! Our problem, and therefore our need for salvation, is that we all have rejected His lordship in our lives. We have violated His commandments; we have contravened His moral imperatives. We have all sinned and come short of the glory of God. Without getting into the whole debate of lordship salvation, it is quite clear from Scripture that we need to repent as His creatures from our rebellion against Him. From the earliest message Jesus preached, we see that we are to repent. That means to turn away from our rebellion and submit to Him, to the obedience of faith.

This is not a promise of obedience, for we can never be 100 percent obedient as a means of salvation. But it does mean that we who have come to a saving knowledge of the Lord Jesus Christ have turned from our wicked ways and turned to the living God, our Creator and our Master. And once that relationship has been straightened out, we are prepared to move to the next stage, that of friendship.

Lord Jesus Christ, Son of God, thank You for choosing me as Your friend.

Friendship with Jesus (cont.)

John 15:15

15 "No longer do I call you slaves, for the slave does not know what his master is doing; but I have called you friends, for all things that I have heard from My Father I have made known to you."

W e can't help but remember Abraham, the "friend of God" (James 2:23). Concerning him, God said, "Shall I hide from Abraham what I am about to do?" (Gen. 18:17). God was about to destroy Sodom because of its wickedness, and He wanted to tell Abraham ahead of time. Friendship has its perks, and insider knowledge is one of them. In our passage today Jesus reveals things to the disciples that are insider knowledge, namely, everything Jesus had heard from the Father concerning His mission on earth. The disciples may not have understood it all, but it was there for them to learn.

A servant, by contrast, does not need to know what the Master is doing, but only needs to know what he, the servant, must do. He doesn't need to know the "why." But a friend, as Jesus now calls the disciples, is invited into the inner circle of counsel. We, along with the Upper Room audience, are asked to join with Christ in His mission, not as automatons who don't think, but as those who engage in thinking about how to execute the mission. The Upper Room teaching, along with all that Jesus taught the disciples, was not intended to be a set or list of itemized marching instructions. His teachings were the guiding principles with which we are to live out and carry on the mission of Christ.

Sometimes it would seem to be easier if the Lord would orchestrate every detail of our lives, to give us writing in the sky or a fleece on the ground to determine His will. Should I take this job or that one? Should I marry this person or not? Should I become a missionary on the foreign field or be a missionary in the workplace at home? But God wants to engage us as partners, as friends who join in with our mind, our ideas, our personalities and our gifts. He leaves much for us to decide and figure out, as though saying, "How do you want to do this?" While this may seem like a dangerous tip of the hat to humanism, keep in mind that Jesus in our passage is speaking to His followers. This is not a group of "Sunday morning only" kind of Christians. These are the ones to whom He says, "You are My friends if you do what I command you" (vs. 14).

So while the mission is determined by God, the details are left up to those who are Jesus' friends, the ones who do as He commanded, namely those who act in love, just as He sacrificed Himself in love.

Lord, thank You for bringing me into Your circle of counsel. I want to use the gifts You have given me to continue Your mission in the world.

WEEKEND READING

Saturday – John 7:25-39
Sunday – Acts 12:20-25

PERSONAL REFLECTIONS

Joyful Dilemma

John 15:16

16 "You did not choose Me but I chose you, and appointed you that you would go and bear fruit, and that your fruit would remain, so that whatever you ask of the Father in My name He may give to you."

Theological debate rages between the so-called Armineans and Calvinists, two opposing theological systems, and today's verse is one of contention. As with most such discussions, there are wide-ranging perspectives between the extremes. One side emphasizes, among other things, the freedom of human will, and the other emphasizes the sovereignty of God. Terminology inexactitudes and caricaturizations abound, clouding the issues, and the arguments wax eloquent and erudite. Historically, those holding these opposing Christian systems of thought killed each other!

Against all this, Jesus simply says, "You did not choose Me but I chose you . . ." Does this mean God chooses some first and then predestines them to believe, or do some believe first and then He chooses them to bear fruit? To answer this fully would invoke more space than we have here. But we must not miss the wonderful, irrefutable truth that regardless of what it means, He does the choosing, not the other way around. It is like being taken number one in the sports draft. We are His first choice! God wants us. He does not play hard to get, waiting for us to make the first move. "For the Son of Man has come to seek and to save that which was lost." (Luke 19:10). He came to choose us *and* to appoint us to bear fruit. Now that is absolutely astounding, and it is wonderful. He came to save sinners because He desired us. He desired me. He desired you!

The old illustrations still convey the message well. Salvation is like a door with a sign on the outside that says "Whosoever will." Once a person enters, he turns and looks back at the door, and the sign now says "Chosen." The intersection of the will of man and the sovereignty of God is impossible for us mere humans to fully comprehend; trying to fully resolve this dilemma now requires denying either full human culpability or God's absolute sovereignty. This mystery finds resolution beyond our finite human comprehension, and only in the eternal dimension of God's mind.

But this limitation of our understanding should not prevent us from enjoying the deep mysteries of God's wisdom. Why did I believe and someone else didn't? I cannot claim to be better because I have believed. I am left to simply rejoice in wonder that God wants me to serve in the mission of His Son.

Lord, what never-ending joy, security and motivation You bring me with this great truth that You desire me as Your own, as Your friend.

No Volunteers Needed

John 15:16 (cont.)

[16] "You did not choose Me but I chose you, and appointed you that you would go and bear fruit, and that your fruit would remain, so that whatever you ask of the Father in My name He may give to you."

"Appoint" means to lay hold of for a purpose. There is no sense of volunteerism or option to accept the appointment. It is for fruit-bearing that the believer has been chosen. The great evangelistic passage of Ephesians 2:8-9 is followed by verse 10, "For we are His workmanship, created in Christ Jesus for good works, which God prepared beforehand so that we would walk in them." God, the Creator of the universe, the sovereign Lord over all that exists, has appointed the followers of Jesus Christ to go and bear fruit with good works.

At once this is also an authorization. Nothing can stand in our way, and therefore we need to go forth and do it. Some have erroneously claimed that Christians are commanded to be faithful, not fruitful, for fruit is not something that can be commanded; it is the result. However, the goal is certainly fruitfulness, not simply obedience. We must not suffer confusion between the means and the ends. Faithfulness is not the goal, as though when it is all said and done, God is looking for obedience, and that is it. No, God is looking for fruitfulness, and that is our motivation for good works.

God's own good works include all of creation, a reflection of His glory. And He wants us to live our lives faithfully, so that the fruit of our faithfulness shows His glory. To do that we must, of course, abide in Christ, as a branch abides in the tree (see earlier in John 15). But the end goal is fruitfulness.

The other great truth we find in this verse, as we have seen earlier in the Upper Room (15:7), has to do with prayer. In our quest for fruitfulness, we have been appointed to ask God the Father for anything in Jesus' name and He will give it to us. Of course, this is not a blank check to use for our selfish purposes; that would not bring fruitfulness for God's glory. But, in our efforts to glorify Him as followers of Jesus Christ, we are given tremendous liberty to ask with the confident expectation that God will supply what we ask for. This confidence comes from being in line with His purposes and His mission.

The problem of prayer is that too often Christians pray for the wrong things or with the wrong motives. James writes, "You do not have because you do not ask. You ask and do not receive, because you ask with wrong motives, so that you may spend *it* on your pleasures" (James 4:2-3). But a life lived for Christ is a life of answered prayer, for His glory.

Lord, show me the things to pray, so that Your glory will be revealed.

New Commandment Repeated

17 "This I command you, that you love one another."

F ive times—count them—Jesus commands Christians to love one another.

"A new commandment I give to you, that you love one another, even as I have loved you, that you also love one another." (John 13:34)

"This is My commandment, that you love one another, just as I have loved you." (John 15:12)

This is His commandment, that we believe in the name of His Son Jesus Christ, and love one another, just as He commanded us. (1 John 3:23)

Now I ask you, lady, not as though I were writing to you a new commandment, but the one which we have had from the beginning, that we love one another. (2 John 5)

When God repeats Himself, He isn't stuttering. Jesus knew the propensity of His followers to miss the mark of our calling in life. We so easily get caught up in our theologies, our efforts of good works, our striving for pride, esteem, respect, acceptance, significance in the world and among people—all designed to somehow enhance our standing in life, in the sight of others or in God's sight. We so easily fail in the most fundamental task of loving others more than ourselves. If there was anything Jesus wanted to convey to the disciples, it was this: "Love one another."

Love is foundational to witnessing. "By this all men will know that you are My disciples, if you have love for one another" (John 13:35). It reflects the love the Father and Son have for each other, which extends beyond the Godhead to the whole world. And the love we have from the Father and the Son is extended to all our brothers and sisters in Christ, and through us to the world. Love is absolutely central and supreme in the Christian life. Without love, as Paul writes, we are nothing. Our theology is nothing more than noise in a noisy world (1 Cor. 13:1-3).

This love is not a touchy-feely sentiment or emotion. It is not a feeling to be enjoyed with those closest to us, who can love us back. Jesus defined love as sacrificing oneself for the sake of others (John 15:13). This is an action, a forgetting about oneself and focusing on the needs of others. The apostle Paul fleshed this out by writing, "Do nothing from selfishness or empty conceit, but with humility of mind regard one another as more important than yourselves . . ." (Phil. 2:3). Oh, that we could be like Jesus who loved with His sacrifice.

Lord, thank You for loving me with such a perfect love. Help me to love others in the same way, sacrificing what I want to do today for the sake of others.

Expecting Hatred

John 15:18

18 "If the world hates you, you know that it has hated Me before it hated you."

Not a very hopeful prognosis, to say the least. But that is only if we pull this verse out of context. The disciples had already been promised a new home in heaven, a reuniting with Christ, another Comforter in the Holy Spirit and answered prayer, fruitfulness and friendship with Christ. Yet laced throughout this Upper Room interaction was prediction of trouble, trials and failure. We can expect to experience hate, just as Jesus did.

This fundamental truth we must embrace: we *will* be persecuted. Although particularly a difficult prospect for those Christians who are tempted to be people-pleasers, this is not something any Christian looks forward to. We are called to love and sacrifice ourselves for others. But even in this, the world will reject us. After all, Jesus demonstrated perfect love in talking with the downcast, touching lepers and accepting sinners, yet there were many who seethed with anger at Him and killed Him.

How can the world reject someone who had perfect love for others? It was because in His love, Jesus also spoke truth, and He spoke about sin. And fundamentally, such talk will always override love in the lives of those who harden themselves against God. It is a miracle that anyone ever believes, considering the hardness of heart that so prevails in humanity.

As Christians, as churches, we must take this reality to heart. Some churches so desperately want to increase attendance numbers that they will preach the feel-good parts of the Gospel story but leave out sin and judgment altogether. Certainly that "sells" well in the marketplace of religion. But Christianity is a religion of truth as well as love. Love certainly is the greatest of virtues, but holding to truth is not a virtue to be compared unfavorably with love. Love is rooted in truth, in reality. Love only has significant meaning because of truth.

And the truth is that God's love extends not to just "good people" but to sinners who have thumbed their noses at God. Without truth, love is just a feeling, a sentiment. But with truth, love is the greatest, because it endures being despised— the suffering and shame of rejection. Love is great because with truth, one acknowledges the evil of one's enemy, but then can truly love that enemy, despite his evil. Any other kind of "love" is limited and will ultimately fail when one's own life is at stake. Biblical love, because it can only be enacted from the bed of truth, will at times be rejected. And we who love truly will be hated by the world, just as Jesus was hated.

Lord, help me to love even those who hate me—just like Jesus did.

Expecting to be Unloved

John 15:19

19 "If you were of the world, the world would love its own; but because you are not of the world, but I chose you out of the world, because of this the world hates you."

"Hate speech" is a phrase bandied about today. If anyone disagrees with another's lifestyle, he is accused of hatred. "Hate crimes" are punished more severely than "regular" crimes. The actual event might be the same, but because the crime was motivated by a person's hatred of another, it becomes particularly heinous. But today, people who disagree with the modern mantra that "all religions lead to God," or disagree with the homosexual lifestyle rather than celebrating people's honesty and courage for "coming out," are considered by the media-driven culture to be "haters." Tolerance is going to seed, to the point that the Christian perspective is no longer tolerated, and Christians are becoming increasingly hated. To be certain, sometimes Christians are hated because of doing unkind things and being hypocritical, without showing love. But there is much rejection of Christians that identifies with the rejection of Christ Himself.

The great judgment of the prophet Isaiah rings out from 2,500 years ago: "Woe to those who call evil good, and good evil; who substitute darkness for light and light for darkness . . ." (Isa. 5:20). God is not fooled, and He is not silent. He is watching and waiting, not willing that any should perish in their rejection of Christ and His followers (2 Peter 3:9). And in the meanwhile, He has left the disciples of Jesus to carry on in a world that will hate them, carrying the message of Christ's love for them despite their sinful rejection of God.

Rejection by the world should not come as a surprise to us if we listen closely to Jesus' teaching in the Upper Room. If the world thinks highly of us, it is possible that we are so much like the world that they see little difference in us. But Christ has chosen His followers to be "not of the world," to endure the hatred that comes with the territory of being Christ followers. Thus, we will at times suffer for our faith in Christ. But to the scattered, persecuted Christians, Peter wrote, "It is better, if God should will it so, that you suffer for doing what is right rather than for doing what is wrong" (1 Peter 3:17). We will suffer from the world's rejection and hatred of us, but we need to continue to speak in truth and love and not worry about whether they accept us or hate us.

It is this kind of love that will win the lost to Christ. It is this kind of love that will mark us out as being like Christ. It is for this reason He left us here.

Lord, help me fulfill Your purpose to love those in
the world without being "of the world."

WEEKEND READING

Saturday – John 7:40-52
Sunday – Acts 13:1-25

PERSONAL REFLECTIONS

Like the Master

John 15:20

²⁰ "Remember the word that I said to you, 'A slave is not greater than his master.' If they persecuted Me, they will also persecute you; if they kept My word, they will keep yours also."

Quoting Himself, "A slave is not greater than his master," Jesus reminds His disciples they should expect the same treatment He received. During an extended discourse recorded in Matthew 10:16-29, He had already warned them about persecution. At that, John the Baptist was incarcerated and executed. Being a disciple of Christ has significant consequences.

Earlier in the Upper Room, He again used the phrase in relationship to serving. If Jesus, their Master, washed their feet, then such humility was not below any of the disciples. Now, capitalizing on this thought, neither should suffering be outside of their expectations. This bears repeating. The Old Testament story of Samuel is instructive. When the people rejected the judgeship system of God, the Lord told Samuel, "They have not rejected you, but they have rejected Me from being king over them" (1 Sam. 8:7). So the same is true for those who represent God to the world. A big part of being a follower of Christ is that we represent Him to the world. What the world does to us, they are doing to Christ—and ultimately to God.

If we are persecuted as His disciples, it is because we represent Him. And if people accept our testimony, they are accepting Christ, the One of whom we bear witness. We simply must accept this as part of the package of discipleship. Too often Christians struggle with being ineffective, or we get puffed up with the "success" of seeing people come to Christ. Our role is simply to bear witness of Him, to point people to Christ. Nothing more, nothing less. Some are gifted evangelists, others not so much so. God at times works through the witness of one person, while not so much through another. But we must accept that the majority of people will reject the message. Jesus Himself said, "Enter through the narrow gate; for the gate is wide and the way is broad that leads to destruction, and there are many who enter through it" (Matt. 7:13).

We Christians should by all means share our testimony and do everything we can to reach the lost world around us. But we should not measure "success" by the number who come to believe in His Word. We will be persecuted; that is not necessarily a sign of failure or that we are doing something wrong. It comes with the territory of being a follower of Christ. He certainly wasn't a failure, and they crucified Him.

Lord, help me not waver in the face of persecution. I believe that when they reject me, they are rejecting You. I so want them to know You.

Remedy the Ignorance

John 15:21

21 "But all these things they will do to you for My name's sake, because they do not know the One who sent Me."

Jesus had just raised the disciples to the status of friends: "You are My friends if you do what I command you. No longer do I call you slaves . . . I have called you friends . . ." (vs. 14-15a). That is true of all followers of Christ. Yet we must never forget that this friendship does not mean we can act independently of the Lord. He is still our Master (Eph. 6:9; Col. 4:1; Jude 4) and Lord. Friendship depends upon our faithfully following Him ("if you do what I command you"). In other words, once our basic relationship to Him as Lord of our lives, Master of our souls, is established, then we move into friendship—but that doesn't leave Lordship behind. He is both Lord and Friend!

But to the point, our persecution, which Jesus predicted, is the result of our representing Him ("for My name's sake"). When people reject God and His Son the Lord Jesus Christ, then they reject all those who represent Him. Rather than be defeated by this, the disciples eventually took persecution as a badge of loyalty. Indeed, after Jesus' ascension and after the Day of Pentecost, Peter and John were incarcerated and beaten, and when they were released with a stern warning to stop witnessing, they had no sense of failure in their mission. In fact, "[t]hey went on their way from the presence of the Council, rejoicing that they had been considered worthy to suffer shame for *His* name" (Acts 5:41). Jesus' predictions had come true very early in their missionary enterprise. But it emboldened them. "And every day, in the temple and from house to house, they kept right on teaching and preaching Jesus *as* the Christ" (Acts 5:42).

The disciples came to understand the import of Jesus' comment to them, that their persecution would be the result of ignorance: "they do not know the One who sent Me." The solution to persecution? Continue to witness of Christ, so that people *will* come to know Him. The idea is, how could anyone reject Christ if they really knew who He was and the God who sent Him? That is why the next day Jesus said on the cross, "Forgive them, Father, for they do not know what they are doing" (Luke 23:34). His executioners were ignorant. One shudders to think of the horror one will experience when he discovers at the judgment seat of God that he had rejected the very One who could have given him forgiveness and eternal life. The tragedy is great. The thought of persecution should never deter the Christian from witnessing to others about Christ. He is their only hope of salvation. We need to remedy their ignorance problem.

Lord, I confess my meager (even lack of) attempts to share my knowledge of Jesus Christ with others. They will only come to know Him if I witness to them.

Rejecting True Knowledge

John 15:22

22 "If I had not come and spoken to them, they would not have sin, but now they have no excuse for their sin."

Now clearly, there was sin in the world already before this, as Paul later wrote, "Therefore, just as through one man sin entered into the world, and death through sin, and so death spread to all men, because all sinned, for until the Law sin was in the world, but sin is not imputed when there is no law . . ." (Rom. 5:12-13). So also Jesus had previously taught essentially the same thing: "This is the judgment, that the Light has come into the world, and men loved the darkness rather than the Light, for their deeds were evil" (John 3:19). But sin was not imputed until they rejected Christ—that is what our verse today addresses.

It is true that all have sinned and come short of the glory of God, deserving death (Rom. 3:23; 6:23). But the full weight of sin is seen in the rejection of Christ. The Jews had seen Jesus' miraculous signs and heard His wonderful teachings. He had shown them the inconsistencies in their teachings and their manipulation of the Law. He uncovered their duplicitous hearts on many occasions. The tragic irony of this is that they rejected the very signs that validated Jesus as the Messiah. In the Nazareth synagogue, He had read the Messianic prophecy in Isaiah, "The Spirit of the LORD is upon Me, because He anointed Me to preach the gospel to the poor. He has sent Me to proclaim release to the captives, and recovery of sight to the blind, to set free those who are oppressed . . ." (Luke 4:18). And then finishing, He proclaimed, "Today this Scripture has been fulfilled in your hearing" (Luke 4:21). Even Nicodemus, himself a Pharisee, admitted to Jesus, "Rabbi, we know that You have come from God *as* a teacher; for no one can do these signs that You do unless God is with him" (John 3:2).

Yes, the Jews rejected their Messiah. There is no excuse. They who knew the Law, and who so easily passed judgment on others with their knowledge of the Law, are themselves condemned by the Law. How ironic that in less than 24 hours, they would be crying out, "His blood be on us" (Matt. 27:25).

Yet despite all this, Jesus, while hanging on the cross, pleaded with His Father, "[F]orgive them, for they don't know what they are doing" (Luke 23:34). Their guilt in knowingly rejecting Christ was fully culpable. But their crucifying Him was a supreme ignorance. It was a chosen ignorance, and pitiable. If only they knew, really knew, they were crucifying their only possible means of restoration with the God of Abraham, Isaac and Jacob. The Lawgiver.

Lord, I want to help others come to the true knowledge of who Jesus Christ is.

Jesus-Hate

John 15:23

23 "He who hates Me hates My Father also."

Jesus-phobia, Jesus-hate. There is coming a day when we will see this in our Western world, where we have long enjoyed a Judeo-Christian culture and morality, infused with the influence of the Bible. It is increasingly difficult to "work around" Jesus' teachings and to try making the problem out to be the hypocrisy, extremism and abuses the world sees and calls Christianity. Until now, the fault has been laid at the feet of Christians, not at the feet of Christ. The assumed answer to the question "What would Jesus do?" is that He'd be loving, non-judgmental, inclusive, celebrating diversity, meek, non-threatening.

Yet the world will have to come to terms with Jesus' righteousness, holiness and exclusivity. For example, it was Jesus who said, "I am the way, the truth and the life; no one comes to the Father but through me" (John 14:6). That is an extremely narrow view of the truth. He claimed for Himself to be the only way to God, not just one of many, taking His place among great religious prophets. He, as a man, accepted worship as God (John 20:8). He didn't accept the promiscuous woman in John 8 as just having an alternative lifestyle but said to her, "Go now and leave your life of sin" (John 8:11 NIV). He was about changing lifestyles to line up with the holiness and righteousness of God.

Jesus unashamedly admired John the Baptist as the greatest of all prophets (Matt. 11:11), yet the Baptist railed against Herod's immoral lifestyle (Matthew 14). Yes, Jesus was a social reformer, endorsing the judgment of God against a permissive culture, using the biblical standard of righteousness. He spoke of moral accountability and judgment by the moral Law-giver. He spoke of absolute truth, even claiming to be "the truth" (John 14:6). None of these things go over well in our "emancipated," post-modern world.

Once the world system figures out that Christians act the way they do because of the teachings of Jesus Christ Himself (however poorly we may represent Him), the world will turn on Christ! They did it when He was physically present with those well-versed in the OT prophecies. They will do it again when there is less common morality, other than tolerance. And then tolerance itself will give way to anarchy or totalitarianism. These things reign in the absence of a belief in the true God.

When people reject Jesus Christ, they reject God Himself. Jesus' words fit well into the terminology of today's culture. "Hate-speech," which is normally thrown around at those who are seen as "intolerant," will ironically and tragically be thrown against Christ and against God.

Lord, I am not ashamed to stand with You or afraid of rejection by the world.

The Unique Jesus

John 15:24

24 "If I had not done among them the works which no one else did, they would not have sin; but now they have both seen and hated Me and My Father as well."

The Judge has spoken. The charge is hate. If Jesus had not come as Messiah, they would not have been guilty of rejecting Messiah. Jesus advisedly uses a strong word. Earlier in His speech on the hillside, He intoned, "Everyone who is angry with his brother shall be guilty before the court; and whoever says to his brother, 'You good-for-nothing,' shall be guilty before the supreme court; and whoever says, 'You fool,' shall be guilty *enough to go* into the fiery hell" (Matt. 5:22). John, probably remembering all this, later wrote, "Everyone who hates his brother is a murderer; and you know that no murderer has eternal life abiding in him" (1 John 3:15).

Jesus is the only one who can pronounce judgment like this. His purpose was not to come into the world and to the Jewish nation to bring judgment, but that through Him they might be saved from their sin (John 3:17). They brought the judgment on themselves, and Jesus is simply acknowledging that they have failed to respond to the Messianic signs of His coming (Luke 4:18-21). The evidence is in; the verdict has been rendered: guilty as charged. Once again, Paul would later elucidate that all are sinners. "All have turned aside, together they have become useless; there is none who does good, there is not even one" (Rom. 3:12; cp. Ps. 53:3). "All have sinned and come short of the glory of God" (Rom. 3:23).

Some might give some leeway to the rejecting Jews for missing the signs. For if they really understood, after all, they would not have rejected Jesus. Why would anyone, thinking clearly, reject the One they had been waiting for? But Jesus gives them no quarter, for they knowingly rejected Him. Just as Adam knowingly rejected God's clearly revealed command to not eat from the forbidden tree, it is of the same piece for the Jews to reject the Word of God in the flesh (see John 1:14).

But, some might say, there were many claiming to be Messiah in those times. We respond that none of them did all the things Jesus did. Like the "magicians" in Moses' day, there will always be imitators. But Jesus raised the dead and healed those who had been blind since birth—miracles even the Jews recognized had never been done before (John 9:32; Matt. 15:31). Sufficient evidence was available; all that remained was for them to act out their hatred.

Lord, I shudder to think of the times I have rejected Your command to me.
Thank You that Your love forgives me for all my sin and has given me new life.

WEEKEND READING

Saturday – John 7:53–8:11
Sunday – Acts 13:26-52

PERSONAL REFLECTIONS

_____

_____

_____

_____

_____

_____

_____

_____

_____

_____

_____

_____

_____

_____

_____

_____

_____

_____

_____

_____

_____

What to Do with Hate Speech

John 15:25

25 *"But they have done this to fulfill the word that is written in their Law, 'THEY HATED ME WITHOUT A CAUSE.'"*

Many today invoke the word "hate" to project the most extreme judgment on the intentions of another person with whom they disagree. Much emotional leverage can be obtained by accusing someone of hate speech. But Jesus, in using this word, does not stoop to making political points, nor does He squelch the speech of those who would disagree with Him. The hate that He speaks of is not a rhetorical device to enflame His followers to violence; He is simply preparing them for the worst and for the best. In a few short hours, the hatred of which He speaks will drive His detractors to crucify Him. But His and His disciples' response would be to confront the worst with their best, namely, genuine love.

How ironic that the Messiah, the Sent-one from God, the very God Himself appearing as a man, the soon-to-be-Savior of the world, would actually be hated! He who came to love, and did indeed demonstrate that love to all without bias, partisanship or prejudice—this one was hated. A relative few responded to His overwhelming love and acceptance, but the majority rejected Him in their hatred of His truth, His holiness, His righteousness. They didn't want His forgiveness, as wonderful as that would be, because they held too tightly to their self-attained "goodness." They would not humble themselves to acknowledge their need. Theirs was a hatred that was born in the great fall of Lucifer himself, who wanted to ascend above the throne of God (Isa. 14:12-13). When confronted with the fullness of the Godhead in bodily form (Col. 2:9), the seed of the serpent burst forth in the hearts of men, in all its colorless blackness. Hatred is the only word strong enough to describe it. Jesus simply but starkly reprised what He had taught them earlier: "For everyone who does evil hates the Light, and does not come to the Light for fear that his deeds will be exposed" (John 3:20). The crucifixion of Jesus would indeed expose their hearts, their deeds, for what they really were: hatred of God. In a few short hours, full expression would be given to that hatred. And without cause!

How are disciples to respond to the inevitability of being hated? Let us recall what our Lord and Master spoke earlier: "You have heard that it was said, 'You shall love your neighbor and hate your enemy.' But I say to you, love your enemies and pray for those who persecute you . . ." (Matt. 5:43-44). It is to this that we testify by our words and by our actions—God's overwhelming love.

Lord, help me as I face the world's rejection of the message of God to respond with Christ-like love, the best response to the worst rejection.

Truth Will Prevail

John 15:26

26 "When the Helper comes, whom I will send to you from the Father, that is the Spirit of truth who proceeds from the Father, He will testify about Me . . ."

Our Western culture values the marketplace of free speech and public debate. Hatred blinds the mind of the one who hates and suppresses the truth against all good conscience and fairness. Hatred cares not for what is right and good, and drives a person to reject the very One who created him. Hatred, extremely powerful, forceful and violent, doesn't seek fair debate or discussion. It seeks to kill and destroy, as demonstrated in the execution of the Logos, the Truth of God (John 1:1, 14).

Mere human effort cannot stand before acrimonious, withering, bitter hatred, which is what the world ultimately heaps on the follower of Christ. If they hated Him, they will hate us. Now, we normally don't see that "emotion" hanging on people's sleeves, but it breaks out from time to time—more so in heavily persecuted areas. But make no mistake, the hatred runs deep below the respectable clothing of the religiously righteous, as is about to become so clearly evident in the Jewish leaders' trial and execution of Christ. Their hatred for the truth was focused on "the way, the truth and the life" (John 14:6), their only hope of salvation. For Jesus exposed their arrogance, pride and self-sufficiency—in short, their desire to be independent of God, the whole while giving Him lip service. Their only recourse was to suppress the truth of God.

This suppression of truth began in the Garden of Eden when Satan, that fallen angel of light, distorted God's word to Eve. Eve and then Adam fell to the lie, and they joined in the big cover-up. Instead of welcoming the Light of the world who came down to walk in the garden "in the cool of the day" and have fellowship with them, they hid in the bushes and covered themselves with leaves. The hatred Satan had and still has for God bred the big cover-up that continues to suppress the truth to this very day.

This lie against the truth of God infiltrates all of life, because Adam's sin passed to all his descendants, "for all have sinned and fall short of the glory of God" (Rom. 3:23). This lie affects not only our relationship with God, but also our relationship with each other, and, insidiously, our relationship with ourselves. Indeed, we struggle with self-deception, ever believing the lie about ourselves, that we are the center of the universe and fully capable of self-determination. This onslaught of the false can only be countered with the overwhelming help of the Trinity of God, Father, Son and Spirit—all working in perfect harmony to advance successfully the truth of God.

Lord, help me always embrace Your truth and not the lies of this world.

Three-Fold Testimony

John 15:26 (cont.)

26 "When the Helper comes, whom I will send to you from the Father, that is the Spirit of truth who proceeds from the Father, He will testify about Me . . ."

W e stand not alone in the quest for truth. God has a vested interest in the march of truth into the blackness of the lie, this fallen world. Even more so today, in our media-driven world, which has saturated the human senses with its imagery and imagination, God has incisively injected the truth. Our role is not as partners, or even as channels of truth. Our role, rather, is to testify about the truth, as the next verse tells us. But what energizes this effort on our part is the effort on God's part.

Enter the Holy Spirit once again into Jesus' final words to His disciples in the Upper Room, on the night before He was crucified. His departure, the thought of which was disappointing to the disciples, would usher in His Replacement. The battle for truth would not abate, but the tag-team of the Son and the Spirit would see to it that the truth would prevail. Actually, the Trinity works closely together, and the gates of Hades cannot prevail against the onslaught of the divine three-fold cord (cp. Eccl. 4:12).

Notice Jesus sends the Helper from the Father. Both the first and the second member of the Trinity send the third member. While the original Nicean Creed says that the Holy Spirit "proceeds from the Father," some later versions write that the Holy Spirit "proceeds from the Father and the Son." Theologians debate about the Spirit's accountability to the Father only or also to the Son. The word "proceeds" applies to the Father's action in sending the Spirit. But it is clear that Jesus "will send" the Spirit. The nuanced subtleties of the difference in these viewpoints is better left to the theologians. But it is clear from this verse that three things—the work of Jesus in sending, the fact that this sending comes from the proximity of the Father's presence, and the clear statement that the Spirit proceeds from the Father—all point to a seamless co-intentionality, reminiscent of Jesus' earlier statement, "I and the Father are one" (John 10:30).

Of particular note are the contrasting verb tenses of our passage today. At the time Jesus spoke these words, the sending of the Spirit was future ("I will send"). But the action of the Father is depicted using a present-tense verb, "proceeds." This "procession," as theologians call it, is an eternal, ongoing activity. We first see the Holy Spirit in Genesis 1:2, where "the Spirit of God was moving across the surface of the waters." Yet the specific action of the Spirit of which Jesus spoke, namely testifying about Jesus, would be future to the time when He spoke these worlds. That would come at the Day of Pentecost.

Lord, I believe in You, Father, Son and Spirit—the three-fold Giver of Truth.

Apostolic Witness

John 15:27

27 ". . . and you will testify also, because you have been with Me from the beginning."

Chosen to be God's instruments in propagating the truth, we followers of Christ have the inestimable privilege of joining with the Trinity in testifying about Jesus Christ. To testify simply means to share what we know, to present the evidence from our own personal perspective. Jesus isn't calling all of us to be evangelists, that is, gifted individuals in the Ephesians 4:11 sense. Even Timothy was not a gifted evangelist, as is evident from Paul's command to him to "do the work of an evangelist" (2 Tim. 4:5)—a gifted evangelist does not need instructions to do so.

However, the apostles were given a unique role as authorized witnesses. After His resurrection and just before His ascension to heaven, the Lord specifically told them, "You will receive power when the Holy Spirit has come upon you; and you shall be My witnesses both in Jerusalem, and in all Judea and Samaria, and even to the remotest part of the earth" (Acts 1:8). This is accentuated by the fact that Judas, the betrayer, had to be replaced. Peter proclaimed, "Therefore it is necessary that of the men who have accompanied us all the time that the Lord Jesus went in and out among us—beginning with the baptism of John until the day that He was taken up from us—one of these *must* become a witness with us of His resurrection" (Acts 1:21-22).

These twelve were the ones authorized to be the official conveyors of Jesus' ministry. It was their teaching to which the early church committed (Acts 2:42). Peter appealed to the validity of his and the other apostles' testimony (Acts 3:15). In fact, he appeals to their partnership with the Holy Spirit: "And we are witnesses of these things; and *so is* the Holy Spirit, whom God has given to those who obey Him" (Acts 5:32).

The importance of this apostolic witness weighed heavily on the formation of the NT canon (the accepted list of inspired writings). If a letter or saying could be verified as being from an apostle, then it was considered authentic. For example, the Gospel According to Matthew and the Gospel According to John were immediately accepted as authentic because of the apostolic authorship. The Gospel According to Mark was considered to reflect the teachings of Peter, of whom Mark was a frequent companion. And the Gospel According to Luke was authoritative because of Luke's association with the apostle Paul (later given the same apostolic authority as the twelve).

Lord, thank You for the faithful witness of Your first followers. I personally validate their writings as authentic by my devotion to the Word.

Not Surprised by Suffering

John 16:1

¹ "These things I have spoken to you so that you may be kept from stumbling.

Jesus uses a common training tool with His disciples, telling them about the problems they will have *before* they get there—so the surprise element won't stumble them. In fact, the entire Upper Room discourse was designed to prepare them for life and ministry and persecution.

Jesus gives them at least three reasons for this Upper Room discourse. First, He wants for them blessing: "If you know these things, you are blessed if you do them" (John 13:17). In other words, His words were intended to help them experience life to the fullest (see John 10:10). Second, "These things I have spoken to you while abiding with you . . ." (John 14:25). His teaching was like a placeholder and would become fully alive to them when the Holy Spirit came. "But the Helper, the Holy Spirit, whom the Father will send in My name, He will teach you all things, and bring to your remembrance all that I said to you" (John 14:26). Third, in our passage today His words are intended to prepare the disciples for things coming which would otherwise stumble them.

The word "stumble" (Greek *skandalizo*) is used 25 times in the gospels, most frequently with the meaning of "be appalled" or "to cause to sin." We can see at the least the first meaning in our English word "scandalize," which means "to shock someone with an action or opinion thought of as immoral or wrong." Jesus doesn't want them to be shocked at the persecution that was going to come. This warning, or should I say preparation, remains for us today. We need to get used to the idea that suffering will come. As followers of the Suffering Servant (Isa. 53), we have signed over our primal claim to a suffering-free life. We take up our place among the "great cloud of witnesses" who have gone before us and suffered for their faith (Heb. 12:1).

The NT speaks so much about suffering that only the most worldly-minded should be surprised when it happens to them. Though we don't desire it by any means, we must expect it. We must be ready for it, by imbibing Jesus' teachings, letting them marinate in our souls—so that we are ready when it comes. Peter could never forget his Master's teaching and passed it on to the persecuted Christians: "Beloved, do not be surprised at the fiery ordeal among you, which comes upon you for your testing, as though some strange thing were happening to you; but to the degree that you share the sufferings of Christ, keep on rejoicing, so that also at the revelation of His glory you may rejoice with exultation. If you are reviled for the name of Christ, you are blessed, because the Spirit of glory and of God rests on you" (1 Peter 4:12-14).

Lord, I anticipate suffering, and I willingly accept this in following You.

WEEKEND READING

Saturday – John 8:12-30
Sunday – Acts 14:1-28

PERSONAL REFLECTIONS

Outcast Christians

2 "They will make you outcasts from the synagogue, but an hour is coming for everyone who kills you to think that he is offering service to God."

Persecution will run extreme, Jesus warns His disciples in the comfort and culinary enjoyment of the Passover meal—a meal ironically designed to be an annual reminder of God's gracious redemption of His people from slavery in Egypt. Yet, here was Jesus, the promised "seed" of the covenant promise to Abraham (Gal. 3:16), telling these few faithful, fellow Jews, that there will be unprecedented difficulties ahead. To be "outcasts from the synagogue" was tantamount to being excommunicated from Jewish life and society! For a Jew, things don't get lower than that. That would be a sign of complete separation from God, abandonment to the Gentile world, and being placed outside of the covenant of God with His people.

What is worse yet, the ones casting them out would do it seemingly as an act of fidelity to God, even of pleasing God. They would be doing it with a sense and confidence of moral and spiritual superiority. They would do everything they could to make these followers of Jesus feel like they were abandoning Moses and the Law, the very life-blood of every Jew and the basis for their relationship with God.

Yes, Jesus readies them, persecution will be worse than they could possibly imagine. And indeed, that time did come. Shortly after Jesus' death and resurrection, the harassment began first with threatening (Acts 4:21), then imprisonment (Acts 5:18) and flogging (Acts 5:40). Peter and John, most likely remembering Jesus' words from the Upper Room, rejoiced that "they had been considered worthy to suffer for His name" (Acts 5:41). Jesus' preparation and the work of the Holy Spirit turned out to be quite effective.

Persecution got worse, however. Stephen, who himself was not in the Upper Room before the cross, had surely heard all about it, and was emboldened to witness bravely for Christ. In faith, he died by stoning, the Jews' punishment for blasphemers (Acts 7:58-60). In his death, he remarkably responded as Jesus did on the cross, when he cried out with his last breath, "Lord, do not hold this sin against them!" (Acts 7:60; cp. Luke 23:34).

We take it on the example of Christ with His disciples that the best preparation for persecution is to study this Upper Room discourse, as though it were Jesus speaking directly to us, the readers. It is His words that are life and wisdom and strength and power. Mark it well, as followers of Christ, we will be persecuted. The goal is not to avoid it, but to give God glory in the midst of it.

Lord, thank You for preparing me for persecution by Your prophetic words.

If Only They Knew

John 16:3

3 "These things they will do because they have not known the Father or Me."

Ignorance is no excuse, so goes the popular saying. And that's true in spiritual things as well, if you think about it carefully. There is no excuse for not knowing God, for He actively seeks out every single human being. Beginning with Genesis 3:8, where God came to walk with Adam and Eve "in the garden in the cool of the day," He has been actively revealing Himself to humankind.

In Romans we find this assessment: "That which is known about God is evident within them; for God made it evident to them. For since the creation of the world His invisible attributes, His eternal power and divine nature, have been clearly seen, being understood through what has been made, so that they are without excuse" (Rom. 1:19-20). God made creation, including humankind, to reflect His glory plainly. His existence is "self-evident" within mankind who, made in His image, has the innate capacity to know God. God's glory in nature resonates with God's image in the human. Therefore, there is no excuse. Paul goes on to say, "For even though they knew God, they did not honor Him as God or give thanks" (Rom. 1:21).

Ignorance not only brings guilt, but it also explains why non-believers persecute believers. They are doing what comes "naturally" to them, as sinners fallen away from a God whom they have rejected. If they reject Christ, then it logically and naturally follows that they will reject those who follow Him. It is not that the unbelieving world rejects us because we *believe* in Christ. It is that we *follow* Christ, that we pattern our lives after Him. There is a difference. Believers, like Christ, seek to carry out His mission in the world. We cannot settle into a comfortable pluralism of "live and let live" with other religions. That is not an option. We have a message of love and freedom from legalism that does nothing to stem the tyranny of sin, a message of humility and forgiveness. Of submission to God.

"Father, forgive them; for they do not know what they are doing," said our Master on the cross (Luke 23:34). Sin blinded His executioners. Had they known who He really was, in the believing sense of the word "to know," they would not have put Him on the cross. The solution, again, is love—thus His desire to forgive them. The disciples in the Upper Room are being prepared to love their persecutors the way Jesus loves sinners. Like Him, we need to be unwilling that any should perish but that all would have eternal life.

Lord, I remember how I lived in ignorance of You and Your perfect love for sinners. You have forgiven me for my ignorance. Thank You!

If Only They Knew (cont.)

John 16:3

3 "These things they will do because they have not known the Father or Me."

A theists assert there cannot possibly be a God. How could that be when there are so many evils in the world: wars, genocides, murder, extortion and sickness? That was the "argument" of one mocking, young unbeliever in his smug defiance of all things Christian. Yet when confronted with and finally embracing the message of Jesus Christ and His forgiveness on the cross, the answer to his seemingly self-convincing questions became quite clear. The reason for all the bad stuff that happens in the world, he came to realize, was not because there is no God, but that people rejected the God who created them. Suffering is not God's "fault," but rather the fault of humans. If people really knew God as He has revealed Himself in Jesus Christ, there would be none of the bad stuff going on. Their lives would be changed.

Theologians attempt to sort out the sovereignty of God and the free will of man, and how those two things figure into salvation, a discussion which can easily sound like the question of which came first, the chicken or the egg. Pre-millennialists, post-millennialists and amillennialists argue whether the world is becoming a better place or is declining toward Armageddon. Jesus said His disciples will be persecuted, things will worsen—and not always because of Christians' failure to influence the world. It will come even to the most faithful. The world is fallen.

Christians tend to berate themselves for the state of the world, as though we are at fault for not being more faithful in our witness and living the character of Christ. We have failed to be salt and light, and that accounts in large part for the moral tsunami taking place. In fact, our society actually celebrates sinful lifestyles and heralds those who "come out" with their alternative sexualities—this moral upheaval is overwhelming our Western world at a break-neck speed.

But is the fault laid at the feet of Christians? When Jesus was physically present in this world, He was the salt and light of the earth, par excellence. No one could be like Christ better than Jesus Himself. Yet the world crucified Him. And it is He who said His followers would be persecuted. The cause of persecution is not Christian political activism, which has fallen under withering criticism. Nor is it Christians' failure to love their "enemies" or those who are "different." The root reason for persecution is ignorance. If people only knew Christ the way the disciples came to know Him, they would not persecute Christians or live immoral lifestyles—they would be fully committed followers of Jesus Christ as well.

Lord, I want to be faithful in my witness to people about Your Son.

When All Seems Lost

John 16:4

⁴ "But these things I have spoken to you, so that when their hour comes, you may remember that I told you of them. These things I did not say to you at the beginning, because I was with you."

No one wrote down what Jesus said while He spoke. Yet they needed to remember it all, and they would—without handwritten notes. The entire Christian enterprise depends upon their testimony. Jesus would declare them to be His official representatives (ambassadors, if you will) just before He ascended to heaven after His resurrection (Acts 1:8). The early church was devoted to the apostles' teachings (Acts 2:42).

The message of Christ was to extend far beyond His physical presence and His own audible voice. He now speaks through the writings of the apostles, which were collected by the early church into what we now know as the New Testament. Much has been written elsewhere on how that came to be, which goes beyond the scope of our purposes here (see "The Formation of the New Testament" by Chuck Gianotti, ECS Ministries).

John, being one of the apostles and Upper Room participants, writing around 60 years hence, penned these very words of Jesus' Upper Room discourse. Memory for most people, especially as they age, is suspect, but memories that are precious are well preserved, etched in our minds and unchangeable. But more significantly, as we have noted earlier, Jesus promised that the Holy Spirit would give the apostles perfect recall of everything He taught (John 14:26). So John recalls for us the details and the nuances of Jesus' words at the last supper before His death.

The memory of Jesus' words would be especially precious and valuable when their commitment to the kingdom of God, as presented in the person of Jesus Christ, would be tested to the max. In a few short hours, Jesus, the One for whom they had left all, and in whom they were risking tirades of the rabbinical interpretation of the Law of Moses, would be arrested and executed with the most merciless, painful, shaming kind of death known to the Romans. By all counts, they were about to experience what was assuredly a complete failure of Jesus' mission. All they had, in the face of everything to the contrary, was Jesus' words. And this was the reason Jesus spoke in the Upper Room as He did. They would need those words when He was taken from them, when God became silent and all seemed lost. We also need these words from the Upper Room so we too have strength to carry on when God is silent and all seems lost.

Lord, Your words and promises are precious to my soul. They sustain me in the darkest times of my life, and I actively seek to meditate on them every day.

Final
Preparation

When Going Is a Good Thing

John 16:5-6

[5] *"But now I am going to Him who sent Me; and none of you asks Me, 'Where are You going?'* [6] *"But because I have said these things to you, sorrow has filled your heart.*

Overwhelmed at His leaving them, the disciples were oblivious to even considering where He might be going. The question was not on their minds. The thought of His absence was too much to handle. It didn't really matter to them where He might be going; what would be the point of knowing that information?

We must give the disciples some slack here, for their devotion to the kingdom of God rested solely in their devotion to Jesus. It was Him they were following, not a system of belief or a political movement that was greater than their leader. The movement was not greater than Him; Jesus *was* the movement they were following. Never has any person lived who has evoked such devotion to himself as the person of Jesus Christ.

Jesus Himself had said, "And I, if I am lifted up from the earth, will draw all men to Myself" (John 12:32). What is it about Him that makes Him so attractive? It is not only His gracious teachings, but also His ultimate gracious act: "When you lift up the Son of Man, then you will know that I am *He* . . ." (John 8:28). The people understood clearly the implications of these words. "Jesus said to them, 'Truly, truly, I say to you, before Abraham was born, I am.' Therefore they picked up stones to throw at Him, but Jesus hid Himself and went out of the temple" (John 8:58-59). He was God in the flesh—this "claim" was clearly understood to be the meaning of His words by those who sought to stone Him (assuming blasphemy for using a self-referential term appropriate to God alone) and ultimately crucify Him.

But in that very act of rejection, He was "lifted up" on the cross, and this is the ultimate attraction of Christ. He was God in the flesh dying for the sins of all people. And that is the attraction of Christianity: Jesus Christ Himself. All other religions follow prophets who point to God, but in Christianity, we have Jesus, who is God Himself. The disciples got it, although in the Upper Room they had not yet comprehended the final and ultimate demonstration of Jesus' personality, that of His sacrificial love. They allowed themselves to be completely abandoned to Him—and the thought of His leaving was cause for sorrow. But they needed to remember what He had already told them: "Do not let your heart be troubled; believe in God, believe also in Me" (John 14:1).

Lord, I too need to calm my troubled heart when You seem silent, when I don't feel Your presence. I believe in You, though my senses tell me You are not there.

WEEKEND READING

Saturday – John 8:31-47
Sunday – Acts 15:1-12

PERSONAL
REFLECTIONS

_____
_____
_____
_____
_____
_____
_____
_____
_____
_____
_____
_____
_____
_____
_____
_____
_____
_____
_____
_____
_____
_____

Is Sorrow Overrated?

John 16:6

6 "But because I have said these things to you, sorrow has filled your heart."

Sorrow in itself is overrated. True, there is genuine sorrow at the loss of things that are precious to us—that is inherent to our human nature. However, sorrow can be eclipsed by hope and joy, engulfed by that which is greater, like light flooding a dark room.

The words of Jesus had a negative effect on the disciples. Knowing that would be their reaction, He spoke with them anyway, because He knew their sorrow was a precursor to joy. Deep joy is generally attained through deep sorrow. That which brings deep joy cannot be comprehended at first, before a visceral reaction to the very thing that is the instrument in gaining joy. Too often the hindrance to greater joy is the prospect of losing a lesser joy, without which we think we cannot live. But that lesser joy must be abandoned, and that is where the sorrow comes in. We let go of the lesser joy in order to gain a better joy.

At a very fundamental level, the creaturely pleasures of life bring us a certain, albeit minimal, level of joy. But to love others as we love ourselves means at times forgoing our creaturely pleasures (e.g. sitting in the easy chair, sipping a cold drink and eating a pizza while watching the playoffs on TV) for the joy that comes from serving others (mowing my sick neighbor's lawn). There is some displeasure in getting off the chair and helping someone else. But the joy of serving obscures that.

Sorrow comes for many reasons: loss of a job or a relationship, illness, failure, guilt over sin and many other things. Jesus said we would have trials, so these things are to be expected. Just like the disciples in the Upper Room would have been ill-advised to ask Jesus to change His mind and not leave them, so we must be careful how we pray concerning our losses. Job's loss of virtually everything turned into double blessing (Job 42:10-17). Patriarch Jacob's limp became a sign of blessing (Gen. 32:30-31). Joseph's sorrow and misfortune of being rejected by his brothers and sold into slavery turned out for the good (Gen. 50:20). Daniel's three friends being thrown in the furnace turned into fellowship with God (Dan. 3:25). David's sorrow over his sin led to two inspired Psalms (51 and 32) rejoicing over God's forgiveness and restoration. Peter and John found joy in their flogging and persecution to discover "they had been considered worthy to suffer shame for His name" (Acts 5:31).

God uses the dark strokes of our life to add texture and depth. Joy now is choosing to anticipate that finished work, and that supersedes our suffering now.

Lord, help me look past the dark strokes in life and see the grand finished work.

Advantage

John 16:7

7 "But I tell you the truth, it is to your advantage that I go away; for if I do not go away, the Helper will not come to you; but if I go, I will send Him to you."

"Read my lips," says the Master. "Focus, people—you are blinded by one of the truths I told you, but wait, there's more, and better news." So we might paraphrase the force of Jesus' words. All the disciples could think of was Jesus' soon departure and His ominous talk of trouble, betrayal and denial. How could they think of anything else? Their world was about to shatter beyond repair. Yet here is their Master telling them that His departure was actually an "advantage."

That advantage, of course, was to be "the Helper," whom we know to be the Holy Spirit. Although hearing that did not seem to help them much at the time, there was coming a time when they would be absolutely transformed, from being fearful, sorrowful, dejected disciples to bold, fearless, joyful proclaimers of Jesus Christ. Yes, the Spirit would transform them, individually and as the foundation for building the Church, carrying on Jesus' mission enterprise into the whole world (Eph. 2:20).

Yes, advantage was the right word. When that word is used in the New Testament it usually conveys the concept of sacrificing something we desire for the sake of something greater. An interesting example of this usage is found in Jesus' earlier teaching, "If your right eye makes you stumble, tear it out and throw it from you; for it is better [lit. "advantage"] for you to lose one of the parts of your body, than for your whole body to be thrown into hell" (Matt. 5:29). The eye is obviously a good thing, but giving it up for something better is a clear advantage or "better for you," namely avoiding hell. Paul uses the word as well: "All things are lawful, but not all things are profitable [lit. "advantage"]. All things are lawful, but not all things edify" (1 Cor. 10:23). The "advantage" goes to those who sacrifice their freedoms for the sake of a "profitable" lifestyle—which, in context, is one lived for the benefit of others.

So also for the disciples, they would be losing a good thing (the physical presence of Jesus) in order to gain a more advantageous thing (the abiding presence of the Spirit). If He had stayed in His pre-ascended state, the team of the apostles would have had to stay in close physical proximity in order to experience His abiding presence. This obviously would have hindered the geographical expansion of the message. The "advantage" of the Spirit would benefit not just them but all the world as they moved out to spread the Gospel.

Lord, thank You for the Spirit's ever-abiding presence in my life. Let me take advantage of that benefit and do my part in reaching the world for Christ.

I've Been Found Out!

John 16:8

⁸ *"And He, when He comes, will convict the world concerning sin and righteousness and judgment . . ."*

Conviction is that inner work of exposing a person to his own true nature. The world was already under God's judgment, and Jesus came to provide a solution. However, it was (and is) needed for people to see their own need for that solution, to participate in the solution. But how?

Being created in God's image includes having the ability to make free choices. We infer this from the commands given to Adam in the Garden of Eden (to manage the creation, enjoy the fruit of the garden, procreate and avoid the tree of the knowledge of good and evil). Sin came when Adam, as an image bearer of God, knowingly and freely chose to disobey his Creator, and in so doing, fell away from Him. Resolving the problem of image bearers having fallen must involve their nature of being image bearers of God in their restoration. The solution cannot ignore the fact that they still exist in God's image and need to respond in God's image, namely choosing freely. Any other way would override and in fact nullify the image of God in them. In other words, redemption requires the full understanding of the depths of their depravity, and therefore, their choice to believe must be taken freely. The image of God did not shine brightly in man's fall, but it does indeed shine brilliantly in man's response to sin in repentance and faith.

Unfortunately, we are fallen beings incapable of functioning fully in the image of God because it was in that image that we acted out in the wrong way—by rebelling against Him. If God were to save us in a way that denies the image of Himself in us (for example, to save us apart from our will), then He would be ignoring the very essence of what it means to exist in His image. Thus the only way salvation could happen would be for us to confront the very thing that caused the downfall to begin with. We must face up to the full awareness of our willful rejection of Him, and do so in the fullness of God's image in us.

But how can we do that when we are in fact fallen, spiritually blind and spiritually dead? "And you were dead in your trespasses and sins . . ." (Eph. 2:1). Enter the Holy Spirit, who brings conviction, that is, exposure and full awareness of our sin. He incites the image of Himself in us to rise up in revulsion against our sin, so that we might experience a truly godly response to our sinfulness. He brings us back to Eden, to confront our original sin, our inner rebellion against God. And now, what will we do differently?

Lord, thank You for the convicting work of Your Spirit. Without Him
I would remain dead in my sins, because of my sinfulness.

I've Been Found Out! (cont.)

John 16:8

[8] "And He, when He comes, will convict the world concerning sin and righteousness and judgment . . ."

This work of conviction belongs to the Holy Spirit alone, not to any human being. Yet it seems to be in human nature the desire to displace the Spirit's work. The fine line between this and "judging" must bear the effort of further thought. Even about Jesus, the Word says, "For God did not send the Son into the world to judge the world, but that the world might be saved through Him" (John 3:17). So being like Christ, as we should be, does not involve judging others or bringing them to conviction.

Yet at the same time, we cooperate with the Spirit to keep in step with Him (Gal. 5:25). The word "convict," while here used in reference to the Spirit's work, is also used in reference to the Word of God: "All Scripture is inspired by God and profitable for teaching, for reproof [or convicting], for correction, for training in righteousness . . ." (2 Tim. 3:16). The underlying word translated "reproof" is the noun form of the same word used in John 16:8, translated in verb form as "to convict." Yet note well it is not the preaching of the Word that brings conviction but the Word itself. This is a crucial distinction.

The first application of 2 Timothy 3:16 is not that Timothy should use the Word to cause conviction in other people. Rather, the Word will bring conviction in Timothy's own life so that he, "the man of God," might be "adequate, equipped for every good work" (2 Tim. 3:17). Timothy's task, of course, was to "[p]reach the word; be ready in season *and* out of season; reprove, rebuke, exhort, with great patience and instruction" (2 Tim. 4:2). Again, the word "reprove" here is the same word, now in verb form. Timothy was to bring conviction to others by preaching the Word! But this convicting was not independent of the Word, not just based on the Word, and not just quoting a verse or two out of context. This convicting is the Word of God at work in people's lives, just like it is the work of the Word of God at work in Timothy's life, and in all of our lives.

The point is that conviction does not come through our own personal assessment and moral judgment of another person's life. We cannot possibly know his or her motives and inner thoughts. But "the word of God is living and active and sharper than any two-edged sword, and piercing as far as the division of soul and spirit, of both joints and marrow, and able to judge the thoughts and intentions of the heart" (Heb. 4:12).

*Lord, help me to not take the place of the Holy Spirit in
judging others and forcing conviction on them.*

Spirit, Not Human, Conviction

John 16:9

⁹ ". . . concerning sin, because they do not believe in Me . . ."

The main problem with lost sinners is not the specific sins they commit. Those are the symptoms of the deeper problem, namely the sin nature. When unbelievers sin (and sometimes they sin in "big" ways), they are doing what sinners naturally do—nothing more, nothing less. Sometimes believers fall into the morass of trying to reform non-believers apart from their being regenerated from death into life. When we try to speak to their immorality, it comes across as judgmental and critical—at least that is how the world sees it. While it is true that acknowledgment of sin, confession and repentance are part of the process of salvation, so often a confusing message conveys the need to reform *before* coming to Christ in faith. This inadvertently communicates the wrong message through a subtle shift of focus.

To be sure, the rich young man was tagged by the Lord to sell all he had and give it to the poor so that he could then follow Jesus. Unfortunately, he was not able to turn from his idolatry of money. Jesus, "knowing what was in each person's heart" (John 2:25 NLT), perceived that the man's love of his riches stood between him and Christ. Some could argue that the young man was being called to discipleship, not to salvation proper. But that begs the point. Jesus wasn't in the ministry of seeking believers apart from seeking disciples. In fact, He had no problem turning away a probable 4,988 men from following as His disciples (John 6:10, 66). His difficult teaching about eating His body and drinking His blood was clearly intended to separate out those who came for the personal benefits of following Christ (John 6:26) versus the true believers, who would leave all to follow Him (John 6:68). He was not interested in the nuances that separate faith and discipleship into two separate callings; He made no room for those who did not turn from their sinful ways. Salvation was all about turning from sin and turning to Jesus.

The call to salvation is a call to repent, not to change. An unregenerate sinner cannot change himself in order to be saved. That would be like a dirty person getting washed up first, before coming to take a bath. Only God can change a person—and that begins with the conviction our passage speaks about, which is the work of the Holy Spirit. This is not an outward focus on a specific symptom of sin, but a focus on the core sin issue: unbelief. That is where true spiritual conviction takes place. Then, when followed by faith, the sinner is regenerated and becomes a new creation (2 Cor. 5:17), and God begins to work the change in the specific areas of sin—inward first, then outward.

Lord, thank You for Your convicting Spirit, who shows me my sinfulness.

WEEKEND READING

Saturday – John 8:48-59
Sunday – Acts 15:13-41

PERSONAL REFLECTIONS

Vindication of Christ

John 16:10

10 ". . . and concerning righteousness, because I go to the Father and you no longer see Me . . ."

Righteousness in God's terms resides not in a set of precepts, but in the life and person of Jesus Christ. He is the "Holy and Righteous One" (Acts 3:14-15). While the religious leaders judged Him to be aligned with Satan (Luke 11:15), God judged Him to be "My beloved Son, in whom I am well-pleased" (Matt. 3:17). But He was rejected and executed as a violator on the shameful and cursed cross (Gal. 3:13). By all accounts, He was considered an unrighteous person, because after all, look at how His life ended! Death is the great consequence of sin. The Scripture makes this very clear: "The soul who sins will die" (Ezek. 18:4). "For the wrath of God is revealed from heaven against all ungodliness and unrighteousness of men . . ." (Rom. 1:18). Did not Job's friends reason that way—bad stuff doesn't happen to righteous people, but to sinners? By that logic, Jesus was a sinner.

Yet the story doesn't end there. His resurrection vindicated His relationship with the God of Abraham and Moses. He was ". . . declared the Son of God with power by the resurrection from the dead, according to the Spirit of holiness, Jesus Christ our Lord." (Rom. 1:4). This was not a new religion that existed in violation of the Mosaic covenant. His death was a complete and absolute fulfillment of God's purposes on earth, a fulfillment of the righteousness required by the Law. Since death could not hold Jesus down, it had no absolute control over Him, and therefore proves that He was not unrighteous, but perfect righteousness.

Going back to the Father (what we call the ascension) would further indicate that Jesus was righteous because He was fully accepted by God. That is why later John could write, "In Him there is no sin" (1 John 3:6). So while the religious leaders declared Him to be worthy of punishment befitting a violator of the Mosaic Law, and therefore presumably under God's judgment, the reality was just the opposite: Jesus is fully accepted by the Father. How ironic that the demons, with whom Jesus was assumed to be in alliance, could declare, "You are—the Holy One of God!" (Luke 4:34). The demons knew; God knew. But the religious leaders did not.

The Holy Spirit used Peter in his second convicting Pentecostal speech to point out this central sin: "You disowned the Holy and Righteous One" (Acts 3:14-15). He is the one who can and will bring awareness that the real issue of sin is rejecting His righteousness in Christ.

Lord, I believe in the righteousness of Your perfect Son, the Lord Jesus Christ.

Here Comes the Judge

John 16:11

11 ". . . and concerning judgment, because the ruler of this world has been judged."

Judgment looms over the world of unbelievers. And it began with the judgment of Satan. The actual event that brought on this judgment was still future to the time Jesus spoke these words, but in today's vernacular, we could say, "It is as good as done." The certainty is not in question. From God's perspective, from which Jesus was now speaking, the future is as certain as the past. The Bible uses this "prophetic past tense" in many statements about future events that are certain and treats them as though they had already passed. For example, Isaiah 53, the prophecy of the "Suffering Servant," speaks of the death of Christ hundreds of years before its historical occurrence using the past tense throughout: "He was oppressed and He was afflicted, yet He did not open His mouth . . ." (Isa. 53:7).

The ultimate judgment will come at the end of time, the Scripture writer records, again using the prophetic past tense: "And the devil who deceived them was thrown into the lake of fire and brimstone, where the beast and the false prophet are also; and they will be tormented day and night forever and ever" (Rev. 20:10). The certainty of this was so fixed in Jesus' mind that He said earlier in the Upper Room, "Now judgment is upon this world; now the ruler of this world will be cast out" (John 12:31).

The march is on; the gates of hades will not prevail (Matt. 16:18) against the onslaught of the Spirit. Satan is judged already, and the evidence is the presence of the Holy Spirit. God has staked out a beachhead in enemy territory, and the conclusion is determined. The die has been cast. There is no hope for the ruler of this world.

Yes, the judgment and verdict have been set, but the sentence has not yet been enforced. Satan is still on the loose (1 Peter 5:8). God is in the process of subduing the devil's power through the image-bearing function of humanity: "Therefore, since the children share in flesh and blood, He Himself likewise also partook of the same, that through death He might render powerless him who had the power of death, that is, the devil . . ." (Heb. 2:14). God could have simply spoken a word and Satan would be gone (Matt. 4:10). But in keeping with His original creation of humans in His image, God would defeat Satan using the essence of humanity, namely the image of God. So in the end, God's purposes in creation are fulfilled, His glory shining brightly as He originally intended—through His image bearers.

Lord, thank You that the judgment of my adversary is complete.

Here Comes the Judge (cont.)

John 16:11

11 "... and concerning judgment, because the ruler of this world has been judged."

F ear of judgment runs deep in the human heart, a foreboding sense of coming up short of what God expects. That is what enlightens our understanding of what Jesus meant when speaking of the third aspect of the Spirit's convicting work. To be certain, Satan knows he is judged, but Jesus is speaking of a wider conviction. Satan's defeat simply validates or confirms to us the certainty of judgment for everyone who follows Satan's rebellious ways. If the leader is judged, will not the pack that follows him also be judged?

This is the classical argument from the greater to the lesser, similar to what the writer of Hebrews wrote: "For if the word spoken through angels proved unalterable, and every transgression and disobedience received a just penalty, how will we escape if we neglect so great a salvation?" (Heb. 2:2-3a). If the pinnacle of God's creation (Ezek. 28:12) fell into the judgment of God because of His rebellion, how shall we escape judgment if we fall into the same pattern of unbelief?

Though humans by their rebellion have darkened their hearts through the callousness that sin produces (Rom. 1:21), though they even mock the idea of God's judgment (2 Peter 3:3), the Holy Spirit can still break through and convict the greatest of sinners. When Paul, the great persecutor of the early church, was confronted on the road to Damascus with the presence of the Lord Jesus Christ, there was no arguing with God's righteousness. Although he once thought of himself as being righteous and blameless under the Law of Moses (Phil. 3:6), he came to see himself as he really was: "formerly a blasphemer and a persecutor and a violent aggressor. It is a trustworthy statement, deserving full acceptance, that Christ Jesus came into the world to save sinners, among whom I am foremost *of all*" (1 Tim. 1:13, 15). The Holy Spirit revealed this to him and convicted him.

Yes, the Spirit of God is in the world convicting people of sin, or righteousness and of judgment. As we observe our culture continuing its downward spiral of sin in rejection of God and His righteousness, and as we anticipate the coming judgment, our thoughts need to turn inward, lest we become like Pharisees and fail to see that our culture is made up of human beings, of which I am. Have I hardened my heart against the convicting work of the Spirit in any area of sin? Have I compromised God's righteousness? Have I lost the fear of His judgment?

Lord, please let Your Spirit continue His convicting work in my life.

Sufficient to Understand

John 16:12

12 "I have many more things to say to you, but you cannot bear them now."

Amazing as it was for the disciples to have sat under the Lord's direct teaching—and amazement was a frequent experience of theirs—there was a whole lot more that Jesus could have taught them, but it would have been counterproductive. Not because of any problem with Jesus' teaching, but because of their limited ability to handle the truth. From the beginning, our human ability to handle the truth has been limited. God knew that Adam and Eve could not handle the knowledge of good and evil, so He forbade them from eating of that tree. The knowledge they gained has caused humans problems ever since. It was not that God wanted to withhold anything good from them, as Satan intimated (Gen. 3:5). He was protecting them from TMI ("too much information") for their own good. You know how that story ended: in rebellion against God's clear commandment not to eat from that tree, their eyes were opened to knowledge in a way that brought their fall.

Yet here we see Christ protecting His disciples from knowledge they were not yet ready for. They had enough for the time being. There was coming a time when the jarring truths of the Upper Room would be easier to handle, that is, from the vantage point of Christ's post-resurrection appearances. Their grief and sorrow at His departure would give way to the glorious understanding of God's wonderful work on the cross and the eternal aliveness and presence of Christ through His Spirit. Hope would be restored and faith re-energized at a new and higher level. But in the Upper Room, they were unable to comprehend much more deep truth. What they had was sufficient to see them through the valley of the shadow of death, which they were about to experience.

The apostle John, chronicler of this gospel account, intimates to his readers a similar thought: "Therefore many other signs Jesus also performed in the presence of the disciples, which are not written in this book; but these have been written so that you may believe that Jesus is the Christ, the Son of God; and that believing you may have life in His name" (John 20:30-31). Sufficient is the story, as it is told, for readers to come to faith in Christ. There is much more to the Christian life than what is recorded here in the Gospel of John, but what has been included has been hand selected by the inspired writer for his purpose of bringing people to faith. John does not focus on the grand theological themes elucidated in other parts of the New Testament, like the role of Melchizedek in salvation history (see Hebrews 5 and 7). That is for later study. For the inquirer, sufficient is the Gospel According to John for the truths necessary to believe.

Lord, help me never overcomplicate the message of salvation in Jesus Christ.

The Great Disclosure

John 16:13

13 "But when He, the Spirit of truth, comes, He will guide you into all the truth; for He will not speak on His own initiative, but whatever He hears, He will speak; and He will disclose to you what is to come."

What a salve this truth must have been to the disciples' confused minds! Jesus promised them a personal guide, mentor, instructor who would help them through not just the imminent events facing them, but also through everything they would ever experience. We take the time to delineate the specifics. First, this Helper is the Holy Spirit. Normally, John refers to Him simply as "the Spirit," but in 14:26, He is called the Holy Spirit. This one, as Jesus taught them, would take over Jesus' role of Teacher in their lives.

Second, the Spirit is personal. In the Greek language, words themselves have gender, and the word "spirit" is a neuter word, which leads some to think the Holy Spirit is a "thing" and not a person, and thus argue against Trinitarian theology. However, the masculine pronoun "he" is used in reference to the Spirit, and that in the original language is definitely a personal pronoun. The Spirit is not a "thing" but a person, who is classically called the "third member of the Trinity." So while the word "Trinity" is not used in the Bible, the concept is there. God exists in three persons: the Father, Son and Holy Spirit. (Note: although the original language in which the NT was written didn't use capital letters at all, most modern translations capitalize the word "Spirit" when used in reference to the Holy Spirit.)

Third, He is the Spirit "of truth" (see John 15:26), the exact opposite of Satan, the consummate purveyor of all that is false, "the father of lies" (John 8:44). His role in teaching believers is through enlightenment as we read the Word, through gifted teachers of the Word, and through our life experiences that we bring to the study of the Word.

Fourth, Jesus promises the disciples that the Spirit would guide them into all truth. And that truth was every bit as important as the truth that Jesus taught. All Scripture, whether quotations of Jesus' teachings as in the gospel accounts or writings of the epistles, is inspired by the Spirit of truth. This promise is somewhat derivative for the rest of us believers, though no less authentic or significant. We have access to the Spirit's truth through the apostolic authority through their teaching. It was the apostles' teaching that formed one of the four pillars on which the early church was built. And praise God, their teaching has been preserved for us today.

Lord, thank You for Your Spirit's teaching of truth in my life today.

WEEKEND READING

Saturday – John 9:1-12
Sunday – Acts 16:1-21

PERSONAL
REFLECTIONS

_____
_____
_____
_____
_____
_____
_____

_____
_____
_____
_____
_____
_____
_____
_____
_____
_____
_____
_____

The Great Disclosure (cont.)

John 16:13

13 "But when He, the Spirit of truth, comes, He will guide you into all the truth; for He will not speak on His own initiative, but whatever He hears, He will speak; and He will disclose to you what is to come."

Combined with the perfect recall Jesus told the disciples about (John 14:26), the promise of "all truth" provides the basis of what we call "apostolic authority." As mentioned before, Jesus appointed them as His authorized and official witnesses (Acts 1:8), and the early church took their teaching as authoritative: "They were continually devoting themselves to the apostles' teachings" (Acts 2:42).

Notice, in our passage today, the Spirit does not do His work independently, but conveys the message, presumably, of God the Father. There is no divergence between the members of the Trinity, but perfect harmony—the Spirit, the Son and the Father all working together, each in His own distinct role, never any variation in purpose or thought. Today, the Spirit acts as the primary agent of the Godhead working in the world. So even when Jesus said, "I am with you always, even to the end of the age" (Matt. 28:20), He was indicating that His presence would be in and through the Spirit.

Christians interestingly struggle in addressing God. Do we exclusively pray to the Father (Matt 6:9; Rom 8:15, etc.)? Is it appropriate to pray to Jesus, the second person of the Trinity? The apostle John seemed to think so, if Revelation 22:20 is any indication: "Amen. Come, Lord Jesus." Paul likewise thought so, writing about those ". . . who in every place call on the name of our Lord Jesus Christ, their *Lord* and ours" (1 Cor. 1:2). And certainly praise is to be directed to the Lord Jesus, as seen in the angels' example in Revelation 5:13.

Non-Christians are amused that we Christians sometimes sound confusing when we believe in one God, yet at times pray to the Father and at other times pray to the Son. Indeed, if we are careless, we might find ourselves erroneously thanking the Father for dying for us, when in fact, God did not die as the Father, but God the Son did die for us. So we Christians need to be mindful of which member of the Trinity we are addressing.

But what about the Holy Spirit? While the Spirit helps us pray "with groanings too deep for words" (Rom. 8:26), we do not find specific teaching or example in Scripture directing believers to pray to the Spirit. Yet if the Spirit is God, how could it be a bad prayer to address Him directly? Yet, the normal practice encouraged in Scripture is to pray to the Father, in Jesus' name, through and with the help of the Holy Spirit.

Come Lord Jesus, make Your presence known in my life through Your Spirit.

The Spirit's Work of Glory

John 16:14

14 "He will glorify Me, for He will take of Mine and will disclose it to you.

The Holy Spirit's role is to glorify the Lord Jesus Christ. Does this make Him lesser than the Son? Not in the least. The Spirit is fully God, just as the Son and the Father are fully God. Each has His role as a distinct person, yet at the same time they are one God. This is the historic, what theologians call the orthodox, understanding of the New Testament teaching: there is one true God (monotheism) who exists in three persons (Trinitarianism), all of whom are equally God. There are not three Gods, but one. Christianity could never have gained a foothold in Judaism, which was fiercely monotheistic. Interestingly, the early Christians were called atheists by the Romans because the followers of Christ refused to worship or acknowledge the plurality of Roman and Greek gods. Their tenacious holding to the belief in one God is why they were persecuted so severely.

Some (like Muslims, Jews and others) charge Christians with a contradiction— that essentially Christians worship three gods, yet claim to be monotheistic. But we don't believe in three gods. And indeed, it would be contradiction to believe there are three gods, yet one God. Further, it would also be a contradiction to believe there are three divine persons, yet one Person. Rather, we believe there are three divine persons, but only one Divinity, that is, one God. That is not a contradiction. To be sure it stretches our human mental limitations, but it is not logically contradictory. Jesus accepted worship as God (John 20:28-29; see also Colossians 1:19; 2:9, etc). That the Holy Spirit is fully God is supported throughout the NT (see for example 2 Corinthians 13:14; 1 Peter 1:2, etc.)

In our passage, Jesus teaches that the Spirit's role involves two related things: "to glorify Christ" and to "take of Mine and . . . disclose it . . ." First, His task is to show, demonstrate, reveal, expose, magnify how great the second person of the Trinity is. This is in keeping with the Father's focus on the Son: "This is my beloved Son, in whom I am well-pleased" (Matt. 3:17). What the Father said concerning the Son was an act of glorifying Christ. As Peter wrote, "For when He received honor and glory from God the Father, such an utterance as this was made to Him by the Majestic Glory, 'This is My beloved Son with whom I am well-pleased'" (2 Peter 1:17). So both the Father and the Spirit work closely together to glorify Jesus, to show the world and all of creation how great He is. The second thing the Spirit does is expose, magnify, make known the teachings of Jesus, which He has done through both the inspiration of the NT writings and the enlightening of our minds and hearts as we read it.

Lord, thank You for the enlightening work of Your Spirit in showing me Christ.

No Fuller Explanation

John 16:15

15 "All things that the Father has are Mine; therefore I said that He takes of Mine and will disclose it to you."

Three in harmony, all working together, the Father, the Son and the Spirit (the "He" in our verse refers to the Spirit as understood from the previous verse). Jesus is taking the disciples into His inner circle by sharing privileged information with them. All knowledge, wisdom and understanding of the Father belong to Jesus. That's why the writer, John, in the beginning of this biography of Jesus, asserted, "No one has seen God at any time; the only begotten God who is in the bosom of the Father, He has explained *Him"* (John 1:18). Jesus came to show who God really is.

The word "explained" translates a word from which comes our theological term exegesis. Jesus has *exegeted,* that is, fully explained or interpreted God for us. There is no fuller explanation of Him than what we find in Jesus.

The Jews knew God as Creator overall and as a God of law, but not so much as a God of grace. They knew Him as Master and Lord, and they knew Him as "father" in a distant sense, but didn't know Him intimately as "Father" in a personal sense. Jesus taught us to begin our prayers, "Our Father . . ." He brought us an understanding of intimacy with God. It is as though He brings us to the tree of intimate and true knowledge of God—a tree of which Adam and Eve could not eat without also knowing the intimacy of evil, for it was not their time to know intimacy of the good in the way Jesus was now revealing about God to the disciples in the Upper Room. Now, they (and we) are given access into the perfect closeness of fellowship of the Father, Son and Spirit.

This sweet communion can only be experienced in the context of a love relationship that finds its ultimate expression in the sacrifice on the cross. Adam and Eve were not yet able to experience this, but it was anticipated in the animal skins God provided for them, symbolic of death required for sin (see Genesis 3:21).

Notice that "all things that the Father has are Mine." Paul explained this further when he wrote, "For it was the *Father's* good pleasure for all the fullness to dwell in Him" (Col. 1:19) and "For in Him all the fullness of Deity dwells in bodily form" (Col. 2:9). Nothing the Father has is lacking in the Son. The Father has given to Jesus the task of fully demonstrating what God is really like. The writer of Hebrews puts it this way: "[Jesus] is the radiance of His glory and the exact representation of His nature, and upholds all things by the word of His power . . ." (Heb. 1:3). That is why Jesus said to Philip, "If you have seen Me, you have seen the Father" (John 14:9).

Lord, I worship You, Father, Son and Holy Spirit, who exist in perfect harmony.

Trinitarianism Makes Sense

John 16:15 (cont.)

15 "All things that the Father has are Mine; therefore I said that He takes of Mine and will disclose it to you."

Trinitarianism stretches our minds, and that makes sense. It goes against the propensity of humans to put God in a box, reduce Him to that which is fully comprehensible, to fit Him into human categories of philosophical thought. It should not surprise any thinking individual that there would be some aspects of the infinite Creator God of the universe that would be beyond human understanding. We believe a basic tenet of rational thought, namely the law of non-contradiction, which states that a thing cannot be true and not true, at the same time and in the same sense. Or to put it another way, nothing can be true and at the same time contradict something else that is true.

One of the core Christian dilemmas has to do with the deity of Christ: how can He be God and at the same time be human? To the Jews that is blasphemy, to Muslims absurdity. But Christians have accepted this from the beginning as a true, if not uncomfortable, tenant of faith, and not without some debate.

The earliest theological debates of the early church revolved around the struggle to understand this dilemma. It wasn't a blind, unthinking, kiss-your-brain-goodbye kind of ignorant faith. The NT documents clearly presented Jesus as God, for the apostles certainly believed that to be true. The question for them was not what the Bible taught on this subject, but what did it mean?

Historians have identified the various attempts at "resolution." There was Modalism, which taught that God is a single person, who reveals Himself in various modes. These modes are "consecutive and never simultaneous." Yet Scripture speaks of the Father, Son and Spirit, often in the same verse at the same time (see Matthew 3:16-17, etc.). There was also Docetism, the belief that Christ only "appeared" to be human. Yet the apostle John wrote, "By this you know the Spirit of God: every spirit that confesses that Jesus Christ has come in the flesh is from God" (1 John 4:2). He excitedly wanted his readers to know about "[w]hat was from the beginning, what we have heard, what we have seen with our eyes, what we have looked at and touched with our hands, concerning the Word of Life" (1 John 1:1). Jesus was not an apparition or ghost. Indeed, "[i]n Him all the fullness of Deity dwells in bodily form" (Col. 2:9).

While a fuller treatment of this doctrine of the deity of Christ is beyond the scope of this writing, suffice it to say the NT clearly teaches that Jesus Christ was fully God and fully man. And that is a wonderful, deep mystery that we will probably spend eternity enjoying and unpacking.

Lord thank You for this wonderful truth of Your Son, the Lord Jesus Christ.

We Will See Him Again

John 16:16

16 "A little while, and you will no longer see Me; and again a little while, and you will see Me."

Again Jesus tells them of His departure. This is certainly not a new thought (John 7:33); in fact, this subject dominated the Upper Room conversation (see 14:18-19 and so on). It bears repeating. Jesus didn't come into this world with the intention of living to a ripe old age. He had a carefully planned exit strategy, and now He is letting the disciples in on it.

So often, within a movement, few have the capacity to see beyond or above the movement. In our contemporary world, many Christian entities enjoy phenomenal growth under the founding leader, with no thought given to life after the founder dies. Often those entities or movements buckle and flounder under their own weight. In a somewhat contrarian manner, Jesus had begun a movement that was dependent on His leaving the movement!

It was better for the "movement," that is Christianity, that the founder vacate His visible, physical presence—this is true on a number of counts. First, His departure speaks initially of His death. And of course Christianity is nothing without the death of Christ. That was the whole reason God sent Him into this world: "This *Man*, delivered over by the predetermined plan and foreknowledge of God, you nailed to a cross by the hands of godless men and put *Him* to death" (Acts 2:23). But as Jesus spoke just previously, His departure would also make way for the Holy Spirit's universal and ever-present role. This would be much better than Jesus' physical presence.

Additionally, just as God placed Adam and Eve in the Garden to tend it on His behalf, as His image bearers, God has now left believers in this world to be His ambassadors (2 Cor. 5:21) and image bearers to reach the lost world of non-believers. As in the Garden, so now also, God desires to work in and through His people.

But there is good news for the human soul. Although it is better that Jesus is not physically with us now, He left this promise: "You will see Me." While this could possibly refer to seeing Him now with spiritual eyesight, Jesus was saying that we would physically see Him at some point. True, the disciples physically saw Him again: "He also presented Himself alive after His suffering, by many convincing proofs, appearing to them over *a period of* forty days" (Acts 1:3). But praise God there is coming a day when we will see Him again: "Beloved . . . we know that when He appears, we will be like Him, because we will see Him just as He is" (1 John 3:2).

"Amen. Come Lord Jesus" (Rev. 22:20).

WEEKEND READING

Saturday – John 9:13-27
Sunday – Acts 16:22-40

PERSONAL REFLECTIONS

Clueless in U.R.

John 16:17-18

[17] Some of His disciples then said to one another, "What is this thing He is telling us, 'A little while, and you will not see Me; and again a little while, and you will see Me'; and, 'because I go to the Father'?" [18] So they were saying, "What is this that He says, 'A little while'? We do not know what He is talking about."

"Some," but not all of the disciples were still in a quandary. They had absolutely no clue in the Upper Room (U.R.). One wonders which ones were not in the quandary. Might John, the writer, have been one of them who, in the midst of all the gloom, had a glimmer of hope through an undying faith in Christ? He was part of the inner three that Jesus took into closer confidence from time to time (see Matthew 17:1; 26:37), the other two being his brother James and Peter. John was the first to recognize the truth of Christ's resurrection: "So the other disciple [i.e. John] who had first come to the tomb then also entered, and he saw and believed" (John 20:8).

Whether or not John had it all figured out (and in all likelihood he did not), the evidence points toward his having a propensity toward faith. Maybe this played into his being "the beloved disciple" (John 13:23; 19:26; 20:2; 21:7, 20). It is no wonder that Jesus on the cross entrusted His own earthly mother to John.

While various named individuals questioned Jesus about what He was saying, here no names are proffered. There was a general foreboding and a resistance to asking Him any further. The thought, any thought, about His leaving them gave them a sense of abandonment. After all, did they not just a week or so earlier enter Jerusalem amidst a crowded throng proclaiming, "'Hosanna to the Son of David; Blessed is He who comes in the name of the LORD; Hosanna in the highest!'" (Matt. 21:9)? Was this not the fulfillment of what He had spoken repeatedly, "The kingdom of heaven is at hand"? And now was He leaving? That made no sense at all to some of the disciples.

Often in our Christian walk, after the newness of our salvation experience tempers down and the humdrum of life picks up, and when the difficulties of life seem to be overbearing, we face a similar conundrum. Some Christians are among those who question why God has abandoned them. How could He go silent at such a time as this? Just like the disciples, they might be tempted to say, "This is not how I envisioned things turning out." But others in faith rest in God, who knows the whole story of our lives, not just the page in which we now live. In faith we keep turning the pages to see how the rest of the story develops.

Lord, thank You that the final chapter of my life has not yet been written. The book of my life is working to a wonderful conclusion.

Mind-Reading Savior

John 16:19

[19] Jesus knew that they wished to question Him, and He said to them, "Are you deliberating together about this, that I said, 'A little while, and you will not see Me, and again a little while, and you will see Me'?"

Some people appear to be mind-readers because of their uncanny ability to extrapolate people's thinking from their facial expressions, voice intonations and body language. Others make a living in carnivals with trickery and mind manipulation techniques. Jesus, however, actually knew what people were thinking as though He were connected to a sensor implanted in their brains. Even more, as God, He knows the thoughts and intents of the heart. "And there is no creature hidden from His sight, but all things are open and laid bare to the eyes of Him with whom we have to do" (Heb. 4:13). Early in His ministry we find, "Jesus knowing their thoughts said, 'Why are you thinking evil in your hearts?'" (Matt. 9:4).

The psalmist writes, "The LORD knows the thoughts of man, that they are a *mere* breath" (Ps. 94:11). David, the man of God's heart, wrote, "O LORD, You have searched me and known *me*. You know when I sit down and when I rise up; you understand my thought from afar. You scrutinize my path and my lying down, and are intimately acquainted with all my ways" (Ps. 139:1-3).

This idea that God can read our minds can be either unsettling or encouraging. If we harbor evil or shameful thoughts, God knows—and we should just as soon bring those out in the open to Him now as wait until the judgment. Some might insist their own thoughts are private, and even God doesn't have a right to know them. But how can the creature say or think such things about the Creator? Of course He has the right; He is our Maker.

But the knowledge that God knows our thoughts can be tremendously comforting. There is relief in being fully exposed before God; there can be no further exposure that God will discover something that will change His love toward me. While I was still a sinner, and while Christ knew every thought of my heart both past, present and future, He died for me (Rom. 5:8). I have absolutely nothing to fear.

God also helps us in the deepest issues of our heart. "The Spirit Himself intercedes for *us* with groanings too deep for words; and He who searches the hearts knows what the mind of the Spirit is, because He intercedes for the saints according to *the will of* God" (Rom. 8:26-27). So like the psalmist, we pray:

"Search me, O God, and know my heart; try me and know my anxious thoughts; and see if there be any hurtful way in me, and lead me in the everlasting way" (Ps. 139:23-24).

Transformative Hope

John 16:20

20 "Truly, truly, I say to you, that you will weep and lament, but the world will rejoice; you will grieve, but your grief will be turned into joy.

Heavy emotions the disciples were experiencing at the thought of Jesus leaving them—but that was nothing compared to what they were about to experience—the reality settling in on them in less than a few hours that Jesus would actually be killed. They would "weep and lament" over the death of their Master, the One for whom they had given up everything to follow, the One who inspired hope that the kingdom of God was finally arriving. Had they not, with the multitude, hailed Him as "the Son of David" a few days earlier as He triumphantly entered into Jerusalem on the ceremonial donkey?

What made matters worse was the thought that the people of Israel would be glad to be rid of Him. The vast crowds that followed Him turned their backs when He went beyond feeding and healing them to teach an all-out commitment to God and to self-sacrifice (John 6:66). The mob at His sentencing, with great hatred, would grant the customary pardon to Barabbas, the guilty criminal, rather than exempt the Holy One of Israel from an unjust execution. With gusto they cried out, "His blood shall be on us and on our children!" (Matt. 27:25).

Lament and grief have not been and will not be an uncommon experience for disciples of any age or time period. Suffering continues on. "And not only this, but also we ourselves, having the first fruits of the Spirit, even we ourselves groan within ourselves, waiting eagerly for *our* adoption as sons, the redemption of our body. For in hope we have been saved, but hope that is seen is not hope; for who hopes for what he *already* sees?" (Rom. 8:23-24).

But the resurrection of Christ renews hope and brings joy. "Weeping may last for the night, but a shout of joy *comes* in the morning" (Ps. 30:5). There is hope that any grieving we have here on earth will be turned into joy. Notice grief is not *replaced* by joy, but it is *transformed* into joy. There is something in the nature of suffering that brings a joy that would not be possible without the suffering. Someone has said, "If we never had problems, we would never know that God could solve them." Suffering provides an opportunity to see the greatness of God. This truth gives us hope that there is meaning in our suffering. But this only comes when we firmly embrace that our ultimate goal is to glorify Him, the beloved Son who is our Savior. For the believer, grief and sorrow are temporary. Our Lord is risen, and He will return to raise us up to be with Him forever. That is our hope and that is our joy. And that is our calling in this broken, fallen world, to give witness to a hope that brings true joy.

Lord, I trust in You in the midst of my struggles. Joy comes in the morning!

God's Glory in a Fallen World

John 16:21-22

²¹ "Whenever a woman is in labor she has pain, because her hour has come; but when she gives birth to the child, she no longer remembers the anguish because of the joy that a child has been born into the world. ²² Therefore you too have grief now; but I will see you again, and your heart will rejoice, and no one will take your joy away from you.

Being the master Teacher, Jesus likened the problem of grief over His soon departure to the pangs of childbirth experienced by an expectant mother. Yes, the teaching itself is amazing—and true. But the way Jesus taught them was equally amazing. He showed deep spiritual truths from everyday life situations that His audience (the disciples in the Upper Room and us today) can more readily understand. The analogy is meant to show us spiritual, abstract truths from earthly, tangible things. This method is quite effective, as anyone who reads Jesus' words will readily admit.

But the reason it is effective is because of the great truth that "the whole earth is full of His glory" (Isa. 6:3). The master Teacher is simply uncovering the glory of God in the normal things of life. As another example, marriage, a quite normal part of life, is unveiled as a reflection of God's glory in the relationship of Christ and the church (Eph. 5:22-27). The Spirit of God is telling us, in that elucidation of the spiritual from the physical, something deeply profound about not only Christ and the church, but also about marriage between one man and one woman.

Marriage thus has been identified particularly as a glimpse of God's glory. In this, many have concluded that marriage is therefore "sacred." However, all of life reveals the glory of God, so therefore all of life is likewise sacred, albeit we don't always recognize it as such. Childbirth is sacred in that sense, in that Jesus used that as a reflection on the spiritual reality that is common to followers of Christ who long for His return. Why is there so much pain in childbirth? To be sure, the curse on Eve (Gen. 3:16) explains this initially. But could it be that God intended the painful labor of childbearing to be a reminder to us image bearers that the pain of disconnectedness will someday be transformed into life and joy?

Yes, Jesus as the great Teacher brings together the physical experience of a woman's labor in giving birth and the disciples' "pain" of facing Jesus' physical withdrawal from them. The unity of spiritual truth with the physical realities all reflect the glory of God and His truth in this fallen world.

Lord, help me today to see Your glory in everything around me.

Joy That Cannot Be Taken

John 16:21-22 (cont.)

21 "Whenever a woman is in labor she has pain, because her hour has come; but when she gives birth to the child, she no longer remembers the anguish because of the joy that a child has been born into the world. 22 Therefore you too have grief now; but I will see you again, and your heart will rejoice, and no one will take your joy away from you.

Like the pains of labor leading up to childbirth, so the disciples should see the prospect of Jesus' leaving them as leading to something greater, which can be likened to the miracle of childbirth. Think of it for a moment—procreation is the actual creation of a new human being! From a simple reflection on the complexity of the human body, this is nothing short of completely and absolutely amazing. Billions of cells unite, each with incredibly complex DNA information stored in each nucleus. With one single breath of air, the newborn's lungs separate out the oxygen and send it coursing through the body, pushed along by the heart, through a vast system of arteries and capillaries, to every single cell in the body. One gulp of milk activates the digestive system and feeds nutrients to the entire body through the same blood system. The nervous system electrically controls the entire operation with multitudes of neurons connecting all movement with the command center, the brain.

Add to all this, in the newborn God has placed the propensity to learn, and thus the new human being has the capacity to grow, to learn and to make moral judgment. Each new human being contains within itself the image of God, the reflection of His glory. In all this, the birth of a child is amazing.

Science with all its PhDs, education and research, in its quest of robotics and artificial intelligence after years of experimentation and engineering, can't even come close to emulating the miracle of what takes place at childbirth. Human birth takes place without any education, research or training. In fact, two people without any education or even high IQs can make it happen! God must chuckle at man's trivial attempts to build new towers of Babel!

Basic to Christian disciples, as Jesus tells His disciples in the Upper Room, is that living by faith without the physical, tangible presence of God is like embracing the labors of childbirth because of what it is leading up to. There is joy and happiness in the end, and therefore we can live with that joy and happiness now—in anticipation. Jesus said, "I will see you again, and your heart will rejoice." No one, nothing can take this joy away from us. No suffering, no pain, no heartbreak—nothing.

Lord, when I doubt Your existence or grieve because of Your silence, I am reminded that You are coming back and I will then physically see You.

WEEKEND READING

Saturday – John 9:28-41
Sunday – Acts 17:1-15

PERSONAL REFLECTIONS

_____

_____

_____

_____

_____

_____

_____

_____

_____

_____

_____

_____

_____

_____

_____

_____

_____

_____

_____

_____

_____

Praying to Father or Son?

John 16:23

23 "In that day you will not question Me about anything. Truly, truly, I say to you, if you ask the Father for anything in My name, He will give it to you."

P rayer is a most enigmatic Christian discipline, but it ought not be so. If there is one thing the Scripture teaches it is this: God wants us to pray. He invites us to pray, and He leans in toward us to hear us pray. He is a communicating God, and that is a two-way street. He wants a conversation.

Too often we hear theologically poor statements like "Say your prayers" or "My prayers are with you." We "say grace" before our meals and then recite some words without thinking. Even evangelicals who criticize others for their repetitious, rote recitations of prayers fall into an almost hypnotic repetition of key words, like legalistically ending all prayers with "in Jesus name," as though it were some magical incantation. We change our tone and pace of talking with God. Some even use a special form of the English language, a sort of King James-ese, sprinkling prayers with many thee's and thou's to the God who "doe-th" and "see-eth" all things. Some are melodic in their prayer "chants." Some resort to a low, solemn voice, while others work up an emotional lather.

When Jesus spoke of prayer, He stripped away any mysterious, esoteric or religious baggage and spoke in down-to-earth terms. In our context today, He addresses how to approach God with our requests. This is probably the most fundamental aspect of prayer, from the human perspective. While prayer certainly can be the expression of praise and worship, at its most fundamental level, we start with ourselves. Whether that is right or not, it is true. And Jesus starts there as He continues to prepare His disciples for His departure.

The simple observation is that with Jesus leaving, where would the disciples go to get their questions about God and life answered? Where would they turn for help once Jesus left? The Lord now wants to reorient them to a direct line of communication with the Father Himself. He leaves them with the confidence of a personal audience with the Sovereign of the Universe. This is the God of Abraham, Isaac and Jacob. The God of Moses, who is the Lawgiver. He is the holy, holy, Holy One of Israel. And Jesus says His followers, in His physical absence, can bring their requests to God directly.

The question of whether to pray to Jesus or to the Father is answered in larger part by Jesus Himself. While it is not precisely wrong to pray to Jesus, particularly when worshipping or praising God, Jesus Himself said that when we have needs we pray to the Father and not the incarnate Son.

Lord, talking about prayer is easy, but actually conversing with You, whom I cannot see, requires my faith. "Lord, I believe; help my unbelief" (Mark 9:24).

Praying in Jesus' Best Interests

23 "In that day you will not question Me about anything. Truly, truly, I say to you, if you ask the Father for anything in My name, He will give it to you."

Whether "that day" refers to the post-resurrection appearances of Christ or to post-Pentecostal life in the Spirit, the impact is the same: the disciples of Christ will have unprecedented access to God the Father. And it is obvious that the life of discipleship continues to be one of learning and requesting. No room here for the self-proclaimed, self-sustaining individual. The Christian life is one of dependency on God, and the words of Christ are a great assurance that such dependency is well placed.

Up until now in the life and experience of the disciples, they had gone to Jesus as the Rabbi par excellence, the ultimate source of spiritual truth and understanding. Oh, would it not be nice today to simply find Jesus in the flesh and ask Him all our questions? Or ask His help for whatever we are dealing with? But no, Jesus says there is something better than going to Him with our questions and requests.

We are invited to God, to the Father, and to do it in Jesus' name! This is truly a profound truth. The Jews had to approach God with their needs by going through the Levitical ritual system, through a priest, using the prescribed and detailed protocol. Any violation was subject to strict punishment. But now Jesus teaches that we can go to God directly with only one protocol to follow, namely that we approach God in Jesus' name. Nothing elaborate or ritualistic about this.

Now what does it mean to ask in Jesus' name? Clearly it must be more than adding the rote addendum to our prayers, "In Jesus' name." Prayer is not just a matter of terminology or legalistic patterns. We go to the Father at Jesus' initiative. We say, "Father, I am coming because Jesus sent me to You. I am coming on Your Son's behalf." It is like, as the old illustration goes, walking into a bank with a check signed by Jesus. It is worth something, not because the bearer of the check is wealthy, but because the person whose name is signed on the check is wealthy.

To go to the Father in Jesus' name means we represent Jesus' interests; our concerns have to do with His purposes and ministry. We are His followers, so we ask relative to our involvement in His work. And the key here is that when we do so, the Father "will give it to" us. The only question that remains is, why we don't do this more often?

Lord, help me to align my requests to Your will, so that my prayers will line up with Your name.

Direct Access to the Father

John 16:24

24 "Until now you have asked for nothing in My name; ask and you will receive, so that your joy may be made full."

Upper Room teaching is not exhaustive, but it is profound. Jesus wasn't saying everything there is to say about prayer at that time, but He was laying down foundational principles that would carry the disciples into their post-physical-presence-of-Christ life. Until this point, the disciples had become used to the idea that Jesus was "the Christ, the Son of the living God" (Matt. 16:16). They were increasingly comfortable with taking all their questions about God to Him. In the Upper Room, questions continued to flow. In response, Jesus had increasingly taken them deeper in their understanding of the spiritual life that God requires.

Yes, they had asked Him many questions. But still He asserted, "Until now you have asked for nothing in My name." This must have left them in a quandary—where was Jesus going with this line of thought? To ask the Father in Jesus' name was a completely new idea, yet probably not a completely foreign concept. He was moving them one step closer to the Father, and did not their hearts burn within them? Their Master, whom they had left all to follow, was inviting them into direct access to God, the Father. Following Christ meant entrance into the presence of God.

We know from later Scripture that Christ is our mediator—our *only* mediator (1 Tim. 2:5)—and our intercessor in relationship to righteousness and judgment (Rom. 8:34). But in relationship to our prayer requests, we do not approach with Jesus as our intercessor or mediator, but we approach in His name. He is sending us on His behalf, with all the full benefits, privileges and prerogatives that He has as the Son. We know that the Spirit intercedes for us when we don't know how we ought to pray (Rom. 8:26-27); that intercession is not in place of our going directly to God, but it is a coming alongside of us as we approach the throne room of God. Likewise we don't pray to Jesus, who then takes our requests to the Father. Jesus sends us to the Father directly! Is that not amazing?! Is that not sobering?

Until then, the disciples, as with all of God's people, approached God through quite the involved ritual, but now we can go in the authority of Jesus, who is the holy One of whom God said, "This is My beloved Son, in whom I am well-pleased" (Matt. 3:16). When we approach God in Jesus' name, God is likewise well-pleased with us as His children (John 1:12).

Father, I come to you in Jesus' name. Teach me to pray more consistently and faithfully, to learn to commune with You daily.

Answered Prayer and Joy

John 16:24 (cont.)

24 "Until now you have asked for nothing in My name; ask and you will receive, so that your joy may be made full."

Promise of answered prayer was not new to the disciples. Neither was the promise of joy. As early as John the Baptist, joy was presented as something sourced in that which is outside of a person. John found great joy in the fact that "He must increase, and I must decrease," and illustrated this by comparing it to the friend of the bridegroom rejoicing for the bridegroom. The joy Jesus spoke of in the Upper Room was set over against the anguish and grief the disciples were anticipating; it was a joy that would reorient their lives, move their center point to a place outside of themselves, and center on Jesus.

Their loss and grief, which they anticipated in the loss of Jesus' presence with them, was centered on themselves, and therefore was self-centered. Yes, joy is something that is experienced personally, but there is a huge difference in the center, the ground (as philosophers might put it) of their joy. Jesus all along had been calling His followers to abandon themselves and a worldview that puts them at the center, and to replace it with Christ as the center. As Paul would later put it, "I have been crucified with Christ; and it is no longer I who live, but Christ lives in me; and the *life* which I now live in the flesh I live by faith in the Son of God, who loved me and gave Himself up for me" (Gal. 2:20). The disciples were not yet there, but Jesus was preparing them for it.

Thus, the joy Jesus spoke of was incomprehensible at the time of the Upper Room, but they would soon discover what He meant by it. This would be a joy like the peace that passes all understanding—in other words, far exceeding our wildest expectations. But it is a joy that can only be found in a life centered on Jesus Christ—that is what discipleship is all about. That is what asking the Father in Jesus' name is all about—asking with Christ at the center of our lives.

Our problem today is that we so easily satisfy ourselves with superficial joys that last only for a moment. Whooping it up over our sports team that wins a championship, discovering an inheritance from a distant relative, being rewarded at work with a promotion or a raise—all make life enjoyable, but they don't last very long, nor do they stand up when life becomes difficult. Forbes' annual list of the richest people in the world is littered with broken relationships, debilitating illness and ruined lives. Money and affluence aren't enough to bring a lasting joy. Every Christian must come to the question sooner or later, "Is Jesus enough? Is He my joy and my song?"

Lord, to use the words of the two inquirers in Jerusalem (John 12:21), "We wish to see Jesus," and to see Him and embrace Him in our daily lives.

God Our Father and Jesus the Son

John 16:25

25 "These things I have spoken to you in figurative language; an hour is coming when I will no longer speak to you in figurative language, but will tell you plainly of the Father."

Figurative language was a common educational technique for Jesus, the master Teacher. He was going beyond factual knowledge to truths that could not be adequately conveyed apart from context. And the context for fully understanding prayer would not come until after the resurrection of Jesus, which truth itself was yet beyond the disciples' comprehension.

Truth is not relative, but absolute; yet trust must be contextually understood. To know absolutely requires something or someone that is bigger than truth; that alone gives a context beyond which there is no greater context. Only then can we know truth absolutely. So Jesus, being God, the originator of all truth, understands perfectly and absolutely all truth.

But when Jesus spoke to His disciples, He modulated His message by using figurative language that His disciples could understand. This is not to say He "dumbed it down." Rather, He framed it in figurative ways to convey a truth that was beyond factual statements or philosophical propositions. He used parables (one of His favorite teaching techniques) at times to hide the truth from unbelievers but at the same time communicate to believers (Matt. 13:10-13). At other times He used parables to clearly communicate the truth in a straightforward manner (Matt. 21:45). He also used illustrations from everyday life, and frequently employed metaphors and similes, such as, "The kingdom of heaven is like . . ." There were times when He used euphemisms, substituting a less offensive word for another, as when He referred to Lazarus as "sleeping" (John 11:11). But then He almost immediately clarified that statement straightforwardly when He added, "Lazarus is dead" (John 11:14).

In the Upper Room, Jesus chose to speak figuratively about prayer. We Christians are so used to speaking of God as Father and Son, we fail to realize that Jesus used very human conventions for picturing to us how to communicate with God. We dare not substitute other imagery, like thinking of God as mother, for example. God is predominantly pictured for us as a Father. Jesus used divine figurative language that God clearly intends us to use. Paul reinforced this when he wrote, "God has sent forth the Spirit of His Son into our hearts, crying, 'Abba! Father!'" (Gal. 4:6). We are not at liberty to change the way God has communicated to us about Himself. And we will understand this better in the context of our growing faith.

Father, I praise You that You are my heavenly Father.

WEEKEND READING

Saturday – John 10:1-21
Sunday – Acts 17:16-34

PERSONAL REFLECTIONS

God's Circle of Love

John 16:26-27

26 "In that day you will ask in My name, and I do not say to you that I will request of the Father on your behalf; 27 for the Father Himself loves you, because you have loved Me and have believed that I came forth from the Father.

Hard to take, but maybe it is beginning to dawn on them—Jesus would no longer "pass on their requests" to God. The disciples had become used to the idea that Jesus had a special relationship with God, and that their access to the Father had something to do with Jesus. But with Jesus leaving them, He says they will now have direct access to God. And it's not a matter of Jesus conveying their concerns to the Father—that will not be necessary. It is not that Jesus doesn't want to intercede for them, or that they can never talk with Him again (for as we have shown before there is a legitimate place for praying to Jesus). It is just that they also have direct access to the Father now, just like Jesus has direct access.

There are many in the world who believe that Christians need to go through various intermediaries, like saints, or even the earthly mother of our Lord, Mary (calling her a mediatrix). The idea is that supposedly such holy individuals would be more likely heard by the heavenly Father than the rest of us average human beings. Some even feel that if Mary makes requests for us, the Lord would never deny His own mother. Such thinking is nonsense and besides having no basis at all in Scripture, completely dismisses the wonderful teaching of our Lord in the Upper Room. Followers of Christ have a direct love relationship with the Father. He loves us and doesn't need anyone else to intercede for us; He will hear us directly. We have a personal, instantaneous, ever-available audience with God.

In human relationships, when two people love each other, they do not require an intermediary to express their intimacies to each other. It may be that a girl in grade school might be embarrassed to express her affections to a boy and so she asks a friend to convey a "love" message for her. That is at best sophomore-ish. As followers of Christ, we can express our love to Him directly. To use a mediator would be an insult to our relationship with Him.

This doesn't mean that Jesus is sidelined as though His role was simply to introduce us to the Father. Rather, it is that we have been brought into the same relationship of love with the Father that Jesus has with Him. The Father loves us because we have loved the Son. And since the Son comes from the Father, we therefore love the Father and He loves us. We have entered the community of love within the Trinity. What a blessed place to be!

Father and Son, I am absolutely privileged to be part of Your circle of love.

Contradiction in Scripture?

John 16:27 (cont.)

27 ". . . for the Father Himself loves you, because you have loved Me and have believed that I came forth from the Father."

An interpretive issue arises in this verse that must not be left unaddressed. Is God's love for us contingent upon our love for Him, as first reading of this verse seems to indicate? What about 1 John 4:19, "We love, because He first loved us"? And did God not "[demonstrate] His own love toward us, in that while we were yet sinners, Christ died for us" (Rom. 5:8)? Some worry over the skeptic's charge that Christians resort to interpretive sleight of hand in order to "explain away" such apparent contradictions. However, there is no need to worry.

First, we believe in the existence of God and that all of Scripture is inspired by Him. Therefore, believing in the non-contradictory nature of God, we believe that what He inspires cannot be contradictory (Heb. 6:18; Rom. 3:4; 1 Tim. 3:16). Does this faith trump "obvious" logical contradictions in the Bible? No, that is not the case. In fact, one can say that the non-believer's faith in the non-existence of God, or the possibility that God can contradict Himself, can trump the clear resolutions of those "contradictions." So both believers and unbelievers begin with faith. We Christians have settled this issue already.

Second, a careful study of John 16:27 shows no contradiction with 1 John 4:19 or Romans 5:8, when we consider the original language in which these passages were written. The English word "love" translates various words in the original Greek. In 1 John 4:19, it is written, "We love (Greek: *agape*) because God first loved (*agape*) us." The same word is used in Romans 5:8. The word *agape* refers to a sacrificial, unilateral love that is based not in any worthiness of the recipient, but solely in the giver of the love. It is this love that originates with God, and which breeds a responsive love in us.

But in our verse today, John 16:28, the word translated "love" is the Greek word *phileo*. This is a brotherly kind of love, a reciprocal sort of fellowship. It is this kind of love that God is looking for us to initiate, and to which He then responds. Jesus in the Upper Room means that when a person responds with *phileo* love to the *agape* love of Christ, God then responds with a *phileo* kind of love to us. And that is the enjoyment of the fellowship in community that the Father and Son enjoy together, and which we can now enjoy.

Yes, we do contribute to the relationship with God, in a reciprocal way. He loves us, we love Him, we love each other. What a fellowship.

Lord, thank You for inviting me into the love relationship with You and Your Son. I want to do my part in loving and having fellowship with You.

The Essential Incarnation

John 16:27 (cont.)

27 ". . . for the Father Himself loves you, because you have loved Me and have believed that I came forth from the Father."

"**B**elief that Jesus came from God" is absolutely essential for a right relationship with God. True Christianity does *not* teach that Jesus the man became God, something which is impossible and the teaching of which would rightly be called blasphemy. Rather, the Son, who is God, became a Man, Jesus. There is a huge difference between these two statements. While it is impossible for man to be God, it is entirely within the realm of God's ability to become human, and to exist with both the full qualities of Godhood and humanity at the same time in the same existence.

One cannot be a follower of Christ and fully experience the love of God without believing that Jesus came from God, and is, in fact, God in the flesh. John expands on Jesus' comment when he wrote about 50 years later, "Whoever denies the Son does not have the Father; the one who confesses the Son has the Father also" (1 John 2:23). Further, he wrote, "By this you know the Spirit of God: every spirit that confesses that Jesus Christ has come in the flesh is from God; and every spirit that does not confess Jesus is not from God; this is the *spirit* of the antichrist, of which you have heard that it is coming, and now it is already in the world" (1 John 4:2-3). In his second letter, John adds, "Grace, mercy and peace will be with us, from God the Father and from Jesus Christ the Son of the Father, in truth and love" (2 John 3).

True faith involves believing that Jesus came from God, that He is God in the flesh, and that His relationship with the Father is as a Son who has been commissioned by His Father to come into the world. He is certainly a Prophet, but not only a mere prophet. His origin is not from among humans, but from God. He is the cosmic and eternal entry point of the Creator into His creation, the Uncreated One taking on the form of His creation. Jesus Christ is the Reality merging with the reflection of reality. The One in whose image we were created, taking on that image in human form.

Paul affirms this when writing to the Colossians: "For it was the Father's good pleasure for all the fullness to dwell in Him [i.e. Christ]" (1:19) and "For in Him all the fullness of Deity dwells in bodily form" (2:9). And because Jesus came from God as a human, therefore, following Christ and believing in Him means ". . . you have been made complete . . ." (Col. 2:10a). We are completely accepted, for we have fully believed in who Jesus is and what He came to do.

Lord, I believe that Jesus is fully God and fully human. And in this faith, I know I am completely accepted and loved by You.

Submission of God?

John 16:28

28 "I came forth from the Father and have come into the world; I am leaving the world again and going to the Father."

Relationship between the three persons of the triune God—that's an issue that taxes the best intellects. Contrary to Muslim thinking (as well as that of all cults that deny the deity of Christ), the Trinity is not a contradiction of terms, as we have pointed out before in this study of the Upper Room. But what does it mean that the Son came from the Father?

If the Son comes from the Father, then the Father sent the Son, and thus there is a subservient element in the relationship. How then can the Son be fully God? The answer, in its simplest form, is that submission does not negate equality, if we understand the submission to be voluntary and not coerced. The Son fully submits to the Father's desires: "Not my will, but Yours be done" (Luke 22:42). As the incarnate God-man, "[a]lthough He was a Son, He learned obedience from the things which He suffered" (Heb. 5:8). According to this verse, the obedience is not inherent in Sonship (the God-aspect of incarnation) but in being human (the man-aspect of incarnation). In taking on human form (Phil. 2:7-8), He "became obedient to death, even the death on the cross."

This accords with 1 Corinthians 11:3, where we read, "God is the head of Christ." The word "head" (Greek: *kephale*) speaks of authority, as in a general being the head of an army. In recent times, contrary to all lexical definitions and etymological studies, there has been an effort to assert that the word *kephale* does not imply authority but rather can take on the meaning of "source." The main argument against that view point is the lack of clear use in ancient Greek of the word ever meaning "source" compared to an abundance of instances where it is used with the sense "head." Plus, no reputable lexicon of the Greek language identifies "source" as a possible meaning. One wonders whether the drive for egalitarianism of the sexes clouds some interpreters' views of 1 Corinthians 11:3, as well as other passages that indicate the husband is the head of the wife (e.g. Eph. 5:23). In trying to strip the authority relationship in the marriage, they must also strip the authority arrangements in the Godhead. But this flies against Scripture.

Authority in relationship, when entered voluntarily, does not negate equality or dignity within the relationship but speaks to functional differences. Just as we functionally pray to the Father in Jesus' name, the Son was sent from the Father. The two teachings are intertwined.

Lord, thank You for the perfect picture of equality in relationship and differentiation in roles.

Absolute Truth and Faith

John 16:29-31

²⁹ His disciples said, "Lo, now You are speaking plainly and are not using a figure of speech. ³⁰ Now we know that You know all things, and have no need for anyone to question You; by this we believe that You came from God." ³¹ Jesus answered them, "Do you now believe?"

A subtle humor sneaks out in this passage. John must have chuckled to himself as he quoted his and the other disciples' words—"We now know . . . we believe . . ." Even Jesus questioned whether they had really gotten the point yet: "Do you now believe?" Really? But at the time, there was probably a genuine dawning of understanding, even though its fullness would not become apparent to them until after the resurrection, some three days away. But a lot had to happen before then, namely the crucifixion!

Yet John, among all the disciples, had a propensity toward faith, even when He didn't fully understand. Peter was more interested in being loyal to Christ, Thomas was more interested in questioning Christ, and the other disciples all had their individual propensities. John records that at the tomb the following Sunday morning, when he and Peter bolted there at the weakest of testimonies that His body was gone, while Peter went in to examine the evidence, John remained outside the tomb and "believed" (John 20:8). Maybe he had secretly, all through the dark three days, had a quiet belief that somehow things were going to work out right, though with no concept of how.

At the same time, it is possible that all the disciples believed, though not as much as they would have liked to think. After all, this is the clearest teaching from Christ about His origins, His deity and His relationship with the Father. If in fact, as they are believing, Jesus was from God, then it follows that He must "know all things." His word is final and not to be questioned as though the truth of His teaching was subject to rabbinical review. At the minimum, the disciples in the Upper Room were stating their faith in His teachings as absolute truth, even if they didn't fully understand all that He said.

Is this not the kind of faith that God requires? "Trust in the LORD with all your heart and do not lean on your own understanding. In all your ways acknowledge Him, and He will make your paths straight" (Prov. 3:5-6). David had that kind of faith when he wrote, "Your word I have treasured in my heart . . ." (Ps. 119:11). Abraham was likewise a man of faith: when God took him outside and compared his promised descendants to the number of stars in the sky, "Then he believed in the Lord; and He reckoned it to him as righteousness" (Gen. 15:6). God is looking for people to simply believe what He says.

Lord, help me to have the simple faith to believe Your Word as absolute truth.

WEEKEND READING

Saturday – John 10:22-42
Sunday – Acts 18:1-17

PERSONAL REFLECTIONS

Companionship of the Conflicted

John 16:32

32 "Behold, an hour is coming, and has already come, for you to be scattered, each to his own home, and to leave Me alone; and yet I am not alone, because the Father is with Me.

The hour Jesus spoke of in John 4:23 when "true worshipers will worship the Father in spirit and truth" has arrived. Yet it begins with persecution: "They will make you outcasts from the synagogue, but an hour is coming for everyone who kills you to think that he is offering service to God" (John 16:2). And now we see in today's passage that the hour in question will also include the scattering of Jesus' disciples, abandoning Him in His time of need. And finally, this hour will include the earthly aloneness of the Savior.

Ironically, earlier in the Upper Room Jesus spoke of His leaving the disciples, yet here He speaks of the disciples abandoning Him. Only with the hindsight of their post-Pentecostal spiritual awakening would they fully understand the impact of Jesus' words. By then, they will have returned to the Savior, but with the indwelling Spirit who began to teach and clarify to them everything Jesus had taught them. Can you hear an echo of the Upper Room in Peter's encouragement to the persecuted believers scattered around the eastern Mediterranean? "For you were continually straying like sheep, but now you have returned to the Shepherd and Guardian of your souls" (1 Peter 2:25).

One of the significant aspects of Jesus' suffering was being abandoned by His closest followers. Judas betrayed Him, Peter would soon deny Him, and they would all fall asleep during His greatest temptation. He would go through His penultimate suffering and His ultimate work by Himself. The disciples were not able to provide for Jesus in any way during the final hours of His passion.

Yet He provided an example for them and all believers afterward, that even in suffering He was not alone, though everyone would abandon Him. He was not alone because "the Father is with Me." Peter got it. And he instructed others just as he had learned for himself: "For you have been called for this purpose, since Christ also suffered for you, leaving you an example for you to follow in His steps . . ." (1 Peter 2:21). As followers of Christ, there will be times when we are alone, with no human companionship to help us through our times of trouble. But we are not truly alone; the Father is with us, even in the darkest times. And rather than blame other Christians for letting us down, we are blessed to follow in the footsteps of Him who, "being reviled, He did not revile in return . . . but kept entrusting *Himself* to Him who judges righteously" (1 Peter 2:23).

Lord, help me to see You in the midst of my trials, for You are always with me.

Expecting Tribulation

John 16:33

[33] "These things I have spoken to you, so that in Me you may have peace. In the world you have tribulation, but take courage; I have overcome the world."

That Christians will suffer in this world is abundantly asserted in the New Testament. Jesus here says it unequivocally—"In the world you have tribulation . . ."—using the present tense, which here carries a sense of enduring experience. This was a very trying time for the disciples, the atmosphere foreboding. Jesus' talk of His departure caused them extreme consternation and grief. He had previously told them that because of Him, they would be hated and persecuted by the world (John 15:18, 20).

Paul speaks to this as well, when he addresses his disciple Timothy: "Indeed, all who desire to live godly in Christ Jesus will be persecuted" (2 Tim. 3:12). Suffering, persecution and trials of all sorts are a by-product of being a follower of Christ. Jesus was not spared from it. Paul was not spared from it. None of us will be spared.

Living in a fallen world is part of the reason for suffering. Being part of the family of God, being a saved, regenerate believer, does not exempt us from the effects of a fallen world. "Bad stuff" happens. Car accidents, trees falling and earthquakes affect believer and non-believer alike. Sickness and dying come to Christian and non-Christian alike. Sometimes "bad stuff" happens as a result of our sin and even our own stupidity, and we have to live with the consequences. Some of our trials are of our own doing.

There are also trials that are a direct result of other people being evil and acting in unjust ways. Peter took this Upper Room teaching to heart when he wrote to the persecuted Christians that when they faced difficulties because of their faith, ". . . this *finds* favor, if for the sake of conscience toward God a person bears up under sorrows when suffering unjustly. For what credit is there if, when you sin and are harshly treated, you endure it with patience? But if when you do what is right and suffer *for it* you patiently endure it, this *finds* favor with God" (1 Peter 2:19-20). We Christians are called to acknowledge, yes, even to embrace hardships as part of our God-given calling, an opportunity for growing in faith.

We must never give in to an obsession with the comforts of life, tying them to our faithfulness to God. We must not emotionally flagellate ourselves when bad stuff happens as though we and we only are the cause of all difficulties in our lives. Such is a self-centered view of life. We will have tribulation. The question is, what we *will* do with that? The first thing: accept it.

Lord, help me to accept the trials in my life and not wallow, "Why me?"

Christic Overcomes

John 16:33 (cont.)

[33] *"These things I have spoken to you, so that in Me you may have peace. In the world you have tribulation, but take courage; I have overcome the world."*

One might be hard-pressed to take Jesus seriously, in context of all that was happening: "I have overcome the world." Right. From outward appearances, Jesus was huddled with His disciples in an Upper Room, speaking of His departure which, if the disciples hadn't figured out by now, would come about by dying.

However, the disciples had witnessed great things where Jesus gave a foretaste of that "overcoming." He routinely mastered the religious leaders with His responses and retorts to the many traps they laid for Him—with the Pharisees, Sadducees and scribes routinely exiting in what came to be their signature slinking-away move.

Jesus commanded the winds and waters, and they obeyed Him as their Master. He had command over every kind of sickness and disability, the only exception being where there was a concerted lack of faith. Demons trembled in His presence, calling Him the "Son of the Most High God."

Why leave, now that He has "overcome the world," at the pinnacle of His mission? The answer is that though He had demonstrated mastery over the world, He had yet to finally overcome death and Satan. It may be true that Jesus was speaking with a prophetic sense of completeness—at the cross and resurrection, He would finally overcome the world. And it is true that Satan was as good as defeated. But we believe that the term "world" does not include death (which is the exit from this world), which would be "swallowed up in victory" (1 Cor. 15:54). Neither does it include Satan, who is "now the ruler of this world" and who "will be cast out" (John 12:31). These are yet to come.

Christ's life on the earth was continually validating Him as the Sovereign of all that lives. He is Master over a broken world, He is Lord over sinners and He is the promised victory over the seed of the Serpent (Gen. 3:15). From our perspective, on the one hand, we can see all this clearly, for God's written revelation is now complete. On the other hand, the disciples had not yet come into the full knowledge of these things. They simply had the word of Jesus, "I have overcome the world."

Today, we can struggle with this concept, though, in view of the decaying morality of our present world and the suffering many experience. His "overcoming" the world must still be taken by faith. The victory is His, even when, from outward appearances, things look dire and out of control.

Lord, help me live knowing that You are in fact, in control!

Christ is Peace

John 16:33 (cont.)

33 "These things I have spoken to you, so that in Me you may have peace. In the world you have tribulation, but take courage; I have overcome the world."

Peace in Christ derives from the most relevant truth for our day: Christ *is* peace. The young unbeliever adamantly opposed to the existence of God asserts, "How can there possibly be a God, a good God, when there is so much hatred, murder, abuse and war in the world?" Indeed, his premise is right on target, but his conclusion misses the mark.

To support the premise, one need not look far in Scripture, for no later than the third chapter (out of 1,189 chapters in the Bible) conflict arises in the Garden, with guilt and interpersonal tension between Adam and Eve over a piece of fruit. To be sure, the causative issue was much greater than the fruit, which is emblematic of all conflict—the presenting problem is usually not the real issue.

The next chapter brings the first murder, Cain's aggression toward Abel. The rest, as they say, is history. Civilizations rise and civilizations fall—all with violence and bloodshed. The Roman Empire, as an example, has left behind a multitude of monuments dedicated to conquests of various military "heroes" carved in marble to testify proudly of victories over the vanquished enemies.

Caesar Augustus, the first emperor of Rome, reigned from 27 BC to AD 14. He himself was not primarily a military man but was supported by Marcus Agrippa, one of the greatest Roman generals. The longest-reigning emperor (41 years), he died at age 75 under somewhat suspicious circumstances (many believe he was fed a poisoned fig by his wife). His famous last words reportedly were, "Have I played the part well? Then applaud as I exit." The month of August in our calendars was named after him. Yet while he unified and solidified Rome's hold on ancient Europe and the Mediterranean, his history is splattered with bloodshed.

There was Pax Romana (Roman Peace), historians tell us, but it was a peace that required an iron fist and a huge army. Augustus was not the Prince of Peace. For despite his accomplishments, his efforts could not bring inner peace either to himself or anyone else. His own family was fraught with difficulty, multiple marriages, his beloved daughter Julia's promiscuous lifestyle and his own pride and need for approval.

Inner peace can only come from Christ, whose birth was announced by angels, "[O]n earth peace, goodwill toward men!" (NKJV). For He is peace.

Lord, I bring my anxious thoughts to You because You promised that the peace of God will guard my heart and mind through Christ Jesus (Phil. 4:6-7).

Take Courage

John 16:33 (cont.)

[33] *"These things I have spoken to you, so that in Me you may have peace. In the world you have tribulation, but take courage; I have overcome the world."*

Seven times in the New Testament this word for courage is used, and always in the imperative, a command—and always spoken by Jesus to His disciples. Peace provides the foundation for courage. We have the ability to be courageous because we are no longer distracted by the inner conflicts that so easily neutralize any spiritual power we might otherwise have.

The word courage means "to be firm or resolute in the face of danger or adverse circumstances, be enheartened, be courageous." The world is a dangerous place, with all kinds of hazards for the Christ follower, being mocked and marginalized because of Christ-like moral behavior. In a few hours the disciples would watch the arrest of their Master and mourn His death.

To be sure, they subsequently saw multitudes baptized on the Day of Pentecost, but the history of the Christian movement is one littered with the martyrdom, suffering and deprivation of millions. Men and women through the centuries have had the courage to witness of Christ despite the prospect of hardships, and even die with the peace of God in their hearts. It is a peace that passes understanding (Phil. 4:7). It is a peace that engenders courage.

And we need this kind of courage. We need courage for evangelism: "For God has not given us a spirit of timidity, but of power and love and discipline. Therefore do not be ashamed of the testimony of our Lord or of me His prisoner, but join with *me* in suffering for the gospel according to the power of God" (2 Tim. 1:7-8). We need courage when facing all kinds of difficulty: "Therefore I am well content with weaknesses, with insults, with distresses, with persecutions, with difficulties, for Christ's sake; for when I am weak, then I am strong" (2 Cor. 12:10). We need courage when facing persecution for our faith: "But even if you should suffer for the sake of righteousness, *you are* blessed. And do not fear their intimidation, and do not be troubled, but sanctify Christ as Lord in your hearts, always *being* ready to make a defense to everyone who asks you to give an account for the hope that is in you, yet with gentleness and reverence" (1 Peter 3:14-15).

We follow a Master who has overcome the world in the truest sense. Because of this we can have peace and be courageous, one of the great and magnificent promises Peter wrote about some 30 years later (2 Peter 1:4).

Lord, thank You for giving me Your peace. I resolve to be more courageous because You have overcome the world.

WEEKEND READING

Saturday – John 11:1-16
Sunday – Acts 18:18-28

PERSONAL REFLECTIONS

High Priestly
Prayer

High Priestly Prayer

¹ Jesus spoke these things; and lifting up His eyes to heaven, He said, "Father, the hour has come; glorify Your Son, that the Son may glorify You . . ."

John 17 is forever titled "Jesus' High Priestly Prayer." Some have called it "the Lord's Prayer," as opposed to "the Disciples' Prayer" (Matt. 6:9-13; Luke 11:2-4). It is the most intimate communication recorded in Scripture of the conversation the Son had with the Father. Though we only hear Jesus' words, we sense from these 26 verses an intimacy that is unparalleled in all of literature. God pulls back the curtain of heaven and invites us to listen as Jesus pours out His requests and petitions.

On the one hand, we might study this chapter as a means to learning how to pray better, by imitating Christ (1 Cor. 11:1). Or we could study it to understand our theology better, particularly the Trinity and the relationship between the Father and Son. Finally, we might study with a view to knowing the heart of Christ—what concerned Him at the deepest level. We shall touch on all these as we progress through this preeminent prayer of the Bible.

Little did the disciples know when they had previously asked, "Lord, teach us to pray," that the lesson was not a static "one time only" deal, but that prayer was a way of life. They had heard Jesus pray on a number of occasions, for example when He thanked the Father for food (John 6:11) and when He addressed God at Lazarus' tomb (John 11:41-42). And He would soon be praying in the Garden of Gethsemane during His final temptation, and finally on the cross where He would pray, "My God, my God, why have You forsaken Me?" and "Father, forgive them; for they do not know what they are doing" and "Into Your hands I commit My spirit."

This Upper Room prayer, as with all His prayers, was perfect, for it was given by the perfect human. No second guessing, no doubts. Confidence bred from familiarity and intimacy and love. And His timing was impeccable (of course). The time for teaching was over; the only thing left was to pray and sing a hymn (Matt. 26:30)—and then the Passover meal would be finished. John, the inspired writer, is the only one to record this prayer, and it must have resonated in His life for the 50-plus years between hearing it and putting it to pen. It was one of the things "we have heard . . . we have seen with our eyes" (1 John 1:1). He was so transformed, he was infused with a driving passion to tell others about "the life [that] was manifested, and we have seen and testify and proclaim to you the eternal life, which was with the Father and was manifested to us" (1 John 1:2).

Lord, thank You for the privilege of hearing Your Son's prayer to You.

The Mind and Heart of Christ

John 17:1 (cont.)

¹ Jesus spoke these things; and lifting up His eyes to heaven, He said, "Father, the hour has come; glorify Your Son, that the Son may glorify You . . ."

"The hour" had finally come for the full revelation of who Jesus really was. From the time of the first miracle, when His earthly mother brought to Him the problem of wine run out at the Canaan wedding, Jesus asserted to His earthly mother, "My hour has not yet come" (John 2:4). When His earthly brothers challenged Him to go to Judea and "show [Him]self to the world" (John 7:4), He responded, "My time has not yet come." When the mob in the temple reacted to His teaching and tried to seize Him, "no man laid his hand on Him, because His hour had not yet come" (John 7:30; 8:20).

In John's rendition of the Upper Room discourse, he records the beginning with these words: "Jesus knowing that His hour had come that He would depart out of this world to the Father, having loved His own who were in the world, He loved them to the end" (John 13:1). And now as their last meal together comes to a close, Jesus prays, ". . . the hour has come." This is it. The die is cast. The complete story of Jesus' life on earth is coming to a conclusion—which is really the beginning of the grand story that His departure is about to launch.

As often has happened in John's writing, the details of a loving observer are evident in his record of Jesus lifting His eyes to heaven. This is an intimate account, and we are invited into the room with our imaginations to listen as Jesus prays. Many times before the disciples heard Jesus pray, but this time so profoundly impacted John that it occupies a large place in his record of Christ's final earthly fellowship with them.

The prayer covers rich ground, beginning with requests for Himself and glory (vss. 1-5). Then He prays for His disciples, setting the bar high in what He wants for them (vss. 6-19). Finally, Jesus intercedes "for those also who believe in Me through their word" (vss. 20-26). These are the things that occupy the Savior's mind and heart, about which He communes with His Father, in the hours before He dies. Volumes have been written on this chapter of Scripture alone, and still the depths have not been fully plumbed. Here, like nowhere else in Scripture, we see the mind of Christ—and we do well to slow down our contemplation in order for it to more fully soak in. If it is true what Paul says, "We have the mind of Christ" (1 Cor. 2:16), then in this prayer we can meditate on that mind.

Father, as I enter into this holy place of meditating on Jesus' prayer, help me learn His mind and heart so that I might think and pray like Him.

The Mind and Heart of Christ

John 17:1 (cont.)

¹ Jesus spoke these things; and lifting up His eyes to heaven, He said, "Father, the hour has come; glorify Your Son, that the Son may glorify You . . ."

With the awaited time arriving, Jesus began with "Father," the same as He taught His disciples to pray (Luke 11:1). Simple, intimate, familial and evocative. No mention of "Abba," as He would soon address God in Mark 14:36 when asking that the Father "remove this cup from Me, yet not what I will but Your will." The tone here is different, not pleading, nor wrestling. In this magnificent prayer, the unity of purpose unfolds, Jesus and the Father on the same page. The time to consummate that purpose has arrived.

It matters not whether Jesus takes the initiative or whether He is simply expressing agreement with the Father's initiative; the unity is beautiful. However we understand His struggle with God's will in the Garden of Gethsemane, we see here a perfect unity of wills. Both the Father and Son desire the glory of the Son and the glory of the Father. There is no reserve or deference implied in the least, only utmost confidence. It is almost as though Jesus is giving the "go-ahead."

Lest this seem perfunctory or self-serving, we must remember that this glory involves a great deal of suffering. How can that be? Where is the glory in that? To glorify someone means "to influence one's opinion about another so as to enhance the latter's reputation." Jesus prayed that the Father would enhance His (Jesus') reputation. The time had come for the world to see Jesus for who He really was. For the Jews, the Messiah; for everyone, the Savior of the world, the One who through His suffering and sacrifice on the cross would bring victory over the curse that was laid down in the Garden of Eden. He was the new High Priest who provides redemption, "whom God displayed publicly as a propitiation in His blood through faith . . ." (Rom. 3:25). He was the One "who was declared the Son of God with power by the resurrection from the dead, according to the Spirit of holiness, Jesus Christ our Lord" (Rom. 1:4).

That is what Jesus prayed for when He asked to be glorified. Pull back the curtains so that all may see who He really was and is. And for this to happen, the Son needed to be tried and tested, and be found holy and perfect. Paul wrote of Jesus setting aside His outward manifestation as God for a time when He humbled Himself to became human, but then be exalted as "Lord, to the glory of God the Father" (Phil. 2:11). Ultimately, His desire for glory had an even greater purpose: to glorify His Father.

Lord, I exalt You and glorify You, both Father and Son, for You are worthy of all praise and adoration. Let others see how great You are through me.

Request for Glory

John 17:1 (cont.)

¹ Jesus spoke these things; and lifting up His eyes to heaven, He said, "Father, the hour has come; glorify Your Son, that the Son may glorify You . . ."

Requesting glory for Himself, Jesus is the only person in the universe who escapes moral guilt for doing so. Such "self-centeredness" in a mere human would be outrageous when spoken in such a bold manner: "Glorify me." Although Jesus, as He often does, refers to Himself in the third person, there is no question to whom "the Son" refers. If Jesus wasn't God, then such a request would be tantamount to blasphemy, the same as saying, "Let me occupy the center of the universe."

Satan had that objective, as Isaiah cryptically wrote: "But you said in your heart, 'I will ascend to heaven; I will raise my throne above the stars of God, and I will sit on the mount of assembly in the recesses of the north. I will ascend above the heights of the clouds; I will make myself like the Most High.' Nevertheless you will be thrust down to Sheol, to the recesses of the pit" (Isa. 14:13-15). Eve and Adam were so tempted in the Garden of Eden by that same evil thought: "For God knows that in the day you eat from it your eyes will be opened, and you will be like God, knowing good and evil" (Gen. 3:5). The desire to be like God, even to replace God, is the heart of sin, the creature taking the place of the Creator.

The irony drips over because humans are made in God's image, so there was no need to strive to "be like God," for they already were like Him, as much so as any creation can possibly be. "God created man in His own image, in the image of God He created him; male and female He created them" (Gen. 1:27). But in their sin, humans "exchanged the glory of the incorruptible God for an image in the form of corruptible man and of birds and four-footed animals and crawling creatures" (Rom. 1:23). What man can't have, man corrupts.

Yet here is Jesus asking for that very glory that man aspires to, that man corrupts. In that desiring, man reveals a sinful heart to supplant God. If Jesus were just a man, then He would have been completely off center and blasphemous to make such a request. But He was not just a man, a creature. He was the Son of God, who, "although He existed in the form of God, did not regard equality with God a thing to be grasped, but emptied Himself, taking the form of a bond-servant, *and being made in the likeness of men*" (Phil. 2:6-7). Jesus was not a man trying to become God and grasp the glory that was not His. No, He was God the Son, who set aside His glory and became man, now requesting His glory back. His purpose in being incarnated was now coming to completion.

Lord, show me Your glory that I might worship You in truth and spirit.

The Mind and Heart of Christ

John 17:1 (cont.)

¹ Jesus spoke these things; and lifting up His eyes to heaven, He said, "Father, the hour has come; glorify Your Son, that the Son may glorify You . . ."

"High Priestly Prayer" is the title often given to this chapter. The high priest in the Jewish religion was the one who represented the people to God, interceding on their behalf—which is what we indeed find Jesus doing in this Upper Room prayer. But His priesthood is different from that of the Jews. The book of Hebrews makes the comparison, eternally favorable in its description of Christ. Of particular relevance there is the connection between Jesus' Sonship and His priesthood: "Christ did not glorify Himself so as to become a high priest, but [God] said to Him, 'You are My Son, today I have begotten You;' just as He says also in another *passage*, 'You are a priest forever according to the order of Melchizedek'" (Heb. 5:5-6). Notice in Jesus' prayer, He refers to Himself as "Your Son." His goal was not ultimately His own glory, but the glory of the Father.

In order to bring glory to the Father, the Son must be glorified Himself, so that the world might know that He is the Messiah, the Savior of the world. "Jesus . . . because He continues forever, holds His priesthood permanently. Therefore He is able also to save forever those who draw near to God through Him, since He always lives to make intercession for them" (Heb. 7:24-25).

So we find Jesus asking for glory on two counts. First, He is God in the flesh, who is now reclaiming that which is rightfully His. Secondly, this glorification of Himself is necessary in order for the Father to be glorified. This is all in accord with God's purposes in Christ: "For this reason also, God highly exalted Him, and bestowed on Him the name which is above every name, so that at the name of Jesus every knee will bow, of those who are in heaven and on earth and under the earth, and that every tongue will confess that Jesus Christ is Lord, to the glory of God the Father" (Phil. 2:9-11).

Yes, Jesus is the only person who can legitimately and rightly ask God to "glorify Me." Athletes may seek that in their trophies, celebrities today in their marquees and Oscars, military heroes in medals on their chests. Jesus sought glory through His death. Essentially, in the introduction to His prayer, He says, "Bring it on"—the very act, the ultimate statement of who He really is—and bring it on in such a way that there will be no mistake that He loves the Father and that He loves the world. His substitutionary sacrifice on the cross is the only hope we creaturely humans have for recovering from our self-centered desire to usurp God's glory.

Father, I worship You because of Your glory revealed in the death of Jesus.

WEEKEND READING

Saturday – John 11:17-29
Sunday – Acts 19:1-20

PERSONAL
REFLECTIONS

Sovereign Authority

John 17:2

2 ". . . even as You gave Him authority over all flesh, that to all whom You have given Him, He may give eternal life."

The request now for glory, which begins Jesus' Upper Room prayer, does not arise out of a vacuum or a whim. He couches this request in the existing relationship He has with the Father. Just as the Father has already given Him authority "over all flesh," so also, in like manner, the Son is asking for glory. In other words, if the Father has already given Him authority, then asking for glory is commensurate with the authority He already has. In a few simple words, much depth is revealed.

First, "authority over all flesh." We know from Jesus' previous teaching that "The Father loves the Son and has given all things into His hand" (John 3:35). And we have seen His authority over the "winds and sea" (Matt. 8:27), the demons (Mark 5:7) and diseases of every kind (Matt. 10:1). This authority is the Father's endowment to His Son. A spiritual analogy will help us understand this. God "has granted to us everything pertaining to life and godliness, through the true knowledge of Him who called us by His own glory and excellence" (2 Peter 1:3). God has equipped Christians to live the life He desires for us, by giving us what we need to succeed at that. In the same way, the Father has granted to the Son all authority over flesh, so that He would succeed in doing all the Father had designed for the Son to do. In order for Jesus to do the glorious work He needed authority over all flesh.

The word for "authority" in the Greek is *exousia*. The KJV renders this as "power," but the idea is not an explosive or physical power in overcoming an enemy. Rather the term conveys delegated authority, which of course is backed by the ability to enforce compliance—the authority of the badge, rather than the club. The Father gave the Son the authority to do what Adam and Eve relinquished in the fall: to rule over creation. Unfortunately, in their rejection of God's authority over them, they discovered that self-rule was not satisfactory. Jesus, as God's solution to man's self-rule, was given the role as God-man to rule over all flesh—not just the animals, but also human flesh.

The Lord Himself put it this way: "If anyone hears My sayings and does not keep them, I do not judge him; for I did not come to judge the world, but to save the world. He who rejects Me and does not receive My sayings, has one who judges him; the word I spoke is what will judge him at the last day" (John 12:47-48). Jesus is God's authoritative Word for all people today (John 1:14).

Lord Jesus Christ, I bow to Your authority, for You are Lord of my life and You are Lord of all flesh. You are my Sovereign and my Master.

Authority Veiled

John 17:2 (cont.)

2 *". . . even as You gave Him authority over all flesh, that to all whom You have given Him, He may give eternal life."*

Authority given to Christ extends to all of creation, including the unseen spiritual angelic world. The writer to the Hebrews explains, "You [God] have made Him for a little while lower than the angels; You have crowned Him with glory and honor, and have appointed Him over the works of Your hands" (Heb. 2:7). That includes everything, even angels and demons. Quoting Psalm 110:1, that writer says, "But to which of the angels has He ever said, 'Sit at My right hand, until I make Your enemies a footstool for Your feet'?" (Heb. 1:13). Though for a time His authority is somewhat veiled, one day all creation will see clearly that He is Lord over all.

In our context of the Upper Room, the word "flesh" extends specifically to humanity, where the most incredible exertion of faith would struggle to see Jesus' authority. The group is secreted in an upper room, with Jesus' foreboding teaching of His upcoming suffering and death. Shortly the mob will be arresting Him, whipping Him beyond the point of recognition and then fastening Him immobile to a Roman cross, a symbol of absolute shame and defeat. When the Romans vanquished their enemies, it was the ultimate insult for the defeated foes, but glory for the Roman victors, to parade the leader of the opposition through the streets of the city and openly execute him. This demonstrated absolute authority over any who opposed Rome. One person mocked, "He saved others, He cannot save Himself" (Mark 15:31). How true—to save Himself would go against what the Father had sent Him to do, and He could not do that.

Yet, though His Lordship was hidden, there is coming a time when "all flesh" will see Him as He really is. "In these last days [God] has spoken to us in His Son, whom He appointed heir of all things, through whom also He made the world" (Heb. 1:2). The apostle Paul wrote, "Being found in appearance as a man, He humbled Himself by becoming obedient to the point of death, even death on a cross. For this reason also, God highly exalted Him, and bestowed on Him the name which is above every name, so that at the name of Jesus every knee will bow, of those who are in heaven and on earth and under the earth, and that every tongue will confess that Jesus Christ is Lord, to the glory of God the Father" (Phil. 2:8-11).

Unlike Roman victors, Jesus doesn't parade and humiliate His enemies. Rather He died for them, taking their shame upon Himself, so that we might be won over not by force, but by love. His authority extends in love.

Lord, I willingly surrender to the authority of Your love. I am Yours.

Authority to Give Life

2 ". . . even as You gave Him authority over all flesh, that to all whom You have given Him, He may give eternal life."

Very specifically, and most importantly, Jesus was given the authority to grant eternal life. God's relationship with His image bearers is the focus of Jesus' coming into this world. Ruling over the earth and the spiritual world is significant, to be sure—all things that were intended for humans. Jesus now, as the new Adam (cf. 1 Cor. 15:20-49), fulfills the image of God perfectly, for He is not made in the image of God; He *is* the image of God. "He is the radiance of His glory and the exact representation of His nature . . ." (Heb. 1:3a). Just as Adam originally was given authority over the earth, now Jesus has been given that authority, but with added measure. What I mean is that the authority given to Jesus extends to redeeming Adam and all his descendants, who have cast aside the authority of God for their own self-defeating authority.

Jesus has the weight of authority to overcome the fall and give humans the opportunity to attain to the "tree of life," as it were. Remember in the Garden of Eden, when the first couple were cast out, they were prevented from returning. "[God] drove the man out; and at the east of the garden of Eden He stationed the cherubim and the flaming sword which turned every direction to guard the way to the tree of life" (Gen. 3:24). Who could possibly go against the cherubim and storm the tree of life with any kind of force or authority? Only the one who created the angel in the first place. Christ now has now been given that authority to give life that was prohibited Adam because of his sin.

The writer of Hebrews aptly quotes from Psalm 45 in showing that Christ is greater than the angels: "But of the Son *[God] says*, 'Your throne, O God, is forever and ever, and the righteous scepter is the scepter of His kingdom'" (Heb. 1:8). And, "To which of the angels has He ever said, 'Sit at My right hand, until I make Your enemies a footstool for Your feet'?" (Heb. 1:13). Yes, Jesus was given the authority over the angels, and that means He has the authority to cause the cherubim to stand down, to allow passage to the tree, as it were.

Consider the reason Adam was prevented from eating from the tree of life. That tree was set in contrast to the tree of the knowledge of good and evil (Gen. 2:9). One tree brought spiritual death, the other; we presume, would have brought spiritual life. Neither the fig leaves (Gen. 3:6) nor the animal skins (Gen. 3:21) gave them authority to eat from the tree of life that would give them life. But Christ, the perfect sacrifice, has the authority to give eternal life.

Lord, You have given me eternal life, and for that I am eternally grateful.

Knowing Jesus Christ

[3] "This is eternal life, that they may know You, the only true God, and Jesus Christ whom You have sent."

Eternal life, what is that? Christians like to think of it as our spiritual fire insurance policy, our "get out of hell" card, a euphemism for salvation. To be sure, genuine Christians indeed are saved from hell, with the judgment against us nailed to the cross (Col. 2:14), a guarantee written in the blood of Christ. We are assured a home in heaven, grounded not in our good deeds, but in the grace of God (Eph. 2:8-9). But eternal life is more than that.

Many Christians enjoy the idea that our salvation is eternal, not temporary. That is, once given, God will never take away our eternal life, for then it would not be eternal. Others relish the thought that eternal life speaks of a quality of life rather than the duration of life. While we hold to the eternal security of the believer, Jesus makes it clear that eternal life has, at its core, a relationship with Christ. It is an unending, eternal relationship. It is knowing "God and Jesus Christ." The Creator of the universe is a God of relationship and restoration. As a relationship, eternal life is alive, dynamic. One believer, when asked if he was saved, said, "Yes, I've known Jesus for over a year." He had the right idea.

The apostle Peter finished his written communication with this summary instruction: "but grow in the grace and knowledge of our Lord and Savior Jesus Christ. To Him *be* the glory, both now and to the day of eternity. Amen" (2 Peter 3:18). To be saved is to know Christ. To know Christ is to grow in the knowledge of Him. A few observations are in order. Growing in grace and growing in the knowledge of Christ are related, and therefore, eternal life is mixed in there as well. Since salvation is by grace alone, then salvation must be eternal in nature. And grace that is perfect is found only in Christ. So, as genuine believers, we need to grow in the nurturing environment of eternally being recipients of God's grace. Grace is not a static, once-for-all thing. God continues to be gracious to us in every way, from the air we breathe to the more obvious blessings we more readily recognize as being from God's hand, all things undeserved.

But growing in the grace and knowledge of Jesus Christ also means growing in our capacity to show grace to others, being a channel of God's grace permeating in us and through us, so that we become the grace of God to other people. This, then, is being like Christ, and reflects the reality of our knowing Him. No wonder Peter instructs us to grow in this way. This makes us look like Christ. In other words, we show the image of God in which we were created.

Lord, how can I ever thank You enough for the grace of eternal life in Christ?

Of Dilemmas and of Christ

John 17:3 (cont.)

3 "This is eternal life, that they may know You, the only true God, and Jesus Christ whom You have sent."

"What would Jesus do?" was a popular saying a few years ago. But many used it to support any feel-good activity or politically correct notion in vogue. In order to ask that question, one must know Jesus Christ on His own terms, not as what one wants Him to be. And here is the rub: Jesus doesn't fit into a box, and as God in the flesh, He acts in very unpopular ways. Knowing Him is knowing true grace. But that doesn't mean He is a pushover.

When the legalists of His day demanded an answer concerning a woman caught in adultery, He refused to bend to what they thought was their clever trap. Those who don't know Christ are quick to jump to the popular quote of Jesus, "He who is without sin among you, let him *be the* first to throw a stone at her" (John 8:7). But there is more about Christ in this story to those who desire to grow in their knowledge of Him.

Those self-righteous Pharisees (John 8:3) paraded their self-exalted morality before the Lord, with the woman being a mere puppet to advance their vendetta against Him. They were trying to corner Jesus for hypocrisy in a no-win dilemma. If Jesus said to let the woman go, He would be guilty of contravening the Law of Moses, under which He was submitting Himself. If He said to stone her, then that would buy into the Pharisees' manipulation and contravene the love that He had been preaching. Is Law greater than love, or is love greater than Law? They were forcing the terms of engagement with Jesus, but Jesus refused to be manipulated.

Christianity's detractors today fall into the same category as the Pharisees, thinking they have the moral high ground, and try to catch Christians in a dilemma. What would Jesus do? He would not bow to their manipulation today, and we should not either. He showed how their guilt was no less than hers (in fact, it takes two to commit adultery, but they only brought the woman—sounds like a political scandal cover-up). The room was filled with guilty sinners.

After they all left, painfully aware of their own threatened exposure, only the woman remained. Since now there was no witness left to accuse her, there was no legal case before the Law of Moses—and therefore no condemnation. But Jesus did imply that the woman was guilty of sinning, for He finished by saying to her, "Go. From now on, sin no more" (John 8:11). He did make a judgment, but not to condemn, but rather to free the woman from her sin.

Lord, help me to know You better so that I might respond to my dilemmas better.

WEEKEND READING

Saturday – John 11:30-46
Sunday – Acts 19:21-41

PERSONAL REFLECTIONS

_____
_____
_____
_____
_____
_____
_____
_____
_____
_____
_____
_____
_____
_____
_____
_____
_____
_____
_____
_____

Shining Jesus Shine

John 17:4

4 "I glorified You on the earth, having accomplished the work which You have given Me to do."

Shining light on the true nature of God was Jesus' goal. And truly that was needed, because since the fall in the Garden of Eden, the knowledge of God grew darker and darker. "For even though they knew God, they did not honor Him as God or give thanks, but they became futile in their speculations, and their foolish heart was darkened. Professing to be wise, they became fools, and exchanged the glory of the incorruptible God for an image in the form of corruptible man and of birds and four-footed animals and crawling creatures" (Rom. 1:21-23).

Monotheism (the belief in one God) became replaced by belief in "other gods," as was characteristic in Abraham's pre-faith days in Ur (Josh. 24:2). Humans began making images of the gods from wood, metal and anything else they could use to represent those gods. Characteristics associated with these so-called gods included vindictiveness (unreasonable desire for revenge), capriciousness (ruling by their whims), arbitrariness, accepting of bribes and even in some cases demanding human sacrifice, temple prostitution and religious orgies. They were seen as territorial, constantly at war with one another. Nations would in effect boast, "Our gods are stronger than your gods."

Even among the Jews, though idolatry was strictly forbidden, the pull toward idolatry was persistent, whether it be worshiping on the high places (universally condemned in Scripture) or committing "spiritual adultery" by worshiping other nations' deities. Solomon offers a prime example of such behavior: "When Solomon was old, his wives turned his heart away after other gods; and his heart was not wholly devoted to the LORD his God, as the heart of David his father *had been*" (1 Kings 11:4).

The darkness of humans' view of God is a direct cause in their own sinfulness. In Solomon's case, he was influenced by his weakness for women. He believed they could provide something that God could not provide, something he felt he could not live without—just as Adam and Eve had bought into the lie that they could not live without the forbidden fruit, that somehow God was keeping something good from them. That "something" became more important to them than God Himself. And that is the most repressive darkness there is. That is the essence of idolatry.

But "[in Christ] was life, and the life was the Light of men" (John 1:4). He came to shine forth the nature of God clearly, that is, to glorify God.

Lord, thank You for helping me see the character of God more clearly.

Exegeting God

John 17:4 (cont.)

4 "I glorified You on the earth, having accomplished the work which You have given Me to do."

S hining light on God's character so that people might see Him as He is—that is the work Jesus came to do. Everything about Jesus—what He taught, the miracles He performed, the conversations in which He engaged—all were designed intentionally to show the true nature of God.

Whereas idolatry reflects the effort of fallen humans to *define* deity (in essence to create a man-made god), Jesus came to *reveal* God. "No one has seen God at any time; the only begotten God who is in the bosom of the Father, He has explained *Him*" (John 1:18). The word "explained" translates the word *exegeomai*, from which comes the theological term "to exegete"—to expound or interpret, to draw the meaning or understanding out of something.

The natural human tendency is to "isogete," that is, to put meaning into deity, to bring one's own ideas about deity into the study of spirituality. But Jesus came not to "give meaning" to the concept of God, but to reveal God, to be the lens through whom we clearly see the God who is really there—the objective reality of the Creator of the universe.

The first "work" which Jesus did was to enter the world. "And the Word became flesh, and dwelt among us, and we saw His glory, glory as of the only begotten from the Father, full of grace and truth. (John 1:14). As the Son incarnate, His birth was the beginning of His work of glorifying the Father. Did not the angels at His birth proclaim, "Glory to God in the highest"? (Luke 2:14).

In Christ, the world discovers a God who is "full of grace." What religion anywhere sees this about God? To the Jews, He was a God of law. To Abraham, He was a God of promise. To Adam, though God desired to reveal Himself "walking in the garden in the cool of the day" (Gen. 3:8), the view of Him became darkened into an austere, forbidding God. But in Jesus, we see the Almighty as a forgiving God, reaching out to the outcasts of society, bypassing the religious elite and extending Himself to the humble of this world.

We see a God who humbled Himself by becoming human, condescending to a creaturely existence. He, the very image of God (Heb. 1:3), came to live among those created in His image. To Thomas, Jesus said, "If you had known Me, you would have known My Father also; from now on you know Him, and have seen Him" (John 14:7). And to Philip, "He who has seen Me has seen the Father . . ." (John 14:9).

Father, I want to study Your Son, so that I may come to know You better.

The Glory and the Will

John 17:4 (cont.)

4 "I glorified You on the earth, having accomplished the work which You have given Me to do."

P ast tense is what Jesus used to describe the work of glorifying God. Yet He had not yet accomplished the greatest work assigned to Him, namely dying on the cross for the sins of the world. What do we make of this statement then? All story-telling involves human conventions of communication, one of the most intriguing of which is the use of time notations—especially when it comes to Holy Scripture written by inspired writers, about a God who is timeless. And here we have a prayer by God the Son to God the Father, a communication of the eternal Godhead, who transcends all sequences of notations like "before" and "after."

It may be, on the one hand, that Jesus referred to the past instances of the work He was called to do, without any reference to the future instances of glorifying God. In other words, "up until this point." Or it may be that Jesus took the whole purview of His earthly existence, including the future crucifixion, as the work given Him to do. In this case, He would be seeing the future (the next few hours) as good as done. The die has been cast; the final stage of His work has been set in motion, Judas being the catalyst by embarking on his betrayal.

Earlier in His ministry, Jesus said to them, "My food is to do the will of Him who sent Me and to accomplish His work" (John 4:34). And God's will was for Him to die for the sins of the world. Paul understood this: "It is a trustworthy statement, deserving full acceptance, that Christ Jesus came into the world to save sinners, among whom I am foremost *of all"* (1 Tim. 1:15). To use modern vernacular, Jesus was all in. He came with a singularity of purpose, and His life was completely at the disposal of this mission. This wasn't just a desire or a willingness; it was the actuality of His life.

In the Garden of Gethsemane, in a couple of hours, He would be wrestling with the final temptation from Satan—would Jesus follow through on obeying the will of the Father and complete the work He was called to do? Matthew records the scene this way: "And He went a little beyond *them,* and fell on His face and prayed, saying, 'My Father, if it is possible, let this cup pass from Me; yet not as I will, but as You will'" (Matt. 26:39). Three times he prayed this; three times He submitted—and He went to the cross.

The question for Christ followers: are we going to do the will of God, namely, to do the work He has given us to glorify Him with our entire lives?

Lord, I renew my commitment to live for Your glory in all I do.

Return to Glory

John 17:5

[5] *"Now, Father, glorify Me together with Yourself, with the glory which I had with You before the world was."*

Togetherness is unity, an important theme in this Upper Room. Unity begins, though, with the Father and the Son. The "work" of glorifying God is a team effort between the two of them. The Holy Spirit, as it were, was revealed to us by Jesus as the silent Partner, whose work it is to "testify about Me"—which is another way of saying "to glorify Christ."

Quite significant in Trinitarian theology, which saturates not only this prayer of Jesus but also the entire Upper Room discourse, is that Jesus was not about to come into a new or added glory. He was not being elevated to divine status, as some errant religions claim. In the context of the ancient Roman times, this was an important distinction. The path to glory for a man followed a prescribed pattern of official offices in the government. The most successful achieved the highest position as senator, and ultimately became one of two consuls who ruled the republic. With Augustus Caesar, the position and honor of emperor superseded all else. But that was the end game, from a human perspective. Upon death, many emperors were elevated by decree to divine status, complete with temples dedicated to their names. Some even assumed this before their death. The ultimate honor and glory a man could achieve was elevation to deity, or so their darkened minds thought.

Jesus was not seeking glory the way human emperors sought it. He was not asking to be deified. Rather, He was requesting the glory He had before His incarnation. The apostle Paul later commented on the incarnation: "Although He existed in the form of God, did not regard equality with God a thing to be grasped, but emptied Himself, taking the form of a bond-servant, *and* being made in the likeness of men" (Phil. 2:6-7). As God, the Son had possessed the glory of God from eternity past. He was asking for what was already His.

Before creation, when all that existed was the triune God, the Son was fully known among the other members of the Trinity. In creation, though, His image bearers rejected the knowledge of God in favor of a godless knowledge and their hearts were darkened. When the Son came into the world, as John wrote earlier, "The Light shines in the darkness, and the darkness did not comprehend it" (John 1:5). God's glory in Christ became veiled. Now, Jesus, completing God's work to shine the light of His knowledge, was ready to return to His previous state of glory, but with the difference that now the world could better comprehend the knowledge of God through His death and resurrection.

Lord, help me see You through the spiritual magnifying glass of Jesus.

The Glory of God

⁵ "Now, Father, glorify Me together with Yourself, with the glory which I had with You before the world was."

Glory, typically, is something we tend to think of in terms of brightness, an apt metaphor or depiction. To see God as He is would certainly be a blinding experience. Abraham experienced God's glory indirectly, for God said to him, "You cannot see My face, for no man can see Me and live!" (Ex. 33:20). But the Lord wanted to reveal *something* of Himself, so He told Abraham, "Behold, there is a place by Me, and you shall stand *there* on the rock; and it will come about, while My glory is passing by, that I will put you in the cleft of the rock and cover you with My hand until I have passed by. Then I will take My hand away and you shall see My back, but My face shall not be seen." (Ex. 33:21-23). Whatever we say about the glory of the Lord, it has to be mitigated in its appearance to us, lest we be destroyed by the sight of it.

When the people of Israel looked up to Sinai at the giving of the Law, we read, "And to the eyes of the sons of Israel the appearance of the glory of the LORD was like a consuming fire on the mountain top" (Ex. 24:17). Moses, after being in the presence of the Lord and descending back to the people, carried the reflection of the glory of God in his face, though it soon quickly faded (2 Cor. 3:7). That same glory of God later came down from the mountain, and "the glory of the LORD filled the tabernacle" (Ex. 40:34). The Jews called this the Shekinah glory, and it was depicted as a blinding light.

We see the glory of God in the various images given to the prophets. Isaiah saw the Lord "sitting on a throne, lofty and exalted, with the train of His robe filling the temple" (Isa. 6:1). And he heard the angels calling out as they hovered around the throne, "Holy, Holy, Holy, is the LORD of hosts, the whole earth is full of His glory" (Isa. 6:3). Ezekiel described his vision: "As the appearance of the rainbow in the clouds on a rainy day, so *was* the appearance of the surrounding radiance. Such *was* the appearance of the likeness of the glory of the LORD. And when I saw *it,* I fell on my face . . ." (Ezek. 1:28).

John, in the Revelation, viewed it this way: "And He who was sitting [on the throne] *was* like a jasper stone and a sardius in appearance; and *there was* a rainbow around the throne, like an emerald in appearance" (Rev. 4:3). This is the glory of the Lord. Like a rainbow with many hues, the glory of the Son of God has many aspects of His character and nature that God desires to reveal to us. This is the glory Jesus asks for in the Upper Room, and He wants all to see it.

Lord, show me Your glory that I might know You better.
Help me see You in all Your colorful glory!

WEEKEND READING

Saturday – John 11:47-57
Sunday – Acts 20:1-16

PERSONAL REFLECTIONS

_____
_____
_____
_____
_____
_____
_____

_____
_____
_____
_____
_____
_____
_____
_____
_____
_____
_____
_____

The Name of God

⁶ "I have manifested Your name to the men whom You gave Me out of the world; they were Yours and You gave them to Me, and they have kept Your word."

The name of God is the most significant word in all of Scripture. What is it that Jesus manifested on earth? Contrary to popular belief, God's name is not "God," although we usually refer to Him as "God." That is really a generic term for deity (translated from "elohim" in the OT and "theos" in the NT) and is used for both God and gods in general. Only in English do we use the capital form to refer to God as we worship Him (the God of Abraham, Isaac and Jacob), for capitalization was not used in either the original Hebrew or Greek to distinguish when the words were used of the true God or false gods.

Of course the earthly name given to the Son of God is Jesus. The term "Christ," properly speaking, is not a name, but a title, which is a transliteration of a Greek word corresponding to the OT title of Messiah. Christian tradition has come to call Him Jesus Christ or in some cases reversing the order, Christ Jesus. But that is not the name Jesus refers to in our verse today.

To the first century audience the reference would be clearer than to us today. The Jews held God's actual name in such high regard, they would not even speak it out of extreme reverence, borderlining on superstition. That name is usually pronounced in English as either Jehovah or Yahweh. The spelling or pronunciation has been lost (the explanation of why this happened is beyond the scope of this essay), but was first elucidated in Exodus 3:14, where Moses encountered the Lord in the burning bush incident:

> God said to Moses, "I AM WHO I AM"; and He said, "Thus you shall say to the sons of Israel, 'I AM has sent me to you.'" God, furthermore, said to Moses, "Thus you shall say to the sons of Israel, 'The LORD, the God of your fathers, the God of Abraham, the God of Isaac, and the God of Jacob, has sent me to you.' This is My name forever, and this is My memorial-name to all generations. (Ex. 3:15)

In the Hebrew, in which this was written, the play on words is unmistakable, with the phrase "I am" corresponding to the "LORD." In most English Bibles, the translators use "LORD" (in all caps or small caps) to indicate the name of God, which we usually pronounce Yahweh or Jehovah. That is His personal name at the most fundamental level. It is His name forever, His "memorial-name." This is the name Jesus manifested on the earth.

Lord, I want to know You better by understanding Your name.

The Name of God (cont.)

John 17:6

⁶ "I have manifested Your name to the men whom You gave Me out of the world; they were Yours and You gave them to Me, and they have kept Your word."

The name of God was revealed to Moses in the burning bush story in Exodus 3:14, but He clarified shortly after:

> *God spoke further to Moses and said to him, "I am the LORD; and I appeared to Abraham, Isaac, and Jacob, as God Almighty, but by My name, Lord, I did not make Myself known to them. (Ex. 6:2-3)*

The name "LORD" actually is used in Scripture before this, but God had not made Himself known by that name. What does that mean? It means God had not manifested His name; He had not yet shown Himself to be the kind of God as His name would indicate. So what does His name mean? According to the best research among biblical scholars, God's name Yahweh ("LORD") means, "I will be for you whatever your need is; I will act on your behalf in a real, tangible way."

So we see from this point forward that when God speaks definitively to His people, He emphasizes His name. For example, when giving the commandments, God begins, "I am the LORD your God, who brought you out of the land of Egypt, out of the house of slavery. You shall have no other gods before Me" (Ex. 20:2-3). He is the One who acted on their behalf by bringing them out of their bondage. All through the giving of the Law of Moses, we see this phrase: "I am the LORD your God."

Yahweh is unlike the false gods in many ways, primarily because He acts in real, tangible ways, whereas the false gods that are simply figments of man's imagination can do nothing, because they don't exist.

> *"I am the LORD, that is My name; I will not give My glory to another, nor My praise to graven images." (Isa. 42:8)*

> *"I, even I, am the LORD, And there is no savior besides Me. It is I who have declared and saved and proclaimed, 'Even from eternity I am He, And there is none who can deliver out of My hand; I act and who can reverse it?'" (Isa. 43:11-13)*

This is the name that Jesus revealed while on the earth—and as we shall soon see, Jesus' applying this name to Himself brought the wrath of the religious leaders, but the allegiance of His followers.

Lord God, help me to reverence Your name because of who You are.

The Name of God (cont.)

John 17:6

⁶ "I have manifested Your name to the men whom You gave Me out of the world; they were Yours and You gave them to Me, and they have kept Your word."

Stoning was what the religious leaders tried to do to Jesus when He "manifested" God's name to them. To manifest something means to bring it out into the open, to make it known. Jesus' brothers wanted to force Jesus' hand, albeit in a somewhat mocking way: "For no one does anything in secret when he himself seeks to be *known* publicly. If You do these things, show Yourself to the world" (John 7:4). It was not yet Jesus' time or the method by which He would fully reveal Himself.

We begin to see glimpses of Jesus manifesting God's name in John 9:3. When His disciple asked about the cause of a man's blindness, Jesus responded, *"It was neither that this man sinned, nor his parents; but it was* so that the works of God might be displayed in him." Jesus' healing of this man was designed to display God's work, in a tangible, real way. Although the name of God, "Yahweh," was not used in this incident, the meaning of His name certainly is evident in the display of God's being active in the man's life.

In fact, earlier in John 8, Jesus actually uses the name of God in reference to Himself, where three times He verbalizes the unique, startling phrase, "I am," without any predicate (by predicate, we mean "I am _____" like the door, bread of life, etc.). Here the phrase "I am" stands alone. The most well-known of these occurrences is, "Truly, truly I say to you, 'Before Abraham was born, I am'" (John 8:58; see also John 8:24, 28). That was very much non-standard Greek grammar. It was startling and unmistakable to the Jewish ear. Such a phrase in their Old Testament Scripture was attributed to and used only of God, where the "I am" is identified with the name of God, "Yahweh." The play on words, first spoken from the mouth of God, was now being spoken from the mouth of Jesus. The Pharisees wasted no time in picking up stones to execute Him for blasphemy, and rightly so if Jesus were only just a man.

But He wasn't just a man. He was God incarnate, showing in human form that God was not silent, He was not inactive. As His name indicates, God was actively working on behalf of His people in whatever way they needed. Their greatest need was forgiveness and healing. And the greatest manifestation of God's name was about to take place, as Jesus would soon make the perfect, satisfactory, substitutionary sacrifice for the sins of the world.

Lord, You are not a god invented by human minds, but are the real Creator of the universe; and You are active in this world—in my world, in my life. Thanks.

The God Who Chooses

John 17:6 (cont.)

⁶ "I have manifested Your name to the men whom You gave Me out of the world; they were Yours and You gave them to Me, and they have kept Your word."

E lection is the theological term used to label the teaching that God has selected some men for special purposes in Scripture. While the teaching has broader application (and controversy among modern theologians), here the prayer of Jesus is clear. The disciples of Jesus were hand-picked, as it were, by God the Father and given to Jesus the Son. In fact, early in the Upper Room the Lord had told them, "You did not choose Me but I chose you . . ." (John 15:16). And it was not just the eleven, but also Judas, as we read Jesus telling His disciples, "Did I Myself not choose you, the twelve, and *yet* one of you is a devil?" (John 6:70). His immediate followers were not volunteers, but chosen by God.

While we cannot let fear of God's ways and the implications thereof prevent us from seeing the clear stark teachings of certain passages, we certainly should investigate these things further. Although we cannot delve exhaustively into these things here, we can certainly ask questions that will help us ponder with gratefulness our blessings. Yes, the ways of God are beyond our human understanding, but good questions can lead us to amazement and wonder over God's grace. Why would Jesus have "chosen" Judas, knowing his name would become synonymous with betrayal? Why would He have chosen Thomas, whose propensity to doubt became legendary? Or why Peter, knowing full well that this one, whom Jesus gave the name Peter because of his rock-like expression of faith and loyalty, would deny the Lord three times upon His arrest?

Why did God chose David of Old Testament fame, the king of Israel who became an adulterer and a murderer and a hypocritical worshiper, as the one whose name Jesus would take, being called "the Son of David"?

Why did God choose not to immediately bring the promised death to Adam and Eve (Gen. 2:18), but instead to provide animal skins to cover their nakedness? Or why choose Solomon, whose many wives turned his heart away from God to worship idols—why use him to pen the inspired books of Proverbs, Ecclesiastes, Song of Solomon and a number of the Psalms? Why would God choose to forgive the Ninevites during Jonah's day?

Yes, God's choices baffle us, but they speak of His amazing grace. The fact that He chooses should give great comfort to those who are chosen!

Lord God, sovereign over all, You chose to create all that exists according to Your good and perfect will. Though overwhelmed by this truth, I worship You.

The God who Chooses (cont.)

John 17:6

⁶ "I have manifested Your name to the men whom You gave Me out of the world; they were Yours and You gave them to Me, and they have kept Your word."

God could have justly snuffed out the entire world, including the first man and woman. He graciously withheld His judgment, when by all rights He could have justly destroyed all humanity—because all have sinned (Rom. 3:23), and through sin all have rightly earned death (Rom. 6:23). As in the days of Noah, so also in our day, salvation from judgment is by God's grace alone! Faith is the means of God's grace becoming effective in our lives, but we are not the initiators of salvation; we do not earn God's favor, for we have absolutely no merit of our own. Faith is not a work, nor is it something of which we can boast. To be sure, we are called to faith and are held responsible for believing or not believing. But we must never forget that "by grace [we] have been saved through faith; and that not of [our]selves, *it is* the gift of God; not as a result of works, so that no one may boast" (Eph. 2:8-9).

God saved Noah and his family, knowing that they were not perfect, but Noah "found favor in the eyes of the LORD" (Gen. 6:8). He did not earn that election to God's salvation from watery judgment, any more than we today earn salvation from God's eternal judgment of hell. We were chosen, we found favor, when we were as guilty as those lost in the flood.

Our faith does not earn us anything. If salvation is not earned, then how did we get it? It is a gift: "For the wages of sin is death, but the free gift of God is eternal life in Christ Jesus our Lord" (Rom. 6:23). It is not your faith that saves you; it is, and always is, God's grace that saves—undeserved, unearned, unmerited. Faith is simply the means; God's grace is the cause of our salvation.

If we say God is not fair in choosing some but not others, we err as creatures in questioning the Creator's goodness. Is God unfair because He doesn't do the "fair" thing and send us all to hell without any grace? Did the parable of the servants working in the field tell us nothing (Matt. 20)? If the farmer chose to pay a full day's wage to those who worked only the last hour, the same as those who worked all day, was he being unfair? In the same way, is God unfair for graciously choosing some out of eternal damnation?

The greatest bafflement of all is this: why did God choose me? I might beg to argue with the apostle who wrote, ". . . Christ Jesus came into the world to save sinners, among whom I am foremost *of all*" (1 Tim. 1:15). I am the chief of all sinners, for my sin makes me worthy of eternal judgment.

Lord, why did You extend Your saving grace to me? Why me? Praise God, me!

WEEKEND READING

Saturday – John 12:1-11
Sunday – Acts 20:17-38

PERSONAL REFLECTIONS

_____
_____
_____
_____
_____
_____
_____
_____
_____
_____
_____
_____
_____
_____
_____
_____
_____
_____
_____
_____
_____
_____

Gift to the Son

John 17:6 (cont.)

6 *"I have manifested Your name to the men whom You gave Me out of the world; they were Yours and You gave them to Me, and they have kept Your word."*

God's gift to Jesus Christ is you and me! Now that's an interesting thought. We sometimes hear the derisive saying, "That person thinks they are God's gift to the world." But to think that I am the Father's gift to the Son is an amazing thing!

Does this apply to us, or just the eleven disciples? After all, God's choosing them, in context, has more to do with their mission as apostles than with their own personal eternity. However, Jesus makes it clear that He extends His prayer to all believers, not just the eleven: "I do not ask on behalf of these alone, but for those also who believe in Me through their word" (John 17:20).

William MacDonald quotes J. G. Bellet, "They were the Father's by election before the world was, and became Christ's by the gift of the Father, and by purchase of blood." What do you give to someone who is God? The Father gave the gift of image bearers of His glory. His gifts are perfect (James 1:17). Bottom line: we are special to God because we are the Father's perfect gift to His Son. This gift was entirely suitable, fitting for the One "for whom are all things, and through whom are all things" who brought "many sons to glory" (Heb. 2:10). The perfect gift for the perfect Savior.

Keep in mind this is the intimate prayer of the Son as He speaks to the Father. While condescending to allow the disciples (and us) to listen in, it nonetheless contains things beyond our comprehension, but not beyond our wonder. To think that I am, that you are, the precious, perfect gift that the Father gave as an expression of His love for His Son—that should stop us in our tracks with an overwhelming sense of honor, privilege and gratitude. How can God see us as a gift? This is beyond mere human understanding but not beyond gratitude, praise and worship of Him whose ways are above ours.

The positive thing Jesus had to say about His followers was, "They have kept Your word." No mention of what they were about to do in abandoning Him. Obedience was not a qualification for their election. It was proof of their faith, of being chosen by God. To miss this distinction brings error and is extremely important on two fronts: salvation does not come by obedience, for it was our disobedience that necessitated the need of salvation in the first place. Salvation comes by grace through faith (Eph. 2:8-9). But on the other hand, a faith not accompanied by obedience is no faith at all (James 2:14, 17, etc.).

Lord, thank You for the desire to obey that You have placed in me.

The Action Name

John 17:6 (cont.)

⁶ "I have manifested Your name to the men whom You gave Me out of the world; they were Yours and You gave them to Me, and they have kept Your word."

Action was the activity of the Lord Jesus Christ, not just verbal teaching. Taking the verse as a whole, we have seen how He manifested God's name to the "given ones," that is, the eleven disciples, in teaching about His Father's character. But He also demonstrated by His actions that His Father is the God who is there, as His name Jehovah (or Yahweh) suggests. Remember, His name means that He will act toward His people in whatever way they need Him to be. This does not make God the image after men's design, but rather He is a God who actually works in physical, tangible ways to meet our needs, as He determines.

Keeping in mind that in the OT, His name was often combined with other words that emphasized certain aspects of God's actions or character, we can readily see how Jesus's ministry manifested God's name. For example, in Exodus 15:26, God reveals Himself as Jehovah Rapha, the Lord who heals. In Jesus, we see God as a healer. Just before He healed the blind man, He was asked about the cause of his blindness. Jesus responded, "It was neither that this man sinned, nor his parents; but it was so that the works of God might be displayed in him. . . . While I am in the world, I am the Light of the world" (John 9:3, 5). This was an opportunity for Jesus to show that He is the God who heals, thus manifesting the name of God, the One who is there for His people's need.

When the woman caught in adultery was paraded shamelessly before Him, He deftly dispersed her accusers and was left alone with her. He is the God who brought peace to her, freeing her from the accusations of her adversaries. He is Jehovah Shalom, the God of peace (see Judges 6:23-24).

Twice we find recorded Jesus' feeding the multitudes, manifesting God's name, Jehovah Jireh, the God who provides (see Genesis 22:14). At His interrogation the secular Roman governor concluded, "I find no fault in Him," demonstrating that Jesus was the God of righteousness, Jehovah Tsidkenu (see Jeremiah 23:6). His continual instruction and defending His disciples against all kinds of difficulties shows that He is Jehovah Raah, the God who is my shepherd (Ps. 23:1). In His final words to the disciples (although not yet spoken at the time of the Upper Room), Jesus said, "I will be with you until the end of the ages." He is Jehovah Shammah, the God who is there (see Ezekiel 48:35).

Lord Jesus, You are my healer, my peace, my provider, my righteousness and my shepherd. You are here in my life. You are Yahweh and I praise You.

Security in His Words

[7] "Now they have come to know that everything You have given Me is from You . . ."

Cryptic is this saying of Jesus in the Upper Room, seemingly redundant: everything given to Jesus by God is from God. Though the original language leaves this verse somewhat ambiguous, as do the majority of English translations, the New Living Translation gives the correct sense: "Now they know that everything I have is a gift from you . . ." Jesus emphasizes that the Father is the source of what has been given Him. The inner workings of and the relationship between.

What we know from the previous verse is that there is no doubt in their minds that they are God's gift to Jesus. Secondly, although they had often misunderstood Jesus and fallen short in their faith, there is no evidence that the eleven in the Upper Room doubted or rejected the truths that Jesus had been teaching them. It may have taken them a while to understand, to comprehend what He taught, but they had certainly come to recognize the divine origin of their Master's teachings: "Now we know that You know all things, and have no need for anyone to question You; by this we believe that You came from God" (John 16:30).

Keep in mind, this comment from Jesus is actually part of His conversation with His Father. The Father knows this, being omniscient, so in this example of prayer, we see that the goal of prayer is not communicating things to God that He doesn't already know. Rather, by including this, Jesus is increasing the focus on the importance of this truth. Jesus had been successful in manifesting the name of God, as we have seen. And now in reviewing the success of His ministry, He brings together the highlights and the implications. M. C. Tenney comments, "The gift was irrevocable and the Father was able to guarantee it. Jesus had no doubt of the final outcome."

Paul puts it this way: "For I am convinced that neither death, nor life, nor angels, nor principalities, nor things present, nor things to come, nor powers, nor height, nor depth, nor any other created thing, will be able to separate us from the love of God, which is in Christ Jesus our Lord" (Rom 8:38-39). Nothing can snatch us from the hand of God. We are secure because we have believed through the testimony of the eleven in the Upper Room (John 17:20).

This is true of everything Jesus said: it was all from the Father, and therefore as sure as the Law of Moses. Shortly, they would come into full realization of the truth of Jesus' puzzling teaching concerning the immediate near future.

Lord Jesus, Your words are truth and life, and I live by them.

Credentialed Proof

John 17:8

8 ". . . for the words which You gave Me I have given to them; and they received them and truly understood that I came forth from You, and they believed that You sent Me."

Enigmatic might be the way to describe how the disciples first saw Jesus—difficult to interpret, hard to understand—but refreshing, attractive. It began with the Baptist's words, "Behold, the Lamb of God who takes away the sin of the world!" (John 1:29, 35-37). Then in Jesus' first message at His hometown synagogue, He read from a messianic passage, "The Spirit of the LORD is upon Me, because He anointed Me to preach the gospel to the poor. He has sent Me to proclaim release to the captives, and recovery of sight to the blind, to set free those who are oppressed, to proclaim the favorable year of the LORD" (Isa. 61:1-2). Jesus concluded, "Today this Scripture has been fulfilled in your hearing" (Luke 4:18-19, 21). He laid out the credentials for identifying the Messiah, concluding, "That is Me; I fulfill those qualifications." He would go on to demonstrate exactly that in His actions and teachings.

After years of living with Roman taxation and repression, and after numerous imposter-messiahs and would-be liberators, many in Israel were unimpressed by just words. What set Jesus apart was what He did, along with words that were wonderfully different from what anyone had ever heard before. "[A]ll were speaking well of Him, and wondering at the gracious words which were falling from His lips . . ." (Luke 4:22). His miracles elicited similar responses: "After the demon was cast out, the mute man spoke; and the crowds were amazed, *and were* saying, 'Nothing like this has ever been seen in Israel'" (Matt. 9:33). His supernatural works were unique, never before accomplished by anyone. The Pharisees could not discredit the testimony of those who had been touched by Jesus' hand. As one person concluded, "Since the beginning of time it has never been heard that anyone opened the eyes of a person born blind. 'If this man [Jesus] were not from God, He could do nothing'" (John 9:32-33).

The disciples were as amazed as everyone else. Early in Jesus' ministry they had left all to follow Him, yet their comprehension grew from befuddlement—"Who then is this, that He commands even the winds and the water, and they obey Him?" (Luke 8:25)—to fuller comprehension—"We have believed and have come to know that You are the Holy One of God" (John 6:69). As Jesus said to His Father, they had indeed come to know He was sent by God the Father.

Lord, help me to comprehend Your teachings and life more deeply that I may bring You greater glory in my world.

Verbal, Plenary

John 17:8 (cont.)

8 ". . . for the words which You gave Me I have given to them; and they received them and truly understood that I came forth from You, and they believed that You sent Me."

Intriguing was the conversation between Father and Son and the words given. What were these words to which Jesus referred? Clearly, Jesus was referring to His own teachings rather than the Old Testament scriptures. He understood His words to be authentically the teachings of the Godhead.

We are tempted to see a reflection of John 1:1: "In the beginning was the Word, and the Word was with God, and the Word was God," but this might be a bit misplaced. While in that case John used the Greek term *logos*, in our passage today the word is *rhema*. *Logos* refers to the wisdom or the concept of God's communication to the world, in a more philosophical sense. It is the idea behind the words being said. *Rhema* carries the sense of the spoken word, or that which goes out from the speaker, "that which is said, a word, saying, expression, or statement of any kind." Jesus has passed on the specific teachings, not just the ideas of God.

This has implications for our understanding of the inspiration of Scripture. "All Scripture is inspired by God and profitable for teaching, for reproof, for correction, for training in righteousness . . ." (2 Tim. 3:16). We believe this extends to what theologians called the verbal, plenary inspiration. God inspires the specific words of human authors, the writers of what has become known as the canon of Scripture, the 27 books of the NT and the 39 books of the OT. Those who hold to a broader understanding of inspiration believe that there may be specific wording errors in Scripture but that the teachings on the whole are inspired by God. This would allow for errors of so-called non-foundational issues, an often too-easy way to deal with the apparent anomalies of Scripture. We disagree with this limited view on a number of fronts.

First and foremost, in Jesus we find verbal, plenary inspiration at work. His *rhema* was given by God, that is, His words as He originally spoke them were the very words given by His Father. Jesus said, "Man shall not live on bread alone, but on every word [*rhema*] that proceeds out of the mouth of God" (Matt. 4:4). Concerning the OT, Jesus taught, "For truly I say to you, until heaven and earth pass away, not the smallest letter or stroke shall pass from the Law until all is accomplished" (Matt. 5:18).

The words that Jesus spoke were given to Him by His Father, and therefore they are true and we can trust them.

Lord, Your words are true. They are the foundation on which I build my life.

WEEKEND READING

Saturday – John 12:12-28
Sunday – Acts 21:1-26

PERSONAL REFLECTIONS

Our Lord Prays for His Own

⁹ *"I ask on their behalf; I do not ask on behalf of the world, but of those whom You have given Me; for they are Yours . . ."*

Prayers of intercession begin with Jesus and are a priestly function. While we see this sort of praying for others in the OT (Abraham, for example, interceding for his worldly nephew Lot in Genesis 18 and Moses praying for the rebellious calf-worshiping Israelites in Exodus 32:11-14), the epitome of communicating with God is found in Jesus praying for His own. He asks "on their behalf" or "concerning them."

This reminds us of the Holy Spirit, who "intercedes for *us* with groanings too deep for words; and He who searches the hearts knows what the mind of the Spirit is, because He intercedes for the saints according to the will of God" (Rom. 8:26-27). What an assurance that God the Son and God the Holy Spirit pray to God the Father for us. What perfect prayer that is because 1) there is no miscommunication between the members of the Trinity, for they know each others' minds perfectly well, and 2) these prayers are "according to the will of God." Jesus would soon give another demonstration of praying according to God's will in the Garden of Gethsemene, where He prayed three times, "Not my will be done, but Yours" (Luke 22:42).

His purpose was to fulfill the will of His Father (John 4:34), and His Upper Room prayer is a continuation of that purpose. We can say, then, not only that it was the Father's will for Jesus to pray for His disciples, but also that the content of His prayer was in line with God's will. One can almost hear Jesus' words at the tomb of Lazarus, "Father, I thank You that You have heard Me. I knew that You always hear Me; but because of the people standing around I said it, so that they may believe that You sent Me" (John 11:41-42). The apostle John, for one, did not forget what he learned about prayer from Jesus, when 50 years later he wrote, "This is the confidence which we have before Him, that, if we ask anything according to His will, He hears us" (1 John 5:14).

Intercession is a priestly activity, and Jesus was the perfect priest according to the book of Hebrews: "Therefore He is able also to save forever those who draw near to God through Him, since He always lives to make intercession for them. For it was fitting for us to have such a high priest, holy, innocent, undefiled, separated from sinners and exalted above the heavens" (Heb. 7:25-26). His prayers therefore are perfect, holy, unmixed with personal ambitions or selfish goals. He perfectly prays for His own. And we are the beneficiaries.

Lord, I praise You for taking my needs to Your Father, for having my needs as the subject of Your conversation—in my best interest.

Our Lord's Selective Prayer

John 17:9 (cont.)

⁹ "I ask on their behalf; I do not ask on behalf of the world, but of those whom You have given Me; for they are Yours . . ."

Popular religion would have us believe that we are all God's children, emphasizing our commonality and unity with all people. If by this it is meant that all humans are created in God's image, there may be a measure of truth to the saying. However, Jesus in His Upper Room prayer clearly delineates between His disciples and the rest of humanity ("the world"). In His eyes a person is either a follower of His or not; there is no in-between. In fact, biblically, not all people are "children of God," as is clear from John's earlier record, "But as many as received Him, to them He gave the right to become children of God, *even* to those who believe in His name" (John 1:12). Only believers, those who "receive" Christ, are children of God.

Even the term "disciple" must be understood correctly. In biblical terminology, there are not two kinds of Christians, as though certain kinds of Christians are more committed to the disciplines of the Christian life, and therefore are "disciples" Conversely, it is thought that those who are not so committed, while being Christians, are not necessarily disciples. The Bible, however, does not use the term disciple in this way. In NT times, a disciple was simply one who followed the teachings of Jesus, at least identifying with Jesus outwardly. Judas, for example, was initially identified as a disciple (Luke 6:12, 16), but proved to be a false one. So also the multitude that followed Jesus and were fed by Him were called disciples, but most of them quit following Christ when His teachings became difficult to swallow (John 6:66).

Jesus here is not praying for Judas, nor for the multitude who stopped following Him. Nor does He pray for superficial disciples who pass themselves off as believers but are not (the tares among the wheat, to use the words of one of Jesus' parables in Matthew 13:36-43). He prays for those "You have given Me," that is, the elect of God. He uses no figures of speech but speaks clearly with very specific words. This is a select group of individuals whom Jesus has in mind, and it is clear from the context that group initially included those in the Upper Room with the Lord. But it also includes "those also who believe in Me through their word" (vs. 20). We who believe today are part of the elect of God.

While God so loves the world (and in John, that word most often refers to the entire world of humanity), Jesus prays for the select (relatively few) image-bearing humans. This is the inner circle of God's family, those privileged to have the Son of God making mention of them to the Father.

Lord, I am overwhelmed that You actually talk to the Father about me. Wow!

More on the Trinity

John 17:9b-10

[9] ". . . for they are Yours; [10] and all things that are Mine are Yours, and Yours are Mine; and I have been glorified in them.

Community in its finest form—that is what the Father and Son experienced. While the Trinity is the most unique and central part of the Christian understanding of God, Jesus here gives the most attention to the communal relationship between Himself and the Father. Earlier He spoke much of the Holy Spirit as bringing to the disciples' memory everything Jesus had taught them. But all three are spoken of as God, in perfect harmony.

Practitioners of other religions deride Christians for not having enough gods (only three) or holding to polytheism (a belief in many gods). Christians believe, though, there is one and only one God. Jesus spoke of the God of Abraham, Isaac and Jacob, and built His teachings on (and never undermined) the monotheism of the Jews. To be sure He removed the barrier between God and man through His incarnation. But that bringing together of God and man into one individual was unique to Him. He was the matchless God-man. As such, at the point of incarnation, it makes sense that there would be things about such a union that would stretch human understanding. And this is, in part, why the Trinity is so easily misunderstood.

This is not to say that the Trinity was dependent upon the incarnation, for the second person of the Trinity has existed before and apart from incarnation. Yet, we can only delve into these things from the human side, and so incarnation is important to our understanding of the Trinity.

So Trinitarian teaching views the Father as being God overall, the ultimate Creator and Judge of all that there is. The Son is viewed best in His incarnation, as God merged with humanity in the single person of Jesus. The two have had and always will have an intimate relationship that is best described as Father and Son. The Holy Spirit is viewed as God working unseen in the world, doing the will of the Father on behalf of the Son. Words fail in describing this triune God. This ought to be expected, for though God can be approximated in human language, He cannot be contained or limited by our inabilities to think or express what we know about Him.

In all cases, He is viewed as one God, not three. Father, Son and Spirit do not exist independently from one another but are in perfect oneness, perfect community: one God in three persons. We are not saying there are three Gods in one God. He is one God, and He exists as three persons.

*Lord, Your mystery and at times incomprehensibility cause
me to fall down and worship You in amazement.*

Sharing with God

John 17:9b-10 (cont.)

⁹ ". . . for they are Yours; ¹⁰ and all things that are Mine are Yours, and Yours are Mine; and I have been glorified in them.

Before anything else existed, God was all there was. Some modern atheists ascribe to the popular notion, "The cosmos is all there is," but that is a greater assertion of faith than the belief in a Creator God. A much more reasonable faith sees that the universe reflects intelligent design, and thus leads us to believe that there is Designer behind it all. Thus, before the cosmos (all of creation) existed, there was God. If we accept what scientists tell us, that time is a measure of change, then we are left with utter amazement and mystery as to what time means when speaking of a God who existed before anything else existed.

Obviously there was a change when creation took place—and that would be, from human perspective, when time began. So even to say "before creation there was God" is a conundrum. Possibly it might be better to speak of God as being outside of time, where He can observe all of time as eternally present to Him, from beginning to end. The universe is finite, it had a beginning, but God is not finite, He had no beginning—for such a notion has no meaning outside of time, where God exists.

Jesus speaks in His Upper Room prayer about all things created being shared between the Father and Son, and this goes beyond the sequence of "before and after" that is the normal way of thinking about time. Therefore, this sharing of all things is a complete and absolute sharing; there is no time when they didn't share them. Fascinating is the thought that in forming creation, God desired to share it all with humanity, His image bearers, as seen in the story of Adam and Eve. He placed them in the Garden of Eden and instructed them to "cultivate" it and eat freely from the trees (Gen. 2:15). Only in one regard did God not want to share with us, and that was the knowledge of good and evil. In fact, that would be a sharing of that which is not shared among the community of the persons of God. For evil is that which is not God—actions done apart from communion with Him. God cannot do that within Himself, that is, act against Himself. But in creating humans as independent image bearers, He created the possibility of evil, of moral agents capable of acting independently of God. That is what the tree represented.

So evil (or sin, to use a related word) is acting apart from full communion with God, seeking to enjoy life apart from Him. That is a violation of the community of sharing in God and His image bearers.

Father, I want to share in the fellowship You enjoy with Your Son.

Glorified in Us

John 17:9b-10

⁹ ". . . for they are Yours; ¹⁰ and all things that are Mine are Yours, and Yours are Mine; and I have been glorified in them.

How was Jesus glorified in the disciples? We must first see that God was glorified and is glorified in His creation. The angels understood this when they hovered around the throne of God, saying, "Holy, Holy, Holy, is the Lord of hosts, the whole earth is full of His glory" (Isa. 6:3). All of creation is designed to illustrate God, to demonstrate what He is like. "Since the creation of the world His invisible attributes, His eternal power and divine nature, have been clearly seen, being understood through what has been made, so that they are without excuse" (Rom. 1:20).

More particularly, when God created humankind in His image (Gen. 1:26), the reflection took on a tangible, embodied form, like a magnifying glass that gives a close-up picture with more details. We humans reflect a God who creates, relates and chooses. And when we do that in community with God, we reflect Him accurately. But when we eat from the tree of the forbidden fruit, we break communion with Him, making a distorted picture. Unity with God is the critical component of reflecting His glory, for that unity among the Father, Son and Spirit is foremost in Jesus' Upper Room teaching and His prayer.

Now as Jesus prays, He is thinking about the disciples who have left all to follow Him. And they are following Him to the end. They have experienced the community of fellowship that has existed in the Trinity since before time. This is what glorifies God. This is what glorified Jesus. Think of this as an ever-increasing focus on God's glory—first in creation, then through mankind in general, and finally with the coming of the Messiah, embodied not just in those created in God's image but now in Jesus, the very image of God—God in the flesh, as it were, substantially. "He is the radiance of His glory and the exact representation of His nature" (Heb. 1:3a). "For in Him all the fullness of Deity dwells in bodily form . . ." (Col. 2:9).

Now Jesus said He has been glorified in His disciples. When people saw them, they recognized them as followers of Christ. Their lives brought attention to the Son of God. Later, when the religious leaders ". . . observed the confidence of Peter and John and understood that they were uneducated and untrained men, they were amazed, and *began* to recognize them as having been with Jesus" (Acts 4:13). The disciples had lived and continued to live in community with the triune God—and they made God known. When we live and act in community with the triune God, He will be glorified in us as well.

Lord, in my life be glorified in me, that I might reflect You to the world around.

WEEKEND READING

Saturday – John 12:29-43
Sunday – Acts 21:27-40

PERSONAL REFLECTIONS

_____

_____

_____

_____

_____

_____

_____

_____

_____

_____

_____

_____

_____

_____

_____

_____

_____

_____

_____

_____

_____

_____

_____

Jesus Not Here?

John 17:11

[11] "I am no longer in the world; and yet they themselves are in the world, and I come to You. Holy Father, keep them in Your name, the name which You have given Me, that they may be one even as We are."

His work on earth was finished; He was no longer part of the worldly scene. Yes, He was still physically in the world for a few more hours, but for all intents and purposes, He was done. He came to do the Father's will, and all that was left was to leave the world, to die. But in that departure would be the salvation of the world. What a grand finale that was going to be. It was as good as done.

Theologians speak of the prophetic past tense, where a prophet refers to future events using the grammatical past tense, as though the events were already completed. The idea is that God, above and beyond all time, is everywhere and always present; He sees the future the same as He sees the past. So in a divine intersection with time and space, Jesus speaks with a sense of finality, for He sees the next few hours as already completed.

He could speak of no longer being in the world though, because His primary prophetic ministry was over—there was no more offer of the kingdom. Not until after His death would the invitation go out again (Acts 3:19-21). Between the Upper Room prayer and His execution, He would not be inviting anyone to "repent, for the kingdom of God is at hand." Only to the thief on the cross did He promise, "Today you will be with me in Paradise" (Luke 23:43), which is distinguished from "the kingdom."

Jesus would no longer be in the world as the pre-crucified Messiah because of His death on the cross. He would no longer be in the world as the pre-resurrected hope of Israel or as as the Son who learned obedience through suffering (Heb. 5:8). He would no longer be veiled in His glory, being made "a little lower than the angels" (Heb. 2:7). No longer would He be "emptied . . . humbled" (Phil. 2:7-8). The pre-glorified incarnation would be a thing of the past, and the specific task for which He came into the world would be completed. His time on earth, like ours, was only temporary.

Since the fall in Eden, death has plagued all of humankind. Life on earth as we know it now became temporary. But there is hope beyond because Jesus who came into this world is "no longer in the world." He did not come to stay, but to be the "first fruits" from the dead, to lead us to eternal life, to fellowship with Him forever (1 Cor. 15:20). Now if He is the first fruits from the dead, then we who are the rest of the harvest will someday no longer be in the world either.

Lord Jesus, I look forward to being with You forever, no longer in this world.

He Left Us Here

John 17:11 (cont.)

[11] "I am no longer in the world; and yet they themselves are in the world, and I come to You. Holy Father, keep them in Your name, the name which You have given Me, that they may be one even as We are."

Skin of an onion—composed of continuous peels, at different levels, all the way down to the core. This describes the challenge of peeling back the various layers of meaning in this Upper Room prayer of our Lord. It is a kaleidoscope of color and beauty in the mind of our Lord, intricately woven thoughts and intimations, a symphony of melodies and descants. Volumes could be written to decipher these 26 verses of Scripture, for we are catching a glimpse into the mind and conversation of God. At every level we learn His thoughts, which are above our thoughts (Isa. 55:9). We must content ourselves with mere superficial reflections for now, awaiting the true glory of the mind of God revealed in the day we see Him face to face. As a friend of mine recently said, "Once we have been in the Lord's presence, we will ask, 'Why didn't You bring me here sooner?'"

Jesus now makes it clear that although He would no longer be in the world, He was planning to leave His disciples in the world. What an irony; what a turnabout for the disciples. In any human scheme, that would seem to be unreasonable—the leader of the movement copping out before achieving the movement's goals, just when the going gets tough. What gives?

This had been the plan all along, for Jesus' leaving was the very thing that would make the goal achievable. He couldn't stay with them as the un-sacrificed Lamb of God, the un-resurrected Messiah. That would have been failure for the mission. However, it was required that His followers remain behind as ambassadors to the world. And they needed to be "in the world" to do that. This was their mission.

Although the disciples in the Upper Room would not have appreciated the significance of this at the time, clearly their memory of this would have been ignited when the post-resurrected Master commanded them, "You will receive power when the Holy Spirit has come upon you; and you shall be My witnesses both in Jerusalem, and in all Judea and Samaria, and even to the remotest part of the earth" (Acts 1:8). Alone among the gospel writers, John, 50 years later, faithfully and lovingly recorded this prayer, fresh in His mind as the day he heard it from the lips of Christ. And His memory as a disciple and his mission as an ambassador of Christ "in the world" remained fresh all those years.

Lord, thank You for leaving me here as an ambassador (2 Cor. 5:20) to represent You in this world. Help me to be faithful in this mission.

In the World, in His Name

John 17:11 (cont.)

[11] "I am no longer in the world; and yet they themselves are in the world, and I come to You. Holy Father, keep them in Your name, the name which You have given Me, that they may be one even as We are."

He is gone; we are here. And now He asked His Father, "[K]eep them in Your name." The gospel writer John used common words and simple grammatical constructions to record Jesus' teachings. However, the concepts conveyed in this Upper Room prayer are anything but simple. What does it mean to "keep them in Your name"?

To answer this we must first note that Jesus reminded His disciples (see John 7:33) through His prayer that His departure had as its destination the heavenly Father's presence. Just as He had a purpose in entering the world, He had a purpose in leaving it. The word "keep" carries the connotation of protection, so Jesus is asking the Father to protect them while He is gone from being with them. That protection comes "in Your name," which, as we have already seen, means that He is the God who will be there for them in whatever need they have. The writer of Proverbs states, "The name of the LORD is a strong tower; the righteous runs into it and is safe" (Prov. 18:10).

First, they needed protection from abandoning all hope in the next few hours and in the next three days. The disciples were about to go through the unimaginable experience of seeing their Master, whom they loved and followed, being executed and buried, bringing to an end their hopes and dreams for the kingdom of God. Second, they needed protection from the hostility of the religious leaders who would now turn against them. Indeed, Christians through the ages have experienced horrific persecution for their identification with Christ. They (and we) also needed protection from the false teachings of the religious leaders, the trials and the temptations of earthly life.

How often do we ask not only, "What would Jesus do?" but also, "Why couldn't Jesus be here to take care of this?" Wouldn't the Christian walk go better if the physical Jesus were still here, and we could go to Him at any time to solve our problems, settle our doctrinal disputes and convince skeptics? But Jesus has left us here for a purpose, to carry on His mission as ambassadors to the world. We must never forget that we are citizens of another country, the Kingdom of God. We are on "foreign assignment," as part of our King's diplomatic corps, temporarily stationed on planet earth. And our heavenly Father is using all the resources at His disposal to protect us, until our mission is completed and He orders us home to heaven.

Lord, I take refuge in Your Name and Your power while I am "in the world."

Unity of Holiness

John 17:11 (cont.)

[11] *"I am no longer in the world; and yet they themselves are in the world, and I come to You. Holy Father, keep them in Your name, the name which You have given Me, that they may be one even as We are."*

"Holy Father"—this is the only time in Scripture God is referred to in this way. Certainly the Father is holy, but we usually read of the third member of the Trinity, the Holy Spirit, spoken about in this way. "Holy Father" emphasizes God's separateness from the world, and in light of His disciples being "in the world," this seems appropriate. The Holy Father is completely "other than," as theologians would describe holiness. He is not tainted by worldliness. One writer puts it this way: He is infinitely high because He is holy, but He is infinitely "nigh" (or close) because He is Father. The disciples being left "in the world" needed God to be both: holy and Father.

Together, the Father and Son desire that His followers would also live holy, separated lives—separate from the sinful desires of the flesh and the self-centered view of life. The disciples may have been encouraged to hear Jesus praying this way, for they really didn't want Him to leave. How would they fend for themselves in a world that was hostile to their Master, and now would be hostile toward them? The Holy Father who is separate, higher than anything in this world, would keep them separate, higher than their circumstances. God draws us up to His level; that is what it means to become holy like He is holy (see 1 Peter 1:16).

Worldliness is to live at the world's level, walking apart from God, rather than apart from the world, as though we are with Adam and Eve, eating from the tree of the knowledge of good and evil. But holy living is to continue following Christ by following the teachings He left for us.

Jesus ties all this in with His request that His followers "may be one even as We are." This does not mean that Christians should join in with the ecumenical movement to bring all churches together and ascribe to one set of doctrines. Such efforts are rooted in diminishing the core doctrines Christ taught, like His uniqueness and deity (John 8:58), His exclusivity (John 14:6; Acts 4:12) and the nature of His sacrificial death on the cross—to name a few. The oneness Jesus prays for is a unity among the true followers of Christ, a unity that comes through understanding and holding fast to the true teachings of Christ, not to every wind of doctrine that is labeled "Christian." In the world, there will be many temptations to quit following Christ. Jesus asks that His followers continue together in living holy lives while still in this world.

Father, help me be holy today as You are holy always.

Preparing for Handoff

12 "While I was with them, I was keeping them in Your name which You have given Me; and I guarded them and not one of them perished but the son of perdition, so that the Scripture would be fulfilled."

L ike a farewell speech, Jesus outlines His final requests to His Father, almost like His dying requests. His ministry of teaching is about done; all that is left is His great and final task of dying as a substitutionary sacrifice for the world. Of course His death is not the end of the story; it is the transition into the next great phase of God's glory being displayed in the world, a transition of God's program from one of life under the Law of Moses, to life under grace. In this transitionary time, Jesus confers with His Father about the handoff of responsibilities. In particular, the handoff at this juncture of His divine communication has to do with the safety of the disciples whom He is leaving behind.

What love and care He has for the eleven, and as we see later in this prayer, also for those who will believe through their testimony. That includes all believers of all time. Jesus is eminently concerned for us all who have left everything to follow Christ. While He was physically on the earth 2,000 years ago, for about three and half years, He protected the twelve disciples, as John records, by keeping and guarding them. These were His intimates, the ones who stayed with Him when all others left (see John 6:66). He had chosen them (John 6:70) and built into their lives through the constant in-person discipling, training. This was of utmost concern to Him. Although He taught the multitudes, He healed many of their ailments, He proclaimed "whosoever will," it was these men in the Upper Room that He was most concerned about.

Modern management gurus would say that a CEO needs to give the most time to developing his top leaders. But that is nothing new—Jesus adapted this mode of operation long ago. But the organization Jesus was building was not a business venture. No, He was building the church of God, the vehicle through which God would reach the world with the message of Christ. The person of Jesus Christ was about to give way to the "body of Christ," the description by which the church is best known. As a physical man there were natural limitations to His reach. But through the corporate body of all believers, His reach would become exponential. And Jesus was discussing with His Father this transition. These men, and by extension we believers today, would become the primary task force for reaching the world.

Lord, thank You for protecting me as I strive to be Your ambassador today.

Weekend Reading

Saturday – John 12:44-50
Sunday – Acts 22:1-30

PERSONAL REFLECTIONS

_____
_____
_____
_____
_____
_____
_____
_____
_____
_____
_____
_____
_____
_____
_____
_____
_____
_____
_____
_____
_____
_____
_____

Keeping and Guarding

John 17:12 (cont.)

12 "While I was with them, I was keeping them in Your name which You have given Me; and I guarded them and not one of them perished but the son of perdition, so that the Scripture would be fulfilled."

K eeping and guarding His disciples, even when they were unaware that was a concern, was a big part of Jesus' ministry on earth. Out of the multitude, He weeded out the curious onlookers, the self-righteous and the comfort seekers. He spoke of total commitment to Him (John 6:32-58). But what really riled His detractors was His concluding statement: "For this reason I have said to you, that no one can come to Me unless it has been granted him from the Father" (John 6:65). He was clearly separating the wolves from sheep!

His teaching caused a great disturbance among the vast majority of people. "As a result of this many of His disciples withdrew and were not walking with Him anymore" (John 6:66). Talk about disciple-reduction! Even then, He gave the twelve an easy out: "You do not want to go away also, do you?" (John 6:67). They could have left at that time, the door was open; Jesus wasn't going to coerce them to stay, or drop the standard.

Jesus was not about gaining a large crowd of followers; He was looking for highly committed disciples, those who would leave all to follow Him. And from the multitude, there were twelve. Peter expressed their commitment well: "Lord, to whom shall we go? You have words of eternal life" (John 6:68).

For many today, it would be considered ministry failure to go from 5,000 to 12 in one day! That's over *minus* 400 percent growth, ending up with 0.2 percent attendance at the Jesus discipleship meetings. God is like that, though. He began a nation with a single man, Abraham. He whittled down the armed forces of Gideon to 300 (Judg. 7). Jesus wanted to launch His worldwide enterprise, the church, with just a few highly committed men.

It was these men whom Jesus kept and guarded. They had given up all to follow Him; He would take care of His own. He protected them from the Pharisees' criticism, for example, when He defended their eating grain as they walked along the fields on a Sabbath day (Luke 6:1-5). He protected them from the temptation of Satan (Luke 22:31). They just may have been the subject of much of His prayer time on earth.

Finally, the Lord protected His disciples by praying for them. This Upper Room prayer shows Jesus' intercessory role (Rom. 8:34) and His advocacy (1 John 2:1) for us. He continues to protect His own against the accusations of Satan.

Lord, I praise You for protecting me and keeping me as Your own.

One Perished, We Shudder

John 17:12 (cont.)

12 "While I was with them, I was keeping them in Your name which You have given Me; and I guarded them and not one of them perished but the son of perdition, so that the Scripture would be fulfilled."

One perished. Jesus kept and guarded all but one. Judas. One can't help but shudder when thinking about this man who was so close, yet so far. He was one of the twelve who had left all to follow Christ. His sacrifice to follow Jesus was great, but it was flawed—as was the sacrifice all of them had made; take note of Peter's impending denial of Christ, which the Master had predicted (John 13:38). The past tense used by our Lord in reference to Judas—and it is clear that this is the one to whom Jesus referred—is an obvious use of the prophetic past tense, where He speaks of Judas' yet-to-come suicide as a past event, good as done.

The failure of Judas, though, was not a failure of Jesus to keep and guard him. From the beginning, He knew the heart of Judas. After all had left Him except the twelve who proclaimed their loyalty, Jesus said, "Did I Myself not choose you, the twelve, and *yet* one of you is a devil?" (John 6:70). At the beginning of the Lord's Supper, as John records it, the devil had "already put into the heart of Judas Iscariot, *the son* of Simon, to betray Him . . ." (John 13:2).

The telltale signs of satanic work appeared as early as the pre-ministry temptation of Jesus in the wilderness (Matt. 4), then in the challenges by demon-possessed individuals, and now through the close-knit, committed band of twelve men. None of the other disciples apparently suspected anything amiss with Judas. Even after that poignant moment in the Upper Room when Jesus said one of them would betray Him, after giving Judas the symbolic morsel, after Judas immediately left the group, none of the other eleven suspected him as a betrayer (John 13:26-30). In fact, each of them was more concerned about himself, whether Jesus thought he was the guilty party (Matt. 26:25).

Much could be written about God's sovereignty ("that Scripture would be fulfilled") and the freedom of Judas' will. But Judas' betrayal *was* a prophetic certainty—and he would be held responsible: ". . . woe to that man by whom the Son of Man is betrayed! It would have been good for that man if he had not been born" (Matt. 26:24). And we shudder again.

The amazing thing here is that Satan was throwing his best (worst?) efforts at Jesus, using corruption in one of His closest followers. And yet all this plays into the hand of God, for the ultimate glorification of Jesus.

Lord, I believe the worst things that happen to me can become opportunities You to be glorified in me. Help me to remember and rest in that.

One Event, Two Intentions

John 17:12 (cont.)

12 "While I was with them, I was keeping them in Your name which You have given Me; and I guarded them and not one of them perished but the son of perdition, so that the Scripture would be fulfilled."

God's ways are higher than our ways—and that perplexes us. How could God, who is not the author of evil, use evil to accomplish His purpose, without diminishing His goodness and righteousness? While we will never solve this dilemma fully, it should not overly concern us if we truly believe we are finite creatures trying to understand the infinite. Our understanding of absolute holiness is limited by our limited holiness. Faith is all about accepting and embracing the difference and living with the seeming anomalies.

That God can use evil is fully established in Scripture. The psalmist prophesied Judas' betrayal: "Even my close friend in whom I trusted, who ate my bread, has lifted up his heel against me" (Ps. 41:9). Judas' treachery was unequivocally wrong, yet he was instrumental in Jesus' going to the cross. One could say God did not *cause* Judas to actually to betray Jesus, but He used his evil action. But that makes it seem like God's whole plan of redemption was dependent or contingent upon Judas' messing up. This carries a great amount of tension in itself. If God simply knew Judas would mess up, then effectively, Judas could have done nothing else. That doesn't sound like free will.

An instructive example is found in the story of Joseph's brothers pleading with him for forgiveness (with the ruse that their recently deceased father wanted them to pass on to Joseph the request to spare them). Joseph responds, "As for you, you meant evil against me, but God meant it for good in order to bring about this present result, to preserve many people alive" (Gen. 50:20). One act, but two different intentions, two different wills. The brothers were fully responsible for their devious actions toward Joseph, but God had a higher purpose in the same activity. So we see that two wills can be working at the same time, in the same event. Both take responsibility for the event, but in the one case evil is assigned, and in the other righteous sovereignty.

Another example is found in Peter's Pentecostal sermon: "This *Man*, delivered over by the predetermined plan and foreknowledge of God, you nailed to a cross by the hands of godless men and put *Him* to death" (Acts 2:23). God planned it; humans willfully acted out their role. One act, two different intentions. God is glorified; man is guilty. The same holds true with Judas: he meant it for evil, but God meant it for good, the salvation of souls.

*Lord, help me to align my will with Yours, so that You may
be glorified in and through me, not in spite of me.*

Into His Presence

John 17:13

13 "But now I come to You; and these things I speak in the world so that they may have My joy made full in themselves."

Many Christians include in their prayer to God, "I come to You." On the one hand, this seems odd in that God is everywhere present, and therefore we are always in His presence. Jesus obviously would have known this better than anyone, and He lived on earth in the constant awareness of this truth. Yet these are the very words He used in praying to His heavenly Father: "I come to You." What do we make of this? Is it a big deal or just incidental words added to flesh out His prayer?

Unfortunately, at times we mere humans do fall into using filler expressions when we "say our prayers," certain formulas and code phrases like finishing our prayers with the automatic, "In Jesus' name we pray." Some even go so far as to recite canned prayers someone else composed. However, Jesus' words carried meanings that He fully intended; this was not ritual, nor was it rote. This should likewise be the case for us who seek to imitate Him.

Jesus prayed, it seems, with an imagery of approaching His Father like someone would approach another being. Obviously, He hadn't physically moved anywhere; He was still in the Upper Room with His disciples. But the image comes to mind of the high priest entering the tabernacle where God is pictured as residing, to make sacrifice for the people. Even then, that Old Testament image (either the tabernacle or the temple) was really a picture of God in His heavenly throne room, for an earthly tent or temple could not contain the infinite God of the universe. Solomon, upon completing the building of the temple, recognized this when he said, "But will God indeed dwell on the earth? Behold, heaven and the highest heaven cannot contain You, how much less this house which I have built!" (1 Kings 8:27). He concluded by asking, "Listen to the supplication of Your servant and of Your people Israel, when they pray toward this place; hear in heaven Your dwelling place" (1 Kings 8:30).

Praying to God who is spirit must involve the use of imagery, which in literary terms involves metaphors, figures of speech. Praying to God should be a conscious focus of our attention on Him, in the same way as one would make the effort to approach God in a physical temple. While the physicality of it is not required (see Jesus' comments to the woman at the well in John 4:21-24), the imagery remains. We do approach God in prayer by focusing more acutely as though we were in His physical presence.

Lord, I do come to You. I am conscious of You right now, though not physically, but spiritually. You are every much as real to me as the chair I am sitting on.

Of Grace and Mercy

[13] "But now I come to You; and these things I speak in the world so that they may have My joy made full in themselves."

God's presence is the place to be. "I come to You." What do we find there? In the context of the Upper Room, we can see that in God's presence there was communication between the Father and the Son. What a place for us to be, as children of God. We are with the One who is not embarrassed to call us His brothers (Heb. 2:11). It is there we find acceptance and belonging, as part of the family. Of course we are speaking spiritually when we say "there." We are there in belief, not in spatial positioning. We are there emotionally and psychologically. And this is just as real—no, more real—than to be physically in a temple or on a high mountain. When we leave here and enter God's presence in heaven, our personal tangible experience may change, but the reality of being in God's presence will not. We are there now through faith.

That is why the writer of Hebrews says, "Let us draw near with confidence to the throne of grace, so that we may receive mercy and find grace to help in time of need" (Heb. 4:16). We need to live in the grace and mercy of God, a constant awareness and appreciation. When we are lonely, we "come to You" and by faith, we imagine with our spiritual mind, to be in God's very presence—because that is where we are, and we believe it to be true.

When we are discouraged, we come to Him, the Encourager who can say to us, "I have been where you are, and I can come along side to walk with you." When we are in pain, we come to the Great Physician, who can heal but also sustains when the healing is delayed. But we know that we can know the fellowship of sharing in His sufferings (Phil. 3:10). When we are arrogant, His presence humbles us as we see Him high and lifted up, with the train of His robe filling the temple (Isa. 6). When we are humiliated, we come to the One who exalts the humble. He lifts us up and puts our feet on solid ground.

When we fear, we come to the One who is our strong tower (Prov. 18:10). When we feel insignificant, we come to the infinite Creator God of the universe, who knows us by name. When we are anxious, we come to the Alpha and Omega, who knows the beginning and the end of everything, including our circumstances—and, as the song writer says, "He holds my hand." So when we feel guilty, we should come to His throne room of grace and mercy. He will meet every need we have.

Lord, "In Your presence is fullness of joy; In Your right hand there are pleasures forever" (Ps. 16:11). Amen.

WEEKEND READING

Saturday – John 18:1-11
Sunday – Acts 23:1-22

PERSONAL REFLECTIONS

_____

_____

_____

_____

_____

_____

_____

_____

_____

_____

_____

_____

_____

_____

_____

_____

_____

_____

_____

_____

Joy in the Midst of Difficulties

John 17:13 (cont.)

[13] "But now I come to You; and these things I speak in the world so that they may have My joy made full in themselves.

Jesus was all about joy, which at this juncture in His tenure on earth might sound a bit macabre. But He actually used that word four other times in the Upper Room (see 15:11; 16:21-22, 24). It is the same word John used to describe his experience in being the announcer, the forerunner, for the Lord's advent, likening it to the joy that a groom's attendant has when the groom arrives for his wedding (John 3:29). In John's case, the coming of Christ meant a decrease in his (John's) significance because someone more important than he had arrived. He would fade to the background, and Jesus would come into prominence. Yet John was filled with joy.

Our problem with joy is that it is usually tainted with a worldly, superficial perspective and is closely tied to our own well-being. Those earthly kinds of joy are dependent upon circumstances and are ultimately fleeting, which in this fallen world means joy is short-lived at best, limited in scope and depth.

But Jesus, like John before Him, saw joy as transcending the brokenness of this world and of our lives. It is not dependent upon our physical well-being, or our material wealth, or our enjoyable experiences. Those, to be sure, are good experiences, and the Scripture never teaches us to look for trouble, as though there is some benefit in spiritual masochism.

But the joy Jesus spoke of relates to the glory of God. He had just spoken to the Father about His chosen disciples, who we know brought Jesus great joy. The Lord, when He looked at His disciples, may have had in mind the words of the prophet, "The LORD your God is in your midst . . . He will exult over you with joy, He will be quiet in His love, He will rejoice over you with shouts of joy" (Zeph. 3:17). In the Upper Room they did not at all experience that joy. But Jesus knew they were listening in on this prayer, and He desired that they would one day look back on this time with great joy. And what a joy it was going to be for the disciples after the resurrection, when they would come to understand that joy of which Jesus spoke. And to realize that this Master whom they had left all to follow, with whom they broke bread, was the "Son of God" (Rom. 1:4) who loved every minute He was with them, like a lover who gazes over the dinner candlelight at his beloved with great joy.

Jesus' prayer was for you and me as well, that we would have a joy that supersedes any adverse or depressing circumstance. For He is with us always.

Lord, restore to me the joy of my salvation, that I might rejoice in You.

An Uncanny Joy

John 17:13 (cont.)

13 "But now I come to You; and these things I speak in the world so that they may have My joy made full in themselves."

More than human joy—that is what Jesus was talking about. A supernatural joy that completely overshadows human experience while not negating that experience. Too often we think joy requires the absence of fallen-world effects. How can there be joy when there is so much suffering in the world? Actually, the joy of which Jesus spoke is magnified precisely when life is darkest. That is the time when only a God-inspired, Jesus-modeled, Spirit-enabled joy will prevail. All other joys will quickly be swallowed up in the bitterness and depression of trying life circumstances.

Notice the joy Jesus spoke of is "My joy." He has overcome the world, and even as He was then facing execution, He continued to have joy, like a light shining in the darkness. It was operative, it superseded, it overshadowed, it more than compensated. In fact, it was a joy that arose in the midst of suffering and blazed brilliantly in relief against the backdrop of the human problem.

This is a joy that led the disciples, after being jailed and tortured for their loyalty to Jesus, to go away "rejoicing that they had been considered worthy to suffer shame for *His* name" (Acts 5:41). The joy was not in the suffering, or in being delivered from the suffering, but it was a joy in the Lord, that the suffering proved they were worthy of the Lord.

Is this not the kind of joy that is rooted in "fixing our eyes on Jesus, the author and perfecter of faith, who for the joy set before Him endured the cross, despising the shame, and has sat down at the right hand of the throne of God?" (Heb. 12:2). Is this not the joy that Jesus spoke about in the parable that motivates us to be faithful? "His master said to him, 'Well done, good and faithful slave. You were faithful with a few things, I will put you in charge of many things; enter into the joy of your master'" (Matt. 25:23).

Was this not the joy of Paul and Silas, after being flogged and jailed, "praying and singing hymns of praise to God, and the prisoners were listening to them . . ." (Acts 16:25)? In like manner, Christians down through the ages have been animated by the joy of the Lord while facing persecution and death.

But this joy does not come easily; the world continually contradicts this kind of inner, overriding happiness. That is why Jesus prayed to His Father, "that they might have My joy made full in themselves."

Lord, help me be joyful in the midst of life's trying circumstances.
I need Your supernatural help to give me a supernatural joy.

The Living Word

14 "I have given them Your word; and the world has hated them, because they are not of the world, even as I am not of the world."

"**W**ord" was the operative term in Jesus' ministry, the *Logos*. The Gospel According to John begins with it: "In the beginning was the Word, and the Word was with God, and the Word was God . . . And the Word became flesh, and dwelt among us, and we saw His glory, glory as of the only begotten from the Father, full of grace and truth" (John 1:1, 14). In the largest, most expansive sense, our Lord Jesus Christ is the Word, the true *Logos*!

Much has been written on what the term *logos* means. The Roman world, in which the gospel writer John was living when he wrote this account of the life of Christ, enjoyed the cultural carry-over from the previous Greek civilization. This was especially true in the arts and literature. Though it is usually translated "word," the term *logos* was not used in the grammatical sense (e.g. referring to a specific part of a sentence) or even to the spoken word (for which Greek has a better word, *rhema*). Rather *logos* conveyed a philosophical concept, involving ideas like knowledge, wisdom or reason. Its actual use and meaning have quite a storied history, being used by various philosophers in different ways. This may provide some background to John's use of the term in referring to Jesus as "the Word."

At the least, learned Greek readers would readily identify what he was conveying, that Jesus, the human being, is the ultimate statement of God. He was with God in the beginning of all time; He was God. And therefore, Jesus Christ eclipses all philosophical endeavors, for they find their end in Him, for He embodies the truth, the reason, the knowledge and the wisdom. In fact, Jesus said, "I am the way, and the truth, and the life; no one comes to the Father but through Me" (John 14:6). He is not just "a" way to truth; He is the "only" way to truth, for God Himself is the summation of all that humans seek in life.

So when Jesus said, "I have given them Your word," He was speaking of more than just the teachings He gave to His disciples. He gave them Himself. Earlier in the Upper Room, as He was preparing to wash their feet, John records, ". . . having loved His own who were in the world, He loved them to the end" (John 13:1). By His own standards He could give of Himself no more than to die for them. "Greater love has no one than this, that one lay down his life for his friends" (John 15:13).

Lord Jesus, You are the living Word, the absolute Truth, the Wisdom of God. You are greater than any philosophy. To know You is to know life.

The Guiding Word

John 17:14 (cont.)

[14] "I have given them Your word; and the world has hated them, because they are not of the world, even as I am not of the world."

We have seen that Jesus is "the Word" of God. In fact, at His second coming, He is pictured as riding on a white horse, "clothed with a robe dipped in blood, and His name is called The Word of God" (Rev. 19:13). But the picture continues, "From His mouth comes a sharp sword, so that with it He may strike down the nations . . ." (Rev. 19:15). This odd imagery is designed to depict the judgment of Christ on those who rebel against God. As the living Word of God, Jesus speaks words that carry great weight. This was true when He lived on earth among His disciples.

The spoken word that came from the living Word is indeed powerful. In Christian history, the phrase "Word of God" has become synonymous with the Bible, the Holy Scriptures (both Old and New Testaments). Two reasons have caused this. First, the Bible is "God-breathed," that is, it is inspired by God Himself (2 Tim. 3:16). Secondly, the Bible as a whole tells us about Jesus Christ, the living Word. On the road to Emmaus, Jesus demonstrated this truth. As Luke describes the event, "Beginning with Moses and with all the prophets, He explained to them the things concerning Himself in all the Scriptures" (Luke 24:27).

Jesus gave a summary of the weight of His words when He said, "He who rejects Me and does not receive My sayings, has one who judges him; the word I spoke is what will judge him at the last day" (John 12:48). In fact, this is what separated the true disciples from the "Sunday disciples." When the multitude of disciples stopped following Jesus because of His requirement for full-out commitment, only the twelve remained. Peter spoke on behalf of the others when he said, "Lord, to whom shall we go? You have words of eternal life" (John 6:68). He got it. He understood that Jesus was the Word, and that His message and teachings were all about eternal life. This answers the questions that philosophers from the earliest times have asked: "What is life all about? What is our purpose? Why do we exist?" As the popular Christian saying of the 1970s put it, "Jesus is the answer!"

And the disciples would be well equipped by the teachings of Christ for life without His physical presence. They would be able to wield "[t]he word of God [which] is living and active and sharper than any two-edged sword, and piercing as far as the division of soul and spirit, of both joints and marrow, and able to judge the thoughts and intentions of the heart" (Heb. 4:12).

Lord, thank You for Your Word, by which You guide me as I live for You.

The Equipping Word

[14] "I have given them Your word; and the world has hated them, because they are not of the world, even as I am not of the world."

The world today has it all wrong. If Jesus was such a non-threatening, non-judgmental, always gentle, accepting person, then why did the world of His day hate Him? That makes absolutely no sense. But when taken at face value, the Jesus of the Bible (contrary to the imagined "Jesus" of moralists) would be just as much hated today as back in the first century. Today's "world" would have found some way to execute Him. Social media would explode with invectives and venom against Him. The political pundits would slam Him for narrow-mindedness, for claiming that He alone was the truth and the way to God. He would be mocked for saying such cultish statements as "You must eat my flesh and drink my blood." He would be roundly labeled as a hypocrite and religious bigot for implying that anyone who believed anything other than His truth was destined for a lost eternity. If He lived today, He would not think twice about walking into a local mega-church and chasing out the carnival barkers, overturning the modern-day money tables of church capital campaigns.

No, Jesus would not have made many friends today. And neither will those who follow closely His teachings. Because the world hates Jesus, it will also hate us. The disciples in the Upper Room were being prepared for this. They would soon enough find out how true Jesus' statement was here. Early Christian history leads us to believe that all of the apostles died as martyrs except John, who died as an old man—and even then he suffered extreme persecution. These were fearless men who spoke the Word of God readily and powerfully. They were well trained and well equipped.

In spite of persecution, "the Word of the Lord kept on spreading" (Acts 6:7; see also 12:24; 19:20). That is how Luke, the writer of the book of Acts, describes the expansion of the Christian mission. It was "the Word" that spread, that increased.

So in a hostile world, we believers today, likewise, are well equipped with the Word of God. On our part, we need to become well trained in the use of the Word. Paul writes, "Let the word of Christ richly dwell within you, with all wisdom . . ." (Col. 3:16a). Using the analogy of the Word being food, the writer of Hebrews challenges us, ". . . solid food is for the mature, who because of practice have their senses trained to discern good and evil" (Heb. 5:14). We need to train ourselves in the Word and meditate on it regularly.

Lord, my desire is to feed on Your Word daily, that I might be fully equipped.

WEEKEND READING

Saturday – John 18:12-27
Sunday – Acts 23:23-35

PERSONAL REFLECTIONS

_____
_____
_____
_____
_____
_____
_____
_____
_____
_____
_____
_____
_____
_____
_____
_____
_____
_____
_____
_____
_____
_____

Culture Or Not

John 17:14 (cont.)

14 "I have given them Your word; and the world has hated them, because they are not of the world, even as I am not of the world."

"Christ and Culture" is the title of a book by theologian H. Richard Niebuhr (1951). Considering the relationship Christians have with the world around them, he analyzed his topic around the themes of 1) Christ against culture, 2) Christ of culture, 3) Christ above culture, 4) Christ and culture in paradox, and 5) Christ transforming culture. His question was "How do or how should followers of Jesus Christ live in this world?"

Is our faith conditioned to some degree by the cultural lenses we all wear? We might, for example, ask whether there is legitimacy to a "black theology" or an "African theology" or a "continental theology." Is there an authentic "Christian theology"? Should we engage culture or isolate ourselves from it; enjoy culture (the benign part of it) or avoid all forms of entertainment except those overtly Christian? Or in the words of our passage today, what does it mean to be "not of the world, even as I am not of the world"?

These are not easy questions, but I think they should not weigh us down in endless deliberations. Jesus enjoyed aspects of the cultural milieu in which He lived. The wedding feast at Cana is one example, and He even made some great wine for it. He hung out with tax collectors and their ilk. The world has wedding celebrations; the world has its "non-Christian" parties. Jesus obviously enjoyed the entertainment of nature, often using the birds, flowers and weather to provide fascinating illustrations for His teachings. Scripture (the NT in particular) is relatively silent about the styles of dress, forms of media entertainment, and specifics about outward lists of worldly do's and don'ts. So Jesus wasn't completely against the culture. Interestingly, along with the Scripture writers, He was more concerned about the moral and spiritual aspects of life rather than legal things and surface behavior.

But there were certain aspects of culture that were accepted as normal, which were in reality signs of rebellion against God. The Pharisees were held in high esteem and made an ostentatious show of their "good" works and rituals. When the culture condemned the woman supposedly caught in adultery (John 8), Jesus turned the culture of Judaism on its ear by not condemning that woman. He was above the lofty self-aggrandizements of the religious-cultural elite. Yet Jesus was also "in" the culture or world of His day, but He was not "of" the world. And that is the difference we will look at next.

Lord, help me not be controlled by requirements of my culture today, but to mold my life after the "culture" of Christ's grace and love.

Preparing for Hatred

John 17:14 (cont.)

[14] "I have given them Your word; and the world has hated them, because they are not of the world, even as I am not of the world."

The world does not take too kindly to Christians. No matter how inoffensive we try to be, no matter how loving we are toward the lost, the world simply can't stand genuine Christians. If they hated Christ, they will treat us likewise. Yes, many found Him fascinating when He fed them, healed them and put the establishment in its place. But when He became more pointed about righteousness and holiness, their attitudes quickly changed.

They ridiculed Him: "The Son of Man came eating and drinking, and they say, 'Behold, a gluttonous man and a drunkard, a friend of tax collectors and sinners!'" (Matt. 11:19). The mob tried throwing Him over a cliff (Luke 4:29), and the experts in the Law continuously tried to discredit Him. Many of those who followed early on abandoned Him completely. And of course, in the end, they crucified Him, with popular opinion agreeing with the verdict, "Let His blood be on us and on our children" (Matt. 27:25).

The bad news for the disciples, it seemed at the time, was that things were only going to get worse for them. Not only was Jesus leaving them, but all the animosity, rejection and hatred the world heaped on Him would transfer to them in His absence! The Good News of the Gospel wasn't sounding too good, and the prayer of our Lord must have added more gloom to the thick air of the Upper Room. Interesting that Jesus allows the disciples to hear Him praying like this. He never pulled punches; life as His follower would not be easy.

However, the thrust of His conversation with the Father was to prepare and equip the disciples for that coming reality. What they didn't realize at this point was that they *would* be very well prepared, not only with the teaching of Jesus, which they would very well remember, as He promised (John 14:26), but also with the Holy Spirit, who would enable them as God's presence after Jesus left them.

Jesus' prediction was true. After the spiritual high experience of Pentecost, when the disciples were "having favor with all people" (Acts 2:47), Peter and John were arrested, then all the apostles were flogged (Acts 5), Stephen was stoned (Acts 8), the disciples were scattered under the fierce persecution of Saul of Tarsus (Acts 8), and then James the apostle was beheaded (Acts 12). Jesus knew what was coming, so He prayed fervently and intensely for His followers. There was absolutely no way they could handle what was coming, apart from divine strength and intervention.

Lord, thank You for praying for me before I fall into my trials.

In, But Not of, the World

John 17:15

15 "I do not ask You to take them out of the world, but to keep them from the evil one.

The well-known phrase "in the world, but not of the world" is one of those pithy statements that has stood the test of time, because it comes from the Upper Room prayer of the Lord Jesus Christ. But Christians wrestle with how that looks in everyday life. For some, it means avoiding so-called "worldly" activities, such as drinking, smoking, R-rated movies, dancing and premarital sex—all lumped together on an evangelical "do not do" list. Then there is a growing claim to "freedom" in many circles to throw off the shackles of the older generation and its cultural "phobias" and enjoy the freedom we have in Christ. "All things are lawful," the Scripture says, after all. Is this freedom or licentiousness? Does the list need adjusting? What about the rest of the saying, "but not all things are profitable" (1 Cor. 6:12; 10:23)?

The word "legalism," often used in this context, actually does not occur in the Bible, though like many theological terms (e.g. Trinity) it has a history of use among Christians. Historically, it has referred to a works-based salvation, that the moral law must be obeyed in order for a person to go to heaven. The apostle Paul, of course, roundly refutes such a notion ("For we maintain that a man is justified by faith apart from works of the Law" (Rom. 3:28, one such summary statement in Paul's treatise on justification).

However, the word "legalism" has also been used in reference to sanctification. Used in this way, it refers to Christian growth and maturity which comes through keeping a set of objective rules, classically termed as a "list of do's and don'ts." Ostensibly, the list is derived from Scripture, but all such lists are notoriously subject to the whims of the religious leaders of the group to which one belongs. The Pharisees, of NT fame, were one such group of list-makers, but today's "church" is not lacking in this either—all under the banner of "in the world, but not of the world."

But that is not what Jesus meant in His prayer about the world. He had made it clear in His teachings that all have come short of legalistic standards. A legalistic approach to God is a self-defeating proposition, for the law condemns us; it does not justify us before God. At one point, when the disciples heard Jesus' reaction to a rich, young ruler, "They were very astonished and said, 'Then who can be saved?' And looking at them Jesus said to them, 'With people this is impossible, but with God all things are possible'" (Matt. 19:25-26).

Lord, You left me in this world to be a follower of Your Son. Help me not to get distracted by the worldly concept of "legalism" as a way to gain Your approval.

Worldly Unbelief

John 17:15 (cont.)

¹⁵ "I do not ask You to take them out of the world, but to keep them from the evil one."

Why do Christians resort to legalism, living by a list of do's and don'ts? Fallen human nature compels us to think we can become good enough to regain God's favor. Yet Scripture teaches us, "In Him you have been made complete" (Col. 2:10). The book of Hebrews encourages us to rest in Jesus' finished, once-for-all-time sacrifice on the cross.

For some Christians, a legalistic approach to sanctification rises from a fear of losing one's salvation. But Scripture makes it clear that our salvation is eternal and can never be taken away from us. The very reason this is so rests in the perfection of Christ's sacrifice. To lose one's salvation would require *another* sacrifice of Christ in order to regain it, since the first one was not sufficient (see Hebrews 6:1-9). Such a notion is absurd and insults Christ and His work on the cross, akin to "trampling underfoot the Son of God" (Heb. 10:29).

Satan, the evil one, would greatly desire us to fall back into worldly, works-based life, because he knows such living is doomed to failure and will bring guilt and defeat. Living like that will not produce the genuine works God desires. He desires works that are motivated by gratitude and love for the One who loved us and gave Himself for us, not motivated by our efforts to benefit ourselves. (And indeed, works-based sanctification is focused on one's own achievements and therefore the rewards one accrues to oneself.)

From another perspective, sometimes Christians *feel* a lack of God's blessing in their lives and look inwardly thinking, "There must be something wrong with me, because God is not blessing me the way I imagined He would or should." Since they cannot change God, they resort to the one thing they can change (or think they can change): themselves. God's withholding blessing must be because they are not living right, doing the right things. So like trying to lose weight on a diet, they try to discipline themselves with all the right "Christian" things to do, in hopes that somehow God will see their faithfulness and in turn bless them.

Yet, this too is worldly, because Scripture has made it clear that "God has blessed us with all spiritual blessings in the heavenly places in Christ" (Eph. 1:3). What we need is not more discipline, but faith to believe that we already are blessed far more than we deserve!

Lord, I do believe You have blessed me far more than I deserve. Help my unbelief, so that I will live a life more fully out of gratitude than out of works.

Worldly Unbelief

John 17:15 (cont.)

15 "I do not ask You to take them out of the world, but to keep them from the evil one."

The evil one—he is the problem with being in the world. Ultimately the battle is not with other Christians or even with ourselves. It's the devil. He has been in the picture from the beginning, tempting the image bearers of God to turn away from His sufficiency to find fulfillment through their own resources. The battle is a spiritual one at the core, not a social, economic or relational one. By not taking us "out of the world," God leaves us exposed to Satan's influence.

A time is coming when temptation will be no more, at the consummation of the ages: "And the devil who deceived them was thrown into the lake of fire and brimstone, where the beast and the false prophet are also; and they will be tormented day and night forever and ever" (Rev. 20:10). But until then, Jesus' desire, as much as we sometimes wish it were to the contrary, is that the Father would not "take them out of the world." There is a reason Christ left His disciples in the world and didn't take them with Him to heaven when He ascended: they had a mission to accomplish on earth, and so do we today. When our mission is over, then God will take us home.

Until then, we are in the world, and we need protection from Satan and his cohorts. He prowls around like a roaring lion (1 Peter 5:8). That is the real battle, and we should not get distracted by lesser skirmishes. Paul wrote, "For though we walk in the flesh, we do not war according to the flesh, for the weapons of our warfare are not of the flesh, but divinely powerful for the destruction of fortresses. We are destroying speculations and every lofty thing raised up against the knowledge of God, and we are taking every thought captive to the obedience of Christ" (2 Cor. 10:3-5).

So we resist the devil (James 4:7), and so keep in step with God's help for us in protecting us from Satan. The prayer of Jesus in the Upper Room assumes that His followers will agree and work in harmony with the Lord's desires. Jesus asks the Father to "keep" us from Satan—but that doesn't mean Satan can't get at us at all. Our protection requires our complicity with God's desire, namely resisting the devil (James 4:7) and keeping "in step with the Spirit" (Gal. 5:25 NIV). That is why God lets us be privy to this prayer of our Lord, so we know what the plan is. God will protect us, so we are motivated to resist Satan, bringing every thought captive to this truth, in obedience to Christ.

Lord, I want my resistance to the devil to come in line with Your desire to keep me from him. I don't want to be deterred from the mission You have given me.

WEEKEND READING

Saturday – John 18:28-40
Sunday – Acts 24:1-27

PERSONAL REFLECTIONS

_____
_____
_____
_____
_____
_____
_____
_____

_____
_____
_____
_____
_____
_____
_____
_____
_____
_____
_____
_____
_____

Not of the World

John 17:16

16 "They are not of the world, even as I am not of the world."

Reality check: we Christians are not of this world! Not the disciples in the Upper Room, not us today. God looks at the human population and sees two kinds or categories of people: those who are His and those who are not, those who are followers of Jesus Christ and those who are not. Christians are not just a "kind" of people, like Muslims, Hindus and others—just one variety among many. No, there is a sharp divide. Jesus referred to the last judgment as a time of separating the sheep from the goats (Matt. 25:32), the wheat from the weeds (Matt. 13:25), the saved from the lost, those who are spiritually alive from those who are spiritually dead. The Bible is very clear about this. And in our passage today, there is "the world" and there are those who follow Jesus Christ. They are "in the world" but not "of the world."

Of the 98 times the term "world" occurs in the gospel accounts, 78 are in the Gospel According to John. A few times, it refers to the physical world and all that is in it (John 13:35). It can refer to the entire population of humanity (as in John 3:16). It can also be used to refer to the whole world system (John 16:26). But there are times when the word "world" seems to refer to the unbelieving populace, which according to Matthew 7:13 is the majority of people. Contrary to the popular songs, we are *not* the world. We are in it, but not part of it.

Jesus left His disciples in the world to be the salt and light (Matt. 5:13-16). We are aliens in this world (1 Peter 2:11) but are here on assignment as emissaries from a heavenly world, and with a message: "Therefore, we are ambassadors for Christ, as though God were making an appeal through us; we beg you on behalf of Christ, be reconciled to God" (2 Cor. 5:20).

Living in the world, we of course have all the same physical, tangible needs as non-Christians, and we live in the same culture as those around us. But we are spiritually different. We are those who have been redeemed through the blood of Christ. When we share the Gospel with others, we are simply sinners showing other sinners where to find forgiveness.

In His prayer, Jesus says our relationship to the world is the same as His. He was in the world, but not "of" the world. And He is still not "of" the world. He is above the world; He is beyond the world. Yet He is very present in the world, reaching out through Christians—through you and me—to a world that desperately needs to know Him.

Lord, I confess that too often I have acted like I was "of" the world. I resolve afresh to be Your ambassador to share the Good News with this fallen world.

Not of the World (cont.)

John 17:16

[16] "They are not of the world, even as I am not of the world."

Jesus was not of this world. He certainly did not run lock-step with the Jewish world in which He lived. Born to a humble Jewish woman, Jesus came into the world through a birth whose circumstances were anything but usual. As was prophetically anticipated, the Bible teaches us that He was virgin-born. At 12 years of age, He was instructing the learned men of Israel. His miracles, teachings and impeccable life made Him stand out as not just unusual, but left people with only two choices: either He was the Messiah, God in the flesh, or He was a blasphemer of the worst kind. A few came to see Him as the former and worshipped Him, but the majority saw Him as the latter and rejected Him. He was not "of" that world.

When the prevailing righteousness was to condemn a woman caught in adultery, He sided with the woman against her hypocritical accusers. He was not "of" that world. He allowed His disciples to pick grain to eat on the Sabbath, going against the prevailing interpretation of the Mosaic laws. He willingly forgave sins, when others would not or could not. He accepted interactions with women and Samaritans. He healed non-Jews and proclaimed them, at times, more faithful than His Jewish countrymen. He was not "of" that world.

In the end, the world rejected Him, because He was not one of them. Tortured, mocked and shamed. Hung on a cross, which according to that world meant complete rejection by humans, and cursing by God.

Today, Christians need to remind ourselves that we, too, are not of this world. We are sojourners, just passing through, as it were. We are on temporary assignment until we are called home to where we really belong. But if we are living like Christ as His followers, we must be aware that the world will not accept us, because we are not "of" this world. To be sure, we need to be good neighbors, showing God's love and kindness to all around us. But the world has an innate rejection for us, no matter how hard we try to win them over by our love and acceptance. For it is not us whom they reject, but Christ. And He was the perfect human being, perfect in love and acceptance of sinners—yet He was still rejected.

Thus, in Jesus' Upper Room prayer, He makes it clear that despite all this, we are left here for a purpose, and we need protection—not from the world's rejection, but from the evil one (vs. 15), the one who can tempt us to doubt God's purpose in our lives here on earth, to knock us off our mission.

Lord, lead us not into temptation and protect us from the tempter. For Yours is the kingdom, and the power, and the glory, forever. Amen.

Set Apart

John 17:17

17 "Sanctify them in the truth; Your word is truth."

What separates Christians from the world? Certainly there is a spiritual separation, in that true believers are spiritually alive, while all others are spiritually dead. There may be cultural differences, in that Christians do some things differently than non-Christians, having different moral standards. Some Christians try to stand out by the way they wear their clothes, or the standard of living they accept.

Jesus here is talking about a dynamic that is at once holy and at the same time grounded in reality. He prays to the Father, "Sanctify them." The word "sanctify" is related to the term "holy." In its most basic meaning, it carries the sense of being separate, to treat differently. As used in the Bible, it most often means to separate something to God, to treat it as special for God. In the Old Testament, when something was sanctified, like a sacrifice, it was given over to God at the temple. To sanctify something was to make it holy, to separate it from its normal use and purpose and set it aside for God's purpose and use.

Jesus was not asking the Father to create a ritual involving the sprinkling of "holy water" as some do today. He prayed that the Father would separate out His followers and treat them as special—not to treat them as simply part of the "human family," but as a separate, holy group of humans, different from the rest. This is not a desire for creating a religious order, a clergy, but a reality for any follower of Christ. We are a separate class of people, all believers.

We are all called to separate from the world because we are not "of" the world. Peter remembered this when he wrote years later, "But you are a chosen race, a royal priesthood, a holy nation, a people for *God's* own possession, so that you may proclaim the excellencies of Him who has called you out of darkness into His marvelous light" (1 Peter 2:9). There should be no clergy-laity distinction in the church today. We are all "priests," with direct access to God.

The term "saint" as used in Scripture is related to the words "holy" and "sanctified." Religions of the world like (erroneously) to distinguish those who are "saints" as being particularly holy, in contrast to the rest of the religious practitioners. But Jesus asked the Father to make us all saints. In fact, Paul uses that word in reference to the carnal Christians of Corinth: "To the church of God which is at Corinth, to those who have been sanctified in Christ Jesus, saints by calling, with all who in every place call on the name of our Lord Jesus Christ, their *Lord* and ours." (1 Cor. 1:2). Yes, God has made us all saints. We are special to Him, even when we fall short of living as saints.

Lord, help me live in the constant awareness that You see me as special to You.

Set Apart by the Word

[17] "Sanctify them in the truth; Your word is truth."

How does God sanctify His people? According to Jesus, sanctification relates to the truth, particularly the truth of His Word. The word "truth" is one of the important words used in the Gospel According to John. It occurs 26 times, first in the prologue: "And the Word became flesh, and dwelt among us, and we saw His glory, glory as of the only begotten from the Father, full of grace and truth" (John 1:14). This was a defining aspect of Jesus Christ, the Son of God. He was the Word in the flesh, and He was full of grace and truth.

What is particularly interesting is that truth is inseparable from grace. In a world that has rejected the Word from the beginning, God continues to inject His truth, the Word, into the world. There is no principle of "fairness" or "ought-ness" to which God must conform. There is no moral imperative in the universe that dictates that God must give us the truth. He does so from within His own being, and for no other reason than He is a gracious God. He provides the truth about our dilemma of being fallen creatures, and He provides the truth of the solution to that problem—the way of salvation, the Person of salvation—that is the Word, the truth. And He provides the way to life. He clarified the cryptic message of the Old Testament, as John writes: "For the Law was given through Moses; grace and truth were realized through Jesus Christ" (John 1:17). Remember, Jesus said, "I am the way and the truth and the life" (John 14:6).

For disciples of Christ, the truth is how God sanctifies us. "But he who practices the truth comes to the Light, so that his deeds may be manifested as having been wrought in God" (John 3:21). In Christ, we worship "in truth" (John 4:23-24). The truth will make us free (John 8:32). Followers of Jesus Christ are completely centered on the Word of God. Simon Peter said it well: "Lord, to whom shall we go? You have words of eternal life" (John 6:68).

What does this mean for us today? Our sanctification is not dependent on our "spiritual disciplines." Religious orders and cults would have us believe that holiness comes through religious activities, rituals, burning of incense, subdued lighting, vows of silence or fasting, self-flagellation, and myriad forms of self-denial. But Jesus, who is the Word and the Truth, points in a different direction. God uses the Word to set us apart. We live by the Word of God. It is our life, our breath, our food, our sustenance. Nothing else will bring true sanctification.

Lord Jesus, I am committed to the truth, the Word of God. For it is through the Word that I grow in my knowledge of and relationship with You.

Your Word is Truth

John 17:17 (cont.)

[17] *"Sanctify them in the truth; Your word is truth."*

The Bible is the Word of God, and it is the truth of God. While we agree with the saying that "all truth is God's truth," the truth of the Word of God is different from other kinds of truth. There is much to learn in the world about life: how to ride a bike, get an education, design and program computers, and a myriad of factual things and skills. There are also scientific facts and theories, which enable us to increase our health and comforts of life, as well as pique our curiosity for how things work in the universe. Those things are all worthy of pursuit as we live in this world. But none of them is even remotely involved in sanctifying Christians.

In the church, the modern endeavor to enliven worship, build relationships, and be relevant to the world around us so that others would be attracted to Christ— these are all good things as well, things to which churches do well to give serious thought. Some resort to sensual experiences like incense, chanting, iconography and pageantry to invoke holiness in people. But Jesus points to none of these things when asking His Father to sanctify His people.

It is God's Word that is truth, and it is God's Word that sanctifies believers. Being sanctified means being set apart to the truth as God defines it, and that requires the work of God to bring conviction of error. "For the word of God is living and active and sharper than any two-edged sword, and piercing as far as the division of soul and spirit, of both joints and marrow, and able to judge the thoughts and intentions of the heart" (Heb. 4:12). So it is through hearing and believing God's Word that we are saved and grow in our faith: "So faith *comes* from hearing, and hearing by the word of Christ" (Rom. 10:17).

In picturing the church as the bride of Christ, Paul writes that Christ died for the church, ". . . so that He might sanctify her, having cleansed her by the washing of water with the word . . ." (Eph. 5:26). The battle is for the mind, and it is through the study and application of God's Word in our lives that we are set apart for victory, ". . . for the weapons of our warfare are not of the flesh, but divinely powerful for the destruction of fortresses. We are destroying speculations and every lofty thing raised up against the knowledge of God, and we are taking every thought captive to the obedience of Christ . . ." (2 Cor. 10:4-5).

This is life by the Book, by the Truth, by the Word of God. Indeed, His words are life giving. All other truth is derivative, inferior. Jesus said, "Heaven and earth will pass away, but My words will not pass away" (Luke 21:33).

Lord, thank You for giving us Your Word, the Bible, so that we have a faithful and unchanging guide for this world in which You have left us as ambassadors.

WEEKEND READING

Saturday – John 19:1-15
Sunday – Acts 25:1-22

PERSONAL REFLECTIONS

_____
_____
_____
_____
_____
_____
_____
_____
_____
_____
_____
_____
_____
_____
_____
_____
_____
_____
_____
_____
_____
_____
_____

The Sent Ones

John 17:18

[18] "As You sent Me into the world, I also have sent them into the world."

Like Christ, like Christians. We are an extension of Him in this world, on assignment. Our being sent into the world is rooted in Jesus' being sent into the world. We are carrying on His mission. The word "sent" in our verse today translates the Greek word *apostello,* the noun from which we get our English word "apostle." Jesus was the first Apostle, the first "sent one"—"Jesus, the Apostle and High Priest of our confession . . ." (Heb. 3:1).

John, interestingly, does not use the noun form of the word *apostellos* as a descriptor of the twelve. But he recorded Jesus later repeating this element of His prayer in commissioning them: "Peace *be* with you; as the Father has sent Me, I also send you" (John 20:21). They are the "sent ones."

Matthew and Mark, in writing to their original audience, used the word "apostle" only once each. This paucity of use is understandable, because they were not actually sent out formally until the end of Jesus' ministry. The gospel writers were using language more in tune with the events as they happened. Luke, as a careful historian, used terminology that was more familiar later in the expansion of Christianity—specifically that the original twelve came to be well known as "the apostles." Thus, he had more fondness for the word, enlisting it six times in his chronicle of the Lord's life. He stands alone in recording that Jesus did in fact name them "apostles" (Luke 6:13).

In the book of Acts, Luke continues to use the word, enlisting it 28 times. In the first 11 chapters, he uses the word 20 times referring to the twelve (Judas was replaced by Matthias, as recorded in Acts 1:26). Then we discover in Acts 14:4 and 14 that Paul and Barnabas are called apostles, expanding beyond the original twelve. The rest of the occurrences in Acts are somewhat ambiguous as to whether the twelve are in mind or more. Luke was not using the word "apostle" carelessly, for the word had come to carry great significance in the early church. Paul and Barnabas carried weight like the original twelve did, though they were not originally part of that group.

Having said this, the original twelve had a unique role that Paul and Barnabas had no part in, and this will never change. The twelve were the recognized eyewitnesses of the life of Christ from the time of John the Baptist until the ascension (Acts 1:22). No one could be added to that number. It will be *their* names written on the foundation stones of the new city of God (Rev. 21:14), not Paul's name, not Barnabas' name. The twelve are the unique "sent ones."

Lord, thank You for the twelve unique men who were faithful in proclaiming You and Your truth at the foundational stages of the church.

The Sent Ones (cont.)

John 17:18

18 "As You sent Me into the world, I also have sent them into the world."

The apostle Paul refers to the twelve as "the apostles" (1 Cor. 15:7; Gal. 1:7), clearly speaking of them as a one-time, not-to-be-expanded group with a unique authority. The term comes to invoke a wider meaning as biblical history unfolds, but it conveys a foundational authority for spreading God's Word.

Of course, Paul is the most well known "sent one" or apostle, outside of the original twelve. That he was specifically sent out is clear from his own testimony: "And [Jesus] said to me, 'Go! For I will send you far away to the Gentiles'" (Acts 22:21). He is first referred to as an apostle in Acts 14, along with Barnabas.

In the book of Galatians, he asserts his authority as an apostle, beginning with introducing himself as "Paul, an apostle (not *sent* from men nor through the agency of man, but through Jesus Christ and God the Father, who raised Him from the dead) . . ." (Gal. 1:1). He refers to those in ". . . Jerusalem . . . who were apostles before me . . ." (Gal. 1:17), putting himself on an equal basis with them. In one of his visits to Jerusalem, Peter and James both affirm his apostleship, though they conveyed no authority, as Paul asserts that his authority and calling came from God directly, not from the other apostles or any other man (see Galatians 2:7-9; 1:15-17).

And then he goes toe-to-toe with the apostle Peter (a.k.a. Cephas), the most prominent of the original twelve, for his hypocritical behavior. Interestingly, Paul refers to him as "Peter," the name Jesus gave him, in the context of Peter's role as an apostle (Gal. 2:7-8). Paul respected Peter's position as a fellow apostle. But when speaking of Peter's hypocrisy, he refers to him by his common Hebrew name, Cephas, possibly emphasizing that Peter's behavior was unbecoming of an apostle. Paul pulls no punches: "But when Cephas came to Antioch, I opposed him to his face, because he stood condemned" (Gal. 2:11)!

The point is that the original apostles in the Upper Room were not given unlimited authority, nor was Peter ever envisioned as being infallible. Certainly, they were all still fallible human beings who could and did sin in grievous ways. But they were Jesus' sent ones, who were commissioned to preach His message, as His representatives. They were to convey the authority of the Word of Christ. They were not *over* the Word, nor did they have equal authority with the Word. They themselves, like all followers of Jesus, were under the authority of the Word.

Lord, Your Word is my ultimate authority, because it is breathed out by You.

The Sent Ones (cont.)

John 17:18

18 "As You sent Me into the world, I also have sent them into the world."

Preparation of the apostles was absolutely critical to the founding of the Christian movement. Their role could not be overstated—thus Jesus spent considerable time preparing them and praying for them. One wonders how much of His other times of prayer focused on these men. When Jesus spoke of Peter being the particular target of Satanic attack, He said, "I have prayed for you . . ." (Luke 22:32). The implication is that this may have been a previous, ongoing prayer. Finally, in the Upper Room we may be given just a peek into the kinds of things He regularly prayed for.

But as to the importance of the apostles, Scripture says to us, ". . . you are God's household, having been built on the foundation of the apostles and prophets, Christ Jesus Himself being the corner stone" (Eph. 2:19b-20). The early church devoted itself to "the apostles' teaching" (Acts 2:42). To this day, Christians rely on the apostolic teaching as foundational to spiritual truth and growth. It was in God's wisdom that Jesus did not physically write the Scriptures for us, but inspired human authors to convey His teachings. Jesus sent these twelve out. They had previously had their short-term internship where they were sent out by Jesus (Mark 6:7-13, Luke 10:1). These initial experiences of ministering without Jesus were simply training sessions to prepare them for the permanent absence of the physical Jesus. After His death, resurrection and ascension, they would carry on permanently without Him. Fast forward to the time after the death of the apostles. The early church had to carry on without the physical Jesus and without the apostles. What were they to do?

First, they had the apostolic writings, inspired by God. Then they had other writings, by non-apostles, which were affirmed by the apostles (the discussion of this goes beyond the scope of our purposes here). But they also had the Holy Spirit. And that was all they needed, for they had the Word of God and God's presence. And the church continues to grow, having been built on the apostles and prophets.

We finish our comments on this verse by noting that nowhere in Scripture do we find the apostles conferring their role to a succession of others. Their function was foundational to the church—the foundation has been laid and is not in need of re-laying over and over again with new apostles. The concept of "apostolic-succession" as taught in some branches of so-called "Christendom" is not biblical. The authority of the apostles was unique and foundational, establishing for all time what the teachings of Christ were.

Lord, thank You for a unique, solid, unchanging foundation in the Word of God.

You, a Saint?

John 17:19

¹⁹ "For their sakes I sanctify Myself, that they themselves also may be sanctified in truth."

How can Jesus sanctify Himself when He is already perfectly holy? The word for sanctify is *hagiazo* and is related to the holy *hagios*. One sanctifies oneself to become holy. But what does this mean for Jesus?

The problem lies with our erroneous understanding of what it means to be holy. The meaning has changed through the centuries, where the church, as it has in many other areas, has strayed toward human traditions. Iconography (the use of visual imagery) has portrayed holy men as having halos above their heads, having been declared saints in some sectors and requiring veneration by the adherents to that religious expression.

To be sure, the word "saint" is used in Scripture, though very rarely in the gospel accounts (see Matthew 27:52). But the apostle Paul used the term frequently, most notably in his letter to the carnal Christians in Corinth: "To the church of God which is at Corinth, to those who have been sanctified in Christ Jesus, saints by calling, with all who in every place call on the name of our Lord Jesus Christ . . ." (1 Cor. 1:2). In fact, his custom was to refer to believers as "saints" as even a superficial survey of the word use in his writings will make clear. In the biblical use of the word, all believers in Jesus Christ are saints, or to put it another way, holy ones.

The word means "to be separated out for God's use." When Jesus came to this earth, He separated Himself out for the Father's purposes. He was fully devoted to the One who sent Him: "You sent Me into the world" (vs. 18). At the famous well of Sychar, Jesus told the disciples, "My food is to do the will of Him who sent Me and to accomplish His work" (John 4:34). This would seem like a matter of course to us, for after all, He was God in the flesh. He could do no other than the will of God.

Yet we see Jesus that very night, shortly after His Upper Room prayer, wrestling in the Garden of Gethsemane, the night before He died. Three times He prayed, "My Father, if it is possible, let this cup pass from Me; yet not as I will, but as You will." The struggle was real. In His own words, He said, "My soul is deeply grieved, to the point of death." Luke, the doctor, perceptively records, "And being in agony He was praying very fervently; and His sweat became like drops of blood, falling down upon the ground." The question of sanctification was at the heart of the issues. Would He set Himself apart from all human desires for self-preservation, to obedience to the Father's will?

Father, like Your Son, I too want to set myself apart for doing Your will.

You a Saint? (cont.)

John 17:19

¹⁹ "For their sakes I sanctify Myself, that they themselves also may be sanctified in truth."

For you and me as believers, Jesus sanctified Himself. He was the Man on a mission to make us saints, both in position and in practice. He set Himself apart so that we might be set apart and so that we might set ourselves apart. He denied Himself the normal "self-preservation" of human nature, so that we would be delivered from spiraling down the vortex of self-centeredness. Sanctification for Christians is a two-layered concept, doubled over. What I mean is that sanctification is a positional concept and also a progressive concept. But there is also the divine side of sanctification and the human side.

First, at salvation God sets us apart (the core meaning of the word sanctification) as members of His family, His children. We are redeemed, regenerated and renewed. In a world that is dead in their sins, given over to the rebellion against God, serving the purposes of Satan. We believers have been made alive, having confessed our rebellion, and believed in Him who obeyed the Father to the point of death on the cross, and now we serve the purposes of God. We have been sanctified. ". . . but you were washed, but you were sanctified, but you were justified in the name of the Lord Jesus Christ and in the Spirit of our God" (1 Corinthians 6:11; see also Hebrews 4:10). Yet sanctification is a progressive thing as well: "May the God of peace Himself sanctify you entirely . . ." (1 Thess. 5:23). We were initially set apart for God's use; we continue to be set apart for greater use.

Our sanctification is a team effort involving God and us. Clearly, He is the one who sets us apart, for He is Creator and Lord. He defines the purposes, and He elects His own. So it follows that He sets apart those whom He chooses—and He does that through our faith (Acts 26:18). But we also have our role, for, "[s]ince we live by the Spirit, let us keep in step with the Spirit" (Gal. 5:25 NIV). So we must sanctify ourselves, that is, set ourselves apart for that which the Lord sets us apart. "Therefore, if anyone cleanses himself from these *things*, he will be a vessel for honor, sanctified, useful to the Master, prepared for every good work" (2 Tim. 2:21). The apostle Paul expressed it this way: "I press on so that I may lay hold of that for which also I was laid hold of by Christ Jesus" (Phil. 3:12). He has laid hold of us to set us apart for God's purposes.

Our cooperation with God's work in our lives is the only true way to carry on God's mission for us in the world. Just as with the disciples in the Upper Room, we have been chosen by God for the mission of Christ.

Lord, I set myself apart to do Your will today, in the tasks laid out before me.

WEEKEND READING

Saturday – John 19:16-30
Sunday – Acts 25:23–26:18

PERSONAL REFLECTIONS

Prayer of Dependence

John 17:20

²⁰ "I do not ask on behalf of these alone, but for those also who believe in Me through their word . . ."

Humility of Christ is on display in this Upper Room prayer. As God incarnate, it was certainly within His realm of ability to perform all the things He asked of the Father. The temptation of Jesus in the wilderness (Matt. 4:1-11) was real for this very reason—He had the ability to act outside of His role as the second person of the Trinity, that of dependency on the Father's will. Theologians have wrestled with this for two millennia, the nature of the Trinity and the relationship of the Son and the Father. In this prayer we clearly see humility in the Son's submission to the Father. A few comments are in order.

First, He was humble in His incarnation. "Being found in appearance as a man, He humbled Himself by becoming obedient to the point of death, even death on a cross" (Phil. 2:8). For One who is "the radiance of His glory and the exact representation of His nature, and upholds all things by the word of His power" (Heb. 1:3) to voluntarily join the ranks of human image bearers—that is humility defined. That is like the tree becoming like the tree's shadow. He subjected Himself to the very human imperative of dependency on His heavenly Father. He resisted the urge to take things into His own hands; He was subject to the Father.

Second, this humility renders, in human form, the humbleness within the Godhead as evidenced by the differing roles of the Trinity members. The Holy Spirit was sent out by the Father and Son (what theologians call the eternal procession), and the Son was sent by the Father into the world, as Jesus acknowledged in this prayer (vs. 18). The humility of submission emanates from the second person of the Trinity into the incarnation.

Third, the character trait of humility is therefore a divine attribute. Indeed, if Christ-likeness is commanded of us, and Jesus Christ exhibited humility in being sent to die for us, then humbleness must be more than just a trait for the human side of Christ. As God, the second person of the Trinity, He is humble. Otherwise, our emulation of Jesus' humility would cease when we are glorified, when we see Him as He is and become like Him (1 John 3:2). Humility is a trait of His perfection.

Humility is one of the most difficult things for us mere human beings to emulate, for at the very core of our fallenness is an independent spirit. Only by humble submission to God can our tendency to self-exaltation be overcome.

Lord, I confess my tendency to not call upon You in dependent prayer.

Prayer of Dependence (cont.)

John 17:20

20 "I do not ask on behalf of these alone, but for those also who believe in Me through their word . . ."

Jesus' intercessory prayer for His disciples showed a humble submission to the Father. In His incarnation, He placed Himself in a completely dependent role with the Father; this was essential to being fully human. So in praying for the disciples, this was a tacit deference to the Father's will. Why ask for something that you could do yourself? It can only mean a humble, voluntary submission.

But in what sense can God, even the second person of the Trinity, be humble if He is, in fact, perfect? We touch on mysteries beyond our full comprehension. How can we say Jesus was humble when He prayed that He might be glorified with the glory He had before His incarnation (John 17:1-4)? It would seem that humility would be necessary for all of creation, but not for God Himself, because He is the center of all creation, having made it all.

But if we define humbleness as Paul describes it, we might gain some traction in our thinking. "For through the grace given to me I say to everyone among you not to think more highly of himself than he ought to think; but to think so as to have sound judgment, as God has allotted to each a measure of his faith" (Rom. 12:3). Humility is not the opposite of glory. And someone who is glorious can indeed be humble, if we are careful with how we see both glory and humility. Jesus sought the glory He had before with an expressed purpose of glorifying the Father. With mere human beings, we would suspect ulterior motives here, but not so with God the Son.

Jesus was not, in fact, thinking of Himself "more highly . . . than he ought to think." He was, in fact, thinking with "sound judgment" or "soberly" as the NKJV renders it. For Jesus to seek glory is only right because that was the Father's desire, namely, to glorify the Son. So Jesus' request in John 17:1-4 was a sober request, appropriate to the Son of God. The fact that He asked for it, rather than to grab it for Himself, was humble, for it was precisely in this He showed His dependence on the Father.

So we can seek God's glory through our successes that may at times involve our prominence and exaltation here on earth, while using that glory to bring glory to God (1 Cor. 10:31). As for praying for His disciples, in our verse for today, He recognized the coming end of His ministry of discipling them, in a sense, turning them back over to the Father who had given them to Him. Jesus' assignment on earth was coming to a conclusion.

Lord, thank You for humbly but confidently praying to the Father for me.

Prayer of Dependence (cont.)

John 17:20

20 "I do not ask on behalf of these alone, but for those also who believe in Me through their word . . ."

Fourth of July is the day the United States celebrates as Independence Day, commemorating the signing of the Declaration of Independence. This is the most hallowed of all holidays for the U.S. But for Christians, the death of Christ is the most hallowed commemoration, enshrined in the Lord's Supper. Yet at the core of the death of Christ was His humble attitude toward the Father. Paul said, "He humbled Himself by becoming obedient to the point of death, even death on a cross" (Phil. 2:8). Christians celebrate this as a day not of independence, but of dependency. Jesus Christ broke the debt of cancelled sin and set us free to come back under the authority of God. He showed the way, He made the way, He is the way back to the Father.

So His prayer for His disciples and for us who believe through their witness is all part of the humbleness of Christ. We actually see Jesus in Scripture praying at other times as well, though we do not always know what He was praying for or about. At Lazarus' tomb, Jesus prayed for the disciples' faith (John 11:41). Another time, after sending the crowds away and the disciples into the stormy night, He had gone up to a mountain to pray (Matt. 14:23). Even the dullest of minds conjectures that He may have been praying for the disciples' faith. The story concludes with Jesus chastising them, "Oh you of little faith. Why did you doubt?" (Matt. 14:31).

In Mark 3:12, we find Jesus praying through the entire night. Many have suggested He may have been consulting with the Father about the choice of His disciples, for the next day He named the twelve. Concerning Peter, Luke records Jesus saying, "I have prayed for you, that your faith may not fail; and you, when once you have turned again, strengthen your brothers" (Luke 22:32). These are the kinds of things Jesus prayed for. And I would suggest He still prays like that. The Scripture says He intercedes for us (Rom. 8:34) and He advocates for us (1 John 2:1). His Spirit intercedes for us, on our behalf, and in fact, prays for us when we don't know how to pray (Rom. 8:26-27).

Finally, in today's verse (John 17:20), Jesus had in mind all believers of all time. For the only way we would know for sure the teachings of Jesus was through the witness of the men in the Upper Room. We, today, are among those who "believe through their word." Jesus did not pray for so-called "Christendom," those with an adherence to Christian tradition, but for those who believe. His Upper Room prayer is for you and for me, just as much as for His disciples.

Lord, thank You for having me in mind 2,000 years ago in the Upper Room.

Accepting the Incomprehensible

John 17:21

21 ". . . that they may all be one; even as You, Father, are in Me and I in You, that they also may be in Us, so that the world may believe that You sent Me."

Eavesdropping on someone's self-talk can be fascinating. Movies reveal what a character is thinking by using a voice-over in the background. In the Upper Room, though, we don't have self-talk, but the communication between two members of the Trinity. Yet this stretches our imagination to have some framework for understanding what is going on here. Or to put the issue in the form of a question, "If Jesus is God, then to whom is He talking?"

Nothing can be more certain than that the Christian faith is monotheistic. We believe the Scripture that says, "Hear, O Israel! The LORD is our God, the LORD is one!" (Deut. 6:4) and, "Before Me there was no God formed, And there will be none after Me. I, even I, am the Lord, And there is no savior besides Me" (Isa. 43:10b-11). Yet Jesus, as the Son of God, is somehow distinct from God the Father. Other religions may see a contradiction, but that is not the case. Historically, theologians have termed it this way: there is one and only one God, who exists in three persons. There are not three gods, but one God. There is not one person, yet three persons. But three persons as one God is not a logical contradiction. A conundrum, to be sure, but not a fallacy.

Does this not stretch credulity past what is logically reasonable? To some, earthbound and finitely limited as they are, maybe yes. But one thing makes absolute sense. For God to become a man (what we call incarnation, and it is entirely possible for God to do so, since He is God after all) would involve an intersection of the infinite and the finite. It should be expected that at the point of that intersection there would be some things not understandable to us mere humans. To even begin to comprehend such a cosmic event would require help from the other side, that is, the divine side, since our limited non-divine intellect and understanding is considerably limited compared to the infinite.

At the incarnation, where God became a man, we are called upon to believe the revelation of God. Scripture presents Jesus as God, talking with His "Father," as here in the Upper Room. This is more than "self-talk." This is God talking "among" Himself, as represented to us as Son with Father. And unity is uppermost in Jesus' mind, a unity in the Godhead that is unbroken, perfect, in complete harmony, knit together inseparably. In human relationships, with our fallen nature, this kind of unity seems impossible. But with God it is perfect. And Jesus wants us followers to have that kind of unity.

Lord, help me do whatever is necessary to be at one with my fellow Christians, even those with whom I disagree.

Unity in Relationship

John 17:21 (cont.)

21 ". . . that they may all be one; even as You, Father, are in Me and I in You, that they also may be in Us, so that the world may believe that You sent Me."

The most intimate conversation between God the Son and God the Father, when it turns to His followers, centers on unity. From a human perspective, we can rejoin, "Man, did He ever call that one right!" Of all the things concerning us that He could have prayed, He knew that unity would be the most difficult for His followers to attain. The history of the church bears testimony to this. Even in the Upper Room, that unity was threatened when the disciples bickered about who was the greatest among them (Luke 22:24).

Our unity as disciples of Christ is to be rooted in the unity of the Father and Son. They worked in perfect harmony. There was no resisting authority of the Father over the Son. No conflict of the wills. To be sure, Jesus wrestled three times when He prayed, saying, "My Father, if it is possible, let this cup pass from Me . . ." but each time He concluded, ". . . yet not as I will, but as You will" (Matt. 26:39-44). The struggle of the human flesh gave way to the divine purpose.

It is not as though Jesus asked three times like Paul did, and God said "No." There is nothing in this passage about God refusing His request, because in the end Jesus did not ask that the cup be removed, but with each of the three wrestlings, He won the temptation against self-will and submitted to what He knew was the Father's will.

In fact, Scripture makes clear Jesus' intent. The writer of Hebrews quotes Psalm 40:7-8 twice and applies it to Jesus: "Behold, I come; In the scroll of the book it is written of me. I delight to do Your will, O my God; Your Law is within my heart" (Psalm 40:7-8; see Hebrews 10:7, 9). Jesus made this clear on a number of occasions in His teaching, that He and the Father "are one" (John 10:30; 17:11).

Some, however, may insist that Jesus' will was different from the Father's, and thus there was disunity—because Jesus said, "not as I will, but as You will." We respond, how could God convey the real experience of Jesus' being tempted? Human language is employed to describe the divine-human anomaly of the incarnation, God in the flesh. And nowhere else do we see the tension of God inserting Himself into the human experience than at the point of Jesus' temptation. The temptation of the flesh toward self-preservation (among other things) was superseded by Jesus' desire to do the Father's will. Unity was proved.

Lord, Your unity encourages me that unity among Christians is possible.

WEEKEND READING

Saturday – John 19:31-42
Sunday – Acts 26:19-32

PERSONAL REFLECTIONS

_____
_____
_____
_____
_____
_____
_____
_____
_____
_____
_____
_____
_____
_____
_____
_____
_____
_____
_____
_____
_____
_____

Unity in Relationship

John 17:21 (cont.)

21 *". . . that they may all be one; even as You, Father, are in Me and I in You, that they also may be in Us, so that the world may believe that You sent Me."*

Fully divine, God in the flesh—that's what Jesus was. Some Christians, in their efforts to defend this teaching, see in our verse for today a proof text in support of that truth. However, Jesus was not speaking about His deity or equality with God, but about His unity of purpose and will with the Father.

Other Scriptures more clearly present His deity: "For it was the Father's good pleasure for all the fullness to dwell in Him . . ." (Col. 1:19); "For in Him all the fullness of Deity dwells in bodily form . . ." (Col. 2:9). Even in the Gospel According to John, the inspired writer begins with:

> *"In the beginning was the Word, and the Word was with God, and the Word was God. He was in the beginning with God. All things came into being through Him, and apart from Him nothing came into being that has come into being." (John 1:1-3)*

Jesus was and is the Creator God, and there is only one Creator God:

> *"I am the LORD, and there is no other; Besides Me there is no God . . . there is no one besides Me. I am the LORD, and there is no other . . ." (Isa. 45:5-6)*

He is not merely "a" god, as some cults would assert. If He is "god" at all, He must be the "God" over all, because there can be no other gods besides the Sovereign God of the universe. Strict monotheism is rooted in Scripture: "Hear, O Israel! The LORD is our God, the LORD is one!" (Deut. 6:4). God is unified, singular in being, exclusive of all other supposed deities. If Jesus were not God, then John and Paul committed the worst of blasphemies, and the Jews would have been right to stone Him.

So we confirm absolutely the deity of Jesus Christ, but we don't look to our verse today to support that. The emphasis in John 17:21 is rather on the unity of mind and purpose of the Son with the Father, and how we followers of Jesus Christ likewise should be unified in mind and purpose. This "practical" theology is a prerequisite to fulfilling the mission God has for us here on earth. We see it affirmed frequently in Scripture. For example, Paul teaches, "[M]ake my joy complete by being of the same mind, maintaining the same love, united in spirit, intent on one purpose" (Phil. 2:2). This was the desire of our Master in the Upper Room prayer.

Lord, like Jesus, I ask You for unity of believers today, with Jesus as the center.

Unity in Evangelism

John 17:21 (cont.)

21 ". . . that they may all be one; even as You, Father, are in Me and I in You, that they also may be in Us, so that the world may believe that You sent Me."

Christians speak of friendship evangelism, sports evangelism, coffee shop evangelism, child evangelism. Jesus prayed for "unity" evangelism. Our unity will actually convince the world that Jesus is the Messiah, God's answer to our fallen human problems. Unity of believers—imagine that.

Unity is one of the most difficult things to experience, as anyone who has studied church history will clearly see, and as anyone who has been a Christian for more than a short period of time will discover. Christians (ostensibly) have fought and killed each other and outlawed those of different theological persuasions. Churches and denominations have split; seminaries have divided. Sometimes Christians sitting in the same church building refuse to speak to each other. Even among the apostles, there was a struggle to be unified (see Paul and Barnabas in Acts 15:36-40). Paul later, in writing to the Philippian church, a relatively mature fellowship of believers, gave an extended discourse on unity (Phil. 2:1-13). He points out two women who had a particularly difficult time getting along (Phil. 4:2-3).

Unity is difficult to achieve but well worth the effort. Why? First of all, because Jesus desires it of us. Imagine the pain a parent feels when his or her children grow up to become estranged from each other. The Lord loves each of us, and it must pain Him to see us not love each other in the same way. Second, unity is well worth the effort because it reflects the sweet, perfect unity of God the Father and God the Son. We become like God when we strive for unity.

Finally, and the point of this verse, is that our unity as followers of Jesus Christ speaks volumes to the world about who Jesus is. What force or principle can bring people of such diverse backgrounds (social, economic, cultural) into alignment with one purpose and mind? A genuine Christian can travel anywhere in the world and make instant connection with any other Christian. Our fellowship and unity do not know boundaries or borders.

When we genuinely follow Christ and seek the unity He prayed for, there will be racial reconciliation. Church fights over musical styles become opportunities for grace and love and submission to the desires of others. When churches across denominational lines can pray for one another, rejoice together and encourage each other's ministry, the world takes notice. Indeed, Jesus said, earlier in the Upper Room, "[A]ll men will know that you are My disciples, if you have love for one another" (John 13:35).

Lord, help me today to seek unity among those with whom I work and worship.

Unity in Glory

John 17:22

22 "The glory which You have given Me I have given to them, that they may be one, just as We are one . . ."

Goal-oriented, God's desire is for we believers to be unified. But it brings no glory to God if our unity means watering down of the truth. The modern ecumenical movement (more prevalent among theologically liberal-minded churches) seeks common ground on the essentials of religious faith: "Don't focus on what divides us, but on what unites us." The problem with that effort is that it reduces all religions to the lowest common denominator, where the only thing that matters is "faith" in some sort of spiritual sense. Even then, the issue is not "what" you believe, but simply "that" you believe. The object of your faith is irrelevant to unity. Why cannot all religions agree to that, we are asked?

Followers of Jesus (as presented in the Bible) will never be able to have unity with other religions. Jesus Himself did not allow for that option in the same conversation in the Upper Room. He said earlier, "I am the way, and the truth, and the life; no one comes to the Father but through Me" (John 14:6). By His own words, He puts off all other ways of spirituality outside of the path to God. No other path leads to truth and life. His statement does not go over well in our pluralistic, multi-religion society. Never has, never will. But true believers are called to follow Him, not to bend to humanistic pressures.

Jesus, when speaking of unity, was not speaking about Christendom in general but about true disciples of His, genuine believers. Through history and even into our present times, many religions self-identify as Christian yet deny the Lord's teachings about Himself and deny His deity. Denominations abound that even deny the unique authority of Scripture, and teach notions completely foreign to what Jesus and His apostles taught, yet hold onto the name "Christian" as a means of referring to their religious tradition. These can hardly be included in the ones Jesus had in mind when He spoke of unity.

Further, even among true Christians, Jesus was not suggesting that we dilute our doctrinal differences or treat them as unimportant. Remember He also said, "You will know the truth, and the truth will make you free" (John 8:32). We dare not enslave ourselves to that which is false by minimizing truth in the quest for unity. No, we absolutely dare not. Having said that, unity must still be sought in the midst of our diversity, without watering down the truth. That is God's glory, and that is what will impact our evangelistic outreach.

Lord, help me be firm in the truth, but gracious in unity toward those with whom I disagree.

Unity in Glorious Truth

John 17:22 (cont.)

22 "The glory which You have given Me I have given to them, that they may be one, just as We are one . . ."

What does it mean for Christians to be united even when there are strong and important disagreements? Doctrinal differences have often resulted in division, new denominations, church splits, inquisitions and executions. Hatred for those who hold different views has often become ugly throughout church history. The heart of fallen man, when cloaked in religious garments, resorts to force in order to gain compliance.

There is some biblical basis for extreme censuring of and separation from individuals in certain situations, as was the case with Alexander and Hymenaeus, whose false teaching was leading people to spiritual ruin (1 Tim. 1:18-20). Serious moral failure requires believers to separate from ". . . any so-called brother if he is an immoral person, or covetous, or an idolater, or a reviler, or a drunkard, or a swindler—[do] not even . . . eat with such a one" (1 Cor. 5:11).

Christians have struggled to reconcile these contrasting attitudes. However, the unity Jesus spoke of was not intended to override the truth. It was a unity that was based on truth. That is the kind of unity He desires, for He Himself is truth. That is the glory He spoke of. It is a truth that unifies. When people are pursuing the truth of Jesus Christ, this leads to unity because they are all aiming for the same destination. As the old illustration goes, as we move closer to Jesus, we invariably move closer to each other. But if we set as our focus moving closer to each other, there is no guarantee of moving closer to Jesus. He is the anchor point, the solid reference point.

The struggle in practice is what do you do when the pursuit of Jesus leads to sharp doctrinal disagreement? We suggest first that movement toward Jesus should not lead to pride of doctrine but to humility. Truth should so overwhelm us that in times of disagreement we bend toward the self-awareness of our own fallenness. Is that not what Galatians 6:1 teaches us? "Brethren, even if anyone is caught in any trespass, you who are spiritual, restore such a one in a spirit of gentleness; *each one* looking to yourself, so that you too will not be tempted" (Gal. 6:1). When I believe another Christian has fallen into a doctrinal "trespass," I must recognize my own proneness to also err in doctrine. My judgment that the other has nefarious motivation in his beliefs should cause me to consider that I, too, could be judged in the same way. Unity comes with great difficulty, for it comes at a cost to our individual self-deceptions. And to recognize this in ourselves sets us on the path to glorious unity.

Lord, search my heart for self-deception and fleshly pride of doctrine.

Unity in Glorious Truth (cont.)

John 17:22

22 "The glory which You have given Me I have given to them, that they may be one, just as We are one . . ."

S ome Christians have so narrowly defined their circle of doctrine that they see themselves as the remnant, the extreme, the very few, the faithful. They insist on conformity, complete with their specific "shibboleths." You will remember the story in Judges 12, where the men of Gilead would test the fugitives crossing the Jordan. Not being able to say the word "shibboleth" properly was a dead giveaway that a person was an Ephraimite and was to be executed. Today, minute doctrinal fidelity in many circles comes down to using specific words that put people into ideological boxes for determining whether they are "one of us" or not. For example, in some groups, using the word "church" instead of the word "assembly" in reference to the local gathering of believers marks a person out as not being "one of us." This would not bode well with the teaching of our Lord in the Upper Room.

We dare not understand Jesus' teaching about unity too narrowly or too loosely. The pendulum continuously swings through church history and among churches today, each extreme knocking people out one way or the other, but neither attaining to the unity of which Jesus spoke.

So what do we do with doctrinal differences? Who decides which doctrines should legitimately divide us? The answer may never be known this side of eternity, but one thing is absolutely clear. Jesus should be the center of our unity—the Jesus of the Upper Room, not a watered-down religious figure of our own manipulations, the lowest common denominator for the sake of ecumenical unity. Neither is this a pharisaical Jesus who dissected the law down to the elimination of grace. Nor is this Jesus of "monkery" or separation who leads people to isolate themselves from the "contamination" of those of lesser fidelity.

The unity Jesus talked about has Him, the biblical, historical Son of God and Son of Man, in the center. Deity in the flesh. Savior, Lord, Master. The Way, the Truth, the Life. He is the hub from which all spokes extrude. The Alpha and Omega, Beginning and End. The Good Shepherd, the Bread of Life, the Door of Salvation, Healer, Teacher, Miracle Worker. He is the I AM. He is where our unity as believers lies—followers of His, redeemed sinners, saved by grace, elect from the foundation of the world. We are part of the household of God, with Jesus as the Head, being built up in unity to the fullness of Christ. As we continually exalt Him and follow Him, we will invariably come closer together in the experience of our unity in Him.

Lord, help us all to see You as the center of our lives, that we might be unified.

WEEKEND READING

Saturday – John 20:1-18
Sunday – Acts 27:1-13

PERSONAL REFLECTIONS

_____
_____
_____
_____
_____
_____
_____

_____
_____
_____
_____
_____
_____
_____
_____
_____
_____
_____
_____
_____
_____

Unity in Glory Revisited

John 17:22 (cont.)

22 "The glory which You have given Me I have given to them, that they may be one, just as We are one . . ."

W e have seen in verse 21 a unity that bears witness to Christ being sent from God. Now looking closely at verse 22, we can see that there is a glory that is given to us. But in what sense?

At one level, a Christian is an attention-getter for being "in" the world, but not "of" the world (vss. 13-14). We are in the truth (vs.19). We are in Christ (21). But though we are in the world, we are not "of" the world, in the sense of being at home here. We are redefined by our relationship with our Savior. And thus we stand out in this fallen world and are "hated" by the world (vs. 14). Just as the world rejects the glory of Christ in its rejection of His truth, it also rejects the reflection of that glory in us, His followers.

Now in the Western world, Christians are normally not persecuted to the point of death. But around the world, testimonies abound of the hardship and martyrdom of Christians. Even in our more civilized countries, where evangelism is active and immorality is challenged, intense hatred often bursts out with charges of self-righteousness, moral smugness, narrow-mindedness, naiveté and fundamentalist fears. Why the extreme reaction?

It is popular among some Christians seeking to appease the world to point out that we often invite such reactions from the world for our hypocrisies and our poor efforts at evangelism. But at the heart of the matter is the glory of God. John spoke of this earlier in his gospel account: "In Him was life, and the life was the Light of men. The Light shines in the darkness, and the darkness did not comprehend it" (John 1:4-5). "[The Word] came to His own, and those who were His own did not receive Him" (1:11). "And the Word became flesh, and dwelt among us, and we saw His glory, glory as of the only begotten from the Father, full of grace and truth" (John 1:14). So if they reject the glory of Christ, they will also reject us when we reflect Christ's glory.

We understand the phrase "[t]he glory . . . I have given to them" to refer to a reflective glory. The more we become like Christ, the more the world sees in us what Christ came to reveal about God. While the world, for example, is attracted to grace, the world reacts strongly to the idea of grace needed. That is, the implication of grace goes deeper than needing a helping hand. But grace strikes at the root of absolute depravity of the heart. It was "while we were yet sinners, Christ died for us." The world accepts the inevitability of sin but rejects the idea of core sinfulness that separates us from God. So they reject Christians.

Lord, help me to reflect Your glory even though the world rejects it.

Unity in Glory Revisited (cont.)

John 17:22 (cont.)

22 "The glory which You have given Me I have given to them, that they may be one, just as We are one . . ."

Another level of the received glory points to the future. Just like Christ's glory was veiled when He lived out His incarnation while on earth until after His resurrection, so also the glory which He has given us is veiled until after our resurrection. Philippians 2:6-8 tells us, "Although He existed in the form of God . . . [He] emptied Himself, taking the form of a bond-servant, and being made in the likeness of men." This speaks of the outward, visible forms—He set aside the outward glory of God. But there is coming a time when His glory will be revealed, when "every knee will bow . . . and every tongue confess that Jesus Christ is Lord, to the glory of God the Father" (Phil. 2:10-11).

The glory of God which is given to us is seen dimly now, but will be fully realized in a future time: "Beloved, now we are children of God, and it has not appeared as yet what we will be. We know that when He appears, we will be like Him, because we will see Him just as He is" (1 John 3:2). Until then, we have the promise of God's transformative power developing glory in us now, "[b]ut we all, with unveiled face, beholding as in a mirror the glory of the Lord, are being transformed into the same image from glory to glory, just as from the Lord, the Spirit" (2 Cor. 3:18). Therefore, we walk by faith in the truth of God's glory in us even though it is not fully evident yet. "While we look not at the things which are seen, but at the things which are not seen; for the things which are seen are temporal, but the things which are not seen are eternal" (2 Cor. 4:18).

As Christians, we have the great hope of what is yet to come, the foretaste of which we can experience now to some small degree. We have, as someone has said, "the echo of heaven" in our hearts. Now, we live by faith that we have "become partakers of *the* divine nature, having escaped the corruption that is in the world by lust" (2 Peter 1:4). We are being "conformed to the image of His Son" (Rom. 8:29). What a glory all this is. Since we have received Christ (John 1:12), we have also received His glory, and the process of glorifying us in Christ has begun and continues until the day He returns. It simply does not get any better than that—a perfect plan, a perfect process and a perfect unity in the future. Until then, we Christians do well to pursue "being of the same mind, maintaining the same love, united in spirit, intent on one purpose" (Phil. 2:2).

Oh Father, continue to draw us to Your Son Jesus, that we may be in harmony with Him, and therefore in harmony with You and with each other.

Unity in Truth and Love

John 17:23

23 I in them and You in Me, that they may be perfected in unity, so that the world may know that You sent Me, and loved them, even as You have loved Me.

"Them" includes us today. Jesus' prayer in the Upper Room transcends future history, extending to all those who believe the message of Christ as communicated through the apostles (vs. 20). We agree with Andreas Kostenberger that "Jesus' concern for His followers' unity is His greatest burden as His earthly mission draws to a close, and it pervades this entire section. Their unity, in turn, is to be rooted in Jesus' own unity with the Father." This unity, along with love, are essentials to carrying on the mission of Jesus Christ after He is physically gone.

Today's church has been caught up in numerical growth strategies, leadership and management principles, and all kinds of "this is how we do it; you should do it this way as well" techniques. It is amazing that Jesus did not leave any of that sort of teaching for His apostles, despite commissioning them to lead the largest and greatest enterprise the world has ever known. The core strategy is love and unity. This is how the world will recognize Christ!

So rather than needless redundancy, Jesus emphasizes the need for unity and love repeatedly in this final prayer of the Upper Room. Their unity draws from the unity of the Son with the Father, as described by "You in Me." In the same way as the Father is "in" the Son, the Son is "in" us. The Father loves us in the same way the Father loves the Son. We are invited into the very inner circle of the Trinity. There is no greater intimacy with God than this, and we are all invited to enjoy and experience that kind of relationship with Him.

Such unity is essential to our witness in the world. The church has suffered from giving an unclear message because of the in-squabbling of Christians over the centuries. To be sure, sin interferes with the unity Jesus prayed for. Pride, erroneous doctrines and sectarianism have been a plague. This is not to say that error should be ignored or minimized, but we should grieve for the disunity. We need to preach Christ and the truth all the more, the real basis of unity. We must never settle for superficial unity, which ultimately leads to apostasy. We must continue to proclaim Jesus Christ as God and Lord and the absolute need for His sacrificial death on the cross, which demonstrates the perfect love of God for us sinners. We can never give way to the sentiments of humanized religions that assume the goodness of humans and the possibility of their being able to reach God on their own merits. God's grace is based in truth, and that is what speaks of God's perfect love and that is what brings true unity in Christ.

Lord, I join Jesus in praying for unity in truth and love.

Unity Incarnate

John 17:23 (cont.)

23 I in them and You in Me, that they may be perfected in unity, so that the world may know that You sent Me, and loved them, even as You have loved Me.

Connection to Christ and His mission is depicted with the imagery of our Lord being physically "in" us. So also is the imagery of the Father being "in" Christ. Scripture speaks of the right hand of God, the eye of the Lord, the face of God—all images given to help us understand God who is spirit and thus has no physical body. This concept of using figurative language is not unique to the Bible—this is a fundamental element of human communication—and it makes the Scriptures no less "literal." We believe in a literal-historical interpretation of the Bible. A literal understanding helps us see, for example, that when we are told that "those who wait for the Lord . . . will mount up with wings like eagles . . . ," it is literal communication using imagery of nature to convey a spiritual truth. When we exercise patience in God's timing, we will rise above our circumstances, like an eagle rises above the earth.

Consider the incarnation for a moment. Jesus is the "Word" who became flesh (John 1:1, 14). He is the ultimate and perfect "anthropomorphism" of God, that is, He pictures for us God in human form. He took on the "form of a bond-servant . . . being made in the likeness of men . . . being found in appearance as a man . . ." (Phil. 2:7-8). The incarnation was very much physical, in that God as a spiritual being became a physical man. Yet, "He is the radiance of [God's] glory and the exact representation of His nature" (Heb. 1:3). While firmly adhering to the real incarnation as a fundamental of the faith (see 1 John 4:1-3; Colossians 1:19; 2:9), we see God using language ("the Word") to convey an understanding of Himself in a way we can grasp. This is what John meant when he wrote, "No one has seen God at any time; the only begotten God [i.e. Jesus, the Word] who is in the bosom of the Father, He has explained *Him"* (John 1:18).

Indeed, although the disciples had Jesus in the flesh, after His departure, they were left with not just the memory of the physical Jesus, but also with the literary picture that language conveys. So together with them today, we are invited by God to picture in our mind's eye that Jesus is "in" us, in a somewhat similar way as Jesus was "in" His physical body 2,000 years ago.

We live in a finite, flat-line world, as compared to the infinite dimensions of the spiritual world. God uses figures of speech and word pictures to help us gain a truer understanding of Himself and His purposes. We dare not dissect these images down to meaningless generalities. The connection of Jesus to us is best conveyed with the image that He is "in" us. We can do no better.

Lord, thank You for being in me and in us, working to bring us to perfection.

Unity in Practice

²³ I in them and You in Me, that they may be perfected in unity, so that the world may know that You sent Me, and loved them, even as You have loved Me.

Enough about unity? No, we can't say enough; this was a high point in Jesus' teaching. And judging from church history and present experience, its importance should not be minimized. Three times Jesus prays, ". . . that they may be one" just as He and the Father are one. Theology of the Trinity demands our unity. In simplest terms, Jesus wants us all to simply get along. The apostles understood this and likewise emphasized it.

At first their unity was very physical. Jesus had told them "not to leave Jerusalem, but to wait for what [i.e. the Holy Spirit] the Father had promised" (Acts 1:4). They remanded themselves to the Upper Room (Acts 1:13) and were "all with one mind continuing to devote themselves to prayer, along with the women, and Mary . . ." (Acts 1:13-14). They remained there until Pentecost (Acts 2:1). And the resulting group of new believers was "continually devoting themselves to the apostles' teaching and to fellowship, to breaking of bread and to prayer" (Acts 2:42). Unity came easily because of the newness of life that drew them together.

Notice, though, that their continued unity revolved around four things, which we take as essential to fulfilling Jesus' prayer for unity. God had impressed upon these early believers to commit themselves to the apostles' teachings with the same level of commitment they had for the Jewish Scriptures before this time, what we today call the Old Testament. Truth, the most critical element, comes first in the list of commitments recorded by Luke.

Another essential was fellowship—the tangible sharing with one another. "The congregation of those who believed were of one heart and soul; and not one of them claimed that anything belonging to him was his own, but all things were common property to them . . ." (Acts 4:32). The believers shared their possessions so that "there was not a needy person among them . . ." (Acts 4:34). The importance of this unity in fellowship was emphasized in Acts 5, where Satan tried to disrupt things by filling the hearts of Ananias and Sapphira to lie about what they were sharing. Unity was also expressed in the frequent experience of the Lord's Supper, also called the breaking of the bread (Acts 2:46; 1 Cor. 10:17), and in prayer (seen in the frequent times of prayer recorded in Acts.)

When we Christians keep our focus on these four essential commitments, we move in harmony with Jesus' prayer to His Father for unity.

Lord, help me focus on these four essentials that encourage unity.

WEEKEND READING

Saturday – John 20:19-31
Sunday – Acts 27:14-44

PERSONAL REFLECTIONS

_____
_____
_____
_____
_____
_____
_____

_____
_____
_____
_____
_____
_____
_____
_____
_____
_____
_____
_____

Unity Perfected

John 17:23 (cont.)

²³ I in them and You in Me, that they may be perfected in unity, so that the world may know that You sent Me, and loved them, even as You have loved Me.

This speaks of intimacy and unity of the highest order—that is what is meant by the little preposition "in." Like in English, the Greek word *"en"* has a broad field of meaning, and the precise rendering depends on the author's use. It can variously be translated as "in, with, by" or "in union with, joined closely to." Obviously not meant as a physical placement, the phrase "I in them" is thought by some to refer to the spiritual presence of the Lord in our life, as taught elsewhere in Scripture (e.g. Matt. 28:20).

Actually, the spiritual presence of God is depicted more as having to do with the third person of the Trinity, the Holy Spirit, who comes in Jesus' absence: ". . . the Spirit of truth, whom the world cannot receive, because it does not see Him or know Him, *but* you know Him because He abides with you and will be in you" (John 14:17). In the Upper Room prayer, Jesus prays for an intimacy that is centered on a unity in purpose. This is the perfect goal He had in mind.

The word "perfect" is used in Scripture in a variety of ways. In this context, Jesus was speaking of communal unity of purpose. We are brought to maturity in Christ through His body, the church, as we worship, fellowship and serve together. Paul rejoins this idea when he writes to the Philippians: "For I am confident of this very thing, that He who began a good work in you will perfect it until the day of Christ Jesus" (Phil. 1:6). We take this to be both a personal promise as well as a corporate promise for the church. To be sure, there is an individual aspect of perfection, but that will remain future, "until the day of Christ." Yet the future aspect did not keep the apostle Paul from striving for it in the present: "Not that I have already obtained *it* or have already become perfect, but I press on so that I may lay hold of that for which also I was laid hold of by Christ Jesus" (Phil. 3:12).

However, there is a sense in which we have already been perfected, in the sense of being made acceptable to God. "For by one offering He has perfected for all time those who are sanctified" (Hebrews 10:14; see also 12:23). In Christ, we have become perfectly acceptable to God; our sins have been forgiven through the sacrifice of a perfect offering. We have been made complete, in that there is nothing further that needs to be done in order to gain salvation. We who believe in the Lord Jesus Christ are already saved and now belong to God. Nothing can separate us from His love.

Lord, thank You for the perfection we have in Christ; help us live in unity.

The Desire of Jesus

John 17:24

24 "Father, I desire that they also, whom You have given Me, be with Me where I am, so that they may see My glory which You have given Me, for You loved Me before the foundation of the world."

There is a certain intensity to Jesus' prayer, "Father, I desire . . ." He had invited His disciples to "ask whatever you wish, and it will be done for you" (John 15:7) and shortly He would surrender His earthly desire, "My Father, if it is possible, let this cup pass from Me; yet not as I will, but as You will" (Matt. 26:39). But in the Upper Room, Jesus was acting in the role of High Priest, pleading before His Father. In the strongest possible terms He expressed His desire. Together with His unity of purpose with the Father (vs. 22), there was no question that Jesus was now praying "according to [the Father's] will"—and He would be heard and answered. Many years later John applied this example of Jesus to all believers: "This is the confidence which we have before Him, that, if we ask anything according to His will, He hears us" (1 John 5:14).

In all of the Upper Room conversation, only in this verse does Jesus use the word "desire" for Himself. Though He would soon be leaving them (which caused the disciples considerable consternation), He nonetheless was passionate for them, desiring not only to see them again, but for them to be with Him again. This passion was rooted in His relationship with His Father.

Jesus desired that the disciples would be with Him 1) because they were a gift from the Father to the Son, 2) so that they would enjoy His glory which the Father had given to the Son, and 3) because the Father loves the Son. We, too, along with the disciples in the Upper Room, are the gift that the Father gave to the Son. In a sense, we are His crowning glory!

One gets the impression that the whole point of Jesus' life, ministry, death and resurrection is the love relationship between Father and Son. This love is completed through the Son's obedience in going to the cross, in time and space, where He sealed for all time the eternal love that God had for us. God first loved His Son. The Son loves us (John 3:16), and as a response, we enter into that love by loving Him back and loving each other (1 John 4:19). Now we can see more clearly why Jesus spoke so much about love—God is love (1 John 4:8), and being His disciples, we need to be all about love also! That is why Jesus said, "By this all men will know that you are My disciples, if you have love for one another" (John 13:35). Love is the identifying trademark of those who believe in Jesus.

Lord, I desire that my love be of the same sort as the Father's love for You.

He Desires Us

John 17:24 (cont.)

24 "Father, I desire that they also, whom You have given Me, be with Me where I am, so that they may see My glory which You have given Me, for You loved Me before the foundation of the world."

ternity in view, Jesus speaks of the foundation of the world and of a future time. This relationship of love between the Father and the Son, which we now share, had its origin "before" the beginning of time. The human construct of time, in its simplest definition, is the measurement of change. Change can only happen when there is something that can change, whether that change is the size or composition of things or the movement of things in relationship to other things. Clearly, by this definition, time began when creation took place, "when" there was only God. Even to use words like "when" or "before" beg the issue, but how else can we mere mortals, who are subject to the sequence of before and after, understand existence where there is no time, that is, "before" creation?

That God is not subject to time is clear from Scripture: "For I, the Lord, do not change; therefore you, O sons of Jacob, are not consumed" (Mal. 3:6). Therefore, the love the Father had for the Son is eternal: it had no beginning and will have no end. It is outside of time, and therefore it does not change. It cannot change. Paul, inspired by the Spirit of God, whom Jesus had promised the disciples, adds, "He chose us in Him before the foundation of the world . . ." (Eph. 1:4). Therefore, the love Jesus has for us is rooted in that eternal love within the Trinity, outside of time! It is a perfect love that transcends everything we know and experience here "on earth." That is why Paul can write,

> *For I am convinced that neither death, nor life, nor angels, nor principalities, nor things present, nor things to come, nor powers, nor height, nor depth, nor any other created thing, will be able to separate us from the love of God, which is in Christ Jesus our Lord. (Rom. 8:38-39)*

So Jesus prays with great desire for us to be with Him for eternity, which He earlier pictured for us as a mansion with many rooms (John 14:1-4). We, as the Father's eternal love gift, were chosen by God. It could almost be said that we believers are God's housewarming present to His Son.

Aside from the academic and theological musings, we must not miss the personal perspective. Jesus actually wants us to live with Him forever. We tend to think of our benefit in salvation, but He is thrilled to save us (Heb. 12:2) and have us as family members for all eternity! Is that not wonderful?

Lord Jesus, I, too, look forward to being with You and the Father for eternity.

Jesus Our Brother

25 "O righteous Father, although the world has not known You, yet I have known You; and these have known that You sent Me . . ."

Six times in this High Priestly prayer and 53 times in the Upper Room, Jesus speaks of His "Father." The family relationship is obvious, and we believers are included, which He affirmed on a number of occasions. Early on, He made it clear, "Looking about at those who were sitting around Him, He said, 'Behold My mother and My brothers! For whoever does the will of God, he is My brother and sister and mother'" (Mark 3:34-35). After His resurrection, He reminded us through His comment to Mary Magdalene, "Go to My brethren and say to them, 'I ascend to My Father and your Father, and My God and your God'" (John 20:17).

The writer of Hebrews records for us that ". . . both He who sanctifies and those who are sanctified are all from one *Father;* for which reason He is not ashamed to call them brethren . . ." (Heb. 2:11). So now, as Paul writes, "Because you are sons, God has sent forth the Spirit of His Son into our hearts, crying, 'Abba! Father!'" (Gal. 4:6). We can know Him intimately as our "Abba" (which is best translated today as the affectionate "Papa").

Notice that He is our "righteous Father." He is Papa to us, but He is righteous and holy. We cannot selectively relate to God in a one-dimensional way. In an effort to compensate for that, "fundamentalism" presents God as angry and men as rank sinners deserving of His condemnation, but the pendulum swings too easily to embrace a soft, tamed-down God who is all about love and warmth. While God's love and forgiveness are beyond our wildest imagination and completely undeserved, we cannot believe in a one-dimensional God. He is righteous, and it is before His throne we will all someday stand. He is the perfect and complete combination of love and righteousness.

So while we call Him "Abba Father," we also call Him "righteous Father." As Jesus taught His disciples how to pray (Matt. 6:9-13), we are to begin with our relationship to God, "Our Father." We move to His sphere of being "in heaven," connecting as it were with eternity (beyond and above time). But we quickly acknowledge His absolute holiness, which is connected to His righteousness—"hallowed be Your name." And "forgive us our debts" because we have transgressed His righteousness. Yes, we approach God as our Father, who is righteous and forgiving. But we approach as being part of His family, with Jesus as our Brother. We approach in His name, for His purposes and for His glory!

Lord, thank You for teaching me how to approach You as my righteous Father.

Knowledge of Him

John 17:25 (cont.)

25 "O righteous Father, although the world has not known You, yet I have known You; and these have known that You sent Me . . ."

Worldly ignorance of God is no excuse because sinfulness has blinded the eyes of fallen man, rendering him incapable of seeing or knowing God. It is true that God has left the evidence:

> *. . . that which is known about God is evident within them; for God made it evident to them. For since the creation of the world His invisible attributes, His eternal power and divine nature, have been clearly seen, being understood through what has been made, so that they are without excuse. (Rom. 1:19-20)*

This is what we call "general revelation"—that God has revealed Himself in a general sort of way through creation. But humankind rejects even that:

> *For even though they knew God, they did not honor Him as God or give thanks, but they became futile in their speculations, and their foolish heart was darkened. (Rom. 1:21)*

The author of this gospel account at the beginning made this point:

> *The Light shines in the darkness, and the darkness did not comprehend it. (John 1:5)*

> *This is the judgment, that the Light has come into the world, and men loved the darkness rather than the Light, for their deeds were evil. (John 3:19)*

The good news, the Gospel, pierces the darkness with what we call "special revelation." And that is the person of Jesus Christ, the Word of God, the revelation of the true knowledge of God. "No one has seen God at any time; the only begotten God who is in the bosom of the Father, He has explained *Him"* (John 1:18). The term "explained" translates the Greek word *exegeomai*, from which we get our English word "to exegete." This means Jesus fully drew out the meaning of who God really is, and made it clear to all who would receive Him and become children of God (John 1:12). The Word became flesh, and through Him we learned the grace and truth of God (John 1:14). The result is that we who believe have come to God through Jesus Christ. Or as Jesus prayed to His Father, ". . . these have known that You sent Me."

Lord, what a joy it is to know You and the Father, grace and truth revealed! I believe that You have been sent by Your Father and that some day You will be coming back for us. I am so looking forward to being with You for eternity.

WEEKEND READING

Saturday – John 21:1-14
Sunday – Acts 28:1-10

PERSONAL
REFLECTIONS

Your Name

John 17:26

²⁶ *". . . and I have made Your name known to them, and will make it known, so that the love with which You loved Me may be in them, and I in them."*

"God"—that is not His name. That is the general term for deity, *Theos* in Greek and *Elohim* in Hebrew. But His name was revealed to Moses in the burning bush incident:

> *God said to Moses, "I AM WHO I AM"; and He said, "Thus you shall say to the sons of Israel, 'I AM has sent me to you.'" God, furthermore, said to Moses, "Thus you shall say to the sons of Israel, 'The LORD, the God of your fathers, the God of Abraham, the God of Isaac, and the God of Jacob, has sent me to you.' This is My name forever, and this is My memorial-name to all generations. (Ex. 3:14-15)*

According to this passage, God's name is "I AM" or "The LORD." What does Jesus mean that He has made that name known to the disciples? We must look more closely at the meaning of God's name as used in the Old Testament.

The Hebrew text (which is the language of the OT), as originally written, included only the consonants of words, but not any vowels. To present-day readers that would make interpreting the words very difficult. Some words have the same consonants, so without the vowels it would be impossible to distinguish between them. The Jews vocalized the text when it was read publically, and thus the meanings were clear. Since the printing press was not invented until the distant future, there was no economically viable means for reproducing copies of God's Word for everyone to have. The people relied on the public reading of Scripture, and the repeated vocalizations preserved the meanings. This is why the reading aloud of the Scriptures was so important in ancient times—that is what preserved the meaning of the text.

To the Jews, the name of God was considered so sacred, they would not verbalize it. When reading, they would say "the name" or use the Hebrew word for Lord, *Adonai*. In the text of Exodus 3:15, "The LORD" (in what we call small caps) in the original Hebrew uses the consonants from "I am" of verse 13 in a clear play on words. His personal name, if you will, is a play on the word (letters) from the Hebrew word "I am." Centuries later when vowels were added to the text, since the vocalization of God's name was lost, the scribes borrowed the vowels of *Adonai*. English translations render it "LORD." But to the Hebrew ear it would sound like "Yahweh" or the older English "Jehovah." That is God's name, as best we can say it. We will next see what this name means.

Lord, reveal Yourself fully to me, as Your name describes You.

Your Name (cont.)

John 17:26 (cont.)

26 ". . . and I have made Your name known to them, and will make it known, so that the love with which You loved Me may be in them, and I in them."

Thirteen times in the Upper Room "the name" is mentioned, eight of those times in reference to Jesus Himself, and five times (all in the prayer of Jesus) referring to the Father. Of all the words in Scripture, this one is arguably the most important one, for it refers to the very character and nature of God.

Of paramount significance is the identification of the name of the Son with the name of the Father: "Holy Father, keep them in Your name, the name which You have given Me, that they may be one even as We are" (John 17:11b). Our unity as believers with each other is rooted in the unity of the Father and Son, a unity that goes even to the sharing of "the name."

We have seen that the name of God is revealed in Exodus 3:14-15. The meaning there is closely associated with the phrase "I am." The Hebrew concept of being is not static, or to use the philosophers' term, ontological. Rather, the name of God signifies God's phenomenal being, that is, His active presence among His people. He is present for them (and for us) in the way we need Him to be, in whatever may be our situation. To use today's vernacular, He is always there for us. In the evangelical terminology of the 1970s, "Jesus is the answer," no matter the question.

This answers the question of who Jesus is: He is the God in Exodus 3:14, speaking out from the bush. He makes the Father's "name known to them" by revealing Himself through His miracles, His teachings and soon His perfect sacrifice on the cross. The good news, the Gospel, has to do with God revealing Himself in Jesus. Jesus is the one who is there for us. He is divinity ready and willing to act on our behalf whatever the need. Not for our selfish desires, but for our real needs, so that we can line up with His purpose and mission. For that is why we were created, as it were, in the image of God.

Jesus accomplished this mission and continues to "make it known," that the world may know about the love of God. God so loved the world (John 3:16), the Father sent the Son, in His name as the "I AM" (see John 8:24, 28, 58). The Jews understood when Jesus used the name in that way, but they missed the significance that God had come upon them to save them from their sins. We, on the other hand, have believed and are saved by His loving sacrifice.

Lord, words can never express my appreciation for Your unremitting love for me, a sinner. How could I have ever said "No" to Your grace?!

Your Name (cont.)

26 *"... and I have made Your name known to them, and will make it known, so that the love with which You loved Me may be in them, and I in them."*

"**I** am," Jesus said on multiple occasions, taking the very name of God. He intentionally applied the revered, unspeakable name of God, which is rooted in Exodus 3:14-15, emphasized throughout the Mosaic Law and abundantly impressed upon Israel throughout the Old Testament. We see, especially in Isaiah 41–49, the stress on the unique monotheism of the God of the Bible, using the formula "I am." For example, "I, the LORD, am the first, and with the last. I am He" (Isaiah 41:4; see also 43:10, 13; 48:12). "I am the LORD . . ." (41:13; 42:6; 43:3, etc.).

In fact, it was this section of Scripture (Isa. 41–49) that would have been the seasonal reading in the synagogues when Jesus made His famous and controversial claim, "Before Abraham was, I am" (John 8:48). The connection was unmistakable. The Greek words Jesus used, *ego eimi,* were the exact words from the version of the Scriptures in use at that time, what we call the Septuagint, written in Greek. That version of Isaiah 41:4, for example, uses the Greek *ego eimi* ("I am") very clearly as a reference to God and closely associates it with "I, the LORD . . ." And it is used that way throughout Isaiah 41–49. Jesus' timing of His "I am" statement was clearly meant to invoke that section of Isaiah, which asserts repeatedly the uniqueness of God. It is one of the strongest passages in the Bible supporting monotheism—that there is one and only one God, and that He is the God of Abraham, Isaac and Jacob, the God of Israel.

That is why the Jews knew full well what He was implying, and therefore tried to execute Him by stoning (vs. 59), typically the appropriate response to blasphemy. The point is that Jesus' contemporaries knew that Jesus was claiming to be divine, that He Himself was the God of the Jews, the one, unique deity, besides whom there is no other.

His point here in the Upper Room was that He revealed God as the one "who would be there for His people." We see this throughout the Gospel According to John. Jesus said, "I am . . ." the bread of life (6:35), the light of the world (8:12), the door of the sheep (10:7), the good shepherd (10:11), the resurrection and the life (11:25), the way, the truth, the life (14:6) and the vine (15:1). Yes, Jesus is the embodiment of the God who is the "I AM," who is there acting on our behalf in the way we need Him to be. Not a static God who just created and sits back passively, but dynamic and alive, at work in the world and in our lives.

Lord, I would be lost without Your active presence in my life. Thank You.

Recapping the Upper Room

John 13:1–17:26

[13:1] Now before the Feast of the Passover, Jesus knowing that His hour had come that He would depart out of this world to the Father, having loved His own who were in the world, He loved them to the end . . . [17:26] ". . . so that the love with which You loved Me may be in them, and I in them."

The Upper Room discourse records for us, by the pen of the apostle John, the most intimate interchange of our Lord Jesus Christ with His committed followers. The themes are many and the topics diverse, but unity is clear, and love is the goal. The Lord was preparing the disciples (and us) for life without Him physically present. That was mind-boggling for those men in the Upper Room, as they were very much people of the earth, seeing life in the most tangible, physical sense. Many of them were fishermen, not given to ivory tower theological discussions that were of the esoteric or otherworldly sort. They had expected an earthly kingdom with Jesus as King. Indeed, did not Jesus Himself teach, "The kingdom of heaven is at hand" (Matt. 4:17)?

Now the disciples were confronted with talk about His betrayal (13:21), His departure (13:33, 36, etc.), Peter's denial (13:38), His taking up new residence in a place where they could not go until some undisclosed time in the future (14:4). He chided them for not rejoicing with Him (14:28), warned them of their being rejected by the world (15:18-20) and predicted they would be scattered (16:32). The atmosphere must surely have been ominous.

He repeatedly taught them that in the midst of depressing news, they should not be troubled (14:1, 27), and this despite the fact that His own spirit was troubled (13:21). They should rejoice now (14:28), for they will rejoice in the future (16:22) when they will see Him again. Hope was offered, infused through the gloom, but faith in Him was required. They must come to see His departure as a good thing—that was the teaching of their Master Teacher.

The Upper Room teaching of our Lord was intended to prepare His disciples for carrying on the mission to which He formally commissioned them in Matthew 28:18-20. The overriding, major theme was preparation for carrying on the movement of Jesus Christ after He is gone. Little did they realize, much less understand, that Jesus' physical time with them was about to find closure after only three and a half years. But the movement was only beginning, the mission was about to begin. He made it possible by revealing God to us, through His teaching and ministry, and now through His substitutionary sacrifice as the Lamb of God who takes away the sin of the world.

Lord, thank You for preparing me to carry on Your mission in the world.

The Message of Love

John 13:1–17:26 (cont.)

¹³:¹ Now before the Feast of the Passover, Jesus knowing that His hour had come that He would depart out of this world to the Father, having loved His own who were in the world, He loved them to the end . . . ¹⁷:²⁶ ". . . so that the love with which You loved Me may be in them, and I in them."

"Love" is the grand theme of Jesus' Upper Room discourse. The story begins with love and ends with love. He loved His disciples (and all who believed through their testimony, as noted in John 17:20) to the end, so that they would experience the same love that He experiences from the Father. For Jesus to be in us is synonymous with having the love of God in us. "Having loved His own who were in the world, He loved them to the end," whether betrayer, denier or doubter.

The Spirit who was at work in the apostle John's writings as he recorded the words of Christ, confirmed this message in the writings of the apostle Paul:

For I am convinced that neither death, nor life, nor angels, nor principalities, nor things present, nor things to come, nor powers, nor height, nor depth, nor any other created thing, will be able to separate us from the love of God, which is in Christ Jesus our Lord. (Rom. 8:38-39)

But now faith, hope, love, abide these three; but the greatest of these is love. (1 Cor. 13:13)

For this reason I bow my knees before the Father, from whom every family in heaven and on earth derives its name, that He would grant you, according to the riches of His glory, to be strengthened with power through His Spirit in the inner man, so that Christ may dwell in your hearts through faith; and that you, being rooted and grounded in love, may be able to comprehend with all the saints what is the breadth and length and height and depth, and to know the love of Christ which surpasses knowledge, that you may be filled up to all the fullness of God. Now to Him who is able to do far more abundantly beyond all that we ask or think, according to the power that works within us, to Him be the glory in the church and in Christ Jesus to all generations forever and ever. Amen. (Eph. 3:14-21)

Christ came as the Word of God made flesh, that we might comprehend the Creator and Sovereign over all. That is the message we carry into the world.

Loving Father, thank You for revealing how much You love us. I commit to being that message to others, the living proof that there is a God who sacrificially loves us.

WEEKEND READING

Saturday – John 21:15-25
Sunday – Acts 28:11-31

PERSONAL REFLECTIONS

_____

_____

_____

_____

_____

_____

_____

_____

_____

_____

_____

_____

_____

_____

_____

_____

_____

_____

_____

_____

_____

_____

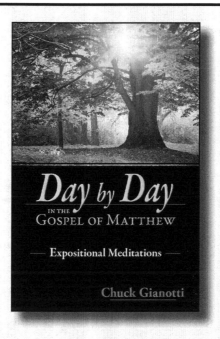

Day by Day in the Gospel of Matthew

by Chuck Gianotti

When Matthew was called to discipleship by Jesus with the simple command, "Follow Me!" he was a Rome appointed tax collector and despised by his fellow Jewish countrymen. Now he holds a place of honor as one of the four authorized biographers of the life and ministry of Jesus Christ.

Matthew's gospel account portrays Jesus of Nazareth as the fulfillment of the Old Testament prophecies, giving ample proof that He was, indeed, the Messiah King whom God had promised to send to reign over His people, Israel.

These daily devotionals (spanning one whole year) follow the gospel of Matthew verse by verse. Each reading is accompanied by a brief commentary and a succinct, devotional prayer to ground your heart and will in an increasing desire to love, honor, and serve the Lord Jesus as one of His disciples today.

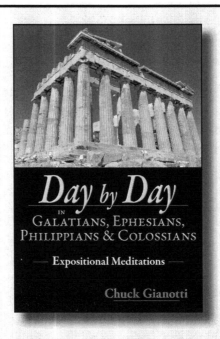

Day by Day in Galatians, Ephesians, Philippians & Colossians

by Chuck Gianotti

These verse-by verse expositional meditations follow the four epistles of Paul to the Galatians, Ephesians, Philippians and Colossians. The Bible text is accompanied by short textual commentaries and devotional thoughts for each day, spanning an entire year.

The reader will notice that the devotionals are divided up to suit a typical five-day workweek. We have included suggested readings for the weekends from the four accounts of the Gospel of Christ: Matthew, Mark, Luke, and John.

May God use these brief daily thoughts to spur you on to greater discipleship of our Lord and King, Jesus Christ, and to enjoy ever-deepening contemplations about His person and work.

Day by Day in Hebrews

by Chuck Gianotti

By comparison with other books of the Bible, Hebrews can *seem* to be not so relevant for our everyday lives. Chapter 11 (the "Hall of Faith" chapter) and a few verses here and there amount to all that many Christians know about the book. In our world of "instant everything," digging for gold takes some effort. In the case of Hebrews, the abundance of spiritual gold to be found there is well worth the effort.

The magnificent Christ emerges from the text: He is better than angels, than Moses, than the High Priest, than the sacrificial system, than the tabernacle. And that mysterious individual Melchizedek turns out to be a very important biblical figure—the reason why is exciting!

May these expository meditations catapult you into greater enjoyment of our Lord Jesus. We can give no greater glory to God than to exalt His Son through our growing appreciation of His glory.

[Jesus] is the radiance of His [God's] glory . . . (Heb. 1:3a)

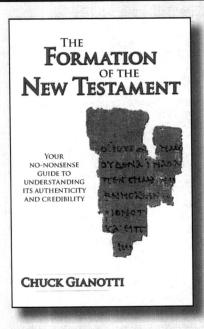

The Formation of the New Testament

by Chuck Gianotti

The Christian faith rises or falls on the historical credibility of the Bible, particularly the New Testament documents. In today's postmodern culture, Christians and those searching for answers face numerous questions including:

> ➤ Are the New Testament writings historically reliable?

> ➤ How do we know those books are authoritative?

> ➤ Who decided which documents to include?

> ➤ What about the apocryphal or deutero-canonical writings?

> ➤ Can we know for certain that the Bible is accurate and complete?

This book reduces the large volume of available (yet very technical) information on the subject by providing a concise analysis of the facts to help you gain confidence in the credibility of the New Testament canon.